MEGASTHENES AND INDIAN RELIGION

Megasthenes and Indian Religion

A Study in Motives and Types

ALLAN DAHLQUIST

MOTILAL BANARSIDASS
DELHI :: VARANASI :: PATNA

Indological Publishers and Booksellers
Head Office : BUNGALOW ROAD, JAWAHAR NAGAR, DELHI-7
Branches : 1. CHOWK, VARANASI-1 (U.P.)
2. ASHOK RAJPATH, PATNA-4 (BIHAR)

First Edition : Uppsala, 1962
Reprint : Delhi, 1977

Printed in India

BY SHANTILAL JAIN, AT SHRI JAINENDRA PRESS, A-45, PHASE-I, INDUSTRIAL AREA, NARAINA, NEW DELHI-28 AND PUBLISHED BY SUNDARLAL JAIN OF MOTILAL BANARSIDASS, BUNGALOW ROAD, JAWAHAR NAGAR, DELHI-7

To my wife

CONTENTS

PREFACE

The preparations for this work extend over rather a long period. It was as early as in 1949 that I asked my teacher, Professor Geo Widengren, for a theme, and he proposed "The figure of Kṛishṇa" or "The Śiva ascetics". I am most thankful to him for giving me considerable freedom in defining more exactly the scope of my task, since my investigation has brought me far from the original subject proposed. On his advice I got in touch with Professor Stig Wikander, who showed such great interest and kindness that he treated Kṛishṇa texts in his Sanskrit lessons for several years afterwards. I have often had the benefit of discussing actual problems with him and have received a great many suggestions from him. Professor Helmer Ringgren and Professor Nils Simonsson have been of the greatest value to me, stimulating and interested as they have been. Other friends to whom I have the pleasure of expressing my hearty thanks for discussing my problems and giving me suggestions are Professor Carl-Martin Edsman, Docent Carl-Gustaf Diehl, Docent Sven Hartman, Docent Bengt Löfstedt, Docent Harry Tegnæus, and Rev. Teol. kand., Fil. mag. Jan Bergman.

Previously I had translated the Greek text into my own language. This translation has been examined, corrected and improved by Fil. lic. Gunnar Bäärnhielm and Fil. lic. Kerstin Bergman. For their help I thank them. It seemed to me pointless to have my own Swedish translation rendered into English, considering there was already a very good English translation by McCrindle. Therefore I have used this existing translation, only stressing at a few points my own differing opinion.

Teol. lic. Eric Sharpe, B.A., has translated my Swedish manuscript. I have written only a few sentences myself. For the most part I have the impression that the translation is a good rendering of what I want to say. The exceptions are generally of little importance. I thank him for his pains.

As to the last labours with printing and proof-reading I extend my most hearty thanks to Mr. A. Eriksson, Almqvist & Wiksells Boktryckeri AB. The librarians of the University Library in Uppsala have always shown extraordinary kindness and obligingness. In particular, I want to express my gratitude to Fil. Dr. A. Melvinger.

I wish also to take this opportunity to extend my special thanks to the Archbishop of Sweden, Gunnar Hultgren, for his inspiring interest. At least once his word alone was the necessary stimulation which enabled me to complete my work.

My clerical colleagues have also shown interest and kindness, for which I thank them most heartily.

Finally, I should like to express my warm thanks to my wife and children for their patience and self-denial, without which I could not have continued my research.

Allan Dahlquist

INTRODUCTION

A. *The Subject*

This investigation will be concerned mainly with Indian religion and not with Megasthenes. But Megasthenes is of the greatest importance for our understanding of Indian religion ca. 300 B.C.

It is common knowledge that the culture of India lacks any historical aspect. We know that important events took place during India's long history, but we do not always know *when* they took place. The extensive literature bears clear witness to the fact that new thoughts and ideas became incorporated into the Indian scheme, but it is usually impossible to decide just *when* a certain concept was first used.[1] It is in this situation that Megasthenes may be of great help to us, for we can determine the exact date of his visit to India: 302–288 B.C.;[2] we know exactly where he lived: Pāṭaliputra, where he was ambassador of Seleukos Nikator to the court of Candragupta; and we are assured of his general reliability: Schwanbeck,[3] Timmer,[4] Truesdall Brown[5] and others have examined the reliability of various aspects of his work, and have found it to be of a high order. Neither these scholars nor any others have however extended their investigations to embrace Megasthenes' statements on Indian religion;[6] this is all the more remarkable in that it is just these passages which form the decisive arguments in the great discussion which, until some fifty years ago, raged among Indologists on the possibility of a relationship between Christianity and Krishnaism. The first time Megasthenes was brought into the discussion was, as far as I have been able to discover, in a passage in Lassen's *Indische Altertumskunde*,[7] where the author maintains Krishnaism to be older than Christianity, since Megasthenes in his *Indica* had clearly described Kṛishṇa

---

[1] For example, we find a number of the ideas of the BhG in the Upanishads: some, but not all. This gives rise to the questions of the origins of these ideas and the age of the BhG. We shall touch upon this question in part IV of this investigation (not printed in this volume), which deals with Megasthenes and the Indian philosphers.

[2] So Garbe, *Indien und das Christentum*, p. 212. Cf. Stein in *PW* s.v. *Megasthenes*.

[3] *Megasthenis Indica*, p. 76.

[4] *Megasthenes en de Indische Maatschappij*, p, 312.

[5] *The Reliability of Megasthenes*, *A.J.P.*, 76, p. 32.

[6] Stein, *PW*. s.v. *Megasthenes*, touches upon the matter, cf. below p. 29 n. 3.

[7] II: 2, p. 1107.

as an *avatar* of Vishṇu, under the name of Heracles. Garbe,[1] referring to this passage in Lassen, supports the latter's argument, but does not appear to have studied it in detail. Lassen's views have since, via *The Cambridge History of India* (I, p. 167), won general acceptance among scholars.

It is interesting to note the difficulties this view has placed in the way of those individual scholars who have been compelled to point out facts in contradiction of the commonly accepted theory. Not all have observed the contradiction between those facts they have advanced and the Megasthenes passages which they reproduce from Lassen. B. C. Law,[2] an outstanding authority on the geography of ancient India, states, with reference to the *Cambridge History*, that in Megasthenes' day Mathurā was known to be a centre of the Kṛishṇa cult. But a few lines later we read, on the authority of H. C. Ray Chaudhuri's *Early History of the Vaishṇava Sect*,[3] that the town ceased to be a stronghold of the Vaishṇava religion during the Śaka-Kushāṇa period. In Law's opinion, the explanation of the decline of the Bhāgavata religion is that a majority of the population was Buddhist.[4] The contradiction is perhaps still not clear. But if we examine the arguments used by Lassen in order to identify the god whom Megasthenes calls Heracles with Kṛishṇa, it becomes perfectly obvious that in the last resort it is Heracles' connection with Mathurā which suggested Kṛishṇa to Lassen, and which forms the foundation of his argument. We shall examine this argument in detail in due course, but it will be useful to summarize the value of this point at this early stage.

1. a) According to Megasthenes, Heracles was worshipped in Mathurā ca. 300 B.C.
   b) Kṛishṇa was worshipped in Mathurā (but in 400 A.D.).
   c) *Therefore* Heracles and Kṛishṇa are identical.

Lassen has himself made use of this conclusion without being entirely clear as to the basis on which it stands. He is thus able in another context to use the following syllogism:

2. a) According to Megasthenes, Heracles was worshipped in Mathurā ca. 300 B.C.
   b) But according to 1 (c) above, Heracles = Kṛishṇa.
   c) *Therefore* Kṛishṇa was worshipped in Mathurā as early as 300 B.C.

This argument is not particularly convincing, but the extent of its illogi-

---

[1] *Indien und das Christentum*, p. 212.

[2] *Tribes in Ancient India*, p. 42, *Historical Geography*, p. 109.

[3] *Op. cit.*, p. 99.

[4] *Tribes ibid.*

cality will perhaps be clear if we replace "Mathurā" by "Rome" and "Kṛishṇa" by "Christ":

1. a) According to Megasthenes, Heracles was worshipped in Rome in 300 B.C.
   b) Christ was worshipped in Rome (but in 400 A.D.).
   c) *Therefore* Heracles and Christ are identical.
2. a) According to Megasthenes, Heracles was worshipped in Rome in 300 B.C.
   b) But according to 1 (c) above, Heracles = Christ.
   c) *Therefore* Christ was worshipped in Rome as early as 300 B.C.

It is obvious that Lassen's logic is seriously at fault, and it is a pity that this has not been pointed out earlier. But if we ask what the reason can have been, the answer is quite simple. When Lassen attempted to identify Heracles in the work of Megasthenes, he took into account only four, or perhaps six, of Megasthenes' statements on Heracles without considering the twenty remaining passages. The result reached by the learned Norwegian-German Indologist on a basis of this unfortunate method was not merely an unimportant matter of detail. On the contrary, his mistake, as we have suggested, has because of its general acceptance brought to an end the discussion of the possible influence on Krishnaism of Christianity.

In order to provide a background to the subject of *Megasthenes and Indian Religion* we must first summarize the discussion—a discussion far too extensive to be capable of exhaustive treatment here. We wish only to demonstrate its general tendency: to let Megasthenes the Greek have the last word on the relative age of the two religions in question, and to accept his verdict in favour of Krishnaism.

B. *Discussion of the Relation between Christianity and Krishnaism*

1. *Before Weber*

Albrecht Weber was the first to make a serious attempt to support the thesis that Krishnaism was no more than a corrupt form of Christianity. More or less amateurish attempts had however been made earlier, notably by P. Georgi, *Alphabetum Tibetanum*, Rome 1762 (pp. 253–263), who considered the name Kṛishṇa to be merely a corrupt form of the Saviour's name. The fact that the essentials of Christianity had not been incorporated into Krishnaism was explained by Georgi as being due to the fact that the name had been borrowed from apocryphal gospels, and from the Manichaeans in particular. In the course of the subsequent discussion, one who contradicted Georgi was Sir William Jones, who believed Kṛishṇa to have been one of the ancient gods of India. But he allowed that Georgi may have been right in certain details, and recognized the possibility that borrowing may have taken place at a later date. For example, the narratives in the apocryphal gospels have been applied to the old story of Keśava, the Apollo of Greece.

P. Paullino à S. Bartolomaeo, *Systema Brahmanicam*, Rome 1791 (pp. 124, 147, 152), contradicted Georgi entirely, in that he maintained that the accounts of Kṛishṇa have to do with events which must have taken place a thousand years or more before Christ. A similarly negative attitude toward the possibility of Krishnaism having borrowed from Christianity was adopted by Kleuker, *Treatise on the History and the Antiquities of Asia*, Riga 1795 (pp. 4, 70); Vol. II, Riga 1797 (pp. 233 ff.). In this case it is interesting to observe a certain alteration in the author's attitude to the problem. In 1795 he not only allows that the same idea may have originated in several places independently, but even goes so far as to suggest that the borrowing might have been by Christianity, for many of the apocryphal writings bear clear traces of Indian doctrine and narrative style. In 1797, however, he follows Jones in supposing Krishnaism to have been influenced in a number of details from Christianity. His attitude to Georgi's thesis is nevertheless for the most part a negative one.

The same views were held by E. Moor, *Hindoo Pantheon*, London 1810 (p. 200), who considered that the myths of the Greeks and others were in fact derived from India; Kṛishṇa—both the name and the myths generally—he believed to be considerably earlier than Christ, and probably contemporary with Homer. Moor has an illustration in which is depicted the child Kṛishṇa at the breast of his mother Devakī. The significance of this is not discussed, the author being content to note the resemblance to Mary and the infant Jesus.

Creuzer, *Symbolik*, 3rd ed. Leipzig 1837, French ed. Paris 1825 (p. 293 in German, p. 212 in French ed.), denies that there is any resemblance between India, Christianity, Greece and Rome. He does though draw a number of parallels with the myth of Osiris. The French edition, prepared by Guignaut, has an interesting addition: the picture which Moor believed to have been of Kṛishṇa at his mother's breast is in fact a representation of the Buddha!

It will be clear from this that Georgi's original tenets met with considerable opposition. But we note that little is advanced against his thesis apart from the bald statement that Kṛishṇa is one of the ancient gods of India. Not one of the scholars made the slightest attempt to produce any evidence for this assertion. It was merely a generally accepted view, which Georgi had—unsuccessfully—attempted to replace. We may perhaps be forgiven for suspecting that the motives which led to the almost unanimous condemnation of the new theory were not particularly scientific. None, though, confessed his personal prejudice so clearly as did Pavie, *Kṛishṇa et sa Doctrine, Bhagavat Dasam Askand*, Paris 1852, who states without more ado that it is humiliating for Christianity to be compared with the Kṛishṇa cult at all.

Weber incorporated these authors and their views into his essay *Über die Kṛishṇajanmāshṭamī*, which brought new life into the discussion; among subsequent participants were many of the leading Indologists of the world.

2. *Weber and the Advocates of the "Borrowing" Theory*

The burden of Weber's monograph is as follows: According to the Bhavishyotta Purāṇa, one of the items in the celebration of Kṛishṇa's birth was the providing of a house for Devakī, the mother of Kṛishṇa, in the form of a byre, filled with shepherdesses. On a bed rests Devakī, asleep, with Kṛishṇa at her breast. At the close of the monograph Weber mentions an interesting paragraph from the Vishṇu Purāṇa: Nanda, the foster-father of Kṛishṇa, was at the time of Kṛishṇa's birth on his way to Mathurā with his pregnant wife, Yaśodā, to pay his taxes. The author has no doubt that borrowing from Christianity has in fact taken place. Further, he attempts to determine the time and the geographical location at which this borrowing took place.

The same author has in another context (*Indische Studien* II, pp. 169) stated his conviction that the Indian system of *avatars* originated as an imitation of the Christian doctrine of the Incarnation.

As we have already indicated, Weber's theory aroused a lively literary debate among scholars. Two years after Weber's essay on the birth of Kṛishṇa came Lorinser[1] with a comparison between the Bhagavadgītā and the New Testament, in which he pointed to what he felt were striking agreements, explicable by a process of borrowing from Christianity. Hopkins, in an essay in *India Old and New*, entitled *Christ in India*, has pointed in particular to a number of points of contact between the Gospel of John and the Bhagavadgītā, which he can only assume to be due to Christian

[1] *Die Bhagavadgita übersetzt und erläutert* von F. Lorinser.

influence in India. An idea of which Hopkins may have been the originator, is that although Kṛishṇa was worshipped at an earlier date, the old, revered Kṛishṇa becomes an entirely new god, just at the critical moment. In Hopkins' view, Kṛishṇa's new characteristics are not to be found in any of the other gods of India: (i) The god of love; (ii) The god who forgives sins; (iii) The god from whom comes forgiveness by faith, and not by works; (iv) Vyāsa = Kṛishṇa: the unborn (= eternal), the only son of God (Mbh XII.350, 4551); (v) Of Kṛishṇa it is said: He, the watcher over his flock, the sinless God, the Lord of the world, agreed that he and his race should die, in order that the words of the seer might be fulfilled (Mbh XVI. 6, 15–16); (vi) Vyāsa = Jesus; (vii) The mote and the beam (Mbh I. 73, 35, 82).[1]

In *J.R.A.S.* for 1907 and 1908 a number of scholars discussed the question raised by Weber. Among them was Grierson, who advanced the same basic thesis as Hopkins, that the ancient Kṛishṇa suddenly changes character.[2] He compares the various *avatars* of Kṛishṇa and finds that the Kṛishṇa *avatar* stands out in comparison with the others. He emphasizes the significance of *bhakti* piety as the new factor, which he considers to be more recent than Christianity. The god Vishṇu, formerly entirely impersonal, suddenly becomes extremely personal, and the attitude taken to him by his worshippers, from being impersonal, becomes deeply personal and even emotional.

Grierson starts with the assumption that there is a core of historical truth in the Thomas legend. It is interesting to note, against the background of the tradition of the Apostle's work in India, that the wave of religious reform which spread over the whole of India, and which confined itself to the various forms of Vishnuism, all seem to have originated in that area of South India, near Madras, where Thomas is said to have laboured.[3] The author can even point to a *bhakti* communion, the character of which resembles the early Christian Eucharist: the bread and water are not only distributed to the laity, but the actual sacred meal (*Mahāprasāda* = the great grace) is followed by a love-feast.[4] Grierson also draws attention to the bloody character of popular Indian religion: there is no room for that love which characterizes Rāmānuja and his followers.[5] He quotes five examples, taken from the *Bhaktamāla*, of expressions which point to the New Testa-

---

[1] *Op. cit.*, p. 158.

[2] *Modern Hinduism and its Debt to the Nestorians*, p. 313 (*J.R.A.S.* 1907).

[3] *Op. cit.*, p. 323.

[4] *Op. cit.*, p. 326.

[5] *Op. cit.*, p. 494.

ment: (i) Be born again (literally); (ii) Turn the other cheek; (iii) Become blind; (iv) Cut off the right hand; (v) Wash the servants' feet.[1]

Another contribution to the debate was made, in an article in the same journal, by Kennedy; his attitude will be clear from the following passage: "Down to a certain date, which. on archaeological grounds, I am inclined to fix at 500 A.D., Kṛishṇa is a warrior hero, originally, perhaps, a nature god personifying the dark sun, whose countenance blinds his enemies, and whose business it is to slay giants and dragons; he is the god of a tribe, and ultimately becomes identified with Vishṇu. And then there comes an entire and sudden change. The new Kṛishṇa is a pastoral and idyllic deity, an infant who grows up to be a boy and a youth, and is throughout a god of love ... The scene is changed from Dwārakā to Bhraj. It is the new Kṛishṇa, the Kṛishṇa bambino, who emerges everywhere victorious."[2]

Elsewhere in the same journal the same author suggests that in Dvārakā Kṛishṇa was a great nature-god of enormous antiquity, worshipped in the Kabul Mountains and in the Indus Valley.[3] The child Kṛishṇa bears no resemblance to the original Kṛishṇa, except in name. But the child Kṛishṇa can be traced to Mathurā, at the beginning of the 6th century, and the identification between Vishṇu and Kṛishṇa is considered to be complete by about 400 A.D. The legends about the child Kṛishṇa in Mathurā agree with neither Buddhism nor Hinduism. On the contrary, Kennedy points out the direct contrast with the Mahābhārata, and says that it is therefore necessary to assume a Christian origin. The Christian material may have been transmitted by Persian hermits and monks.[4]

We need hardly point out that certain aspects of the works here summarized are somewhat speculative in character. This is particularly true of Hopkins' coupling of the names Vyāsa and Jesus; Vyāsa is not another name for the *god* Kṛishṇa, but for his namesake, the mythical author of the great epic. The authors we have quoted belong to the front rank of Indologists, outstanding for their learning and their reliable judgment. In this case, however, they have fallen into the trap—though no doubt unconsciously—of seeing resemblances where there are none to be seen. We find that there is virtual unanimity on one point: that Kṛishṇa was one of the ancient gods of India who changed character completely as a result of Christian influence. The first factor which drew attention to the possibility of a link between Kṛishṇa and Christ was the similarity in their names,

---

[1] *Ibid.*

[2] *Modern Hinduism*, p. 486 (*J.R.A.S.* 1907).

[3] *The Child Kṛishṇa, Christianity, and the Gujars*, p. 951 (*J.R.A.S.* 1907).

[4] *Modern Hinduism*, p. 480 (*J.R.A.S.* 1907).

particularly since in certain dialects Kṛishṇa was pronounced Kṛishṭa—which was also the way the name 'Christ' was pronounced. But if we inquire as to the origin of the popular conception of Kṛishṇa's great antiquity, we are placed in a quandary. Not one of the authors quoted gives any reason for this assumption, but their prejudice has never been challenged. Opposition was however aroused by the two theories that Kṛishṇa had changed character, and that Christianity had contributed something new to Indian religion.

3. *Opponents of the "Borrowing" Theory*

Auguste Barth, whom Grierson and others considered to be the foremost opponent of Weber's theory, says in his book *Religions de l'Inde* that *bhakti* piety marks the coming of something new into the religious life of India. Previously, the way of salvation was by knowledge (*veda*, *jñāna*); now comes *bhakti*, *prasāda*, *śraddhā* (already known in the Vedas, though not with its later emphasis). Barth considers that the essence of Krishnaism is no different from that of any religion which reaches the stage of monotheism. Enthusiasm, *bhakti*, is self-evident when several religions exist side by side. "Ce n'est donc pas sur la possibilité d'un emprunt, mais sur l'emprunt même, tel qu'on l'affirme, que portent nos objections."[1]—"Or M. Weber n'entend nullement que dans Kṛishṇa, chez qui il n'y a pas trace ni du dogme de la Rédemption, ni des récits de la Passion, la vrai source et substance de la foi chrétienne, l'Inde ait jamais adoré Jésus."[2] These quotations give us the heart of Barth's criticism. The last passage points out that it is only in unimportant details that the two really resemble each other; the nucleus and nerve of Christianity, on the other hand, is missing from Krishnaism. Had borrowing from Christianity really taken place; this nucleus should have been the constitutive element. But there is no such trace, either in the form of an accepted view or of polemic. This seems to Barth to exclude the two religions having had any contact. Barth is so eager to make his point that he goes so far as to deny later influence. The expression 'God is love', which occurs in both, has been misunderstood in certain circles in India, and a more thorough consideration of the implications of the expression has deepened the bearing of the expression.[3] That is the explanation of *bhakti*, devotion and *prasāda*, grace. Speculation about salvation by the grace of God marks a later stage in religious thought, at

---

[1] *Op. cit.*, p. 132 (Barth, *Œvres*, p. 194, Engl. ed., p. 221).

[2] *Op. cit.*, p. 133 (*ibid.*)

[3] *Op. cit.*, p. 135 (*Œuvres*, p. 197 f., Engl. ed., p. 225 f.).

which the two main tendencies tend to favour the 'monkey' and 'cat' ideas respectively. The mother cat carries her young by the scruff of its neck, and the kitten is relieved of all responsibility in the matter; the young monkey, however, must keep tight hold of its mother, who carries it, seemingly careless of its presence, to the desired destination. In both cases it is the mother who takes the young where she wishes. These two viewpoints can be explained, says Barth, without having to refer to the controversy between Christian theologians. The thought that the two religions, independently of each other, "gave the same answer to the same question", as Kurt Hutten[1] put it, seems since to have won the widest support.

Furthermore, not even Kennedy, whom we have already said was a supporter of Weber, denied that the essence of Krishnaism, *bhakti*, was pre-Christian in India. On the contrary, Kennedy could find evidence of the existence of *bhakti* in the Rig Veda.[2] A. Berriedale Keith also pointed out that a form of piety strongly reminiscent of *bhakti* was to be found in both Roman and Greek religion; it is therefore possible that it may have developed in India irrespective of external influences.[3] But what must be considered to be the most important point in the whole discussion is Keith's argument against Grierson. The common elements noted by Grierson are not typical of Christianity; they are superficial rites *which are older than Christianity*, and which are to be found outside Christianity.[4] On the other hand Keith points to a fact we have already noticed in Barth, that there is no trace of a doctrine of the Atonement, which is the most typical aspect of Christianity.

Although Kennedy places such emphasis on the figure of the child Kṛishṇa, the universal conqueror, Bhāṇḍārkar states that this detail of Krishnaism, which is acknowledged to be due to Christian influence (!) is of as little importance in Krishnaism as it is in Christianity.[5] The essential doctrine is *bhakti*, which Bhāṇḍārkar believes can be traced in pre-Christian texts. He points out one interesting fact: that *bhakti* in the west has originated from the Upanishads, as have Buddhism and Jainism in the east—and all three have arisen in the Kshatriya caste. But if we consider the figure of Kṛishṇa and its antiquity, we find him assuming the identity of Kṛishṇa and Vāsudeva, saying that "Kṛishṇa, Janārdana and Keśava do not appear to be Vṛishṇi names and were given to Vāsudeva in subsequent

[1] *Die Bhaktireligion und der christliche Glaube im N.T.*, p. 12.

[2] *Modern Hinduism*, p. 482 f. (*J.R.A.S.* 1907).

[3] *Modern Hinduism*, p. 490 (*J.R.A.S.* 1907).

[4] *Op. cit.*, p. 492.

[5] *Vaishnavism, Śaivism and minor religious systems*, pp. 35–38.

times when his worship had widely spread"[1]. The time at which this took place can be indicated only approximately, and then only on a basis of the fact that the name occurs in Patañjali and in Kāśikā; this means that the oldest evidence for these names takes us to the 2nd century B.C. On the cult of Vāsudeva, Bhāṇḍārkar considers that the famous and much-discussed passage in the Pāṇini Sūtra IV.3.98, *Vāsudevārjunābhyām* vun, can be brought in as evidence: this would fix the cult in the 5th century B.C.[2]

Unlike the scholars whom we have quoted earlier, Bhāṇḍārkar has studied the question of the age and origin of Krishnaism; he is not primarily interested in the possibility of a relationship between Christianity and Krishnaism, but his investigation has naturally proved to be of the greatest importance for this latter question, too. He is, as far as I am aware, the first to have produced factual evidence for the existence of Krishnaism in pre-Christian times,[4] viz. the mention of the name of Kṛishṇa in Pāṇini's Vāsudeva Sūtra, and in the works of Patañjali and Kāśikā. We must however point out that neither the Pāṇini passage nor the two other passages are of the slightest practical value as sources of information about the gods, the nature of such gods or the myths connected with them. But the Indian scholar has made a serious attempt to support a judgment previously accepted by scholars on entirely inadequate grounds.

After Bhāṇḍārkar had laid what we may well call the foundations, it was relatively easy for Garbe to have the last word, and explode Weber's theory once and for all. Having read Garbe's penetrating book *Indien und das Christentum*, one is tempted to regard further discussion as unnecessary. What, then, does Garbe contribute? He says, *inter alia*, that euhemerism is correct, with a view to Kṛishṇa and Rāma: first demi-gods, then all-gods.[4] The slaughter of the innocents, with its obvious connections with the gospel narrative, as quoted by Weber in his essay on the birth of Kṛishṇa, is considered by Garbe to be supported by Patañjali in his Mahābhāshya.[5] Garbe therefore claims, on a basis of this Mahābhāshya passage, that the infant Kṛishṇa was already of some importance in the 1st century B.C., and was even worshipped as a god in the 6th century in the Buddha's native country. This particular assertion he bases on archaeological discoveries made in Rummindei (Rukminī devī, the goddess Rukminī: the name of one of

---

[1] *Op. cit.*, p. 11.

[2] *Op. cit.*, p. 3.

[3] With the exception as we have already indicated, of Lassen (see above, p. 9 and below, p. 20).

[4] *Op. cit.*, p. 213.

[5] *Op. cit.*, p. 222.

Kṛishṇa's wives; a common place-name in Buddhist texts).[1] This removes all possibility of influence from Christianity. That Christian elements entered Krishnaism at a later stage in its development is unmistakable, and is disputed by no Indologist.[2] Such influence however belonged to a much later epoch than either Weber or Grierson had supposed. Garbe dismisses the entire legend of Thomas as incredible, even going so far as to attribute its origin to Buddhism, and its content to the teaching of the Buddha.[3] The earliest date at which direct Christian influence on Indian religion is conceivable in theory is 635 A.D., when the Nestorians began their mission to North India. And by that time the entire Mahābhārata, including the Bhagavadgītā, was definitive in both form and content; this implies that Krishnaism as a religion was also complete.[4]

This is Garbe's basic thesis. He has in general handled his material in an exemplary fashion, and his conclusions seem incontestable. There is however one criticism which may be advanced against what he has to say. Is it necessary to understand Patañjali's reference to Kṛishṇa as referring to the *god* Kṛishṇa? Although Vāsudeva or Kṛishṇa is stated by Patañjali to be the killer of Kaṁsa his uncle, it does not necessarily follow that Patañjali accounted the one who did the deed as being of divine nature. Garbe has maintained energetically, expressing his surprise at the opinions of certain other scholars, that Kṛishṇa was originally an ordinary human being, and that he was only deified at a much later date.[5] The Kṛishṇa mentioned by Patañjali may therefore have been a perfectly ordinary man. We must however be content with this selection from Garbe's excellent book; we have drawn attention to the above problem merely to emphasize the risky and uncertain nature of the entire complex of questions dealt with here.

4. *The Importance of Megasthenes for the Discussion*

Garbe produces one passage in favour of Kṛishṇa's divine character in pre-Christian times; but only one, viz. the passage from Lassen with which we began our discussion. In Garbe's words: "It is true that Kennedy had disputed that this (i.e. the declaration of Kṛishṇa as an *avatar* of Vishṇu) took place no later than the 4th century B.C.; but this is clear from the well-known fact that Megasthenes, who was Seleukos Nikator's ambassador at the court of Pāṭaliputra from 302 to 288 B.C., makes unmistakeable

---

[1] *Op. cit.*, p. 224.
[2] *Op. cit.*, p. 218.
[3] *Op. cit.*, pp. 141–143.
[4] *Op. cit.*, p. 192.
[5] *Op. cit.*, p. 213.

mention in his narratives of Kṛishṇa, under the name of Heracles, as an *avatar* of Vishṇu by the side of Dionysos (= Śiva)."[1]

We thus find in the last resort, that the whole question of the possible influence of Christianity on the nucleus of Krishnaism rests on the evidence of the Greek ambassador in the 4th century B.C. But this evidence is not confined to a mere name—he mentioned no Indian name at all—but takes the form of a fairly detailed description of the two Indian gods whom he found to be accorded the most reverence and worship during his stay at the court of Candragupta. The importance of Megasthenes for our discussion deserves to be attested by examples drawn from other contributors to the debate.

We have already said that Christian Lassen was the first to bring Megasthenes into the discussion. Weber's theory of the origin of the Indian *avatar* concept as an imitation of the Christian doctrine of the Incarnation, prompted Lassen to make the following statement, taken from Vol. II of his *Indische Altertumskunde*: "Wenn diese Ansicht haltbar wäre, würde eines der wichtigsten Dogmen der Indischen Religion, wie sie zur Zeit der letzten Bearbeitung der zwei alten epischen Gedichte herrschend war, fremder Herkunft seyn. Sie muss daher zuerst einer Prüfung unterzogen werden. — Glücklicher Weise sind wir im Stande nachzuweisen, dass Kṛishṇa schon während der Regierung des Candragupta als eine Verkörperung Vishṇus gedacht worden ist; denn wenn Megasthenes vom Indischen Herakles berichtet, dass er die ganze Erde und das ganze Meer durchzogen und vom Übel gereinigt hatte, so wird, wie mich dünkt, kein durch Voreingenommenheit für andere Ansichten befangener Forscher in diesen Worten das Indische Dogma verkennen, welches am kürzesten ausgedrückt so lautet: 'So oft eine Erschaffung des Gesetzes und eine Erhebung des Unrechts eintreten, erschafft Vishṇu sich selbst.' Megasthenes wird in andern Fällen mit dem Namen Herakles den Vishṇu im Allgemeinen bezeichnet haben, in den vorliegenden Fällen jedoch gewiss den Kṛishṇa, weil er auch erwähnt hatte, dass Herakles vorzugsweise von den śūrasena, deren Hauptstadt seine Geburtstadt Mathurā war, verehrt ward .... Ich trage daher kein Bedenken zu behaupten, dass das Dogma von Vishṇus Verkörperungen schon drei Hundert Jahre vor Chr. G. sich gebildet hatte, obwohl ihre Zahl und ihre Reihenfolge erst später festgesetzt worden sind."[2]

Barth says: "From the date of the second century before our era, the story of Kṛishṇa was the subject of dramatic representations similar to those

---

[1] *Op. cit.*, p. 224.

[2] P. 1107. (Spelling and grammar as in the original version.)

connected with the festival in honour of Bacchus and our ancient mysteries. Besides, there is good ground for regarding this personage as the Indian Hercules, the worship of whom Megasthenes found prevailing in the valley of the Ganges at the beginning of the third century before Christ."[1]

Hopkins sees Megasthenes as a complicating factor: "A fact of some importance, to be set beside Megasthenes' distinction between a great god Dionysos (Śiva) and a demi-god Heracles (Kṛishṇa), is that Kṛishṇa is unknown in the older Buddhistic literature, which could scarcely have ignored him (in favour of Brahman) if he was already a great god."[2]

Another author who finds that Megasthenes causes certain difficulties is Kennedy, who is to some extent guilty of working against himself. He starts with an excursus on the Greeks' methods of identifying the foreign gods they mention, by using the most peculiar principles, either of resemblances—which did not need to be particularly striking—between names, or of other common characteristics.[3] He states eventually that the Indian Heracles was the object of particular veneration among the Śibi, a people who, according to Megasthenes, dressed in animal skins, carried clubs as weapons and marked their cattle with the sign of the club. Kennedy concludes that it is self-evident that the god worshipped by the Śibi must be Śiva. He does not however undertake to examine this situation in more detail, nor does he produce any more evidence in favour of his views. One might have expected, remembering Kennedy's opposition to Lassen and others, that this new identification would be supported by some more conclusive evidence. One might also have expected Kennedy to have used this tentative result to support the "borrowing" theory; this should have been possible, since he had asserted that Megasthenes was not referring to Kṛishṇa under the name of Heracles, but to Śiva. But Kennedy does not make use of this potential argument. Instead, when he considers the identity of Dionysos, he comes to the unexpected conclusion that Dionysos is Kṛishṇa. One of the main arguments in favour of this thesis is that the followers of Dionysos wear their hair long, as did the god himself, according to Megasthenes.[4]

We shall bring this section to a close by quoting a name which has not previously been mentioned among those scholars who have dealt with the problem of Kṛishṇa. Walter Ruben, in a monograph on this subject, has gathered together various motives connected with Kṛishṇa, and has analysed them from an atomistic point of view. He has paid careful attention

---

1 *Religions de l'Inde*, p. 100 (Barth, *Œuvres*, p. 152, Engl. ed., p. 168).

2 *India Old and New* ("Christ in India"), p. 158 n. 1.

3 On the Greeks' methods of identification, see below, p. 36 f.

4 *The Child Kṛishṇa, Christianity, and the Gujars*, p. 967 (*J.R.A.S.* 1907).

to the occurrence of the theme among a number of peoples, but he has made no attempt to give an overall view of the problem. What is of particular interest to us is his treatment of Megasthenes' information about Heracles, which is, as yet, the most detailed treatment these passages have received: rather more than three pages. He states by way of introduction that "it is evident at first sight that Megasthenes represents Kṛishṇa by the side of Dionysos–Śiva as the only great god of India; that is the situation which is in fact confirmed by the Mahābhārata. Without the evidence of Megasthenes we should have had difficulty in believing it to be so ancient".[1] After having discussed a number of passages in Megasthenes, of which six are used to show that Heracles must be identical with Kṛishṇa, while twelve or more are extremely difficult to combine with Kṛishṇa, Ruben concludes his chapter on Megasthenes in these words: "Megasthenes' writings provide invaluable documentary evidence, for they support the dating of Kṛishṇa, on a basis of the Bhagavadgītā, to Kauṭilya's time, and confirm the books (*grantha*) mentioned by Patañjali as referring to Kṛishṇa. They also confirm the end of the period of purely oral tradition about a local god, and the existence of a recognized religion based on the great god Krishṇa in the 4th century B.C."[2] This idea, of the antiquity of the Kṛishṇa cult, which the author expresses on a number of occasions in this monograph, is also found in his book *Eisenschmiede und Dämonen in Indien*. Ruben is another who considers this to be axiomatic, and to need no further proof. Had we believed Kṛishṇa to be originally no more than a minor tribal deity, we are put right by Megasthenes, says Ruben, informing us that Kṛishṇa was the dominant deity, at least in the Ganges Basin, as early as 300 B.C. So we see that everyone who has broached the subject of the antiquity of Kṛishṇa has had to fall back upon Megasthenes. Ruben's is perhaps the strongest expression of the idea; it is common knowledge that without Megasthenes, we should never have believed Krishnaism to be so ancient—at least as a significant religion.[3] Unfortunately, no one says just *why* we should not have believed it—perhaps because no other absolutely trustworthy proof or evidence of its early existence can be produced?[4]

---

[1] *Kṛishṇa*, p. 278.

[2] *Op. cit.*, p. 281.

[3] *Kṛishṇa*, p. 278.

[4] Cf. this statement in *The History and Culture of the Indian People* II, p. 432: "The earliest reference to devotion to, and worship of, a personal god, out of which Vaishnavism arose, may be traced to *the Ashṭādhyāyī* of Pāṇini (fifth century B.C.) which offers the rule for the formation of the word '*Vāsudevaka*' in the sense of 'a person whose object of *Bhakti* is Vāsudeva'. It is generally agreed that *Bhakti* here probably, *though*

5. *Pāṇini's Vāsudeva-sūtra* (IV.3.98)

We have already emphasized that prior to Megasthenes' mention of Heracles, no proof or evidence of the existence of Krishnaism as an important religion had been produced. In fact the only argument which is normally used, apart from that provided by Megasthenes, has been bitterly contested. This is the passage in Pāṇini's sūtra IV.3.98, which reads: *Vāsudevārjunābhyām vun.* The context of this passage is that it is headed *Bhaktiḥ,* which naturally suggests *bhakti* piety. U. C. Bhattacharjee, in an article in the *Indian Historical Quarterly* I (1925), pp. 483–489, entitled *The Evidence of Pāṇini on Vāsudeva-Worship,* has shown the unreliability of any argument based on this sūtra which attempts to prove that Vāsudeva was a god worshipped at the time of Pāṇini. It is true that P. Bonnerjee has attempted to discuss Bhattacharjee's objections, but in

---

not certainly, is to be taken in the sense of religious adoration. But that Vāsudeva was the object of such devotion, at least as early as the fourth century B.C., is proved by the statement of Megasthenes that the Sourasenoi, i.e. the people of the Mathurā region, held Heracles in special honour; for there is no doubt that Heracles was the Greek analogue of Vāsudeva-Kṛishṇa ... In the light of Megasthenes's statement referred to above, we may place the foundation of the Vāsudeva cult in the fourth century B.C., if not much earlier still." And p. 437: "Although, therefore, the Bhāgavata sect, worshipping Vāsudeva, was known probably to the grammarian Pāṇini of Gandhāra and certainly to Megasthenes, it was apparently not so prominent outside the Mathurā region and the neighbouring land towards the north-west about the third century B.C."

Chaudhuri, in his paper *The Indian Cowherd-God,* expresses the opinion that the original Kṛishṇa, the herdsman, is to be seen in the Purāṇas, while the Mbh has another version of Kṛishṇa, without any reference to the herdsman. He claims that "Gopāla-Kṛishṇa was a tribal nero of the Ābhīras" (p. 71). The Mbh however represents the Ābhīras as the *enemies* of Kṛishṇa-Vāsudeva.

Hutton takes up the question in *Census of India,* 1931, Vol. I, p. 457: "Slater has aptly pointed out that Kṛishṇa himself was of Naga descent and the traditional blue colour in which Hindu art depicts him possibly represents the brunette colouring of the Mediterranean as distinguished on the one hand from the blond Aryans and on the other from the dusky aboriginals." (Cf. Slater, *The Dravidian Element in Indian Culture.*) Przyluski has explained Vishṇu as a Dravidian god originally, and his name as being non-Indo-European (A. O. IV, 2, Aug. 1932; I. A., Jan. 1933).

Both Kennedy (*J.R.A.S.* 1907, p. 968) and Iyengar (*History of the Tamils,* pp. 202–206) quote as proof of the great age of the cult of Kṛishṇa the following: "In the time of the first Arsacide monarch of Armenia, Valarshak (149–127 B.C.), two Indian chiefs established a colony at Vishap on the Western Euphrates, west of Lake Van and founded temples for the worship of Gisani (Kṛishṇa) and Demeter (Baladeva)."

Sastri, in his book *The Vaishnava Cult in India,* traces the key-ideas in the Rigveda, according to a review in *Man in India* XIX, 1939, p. 73; Goswami Kunja Govinda's *A Study of Vaishnavism* deals with the origins and first period of the cult of Vishṇu, ca. 200 B.C.–ca. 600 A.D. (the Śuṅga and Gupta periods).

my opinion, without seriously challenging the validity of his results.[1] Before ever having seen Bhattacharjee's article I had myself considered the same objections and had come to substantially the same result. But Pāṇini's evidence is more than a century older than that of Megasthenes, and I consider that it would be valuable to summarize at this point exactly what Pāṇini said, and how his words have been interpreted. Not until this has been done shall we be in a position to appreciate Megasthenes' great—and in fact decisive—importance for the discussion, since it will become perfectly clear that he stands as an entirely isolated witness to the great antiquity of the Kṛishṇa cult, amid an overwhelming mass of texts and archaeological material which say nothing whatever about it. This will also demonstrate that the subject of the present study is extremely important for the entire chronology of the religious history of India.

Sir R. G. Bhāṇḍārkar writes: "In his comment on Pāṇini IV.3.98, Patañjali distinctly states that the Vāsudeva contained in the Sūtra is the name of the 'worshipful', i.e. of one who is pre-eminently worshipful, i.e. God. The worship of Vāsudeva must be regarded to be as old as Pāṇini."[2]

Rāmaprasād Chanda, in his article on *Archaeology and Vaishṇava Tradition*, not only accepts this viewpoint; he goes much further. He writes: "If Vāsudeva in Pāṇini's aphorism IV.3.98 is a god and not a kshatriya, it follows that the other person named in the sūtra, Arjuna, is also a god and not a kshatriya ... Vāsudeva and Arjuna were not only recognised as gods at the time of Pāṇini, but also as a divine pair as described in the Mahābhārata."[3]

Barth, in his *Religions de l'Inde*,[4] has also expressed the view that Arjuna was considered to be a god; his argument is similar. He also states that the Mahābhārata contains traces of the worship of Arjuna, but produces no evidence in support of this statement. Bhattacharjee, whom I am following here, can find no evidence that this was so. Nor have I, in my reading of the Mahābhārata, found anything to support Barth's assertion. On the contrary, the situation is such, that it is mainly the Pāṇḍavas who treat Kṛishṇa as a god, and show their clear dependence upon their divine friend. We may quote a representative example: after Kṛishṇa's death, Arjuna was not able so much as to stretch his bow, so dependent was he on Kṛishṇa.[5]

---

[1] *Some observations on the interpretation of the Pāṇinisūtra Vāsudevārjunābhyām vun and the antiquity of the Bhāgavatas* (*J.B.R.S.* XL 1954, p. 74–79).

[2] *Vāsudeva of Pāṇini* IV, iii, 98 (*J.R.A.S.* 1910, p. 168–170).

[3] *Op. cit.*, p. 151.

[4] Engl. ed., p. 172 note 2.

[5] *Mbh* XVI.

Kṛishṇa is clearly the object of purely religious faith, both from the five brothers and their wife. This is not the case with Arjuna, who is never afforded religious adoration and prayer. In other words, there is no evidence in the Mahābhārata for the existence of an ancient cult of Arjuna which later disappeared.[1] The only evidence of such a cult is the Pāṇini sūtra under discussion. And it is only reasonable to suppose that if we allow the sūtra to be adequate evidence for the existence of the cult of Vāsudeva, then we are virtually compelled to allow the same sūtra as evidence of an Arjuna cult, since the two names are found in the same compound word. But even that is insufficient. We must in the name of logic accept the Pāṇini sūtra as evidence for the worship of other figures named under the same heading.

The heading of the rule with which we are at present concerned, IV.3.98, is to be found in IV.3.95, and reads *Bhaktiḥ*. Its meaning in this context is that a word or name having the suffix *-ka*, etc., means: he who has *bhakti* for the bearer of the word or name in question. Thus *Vāsudevaka* means: he who has *bhakti* for *Vāsudeva*; *Arjunaka*: he who has *bhakti* for *Arjuna*. This has automatically been interpreted to mean: worshipper of Vāsudeva and Arjuna respectively.

The rule laid down in IV.3.95 applies also to 96, 97, 99 and 100. What is it, then, which is said to be the object of *bhakti* in those passages? In 96: cakes and milk products; in 97: The Mahārāja (the great king); in 99: all Kshatriya and Gotra names, like Nakula; and finally, in 100: countries and Kshatriyas, like the kingdom of Aṅga and the Aṅga Kshatriyas. It is not seriously to be expected that everything under the rule of IV.3.95 should ever have been worshipped in India.[2] And there is no reason to regard the word *bhakti*, as used here, as being of particular significance. It seems perfectly obvious that we are here dealing with a mis-translation. Stated summarily: if we have no right or duty to allow the existence of worshippers of these others, what right have we, from this particular sūtra, to allow the existence of cults of Vāsudeva and Arjuna?

That portion of Bhattacharjee's argument which we have summarized here, and which contains nothing that any reader of the passage in question cannot immediately observe for himself, should serve our purpose of showing that the evidence of Pāṇini is insufficient proof of the existence of a Vāsudeva cult during the 5th century B.C.

---

[1] That there is a cult of the Pāṇḍavas in South India is irrelevant in this context.

[2] It is difficult to understand the view put forward on this subject by Agrawala, in *India as known to Pāṇini*.

In order to bring what has been said into sharper relief we shall quote finally from Bhattacharjee what must be the definitive judgment, that there is no possible reference to the history of Indian religion to be found under IV.3.95–100: the passage in question has nothing which we can be sure refers to the name of a god. The names of the gods are collected under the heading *sā asya devatā*: this is his god, IV.2.22. If Vāsudeva, Arjuna, Nakula and others were in fact the names of gods in Pāṇini, then they would not be found under the heading of *bhakti* (IV.3.95 ff.) but under *sā asya devatā* (IV.2.22). Furthermore, the author ends by pointing out that Nārada and Śāṇḍilya (Bhakti-sūtras) explain *bhakti* as meaning "a feeling related to '*anurakti*'", i.e. preference for.

But the most decisive point is the question: Is it possible to produce any example of word-formation in the whole of the literature where the suffix *-ka* has this function? A worshipper of Śiva is called Śaiva, of Vishṇu Vaishṇava, of Buddha Bauddha, of Jina Jaina, and so on. It is common knowledge that the normal use of *-ka* is to denote the diminutive or affinity (Whitney § 1222). This shows how those carrying on the discussion have ignored the most natural method of understanding Pāṇini's obscure sūtra correctly: by starting from the known in order to illuminate the unknown.

We have no reason to spend more time on Pāṇini's supposed evidence for the Vāsudeva cult. It need hardly be said that such a cult might have existed, although Pāṇini provides no straightforward evidence on the subject.

Finally, for the sake of completeness, I should like to call attention to the words of Gonda, in *Aspects of Early Vishnuism*: "How are we to know for sure that Vāsudeva of Pāṇini was already identified with Kṛishṇa?"[1] It is clear that the author is here reckoning with two different figures, having different names, who were later combined into one. That possibility is of course not excluded. It may even appear to be the most plausible solution of a complex problem.[2]

C. *Megasthenes' Reliability*

If we are compelled to dismiss Pāṇini as a witness, then the importance of what Megasthenes has to say will be all the greater. Will he stand up to such an examination? Is he sufficiently reliable to be believed? Can his

---

[1] *Op. cit.*, p. 160.

[2] Cf. Bhandarkar, *Vaishnavism, Śaivism*, pp. 2, 11, 35 *et al.*

evidence be accepted, even though he stand as a lone witness in favour of the common belief in the great antiquity of Krishnaism, and though he be contradicted by a mass of silent witnesses, who by their very silence seem to deny the existence of Kṛishṇa as a great god before the middle of the 2nd century B.C.?

The subject of the reliability of Megasthenes has inspired a number of studies, of which I should like to give a short summary here. In 1846, Schwanbeck gathered together passages from classical authors containing quotations from Megasthenes.[1] His Latin preface states in all simplicity that the value of later writers on India stands in direct proportion to the accuracy with which they reproduce Megasthenes.[2] This statement is regarded with full approval by Truesdall S. Brown, who was nevertheless able to produce a by no means unimportant negative criticism. Emphasizing, as Arrian had done before him, that Megasthenes visited only a small part of India, he points out that his observations are for the most part not first-hand, but rest on the evidence of others he met at the court of Candragupta; these eyewitnesses were presumably not all one hundred per cent reliable.[3] We must remember here that Brown was talking about Megasthenes' entire literary output, which stretched over geography, biology and many other subjects; he lays no particular emphasis on the passages dealing with religion—if he considers them at all. He continued his criticism by pointing out that the Greek ambassador was probably not acquainted with the local language, and had to rely on interpreters who were probably not always able to produce the right word in the right situation; this, then, may have constituted a distinctly misleading source.[4] Brown's most severe negative criticism, however, is that there existed a Greek literary tradition from which Megasthenes was not entirely free.[5] Despite the fact that he turns his back on the work of Ctesias, written a century earlier in Persia, he reproduces myths every bit as improbable.[6] He had no critical sense, in the modern meaning of the term, but he can hardly be blamed for that. His information on a number of points nevertheless appears particularly valueless. But modern research cannot afford to ignore him.

Brown concludes his acute estimation of Megasthenes as a historical source in these words: "Nevertheless, Schwanbeck's statement is still

---

[1] On other Megasthenes editions see Bibliography.

[2] *Op. cit.*, p. 76.

[3] *The Reliability of Megasthenes* (*A.J.P.* 76, p. 32).

[4] *Op. cit.*, p. 21.

[5] *Op. cit.*, p. 28 f.

[6] *Ibid.*

defensible, that later writers on India owe their value to the fidelity with which they reproduce Megasthenes; Megasthenes also shows up pretty well in our negative test, for he seems, more often than not, to have turned his back on Ctesias."[1]

And despite his criticism, Brown is evidently far from willing to subscribe to the views of Strabo: "Generally speaking, the men who have hitherto written on the affairs of India were a set of liars,—Deimachos holds the first place in the list, Megasthenes comes next; while Onesikritos and Nearchos, with others of the same class, manage to stammer out a few words (of truth). Of this we became the more convinced whilst writing the history of Alexander. No faith whatever can be placed in Deimachos and Megasthenes."[2]

An author who has paid particular attention to Megasthenes' reliability is Timmer who, in her thesis on *Megasthenes en de Indische Maatschappij*, comes to the result that "Megasthenes confuses Indian facts with Indian theory".[3] In other words, he on the one hand reproduced correctly what his own eyes had seen; and on the other, what his Indian informants told him. The evident mistakes he makes and the fantastic element in what he has to say are to be traced, not to the author himself, but to the land he is describing.

To this category belongs another work, though it makes no claim to deal with the question of Megasthenes' reliability. This is Otto Stein's *Megasthenes und Kauṭilya*, which sets out to examine, by means of a comparison between, on the one hand, the facts recorded by Megasthenes and, on the other, the facts contained in Kauṭilya's Arthaśāstra, whether the old tradition identifying the author of the Arthaśāstra and Candragupta's minister is substantially correct. Those facts which agree in the two writings are those which have never been altered; those which are known to have been altered seldom agree at all. From this, Stein draws the conclusion that the author Kauṭilya must be different from the minister, contemporary with Megasthenes.

This result has not gone unchallenged. In an article entitled *The Indica of Megasthenes*, in *J.A.O.S.* 1958 (Oct.–Dec.), R. C. Majumdar subjects Stein's work to critical examination. He shows that Stein has not proved the authenticity of the Megasthenes quotations from which the vital pieces of information which disagree with Kauṭilya have been drawn. All the passages

[1] *Op. cit.*, p. 33.

[2] Strabo 70. Quoted in McCrindle, *Ancient India as described by Megasthenes and Arrian*, p. 18 f.

[3] *Op. cit.*, p. 312.

which do not agree with Kauṭilya are included in sections which are not expressly said to have originated from Megasthenes. This touches upon a particular difficulty in our text: that we are not in possession of a single line of Megasthenes' original work, but must rely on more or less careful and reliable quotations or accounts in other classical authors.[1]

There is only one point on which Schwanbeck finds the content of the preserved fragments to be unreliable, and that is their account of the Indian gods. He does not go into detail on the subject, but one is left with the impression that he considers Kṛishṇa to be unlike Megasthenes' description of Heracles, and Śiva to be unlike Megasthenes' description of Dionysos. The myths related by the Greek ambassador about Heracles and Dionysos are not told by the Indians about Kṛishṇa and Śiva.[2]

We therefore pause at this point to examine the question of Megasthenes' reliability as a historian of religion.

Earlier attempts to get to grips with our problem have dealt with Megasthenes' religio-historical passages on a basis of his own Greek background.[3] This view seems to be generally accepted, and we shall therefore briefly consider this Greek background.

In the first place, it was not Megasthenes who identified Heracles and

---

[1] Majumdar's criticism of Megasthenes, and particularly of his 'reporter' Diodorus, has been answered by Sethna in *J.A.O.S.* 1960, in an article strongly advocating both Megasthenes' reliability and Diodorus' absolute dependence. He absolves Schwanbeck's edition of Megasthenes' *Indika* from the criticism directed against it by Majumdar. Majumdar himself later answered: "I have never denied *Indika* 'a wide mass of factuality or accurately reported fable', but I have stressed the necessity of taking pains to find out what is fable and what is fact in the accounts of Megasthenes, since he did not always distinguish between the two and did not possess a sufficiently critical mind to enable him to do so." This implies that we do not have a presentation of the way the *Greeks* understood the Indians' religion. Megasthenes' objectivity is a great advantage to us.

[2] *Op. cit.*, p. 61 and 76 (McCrindle, pp. 20 and 27).

[3] Stein, *Megasthenes*, in Pauly–Wissowa XV: 1, col. 256 ff.: "Es ist somit sicher, dass M. an die allgemein-griechische, insbesondere an die Alexandermythe angeschlossen hat; es kommen jedoch bei ihm einige Züge hinzu, die teils seinen Beobachtungen, teils entsprechend geänderten religiösen Tatsachen Indiens entsprechen." Cf. col. 258: "Abschliessend lässt sich über den Dionysos- und Heraklesbericht des M. sagen: anknüpfend an die Alexanderhistoriker hat M. die Züge des Dionysos und Herakles für historisch gehalten, beeinflusst von allgemein-griechischen Vorstellungen über deren Tätigkeit als Kulturbringer, bestärkt durch die vor ihm liegende Tradition der Alexanderzeit, überzeugt durch analoge Erscheinungen auf indischem religiösen Gebiete." Col. 323: "... so wie er — vielleicht nur aus eigenem Erleben heraus — die Schranken zwischen Ārya und Mleccha, den Barbaren, übersehen hat ..." Cf. our treatment of Dionysos, below p. 190 f.

Dionysos with two Indian gods: the actual identification was created during the course of Alexander's Indian campaign. If we then ask why this identification was made, we find a number of reasons. First, that Alexander was regarded as standing in a very special relationship to these gods; they were in fact his ancestors. Secondly, there existed a number of traditions according to which these gods had themselves conducted victorious campaigns in various parts of the world; Alexander sought to emulate these, and if possible to surpass them. And thirdly, although Alexander worshipped many gods, Dionysos and Heracles held a special place in his devotion.

We may illustrate this with a number of quotations.

Kern writes: "Der προπάτωρ, der Urahn, von dem alle Makedonen abstammen sollen, ist der Zeussohn Herakles."[1] Berve informs us that "... wie er denn auch den Heiligen der kynischen Sekte, Herakles, nicht nur als Ahnherrn verehrte, sondern zum Vorbild nahm."[2] All rulers did not however worship Heracles or Dionysos as their patron deities; Seleucus Nicator I, for example, reckoned himself as being descended from Apollo, while the chief gods of the Seleucids were Zeus and Apollo.[3] But Nilsson, writing of the Diadochs, the Epigones and the Ptolemaeans, says: "Alle drei Dynastien knüpften anfangs an das makedonische Königshaus der Argeaden an, das sich von Herakles herleitete."[4] Tarn completes the picture by mentioning that both Heracles and Dionysos were regarded as being Alexander's forefathers, thus explaining why Alexander's name was connected with them in this particular way.[5] But though their deeds were great, Alexander surpassed them in every way,[6] thus earning the right to be worshipped as divine.

Nilsson writes, referring to Alexander's attempts to emulate his divine ancestors: "Es wird gesagt, dass sein (Alexanders) Zug zum Ammonsorakel dem Wunsche, Perseus und Herakles nachzueifern, entsprungen sei und dass er am Hydaspes dem Herakles als seinem Ahnherrn geopfert, ja, überhaupt, dass er Herakles und Dionysos nachgeahmt habe."[7]

On the subject of the position of the two gods in the religious life of Alexander, and of Greece generally, we may quote: "Als Grund seiner Belagerung von Tyrus wird die Weigerung der Tyrier angegeben, ihn in die

---

[1] *Griechische Religion* III, p. 45.

[2] *Das Alexanderreich*, p. 67.

[3] Martin P:son Nilsson, *Geschichte der Griechischen Religion* II, p. 157 f.

[4] *Op. cit.*, p. 145.

[5] *Alexander the Great* II, p. 55(–62).

[6] *Op. cit.*, p. 56 f.

[7] Nilsson, *op. cit.*, p. 11.

Stadt hineinzulassen, um dem Herakles zu opfern; Alexander soll geträumt haben, dass Herakles ihn bewillkomne und in die Stadt einführe."[1] Once the town had been captured, Alexander sacrificed to Heracles.

Further evidence of Alexander's special devotion to Heracles is the fact that he founded a town which he named Herakleia, and that he named his son Heracles. Later "wurde Herakles in den Gymnasien verehrt".[2] This later period is also touched upon by Nilsson in another context: "Kein Gott beherrschte das griechische Vereinsleben in gleichem Masse wie Dionysos."[3] It is not however clear when and how the cult of Dionysos attained this position. "Berves Meinung, dass während dem Feldzug im Osten Dionysos mehr hervorgetreten sei, wird mit guten Gründen bestritten von Nock."[4]

It is clear that Dionysos was an important god in Alexander's day; Alexander's mother Olympias was deeply devoted to Dionysos. Further evidence of this is provided by the fact that when in 324/323 Alexander was adopted into the official civil pantheon of Athens, he was received as "the second Dionysos"; Dionysos' position was thus strong, but we know nothing of how it became strong.[5]

This should suffice to demonstrate the prominent position occupied by these two gods in the religious life of Greece at the time of Alexander the Great. We must now proceed to a brief summary of the myths related of these gods, and a brief review of their cultus.[6]

Dionysos

The mother of Dionysos died before he was born. The foetus being transferred to the thigh of Zeus his father, Dionysos was born out of his father's thigh. He was then taken to Mount Nysa, where he was looked after by nymphs, principally the nymph Nysa. According to Euripides—i.e. more than a century before Alexander—Dionysos was "the promotor of civilization, a law-giver, and a lover of peace".[7] He is also said to have campaigned and conquered all over Asia. Euripides mentions a number of countries, among them Persia, Bactria and Arabia, but not India. Dionysos'

---

[1] *Op. cit.*, p. 12.

[2] *Op. cit.*, p. 118.

[3] *Ibid.*

[4] *Op. cit.*, p. 12, n. 9.

[5] Kern, *Griechische Religion* III, p. 46.

[6] The following mainly report of Nilsson, *op. cit.*, I², p. 564–601 (on Dionysos), and Smith, *Dictionary*, s.v. *Dionysos* and *Heracles*.

[7] Bacch. V 55, 85 ff., and 13 ff.

Indian campaign is however considered to have been invented in imitation of Alexander's campaign or at least after it.[1]

Dionysos is represented in art as being surrounded by bacchantes (graces and charities), silenes, panes, satyrs and centaurs. His most outstanding gifts to mankind are the various kinds of tree, principally the grapevine. Others are the fig and the ivy. The close connection between this god and trees is seen in a number of his epithets. It is possible that this is the primary trait of his character, out of which his connection with the vine and the ivy has subsequently developed.[2] He has never been connected with agrarian fertility.[3]

The most outstanding features of his cultus were the role played by women, and its orgiastic character. The bacchantes proceeded in a state of ecstasy to the hills and forests, with torches and staves; they killed and tore apart any animal they encountered, and ate the flesh raw. Women were even known to dismember their own children in their ecstasy. The slaughtered animal was regarded as being the god himself, and to wear its skin was to identify oneself with the god. The wearing of masks was also common in the Dionysos cult—more so than in the cult of any other god. Dionysos himself was believed to appear in the form of a bull.

It is of special significance that Olympias, the mother of Alexander the Great, was a Dionysos worshipper. She was from Thrace, the district in which his cult originated. Some scholars believe however that the Dionysos cult did not achieve prominence until after Alexander's Indian campaign. When it was accepted as an official religion its orgiastic character became considerably modified.

The cult of Dionysos had no element of asceticism or self-inflicted suffering. Processions were a prominent element; one is described as follows: first came a person carrying an *amphora* containing wine, and a grapevine; next a worshipper leading the sacrificial animal, a he-goat, followed by another carrying a basket of figs. Lastly in the procession was borne a *phallos*. Other processions are known to have taken place in which each participant carried a *phallos* (or in which each was ithyphallic). Dionysos alone lacks this symbol. He was sometimes carried on a cart, which resembled a ship, surrounded by silenes. A tent was then set up in which a *hieros gamos* was celebrated between Dionysos and the queen.

According to later texts, Dionysos stood in relation to the dead as

---

[1] Nilsson, *op. cit.* I, p. 578.

[2] Otto, *Dionysos*, has pointed out that Dionysos has connexion exclusively with humid trees.

[3] Nilsson, *op. cit.* I, pp. 585 and 601.

psychopomp. And finally, Nilsson has shown that the mysteries of Dionysos are of very late date. The festival of Dionysos was celebrated in winter, in the month Lēnaion, and was called Lēnaia.

Smith writes that ancient writers were "driven to the supposition that there were originally several divinities which were afterwards identified under the one name of Dionysos. Cicero distinguishes five Dionysi, and Diodorus three".

If we take account only of this description of the *Greek* Dionysos, we find a number of incontestable resemblances between Dionysos and Śiva; it is easy to understand why the two have been so often identified. But we are nevertheless led to ask whether sufficient account has been taken of Megasthenes' description of the *Indian* Dionysos.

Heracles

The Heracles worshipped by Alexander the Great, and which he and his men considered they had encountered at various stages of their campaign, may be briefly described as follows:

Heracles was born the son of Zeus. On the following night his mother gave birth to a twin brother, Iphicles, whose father was however the husband of his mother. Hera, wife of Zeus, became jealous, and this soon became an influence in the boy's life. It is said that on one occasion he came by chance to rest in her arms, and fed on her milk while she slept. When she woke up, she thrust him aside, spilling her milk. This was the origin of the Milky Way. While he was still in the cradle, Hera sent two snakes to kill the child, but he strangled both of them.

The young Heracles is the hero of a number of adventures which took place during his time as a herdsman of Amphitryon. Most originated in the jealousy of Hera, and the measures which she took to dispose of the youth.

On one occasion he made an alliance with King Thespius, who gave him his fifty daughters to wife. But he married many other women, by whom he had a large number of children. Many sons are known by name, but only one daughter, Macaria, whose mother was Deianeira.

Heracles received various weapons from various gods. From Hermes he received a sword; from Apollo bow and arrows; from Hephaistos a suit of golden armour; from Athena a *peplus*. His most characteristic weapon was the club; this he either made or received from Hephaistos.

Toward the end of his life he became insane, killing his own children by Megara and two of the children of Iphicles. His life ended tragically; he mounted the funeral pyre of his own free will after having been given a poisoned shirt by his unsuspecting wife.

The course of his life is normally summed up in his twelve deeds. These are:

1. The fight with the Nemean lion.
2. The fight against the Lernean hydra.
3. The stag of Ceryneia in Arcadia.
4. The Erymanthian boar.
5. The stables of Augeas.
6. The Stymphalian birds.
7. The Cretan bull.
8. The mares of the Thracian Diomedes.
9. The girdle of the queen of the Amazons.
10. The oxen of Geryones in Erytheia.
11. The golden apples of the Hesperides.
12. Cerberus.

Again, if we take account only of the Greek Heracles, we might well suppose the Indian Heracles to have been Kṛishṇa, who had a series of adventures similar to those we have listed. This we say in advance in order to mark the different method we have used in our study, when compared with earlier investigations of Megasthenes' religio-historical passages. We shall see that Megasthenes has little to say about these characteristics of the Greek Heracles in his description of the Indian: but he mentions a great deal which is related neither of the Greek Heracles nor of Kṛishṇa. It is therefore necessary to re-examine the evidence on a basis of what is in fact said about the *Indian* Heracles.

One last point. We know that these two gods were extremely prominent in the thought-world of Alexander and his men; it is possible, with this in mind, that they exerted themselves in order to identify these gods *and no others* in India. So they may have applied a process of eclecticism, choosing one characteristic from one god, another from another god, and so on, until they had satisfied themselves that Heracles was in fact in India; the same applies to Dionysos. We might play with the idea that both Kṛishṇa and Śiva were capable of suggesting Heracles, since both wielded the club, one wore an animal-skin, the other had many wives and had adventures reminiscent of Heracles' deeds. In the same way both can be shown to have had characteristics suggestive of Dionysos, so that Alexander could have recognized Dionysos in a combination of the same gods. Stein has touched upon this idea in his identification of Dionysos and Manu.[1]

But this theory is contradicted by the fact that Megasthenes described the Indian gods in great detail, and included a number of characteristics which have no Greek parallel. This rules out the possibility of the Greeks having transferred attributes from the Greek to the Indian Heracles–Dionysos. A further possibility is that there in fact exists a common cultural heritage in which some Indian ethnic group and some Greek ethnic group share a common ancestry and a common religion.

We must therefore begin by examining the evidence, in order to see whether the descriptions of the Indian gods Heracles and Dionysos contain characteristics which can be paralleled *in India*, before we regard it as proven that there has been a transfer from Greece to India. Not until it has been proved impossible that there should be an Indian parallel shall we reckon with the possibility of transference.

D. *The Reliability of Megasthenes' Reporters*

Timmer has also examined the reliability of those who quote Megasthenes, and has come to the result that "Megasthenes' terminology is best preserved in Strabo and Diodorus, the construction of his work by Arrianus and Diodorus, and the construction of the fragments by Strabo".[2] Nothing is said about the contents, probably because Schwanbeck has succeeded in giving excellent characterizations of the four most important of those quoting Megasthenes. The three we have mentioned share the desire to write easily, pleasantly and enjoyably; they therefore abridge Megasthenes deliberately, but without, in Schwanbeck's view, distorting him in the process. What is a pity, from the point of view of the later reader, is that almost everything which might have been of value for the study of ancient India has been omitted, since the Greek authors and their readers considered such material to be totally lacking in interest. From this point of view, Pliny comes as a valuable complement, since he is not afraid to include dry and uninteresting lists of geographical names, and the like. But what Pliny has to say is not seldom valueless, declares Schwanbeck: so much so that "if we compare his accounts of Taprobane and the Kingdom of Prasii, we might well believe that he lived in two different epochs".[3]

---

[1] *Megasthenes*, in Pauly-Wissowa XV: 1, col. 309 f.

[2] *Op. cit.*, p. 312.

[3] *Op. cit.*, p. 58 (McCrindle, p. 19 note).

E. *Method and Disposition*

In the last resort, there is only one possible way of approaching this vital source of our knowledge of Indian religion in the 4th century B.C. We shall first give a systematic summary and presentation of the passages incorporated into the fragments available to us, and which may be supposed to derive from Megasthenes; and secondly, we shall compare these passages with Indian literature through the ages.

It may prove to be the case that certain of the Megasthenes passages can be supported by relevant material from certain literary groups: the Rig Veda, the Brāhmaṇas, the Upanishads, the Epics or the Purāṇas—in a number of places or within only one of these groups. Should the latter situation arise, then Megasthenes' importance for the history of Indian literature would increase correspondingly.

But it may equally well happen that certain passages cannot be paralleled in any Indian text. In such cases the first step will be to establish the authenticity of the passage in question, if this has not already been done; there is always a possibility that a passage may have been attributed to Megasthenes by mistake. But there is another possibility. The passage may refer to an ethnic group other than the one having the literature. The ethnologists will then be called in to clarify the situation.[1]

Before proceeding, we must however point to a couple of methodological issues. In the first place, one of the most striking things about Greek and Latin authors' accounts of other peoples' religions is the fact that they never refer to the strange gods under their own names. We have already hinted at this.[2] On this point we should like to quote an author who gives us a number of pieces of factual information which may help towards our understanding of which Indian gods are referred to by the Greek names Dionysos and Heracles. When we have identified the gods in question, if we compare them with the following quotation, we shall find that our tentative identification fits in extraordinarily well with the scheme of *interpretatio graeca*.

---

[1] There must be a reason why we do not earlier examine the authenticity of this statement. We see that the name of Megasthenes is quoted very seldom indeed. It follows that only in a few cases can we be absolutely certain that the statement in question comes from him. Other texts are sometimes supposed to be based on information derived from Megasthenes; this is motivated by saying that they contain themes which other authors have claimed to come from Megasthenes' *Indika*. For other principles followed in the choice of texts, see Schwanbeck's introduction to his edition of Megasthenes and the article by Majumdar, quoted above.

[2] P. 21.

Mordtmann, in *Mythologische Miscellen*, writes as follows: "Griechische und römische Schriftsteller, selbst in rein wissenschaftlichen Werken, haben es mit ängstlicher Scheu vermieden, barbarische Wörter zu gebrauchen, indem sie es vorzogen, dieselben, wo immer es nur ging, durch Ausdrücke der eigenen Sprache zu ersetzen; so vor allem bei den Namen der barbarischen Gottheiten, bei denen sich schliesslich ein feststehender Usus ausgebildet hat. Gerade wie man Athene mit Minerva, Hera durch Juno usw. regelmässig übersetzte, so verfuhr man auch mit den fremden Göttern; die Wiedergabe des semitischen El durch Krónos Saturnus, Baal durch Zeus Jupiter, Baaltis durch Héra Juno, der phoenicischen Astarte durch Afrodíte Venus, Eschmun durch Asclepius Aeschulapius, Melkart durch Herakles Hercules ist fast ausnahmslos zu nennen. So weit liesse sich nichts gegen dies Verfahren einwenden; dagegen gerathen wir in nicht geringe Verlegenheit, wo uns andere Gottheiten wie Artemis, Dionysos etc. entgegentreten; einmal lässt sich nämlich nachweisen, dass z. B. dieselbe Gottheit bald durch Artemis bald durch Athene, eine andere bald durch Helios bald durch Dionysos, oder ganz verschiedene Gottheiten durch einen Namen wiedergegeben werden; dann aber herrscht manchmal eine grosse Ungewissheit, ob überhaupt hinter einem solchen Namen ein einheimischer Cult zu suchen ist?"[1]

What is perhaps the most striking fact about this survey is that the same god is sometimes called Dionysos, and sometimes Helios. May this tentative link with the sun help us to understand the Indian Dionysos? But on the whole this quotation shows that we cannot recognize the god concealed behind the Greek name without some difficulty. The most that can be undertaken in confidence is to reckon out what can, and what cannot, be considered to fit in. It therefore seems to be the case that the only way of making sure is to gather together all passages referring to the god in question, and from the result proceed to consider where in the history of Indian religion we encounter the same overall picture, and the largest number of congruent details. But the overall picture and the details must be taken into consideration if any attempt at identification is to be made with confidence. If a god grows in importance, he takes over names, epithets and emblems from other gods, and it would obviously lead us sadly astray if we were to try and identify a god by means of such borrowed plumage, particularly if the attribute in question happened to have been taken over at a later date. We shall, however, return to this topic in due course; here we shall do no more than remark that the questions of methodology and disposition are closely related.

[1] *Z.D.M.G.* XXXII 1878, p. 552. (III. Der semitische Apollo.)

On the matter of the arrangement of this book, it may strike the reader as a little incongruous that the Dionysos fragments should be set out before the Heracles fragments, and then dealt with in the reverse order. An explanation would seem to be called for.

In the present state of the Megasthenes fragments, the entire text is arranged in such a way as to demand the same chronological order as Megasthenes himself followed: Dionysos before Heracles. We had originally intended to follow this order, but it proved to be virtually impossible to establish the identity of Dionysos before being sure of the identity of Heracles. In addition, the whole of the motive for this investigation, as set out above, pp. 19 ff, makes the question of the identity of Heracles primary; we therefore feel perfectly justified in beginning with this question. A further reason is to be seen above, pp. 22 f.: the point that Kṛishṇa never appears to be mentioned as a god in any pre-Christian text, coupled with our doubts as to the accuracy of the current identification.

It had struck me that no one had made use of *all* of the many passages in which Megasthenes had mentioned Heracles and Dionysos. It soon became clear that the reason was a simple one, viz. that virtually all the points mentioned by the Greek author as characteristics of Dionysos and Heracles are not only difficult to relate to the gods in question, but are even impossible to fit into the picture. I therefore felt it necessary to examine carefully all the characteristics and traditions mentioned by Megasthenes, and to compare them with the whole of the religious literature of India. What I have not done is to choose isolated points which might be expected to support a thesis or theory worked out in advance. I have noted down every detail in the descriptions of the two gods, and compared them with descriptions of all the gods in the Indian religious literature. It naturally soon proved to be the case that a number of gods could be deleted from the list. An account will be found here of all those which remain for comparison.

When examining Dionysos I found the information given in the Sanskrit literature most unsatisfactory. There was no god in the whole of this mighty literature which one could confidently identify with the god described by Megasthenes. I was therefore forced to look elsewhere, outside the bounds of Aryan literature; this concerned first and foremost the Dravidians, the second largest ethnic group in India. But among the Dravidians, especially the Tamils of South India, Hinduism occupies the same position as with the Aryans. And Hinduism seems to be of a quite different class from the religion of Heracles and Dionysos. I therefore extended the bounds of my investigation to the Muṇḍa peoples; this however implied abandoning literary investigation and proceeding along ethnographical lines. This obviously gives rise to certain risks. Is there the least theoretical possibility that we can have any knowledge of myths and traditions which may have formed the basis of an author's work ca. 2,250 years ago? I am well aware of the force of an argument such as this, and must therefore state briefly just why I am prepared to make use of traditional material noted down in modern times.

My main point is this: that so long as we are unable to prove that Sanskrit literature contains those myths and traditions which seem to have formed the foundations of Megasthenes' passages, it would seem to have been out of the question for the primitive tribes in the mountains of India to have taken over traditions identical with those described by Megasthenes, from their more literate neighbours. If we find a passage which cannot be paralleled in any Sanskrit text, whether Hindu or Vedic-Brahmanic, but which is on the other hand a living thought, constantly recurring in primitive tradition, can we come to any other conclusion than that Megasthenes' knowledge of the tradition in question was derived from a people in whose lore it lives on today? If the tradition had been taken over from anywhere else, it might have been from another primitive people; this possibility cannot be excluded. It is of course impossible for everything that Megasthenes noted down to be confirmed by modern study and discovery, but what is essential is not the individual detail as such. The vital factor is to see if we are able, by demonstrating agreements in detail, to prove a basic agreement on the nature of the world and the supernatural between the peoples of the Indian mountains today and the peoples from whom Megasthenes obtained the information on which he based his description of Dionysos. It is this which must be our task in our section on Dionysos, since it is evident that the ideas behind Dionysos and Hinduism are widely divergent.

After I had worked for some time on the Dravidian and Muṇḍa traditions, with excursions into the religious world of other primitive peoples, it became obvious that this work would be so extensive that I should not be able to include a projected third section on Megasthenes and the Indian philosophers. The "philosopher-fragments" cover such a wide area, and the points requiring treatment are so many, that this section seemed likely to be bigger than the rest of the work put together. I therefore hope to be able at some future date to complement this investigation by publishing a further volume covering Part IV, Megasthenes on the Indian philosophers. It may well be that it is just this last part which is of the greatest general interest since in it we shall compare Megasthenes with the entire course of Indian philosophy, the Upanishads, the Bhagavadgītā and the orthodox systems. One problem which will come up for discussion then, and which is likely to prove of considerable interest, is this: Does Megasthenes refer to any thought which is to be found in the Bhagavadgītā, but which is missing from the Upanishads? Should such prove to be the case, it would thereby be proved that India's most sacred text was already in existence in Megasthenes' day, 300 B.C.; this has hitherto been incapable of proof. It is true that a number of scholars, of whom Ruben is one, have assumed that the Bhagavadgītā was in fact in existence at that time, but this view has not been arrived at scientifically, but intuitively—using the same scientific instruments as those with which Lassen proved that Heracles is Kr̥ishṇa and Dionysos Śiva. But on the other hand, were we able to find nothing whatever in Megasthenes to distinguish the Bhagavadgītā from the Upanishads, then we should have nothing on which to base a dating of the former; the only effect would be to leave the question open: the Bhagavadgītā *may* be more recent than 300 B.C. This is an important question, in a large context, both as applied to the problem of the age of Krishnaism and that of the possibility of Christian influence on Krishnaism.

PART ONE

Greek and Latin Texts with Translation

Passages in Classical Authors Quoting Megasthenes on Indian Religion

I. Source, author and passage. — II. Number of fragment, page and line in Schwanbeck. — III. Number of fragment, page and line in Fontes. — IV. Page and line in McCrindle. — V. Content. — VI. Number of fragment here.
(Note, the passages on the Indian philosophers included in this scheme.)

I.	II.	III.	IV.	V.	VI.
Abydenus apud *Eusebius pamphili:* Praep. evang. (ed. Colon. 1688)					
(2nd cent. A.D.)	(265–340 A.D.)				
IX: 41	49 p. 146: 19–22	—	114: 23–27	Heracles	B 8
Claudius Aelianus: De natura animalium (= Historia animalium)					
(170–235 A.D.)					
XVI: 5	59: 7–10 171: 17–172: 14	141: 25–142: 28 (not under Meg.)	166: 11–168: 4	Myth of the hoopoe and of reverence for parents	C 18
Flavius Arrianus: Alexandrou anabasis					
(95–175 A.D.)					
VII: 2: 3–9	45 p. 141: 4–27	91: 30–92: 2 (not under Meg.)	116: 15–117: 19	Calanos and Mandanis	C 14
Flavius Arrianus: Indika					
V: 4–9	47: 1–7 142: 20–144: 21	21 20: 20–29 (only V: 7)	200: 25–201: 18	Dionysos	A 5
V: 10–13	47: 8–9 144: 21–34	21 20: 29–21: 12	201: 18–202: 12	Heracles	B 4
VII: 1–VIII: 3	50: 1–12 147: 4–148: 17	23 21: 19–22: 20	204: 9–206: 4	Dionysos	A 6
VIII: 4–IX: 12	50: 13–27 148: 20–152: 9	23 22: 21–24: 3	206: 4–209: 12	Heracles	B 9
X: 1	26: 1 112: 9–12	26 24: 14–17	67: 4–8	Funeral custom	C 3
XI: 1–8	32: 1–3c 121: 6–122: 19	35 25: 1–28	214: 1–216: 4	Philosophers	C 8

Titus Flavius Clemens Alexandrinus: Stromata					
(150–212 A.D.)					
I 15: 71: 3-6	43 139: 24–31	41 b 30: 18–25	104: 23–105: 10	Philosophers	C 12
I 15: 72: 5	42 137: 30–34	41 a 30: 7–10	103: 21–25	Philosophers	C 11
Diodorus Siculus: Bibl. hist.					
(ca. 60–30 B.C.)					
II 36: 6	1: 14 87: 9–18	1 17: 22–23	31: 28–32: 10	Agriculturists holy	C 1
II 38: 3–39: 1	1: 25–33 89: 1–90: 16	1 17: 23–18: 31	34: 18–37: 2	Dionysos	A 1
II 39: 1–4	1: 34–38 90: 16–91: 13	1 18: 31–19: 15	37: 2–38: 2	Heracles	B 1
II 40: 1	1: 40–43 91: 22–92: 5	1 19: 16–35	38: 15–39: 11	Philosophers	C 2
III 63: 2–5	1 B 89: 24–90: 35	37: 8–29 (not under Meg.)	34: 25–35: 31	Dionysos	A 2
Flavius Josephus: Antiquitates Iudaicae					
(37–100 A.D.)					
X 2: 1 (= X 227)	48 B 145: 15–146: 2	22 21: 14–18	113: 16–114: 6	Heracles	B 6
Flavius Josephus: Contra Apionem					
I 20: 144	48 145: 8–12	—	113: 8–13	Heracles	B 5
Palladius episcopus helenopolitanus: Περὶ τῶν τῆς Ἰνδίας ἐθνῶν καὶ τῶν βραχμάνων III: 9					
p. 8. 20	55 156: 17–160: 12	(179: 11–13) (not under Meg.)	123: 18–127: 5	Philosophers, Calanos and Mandanis	C 16
Phlegon: Mirab.					
(unknown date)					
33	51 150: 27–28	24 A 24: 5–7	209: 15–17	Heracles	B 9 b

I.	II.	III.	IV.	V.	VI.
Caius Plinius Secundus Maior: Historia naturalis					
(23–79 A.D.)					
VI 21: 4–5	50 C 151: 25–27	(62: 1–2) (not under Meg.)	115: 27–116: 3	Dionysos	A 7
VI 23: 6	56: 23 166: 13–15	(62: 13–15) (not under Meg.)	150: 11–151: 3	Heracles	B 10
VI 23: 9	56: 29 167: 18–20	(62: 16–18) (not under Meg.)	156: 10–13	Dionysos	A 8
Polyaenus: Strateg.					
(ca. 162 A.D.)					
I 1: 1–3	57 168: 13–169: 19	(95: 20–96: 16) (not under Meg.)	162: 12–163: 24	Dionysos	A 10
I 3: 4	58 169: 24–30	24 B 24: 7–13	163: 29–164: 8	Heracles	B 12
Pseudo-Ambrosius: De moribus Brachmanorum (= Latin translation of Palladius)					
(6th cent. A.D.)					
(P. 62,68 sqq.)	45 B 156: 26–160: 23	—	127: 19–129: 25	Philosophers, Calanus and Mandanis	C 17
Pseudo-Origenes: Philisoph.					
(unknown date)					
24	54 155: 7–156: 10	—	120: 12–123: 12	Philosophers	C 15
Caius Iulius Solinus: Coll. rer. mem.					
(3rd cent. A.D.)					
52: 5	50 C 151: 29–34	(149: 13–18) (not under Meg.)	116: 5–11	Dionysos	A 7
52: 15	56 B: 23 166:27–167: 28	(150: 5–6) (not under Meg.)	161: 21–23	Heracles	B 11
52: 16	56 B: 29 167:28–168: 24	(150: 6–9) (not under Meg.)	161: 23–162: 4	Dionysos	A 9

Strabo: Geographicus

(65 B.C.–20 A.D.)

XV 1: 6–8 a	46: 1–7 142: 7–144: 5	20 20: 8–18 + (49: 1–10) (not Meg.)	107: 24–111: 13	Dionysos	A 4
XV 1: 8 b	46: 8–10 144: 5–145: 3	20 (49: 10–25) (not Meg.)	111: 13–112: 14	Heracles	B 3
XV 1: 39	33: 1–3 121: 17–122: 28	36 26: 3–14	83: 9–26	Philosophers	C 9
XV 1: 53	27: 4 113: 18–19	27 24: 18–19	68: 23–24	Sacrifices	C 4
XV 1: 54	27: 9 114: 9	27 24: 21	69: 13–15	Funeral customs	C 5
XV 1: 54	27: 11 115: 3–5	27 24: 22–24	69: 30–70: 2	Sacrifices	C 6
XV 1: 55	27: 16–17 115: 18–116: 3	27 24: 25–30	70: 21–71: 13	Offices of the king	C 7
XV 1: 58	41 135: 21–29	40 27: 6–15	97: 5–18	Dionysos	A 3
XV 1: 58	41 135: 30	40 27: 15–16	97: 18–19	Heracles	B 2
XV 1: 58 c–60	41: 3–24 135: 30–140: 7	40 27: 16–30: 3	97: 20–103: 9	Philosophers	C 10
XV 1: 68	44 140: 13–29	42 30: 27–31: 12	106: 4–107: 14	Philosophers	C 13

Georgius Syncellus: Chronograph. ad mundi A. 4888 (ed. Bonn)

(ca. 800 A.D.)

I p. 419	48 D 146: 11–13	—	114: 15–18	Heracles	B 7

B. GREEK AND LATIN TEXTS

A 1.

Μυθολογοῦσι δὲ παρὰ τοῖς Ἰνδοῖς οἱ λογιώτατοι, περὶ ὧν[1] καθῆκον ἂν εἴη συντόμως διελθεῖν. φασὶ γάρ, ἐν τοῖς ἀρχαιοτάτοις χρόνοις, παρ' αὐτοῖς ἔτι τῶν ἀνθρώπων κωμηδὸν οἰκούντων, παραγενέσθαι τὸν Διόνυσον ἐκ τῶν πρὸς ἑσπέραν τόπων ἔχοντα δύναμιν ἀξιόλογον· ἐπελθεῖν δὲ τὴν Ἰνδικὴν ἅπασαν, μηδεμιᾶς οὔσης ἀξιολόγου πόλεως /τῆς/[2] δυναμένης ἀντιτάξασθαι. ἐπιγενομένων δὲ καυμάτων μεγάλων, καὶ τῶν τοῦ Διονύσου στρατιωτῶν λοιμικῇ νόσῳ διαφθειρομένων, συνέσει διαφέροντα τὸν ἡγεμόνα τοῦτον ἀπαγαγεῖν τὸ στρατόπεδον ἐκ τῶν πεδινῶν τόπων εἰς τὴν ὀρεινήν· ἐνταῦθα[3] δὲ πνεόντων ψυχρῶν ἀνέμων, καὶ τῶν ναματιαίων ὑδάτων καθαρῶν ῥεόντων πρὸς αὐταῖς ταῖς πηγαῖς, ἀπαλλαγῆναι τῆς νόσου τὸ στρατόπεδον. ὀνομάζεσθαι δὲ τῆς ὀρεινῆς τὸν τόπον τοῦτον Μηρόν, καθ' ὃν ὁ Διόνυσος ἐξέτρεψε τὰς δυνάμεις ἐκ τῆς νόσου· ἀφ' οὗ δὴ καὶ τοὺς Ἕλληνας περὶ τοῦ θεοῦ τούτου παραδεδωκέναι τοῖς μεταγενεστέροις, τεθρᾶφται τὸν Διόνυσον ἐν μηρῷ[4] μετὰ δὲ ταῦτα τῆς καταθέσεως[5] τῶν καρπῶν ἐπιμεληθέντα[6] μεταδιδόναι τοῖς Ἰνδοῖς, καὶ τὴν εὕρεσιν τοῦ οἴνου καὶ τῶν ἄλλων τῶν εἰς τὸν βίον χρησίμων παραδοῦναι. πρὸς δὲ τούτοις, πόλεών τε ἀξιολόγων γενηθῆναι κτίστην, μεταγαγόντα τὰς κώμας εἰς τοὺς εὐθέτους τόπους, τιμᾷν τε καταδεῖξαι τὸ θεῖον καὶ νόμους εἰσηγήσασθαι καὶ δικαστήρια, καθόλου δὲ πολλῶν καὶ καλῶν ἔργων εἰσηγητὴν γενόμενον θεὸν νομισθῆναι καὶ τυχεῖν ἀθανάτων τιμῶν. ἱστοροῦσι δ' αὐτὸν καὶ γυναικῶν πλῆθος μετὰ τοῦ στρατοπέδου περιάγεσθαι, καὶ κατὰ τὰς ἐν τοῖς πολέμοις παρατάξεις τυμπάνοις καὶ κυμβάλοις κεχρῆσθαι, μήπω σάλπιγγος εὑρημένης. βασιλεύσαντα δὲ πάσης τῆς Ἰνδικῆς ἔτη δύο πρὸς τοῖς πεντήκοντα γήρᾳ τελευτῆσαι. διαδεξαμένους δὲ τοὺς υἱοὺς αὐτοῦ τὴν ἡγεμονίαν ἀεὶ τοῖς ἀφ' ἑαυτῶν ἀπολιπεῖν τὴν ἀρχήν: τὸ δὲ τελευταῖον, πολλαῖς γενεαῖς ὕστερον καταλυθείσης τῆς ἡγεμονίας, δημοκρατηθῆναι τὰς πόλεις.

περὶ μὲν οὖν τοῦ Διονύσου καὶ τῶν ἀπογόνων αὐτοῦ τοιαῦτα μυθολογοῦσιν οἱ τὴν ὀρεινὴν τῆς Ἰνδικῆς κατοικοῦντες.[7]

---

[1] Fontes and Fr. G. H.: οὗ.

[2] Fontes and Fr. G. H.: τῆς in brackets. [3] Fontes and Fr. G. H.: 'ἐν ταύτῃ.

[4] (ἐπιγενομένων line 5– ἐν μηρῷ line 13) according to Fr. G. H. perhaps Diodor's addition. [5] Fontes and Fr. G. H.: παραθέσεως. [6] Fontes: ἐπιμεληθήντα.

[7] (οἱ ... κατοικοῦντες) according to Fr. G. H. perhaps Diodor's addition. Why? Cf. Strabo here frg. A 3 and B 2!

MC CRINDLE'S ENGLISH TRANSLATION

A 1. Diodorus Siculus: Bibl. Hist. II: 38: 3–39: 1[1]

The men of greatest learning among the Indians tell certain legends, of which it may be proper to give a brief summary. They relate that in the most primitive times, when the people of the country were still living in villages, Dionysos made his appearance coming from the regions lying to the west, and at the head of a considerable army. He overran the whole of India, as there was no great city capable of resisting his arms. The heat, however, having become excessive, and the soldiers of Dionysos being afflicted with a pestilence, the leader, who was remarkable for his sagacity, carried his troops away from the plains up to the hills. There the army, recruited by the cool breezes and the waters that flowed fresh from the fountains, recovered from sickness. The place among the mountains where Diosysos restored his troops to health was called Mêros; from which circumstance, no doubt, the Greeks have transmitted to posterity the legend concerning the god, that Dionysos was bred in [his father's] thigh.[2] Having after this turned his attention to the artificial propagation of useful plants, he communicated the secret to the Indians, and taught them the way to make wine, as well as other arts conducive to human well-being. He was, besides, the founder of large cities, which he formed by removing the villages to convenient sites, while he also showed the people how to worship the deity, and introduced laws and courts of justice. Having thus achieved altogether many great and noble works, he was regarded as a deity and gained immortal honours. It is related also of him that he led about with his army a great host of women, and employed, in marshalling his troops for battle, drums and cymbals, as the trumpet had not in his days been invented; and that after reigning over the whole of India for two and fifty years he died of old age, while his sons, succeeding to the government, transmitted the sceptre in unbroken succession to their posterity. At last, after many generations had come and gone, the sovereignty, it is said, was dissolved, and democratic governments were set up in the cities.

(39.) Such, then, are the traditions regarding Dionysos and his descendants current among the Indians who inhabit the hill-country.

---

[1] Schw. frg. 1: 25–33, p. 89: 1–90: 16, Fontes frg. 1, p. 17: 23–18: 31, Jacoby 3 C 2, p. 608: 23–609: 8, McCrindle p. 34: 18–37: 2.

[2] verbally: was bred in a thigh.

A 2.

Ἔνιοι δέ, καθάπερ προεῖπον, τρεῖς ὑποστησάμενοι (sc. Bacchos) γεγονέναι κατὰ διεστηκότας χρόνους, ἑκάστῳ προσάπτουσιν ἰδίας πράξεις· καί φασι, τὸν μὲν ἀρχαιότατον Ἰνδὸν γεγονέναι, καὶ τῆς χώρας αὐτομάτως διὰ τὴν εὐκρασίαν φερούσης πολλὴν ἄμπελον, πρῶτον τοῦτον ἀποθλῖψαι βότρυας καὶ τὴν χρείαν τῆς περὶ τὸν οἶνον φύσεως ἐπινοῆσαι· ὁμοίως δὲ καὶ[1] τῶν σύκων καὶ τῶν ἄλλων ἀκροδρύων τὴν καθήκουσαν ἐπιμέλειαν[2] ποιήσασθαι, καὶ καθόλου τὰ πρὸς τὴν συγκομιδὴν <καὶ παράθεσιν>[3] τούτων τῶν καρπῶν ἐπινοῆσαι[4]. τὸν αὐτὸν δὲ καὶ καταπώγωνα λέγουσι γενέσθαι[5] διὰ τὸ τοῖς Ἰνδοῖς νόμιμον εἶναι μέχρι τῆς τελευτῆς ἐπιμελῶς ὑποτρέφειν[6] τοὺς πώγωνας. τὸν δ' οὖν Διόνυσον ἐπελθόντα μετὰ στρατοπέδου πᾶσαν τὴν οἰκουμένην, διδάξαι τήν τε φυτείαν τῆς ἀμπέλου καὶ τὴν ἐν ταῖς ληνοῖς ἀπόθλιψιν τῶν βοτρύων· ἀφ' οὗ Ληναῖον αὐτὸν ὀνομασθῆναι. ὁμοίως δὲ καὶ τῶν ἄλλων εὑρημάτων μεταδόντα πᾶσι, τυχεῖν αὐτὸν μετὰ τὴν ἐξ ἀνθρώπων μετάστασιν ἀθανάτου τιμῆς παρὰ τοῖς εὖ παθοῦσιν. δείκνυσθαι δὲ παρ' Ἰνδοῖς μέχρι τοῦ νῦν τόν τε τόπον, ἐν ᾧ συνέβη γενέσθαι τὸν θεόν, καὶ προσηγορίας πόλεων ἀπ' αὐτοῦ κατὰ τὴν τῶν ἐγχωρίων διάλεκτον· καὶ πολλὰ ἕτερα διαμένειν ἀξιόλογα τεκμήρια τῆς παρ' Ἰνδοῖς γενέσεως, περὶ ὧν μακρὸν ἂν εἴη γράφειν.[7]

A 3.

Περὶ δὲ τῶν φιλοσόφων λέγων τοὺς μὲν ὀρεινοὺς αὐτῶν φησιν ὑμνητὰς εἶναι τοῦ Διονύσου, δεικνύντας τεκμήρια τὴν ἀγρίαν ἄμπελον παρὰ μόνοις[8] φυομένην καὶ κιττὸν καὶ δάφνην καὶ μυρρίνην καὶ πύξον καὶ ἄλλα τῶν ἀειθαλῶν, ὧν μηδὲν εἶναι πέραν[9] Εὐφράτου, πλὴν ἐν παραδείσοις σπάνια καὶ μετὰ πολλῆς ἐπιμελείας σωζόμενα. Διονυσιακὸν δὲ καὶ τὸ σινδονοφορεῖν καὶ τὸ μιτροῦσθαι, καὶ μυροῦσθαι καὶ βάπτεσθαι ἄνθινα καὶ τοὺς βασιλέας κωδωνοφορεῖσθαι καὶ τυμπανίζεσθαι κατὰ τὰς ἐξόδους.

---

[1] Schw.: + τὴν.

[2] Schw.: + καὶ παράδοσιν.

[3] Schw.: — καὶ παράθεσιν, Fontes: in brackets.

[4] Schw.: + διὸ καὶ Ληναῖον ὀνομασθῆναι.

[5] Schw.: — γενέσθαι.

[6] Schw.: ἀνατρέφειν.

[7] This fragment lacking in Fr. G. H., in Schw. in brackets, in Fontes not under Megasthenes.

[8] Schw. and Fr. G. H.: μόνοις αὐτοῖς.

[9] Schw. and Fr. G. H.: πέραν τοῦ.

A 2. Diodorus Siculus: Bibl. Hist. III: 63: 2–5[1]

Now some, as I have already said, supposing that there were three individuals of this name, who lived in different ages, assign to each appropriate achievements. They say, then, that the most ancient of them was Indos, and that as the country, with its genial temperature, produced spontaneously the vine-tree in great abundance, he was the first who crushed grapes and discovered the use of the properties of wine. In like manner he ascertained what culture was requisite for figs and other fruit trees, and transmitted this knowledge to after-times; and, in a word, it was he who found out how these fruits should be gathered in.[2]

This same [Dionysos], however, they call also Katapôgôn, since it is a custom among the Indians to nourish their beards with great care to the very end of their life. Dionysos then, at the head of an army, marched to every part of the world, and taught mankind the planting of the vine, and how to crush grapes in the winepress, whence he was called Lênaios. Having in like manner imparted to all a knowledge of his other inventions, he obtained after his departure from among men immortal honour from those who had benefited by his labours. It is further said that the place is pointed out in India even to this day where the god had been,[3] and that cities are called by his name in the vernacular dialects, and that many other important evidences still exist of his having been born in India, about which it would be tedious to write.[4]

A 3. Strabo: Geograph. XV: 1: 58[5]

Speaking of the philosophers, he (Megasthenês) says that such of them as live on the mountains are worshippers[6] of Dionysos, showing as proofs [that he had come among them] the wild vine, which grows in their country only, and the ivy, and the laurel, and the myrtle, and the box-tree, and other evergreens, none of which are found beyond the Euphrates, except a few in parks, which it requires great care to preserve. They observe also certain customs which are Bacchanalian. Thus they dress in muslin, wear the turban, use perfumes, array themselves in garments dyed of bright colours; and their kings, when they appear in public, are preceded by the music of drums and gongs.[7]

---

[1] Schw. frg. 1 B, p. 89: 24–90: 35, Fontes p. 37: 8–29 (not under Meg.), Jacoby —, McCrindle p. 34: 25–35: 31.

[2] Schw. adds: whence also he was called Lênaios.

[3] Wrong; must be: had been born. Cf. below p. 199.

[4] The beginning of this last sentence says: It is further said that both the place in India, where the god happened to be born, and the names of the cities (called by his name) in the vernacular dialects are pointed out.

[5] Schw. frg. 41, p. 135: 21–29, Fontes frg. 40, p. 27: 6–15, Jacoby 3 C 2, p. 636: 1–8, McCrindle p. 97: 5–18.

[6] verbally: singers.

[7] The meaning of the different words not clear: μιτροῦσθαι can mean: to wear a girdle, σινδονοφορεῖν rather: to wear linen clothes, βάπτεσθαι ἄνθινα uncertain meaning.

A 4.

['Ημῖν δὲ τίς ἂν δικαία γένοιτο πίστις περὶ τῶν 'Ινδικῶν ἐκ τῆς τοιαύτης στρατείας τοῦ Κύρου ἢ τῆς Σεμιράμιδος;][1] συναποφαίνεται δέ πως καὶ Μεγασθένης τῷ λόγῳ τούτῳ, κελεύων ἀπιστεῖν ταῖς ἀρχαίαις περὶ 'Ινδῶν ἱστορίαις· οὔτε γὰρ παρ' 'Ινδῶν ἔξω σταλῆναί ποτε στρατιάν, οὔτ' ἐπελθεῖν ἔξωθεν καὶ κρατῆσαι πλὴν τῆς μεθ' 'Ηρακλέους καὶ Διονύσου καὶ τῆς νῦν μετὰ Μακεδόνων. [Καίτοι Σέσωστριν μὲν τὸν Αἰγύπτιον καὶ Τεάρκωνα τὸν Αἰθίοπα ἕως Εὐρώπης προελθεῖν. Ναυοκοδρόσορον δὲ τὸν παρὰ Χαλδαίοις εὐδοκιμήσαντα 'Ηρακλέους μᾶλλον καὶ ἕως στηλῶν ἐλάσαι. Μέχρι μὲν δὴ δεῦρο καὶ Τεάρκωνα ἀφικέσθαι· [...] ἐκεῖνον δὲ καὶ ἐκ τῆς 'Ιβηρίας εἰς τὴν Θρᾴκην καὶ τὸν Πόντον ἀγαγεῖν τὴν στρατιάν. 'Ιδάνθυρσον δὲ τὸν Σκύθην ἐπιδραμεῖν τῆς 'Ασίας μέχρι Αἰγύπτου. Τῆς δὲ 'Ινδικῆς μηδένα τούτων ἅψασθαι· καὶ Σεμίραμιν δ' ἀποθανεῖν πρὸ τῆς ἐπιχειρήσεως. Πέρσας δὲ μισθοφόρους μὲν ἐκ τῆς 'Ινδικῆς μεταπέμψασθαι[2] 'Υδρακας, ἐκεῖ δὲ μὴ στρατεῦσαι, ἀλλ' ἐγγὺς ἐλθεῖν μόνον, ἡνίκα Κῦρος ἤλαυνεν, ἐπὶ Μασσαγέτας.][3]

Καὶ τὰ περὶ 'Ηρακλέους δὲ καὶ Διονύσου Μεγασθένης μὲν μετ' ὀλίγων πιστὰ ἡγεῖται· [τῶν δ' ἄλλων οἱ πλείους, ὧν ἐστι καὶ 'Ερατοσθένης, ἄπιστα καὶ μυθώδη, καθάπερ καὶ τὰ παρὰ τοῖς 'Ελλησιν. κ.τ.λ.].[4] ...

['Εκ δὲ τῶν τοιούτων Νυσσαίους[5] δή τινας ἔθνος προσωνόμασαν καὶ πόλιν παρ' αὐτοῖς Νύσσαν[6], Διονύσου κτίσμα, καὶ ὄρος τὸ ὑπὲρ τῆς πόλεως Μηρόν, αἰτιασάμενοι καὶ τὸν αὐτόθι κισσὸν καὶ ἄμπελον οὐδὲ ταύτην τελεσίκαρπον· ἀποῤῥεῖ γὰρ ὁ βότρυς, πρὶν περκάσαι, διὰ τοὺς ὄμβρους τοὺς ἄδην· Διονύσου δ' ἀπογόνους τοὺς 'Οξυδράκας ἀπὸ τῆς ἀμπέλου τῆς παρ' αὐτοῖς καὶ τῶν πολυτελῶν ἐξόδων, βακχικῶς τάς τε ἐκστρατείας ποιουμένων τῶν βασιλέων καὶ τὰς ἄλλας ἐξόδους μετὰ τυμπανισμοῦ καὶ εὐανθοῦς στολῆς, ὅπερ ἐπιπολάζει καὶ παρὰ τοῖς ἄλλοις 'Ινδοῖς.][7]

A 5.

[Οὗτος ὦν ὁ Μεγασθένης λέγει, οὔτε 'Ινδοὺς ἐπιστρατεῦσαι οὐδαμοῖσιν ἀνθρώποισιν, οὔτε 'Ινδοῖσιν ἄλλους ἀνθρώπους· ἀλλὰ Σέσωστριν μὲν τὸν Αἰγύπτιον, τῆς 'Ασίας καταστρεψάμενον τὴν πολλὴν, ἔστε ἐπὶ τὴν Εὐρώπην συν

---

[1] Lacking in Fr. G. H., brackets in Schw.

[2] Schw.: μεταμέμψασθαι — misprint?

[3] (καίτοι line 6–Μασσαγέτας line 14) lacking in Fontes.

[4] Brackets in Schw.

[5] Fontes and Fr. G. H.: Νυσαίους.

[6] Fontes: Νῦσαν, Fr. G. H.: Νύσαν.

[7] ('Εκ δὲ τῶν line 18–'Ινδοῖς line 25) in brackets in Schw., put under Strabo in Fontes, under "Anhang" in Fr. G. H.

A 4. Strabo: Geograph. XV: 1: 6–8[1]

[(6. But what just reliance can we place on the accounts of India from such expeditions as those of Kyros and Semiramis?)] Megasthenês concurs in this view, and recommends his readers to put no faith in the ancient history of India.[2] Its people, he says, never sent an expedition abroad, nor was their country ever invaded and conquered except by Heracles and Dionysos [in old times], and by the Makedonians in our own. [(Yet Sesôstris the Egyptian and Tearkôn the Ethiopian advanced as far as Europe. And Nabukodrosor, who is more renowned among the Chaldaeans than even Ḥêrakles [among the Greeks], carried his arms to the Pillars, which Tearkôn also reached, while Sesôstris penetrated from Ibêria even into Thrace and Pontos. Besides these there was Idanthyrsos the Skythian, who overran Asia as far as Egypt. But not one of these great conquerors approached India, and Semiramis, who meditated its conquest, died before the necessary preparations were undertaken. The Persians indeed summoned the Hydrakai from India to serve as mercenaries, but they did not lead an army into the country, and only approached its borders when Kyros marched against the Massagetai.)]

7. The accounts about Hêrakles and Dionysos, Megasthenês and some few authors with him consider entitled to credit, [(but the majority, among whom is Eratosthenês, consider them incredible and fabulous, like the stories current among the Greeks ...)].

[(8. On such grounds they called a particular race of people Nyssaians, and their city Nyssa,[3] which Dionysos had founded, and the mountain which rose above the city *Mêron*[4], assigning as their reason for bestowing these names that ivy grows there, and also the vine, although its fruit does not come to perfection, as the clusters, on account of the heaviness of the rains, fall off the trees before ripening. They further called the *Oxydrakai* descendants of Dionysos, because the vine grew in their country, and their processions were conducted with great pomp, and their kings on going forth to war and on other occasions marched in Bacchic fashion, with drums beating, while they were dressed in gay-coloured robes, which is also a custom among other Indians.)]

A 5. Flavius Arrianus: Indika V: 4–9[5]

[(This same Megasthenês then informs us that the Indians neither invade other men, nor do other men invade the Indians: for *Sesostris* the Egyptian, after having overrun the greater part of Asia, and advanced with his army as

---

[1] Schw. frg. 46: 1–7, p. 142: 7–144: 5, Fontes frg. 20, p. 20: 8–18 and p. 49: 1–10, Jacoby 3 C 2, p. 615: 24–616: 18 and 3 C 2, p. 657: 18–28, McCrindle p. 107: 24–111: 13.

[2] more correct: "earlier accounts of India".

[3] more correct: "and a town of theirs Nyssa".

[4] more correct: "*Mêros*".

[5] Schw. frg. 47: 1–7, p. 142: 20–144: 21, Fontes frg. 21, p. 20: 20–29 (only from V: 7), Jacoby 3 C 2, p. 615: 23–616: 14, McCrindle p. 200: 25–201: 18.

στρατιᾷ ἐλάσαντα, ὀπίσω ἀπονοστῆσαι· Ἰνδάθυρσιν[1] δὲ τὸν Σκύθεα ἐκ Σκυθίης ὁρμηθέντα πολλὰ μὲν τῆς Ἀσίης ἔθνεα καταστρέψασθαι, ἐπελθεῖν δὲ καὶ τὴν Αἰγυπτίων γῆν κρατέοντα· Σεμίραμιν δὲ τὴν Ἀσσυρίην ἐπιχειρέειν μὲν στέλλεσθαι εἰς Ἰνδούς, ἀποθανεῖν δὲ πρὶν τέλος ἐπιθεῖναι τοῖσι βουλεύμασιν·][2] ἀλλὰ Ἀλέξανδρον γὰρ στρατεῦσαι ἐπὶ Ἰνδοὺς μοῦνον· καὶ πρὸ Ἀλεξάνδρου, Διονύσου[3] πέρι πολλὸς λόγος κατέχει, ὡς καὶ τούτου στρατεύσαντος ἐς Ἰνδοὺς καὶ καταστρεψαμένου Ἰνδούς. Ἡρακλέους[4] δὲ πέρι οὐ πολλός· Διονύσου μέν γε καὶ Νῦσα[5] πόλις μνῆμα οὐ φαῦλον τῆς στρατηλασίης καὶ ὁ Μηρὸς τὸ ὄρος καὶ ὁ κισσὸς ὅτι ἐν τῷ ὄρει τούτῳ φύεται, καὶ αὐτοὶ οἱ Ἰνδοὶ ὑπὸ τυμπάνων τε καὶ κυμβάλων στελλόμενοι ἐς τὰς μάχας, καὶ ἐσθὴς αὐτοῖσι κατάστικτος ἐοῦσα κατάπερ τοῖ Διονύσου τοῖσι βάκχοισιν.[6]

Α 6.

["Εθνεα δὲ Ἰνδικὰ εἴκοσι καὶ ἑκατόν τι ἅπαντα[7] λέγει Μεγασθένης δυοῖν δέοντα. [[Καὶ πολλὰ μὲν εἶναι ἔθνεα Ἰνδικὰ καὶ αὐτὸς ξυμφέρομαι Μεγασθένει· τὸ δὲ ἀτρεκὲς οὐκ ἔχω εἰκάσαι ὅπως ἐκμαθὼν ἀνέγραψεν, οὐδὲ πολλοστὸν μέρος τῆς Ἰνδῶν γῆς ἐπελθών, οὐδὲ ἐπιμιξίης πᾶσι τοῖς γένεσιν ἐούσης ἐς ἀλλήλους]].[8]

Πάλαι μὲν δὴ νομάδας εἶναι Ἰνδοὺς κατάπερ Σκυθέων τοὺς οὐκ ἀροτῆρας, οἳ ἐπὶ τῇσιν ἁμάξῃσι[9] πλανώμενοι ἄλλοτε ἄλλην τῆς Σκυθίης ἀμείβουσιν, οὔτε πόλιας[10] οἰκέοντες οὔτε ἱερὰ θεῶν σέβοντες· οὕτω μηδὲ Ἰνδοῖσι πόλιας[10] εἶναι μηδὲ ἱερὰ θεῶν δεδομημένα· ἀλλ' ἀμπέχεσθαι[11] μὲν δορὰς θηρίων[12] ὅσων κατακαίνοιεν·[13] σιτέεσθαι δὲ τῶν δενδρέων τὸν φλοιόν· καλέεσθαι δὲ τὰ δένδρεα ταῦτα τῇ Ἰνδῶν φωνῇ τάλα· καὶ φύεσθαι ἐπ' αὐτῶν κατάπερ τῶν φοινίκων ἐπὶ τῇσι κορυφῇσιν οἷά περ τολύπας. Σιτέεσθαι δὲ καὶ τῶν θηρίων ὅσα ἕλοιεν ὠμοφαγέοντας, πρὶν[14] δὴ Διόνυσον ἐλθεῖν ἐς τὴν χώρην τῶν Ἰνδῶν. Διόνυσον δὲ ἐλθόντα, ὡς καρτερὸς ἐγένετο Ἰνδῶν, πόλιάς[10] τε οἰκῆσαι[15] καὶ νόμους θέσθαι τῇσι πόλεσιν, οἴνου τε δοτῆρα Ἰνδοῖς γενέσθαι κατάπερ Ἕλλησι, καὶ σπείρειν διδάξαι τὴν γῆν διδόντα αὐτὸν σπέρματα· ἢ οὐκ ἐλάσαντος ταύτῃ Τριπτολέμου, ὅτε περ ἐκ Δήμητρος ἐστάλη σπείρειν τὴν γῆν πᾶσαν· ἢ πρὸ Τριπτολέμου τις οὗτος Διόνυσος ἐπελθὼν τὴν Ἰνδῶν γῆν σπέρματά σφισιν ἔδωκε καρποῦ τοῦ ἡμέρου· βόας τε ὑπ' ἀρότρῳ[16]

---

[1] Fr. G. H.: Ἰδάνθυρον. Cf. frg. A 4!

[2] (Οὗτος line 26, p. 50–βουλεύμασιν line 4) lacking in Fontes.

[3] Fr. G. H.: +μὲν. [4] Fontes and Fr. G. H.: Ἡρακλέος. [5] Schw.: Νύσσα.

[6] (Διονύσου μέν γε line 7–βάκχοισιν line 11) lacking in Fr. G. H.

[7] Fr. G. H.: τὰ πάντα.

[8] ("Εθνεα line 12–ἀλλήλους line 15) lacking in Fontes, (καὶ πολλὰ line 13–ἀλλήλους line 15) in brackets also in Schw. and Fr. G. H. [9] Fontes: ἀμάξῃσι.

[10] Fontes and Fr. G. H.: πόληας. πόληάς. [11] Fontes and Fr. G. H.: ἀμπίσχεσθαι.

[12] Fr. G. H.: θηρείους. [13] Fontes and Fr. G. H.: κατακάνοιεν.

[14] Fontes and Fr. G. H.: πρίν γε. [15] Fontes and Fr. G. H.: οἰκίσαι.

[16] Fontes and Fr. G. H.: ἄροτρον.

far as Europe, returned home: and **Idanthyrsos** the Skythian issuing from Skythia, subdued many nations of Asia, and carried his victorious arms even to the borders of Egypt; and **Semiramis**, again, the Assyrian queen, took in hand an expedition against India, but died before she could execute her design:)] and thus Alexander was the only conqueror who actually invaded the country. And regarding **Dionysos** many traditions are current to the effect that he also made an expedition into India, and subjugated the Indians before the days of Alexander. But of **Heraklês** tradition does not say much. Of the expedition, however, which Bakkhos led, the city of **Nysa** is no mean monument, while Mount **Mêros** is yet another, and the ivy which grows thereon, and the practice observed by the Indians themselves of marching to battle with drums and cymbals, and of wearing a spotted dress such as was worn by the Bacchanals of Dionysos.

A 6. Flavius Arrianus: Indika VII: 1–VIII: 3[1]

[(The Indian **tribes**, Megasthenês tells us, number in all 118. [[And I so far agree with him as to allow that they must be indeed numerous, but when he gives such a precise estimate I am at a loss to conjecture how he arrived at it, for the greater part of India he did not visit, nor is mutual intercourse maintained between all the tribes.]])] He tells us further that the Indians were in old times nomadic, like those Skythians who did not till the soil, but roamed about in their wagons, as the seasons varied, from one part of Skythia to another, neither dwelling in towns nor worshipping in temples; and that the Indians likewise had neither towns nor temples of the gods, but were so barbarous that they wore the skins of such wild animals as they could kill, and subsisted on the bark of trees; that these trees were called in Indian speech **tala**, and that there grew on them, as there grows at the tops of the palm-trees, a fruit resembling balls of wool; that they subsisted also on such wild animals as they could catch, eating the flesh raw,—before, at least, the coming of **Dionysos** into India. Dionysos, however, when he came and had conquered the people, founded cities and gave laws to these cities, and introduced the use of wine among the Indians, as he had done among the Greeks, and taught them to sow the land, himself supplying seeds for the purpose,—either because **Triptolemos**, when he was sent by *Dêmêter* to sow all the earth, did not reach these parts, or this must have been some Dionysos who came to India before Triptolemos, and gave the people the seeds of cultivated plants. It is also said that Dionysos first yoked oxen to the plough, and made many of the Indians husbandmen instead of nomads, and furnished them with the implements of agriculture;[2] and that the Indians worship the other gods, and Dionysos himself in particular, with cymbals and drums, because he so taught them; and that he also taught them the Satyric dance, or, as the Greeks call it, the **Kordax**; and that he instructed the Indians to let their hair grow long in honour of the

---

[1] Schw. frg. 50: 1–12, p. 147: 4–148: 17, Fontes frg. 23, p. 21: 19–22: 20, Jacoby 3 C 2, p. 616: 20–617: 21, McCrindle p. 204: 9–206: 4.

[2] more correct: "implements of warfare". See p. 210 n. 8.

ζεῦξαι Διόνυσον πρῶτον, καὶ ἀροτῆρας ἀντὶ νομάδων ποιῆσαι Ἰνδῶν τοὺς πολλοὺς καὶ ὁπλίσαι ὅπλοισι τοῖσιν ἀρηΐοισι. Καὶ θεοὺς σέβειν ὅτι ἐδίδαξε Διόνυσος ἄλλους τε καὶ μάλιστα δὴ ἑωυτὸν κυμβαλίζοντας καὶ τυμπανίζοντας· καὶ ὄρχησιν δὲ ἐκδιδάξαι τὴν σατυρικήν, τὸν κόρδακα παρ' Ἕλλησι καλούμενον· καὶ κομᾶν Ἰνδοὺς τῷ θεῷ, μίτρηφορέειν τε ἀναδεῖξαι καὶ μύρων ἀλοιφὰς ἐκδιδάξαι, ὥστε καὶ εἰς Ἀλέξανδρον ἔτι ὑπὸ κυμβάλων τε καὶ τυμπάνων ἐς τὰς μάχας Ἰνδοὶ καθίσταντο.

Ἀπιόντα δὲ ἐκ τῆς Ἰνδῶν γῆς, ὥς οἱ ταῦτα κεκοσμέατο, καταστῆσαι βασιλέα τῆς χώρης Σπαρτέμβαν[1], τῶν ἑταίρων ἕνα τὸν βακχωδέστατον· τελευτήσαντος δὲ Σπαρτέμβα[1] τὴν βασιλείην[2] ἐκδέξασθαι Βουδύαν τὸν τούτου παῖδα· [καὶ τὸν μὲν πεντήκοντα καὶ δύο ἔτεα βασιλεῦσαι Ἰνδῶν, τὸν πατέρα· τὸν δὲ παῖδα εἴκοσιν ἔτεα· καὶ τούτου παῖδα ἐκδέξασθαι τὴν βασιλείην Κραδεύαν· καὶ τὸ ἀπὸ τοῦδε, τὸ πολὺ μὲν κατὰ γένος ἀμείβειν τὴν βασιλείην, παῖδα παρὰ πατρὸς ἐκδεχόμενον· εἰ δὲ ἐκλείποι τὸ γένος, οὕτω δὴ ἀριστίνδην καθίστασθαι Ἰνδοῖσι βασιλέας.][3]

A 7.

Indi enim prope gentium soli nunquam migravere finibus suis. Colliguntur a Libero patre ad Alexandrum magnum reges eorum CLIV., annis VI. M. CCCCLI. adiiciunt et menses tres.

Indiam Liber pater primus ingressus est, utpote qui Indis subactis omnium primus triumphavit. Ab hoc ad Alexandrum M. numerantur annorum sex millia quadringenti quinquaginta unus, additis et amplius tribus mensibus, habita per reges computatione, qui centum quinquaginta tres tenuisse medium aevum deprehenduntur.

A 8.

Nec non et Nysam urbem plerique Indiae adscribunt, montemque Merum Libero Patri sacrum, unde origo fabulae, Iovis femine editum.

A 9.

Et Nysa urbs regioni Isti datur. Mons etiam Iovi sacer, Meros nomine, in cuius specu nutritum Liberum patrem veteres Indi adfirmant, ex cuius vocabuli argumento lascivienti famae creditur, Liberum patrem femine natum.

---

[1] Fontes and Fr. G. H.: Σπατέμβαν, Σπατέμβα.

[2] Fontes and Fr. G. H.: βασιληίην.

[3] (καὶ τὸν line 10–βασιλέας line 15) lacking in Fontes.

god, and to wear the turban; and that he taught them to anoint themselves with unguents, so that even up to the time of Alexander the Indians were marshalled for battle to the sound of cymbals and drums.

VIII. But when he was leaving India, after having established the new order of things, he appointed, it is said, Spatembas, one of his companions and the most conversant with Bakkhic matters, to be the king of the country. When Spatembas died his son Boudyas succeeded to the sovereignty; [(the father reigning over the Indians fifty-two years, and the son twenty; the son of the latter, whose name was Kradeuas, duly inherited the kingdom, and thereafter the succession was generally hereditary, but that when a failure of heirs occurred in the royal house the Indians elected their sovereigns on the principle of merit;)].

A 7. C. Plinius secundus maior: Nat. Hist. VI: 21: 4–5[1]

For the Indians stand almost alone among the nations in never having migrated from their own country. From the days of Father Bacchus to Alexander the Great their kings are reckoned at 154, whose reigns extend over 6451 years and 3 months.

C. Iulius Solinus: Coll. rer. mem. 52, 5[2]

Father Bacchus was the first who invaded India, and was the first of all who triumphed over the vanquished Indians. From him to Alexander the Great 6451 years are reckoned with 3 months additional, the calculation being made by counting the kings who reigned in the intermediate period, to the number of 153.

A 8. C. Plinius Secundus maior: Nat. Hist. VI: 23: 9 (= VI: 79)[3]

Many writers further include in India even the city Nysa and Mount Merus, sacred to Father Bacchus, whence the origin of the fable that he sprang from the thigh of Jupiter.

A 9. C. Iulius Solinus: Coll. rer. mem. 52: 16[4]

The city Nysa is assigned to this region, as is also the mountain sacred to Jupiter, Mêros by name, in a cave on which the ancient Indians affirm Father Bacchus was nourished; while the name has given rise to the well-known fantastic story that Bacchus was born from the thigh [of his father].[5]

---

[1] Schw. frg. 50 C, p. 151: 25–28, Fontes p. 62: 1–2, Jacoby —, McCrindle p. 115: 27–116: 3.

[2] Schw. frg. 50 C, p. 151: 30–34, Fontes p. 149: 13–18, McCrindle p. 116: 5–11, (Jacoby —).

[3] Schw. frg. 56: 29, p. 167: 18–20, Fontes p. 62: 16–18, Jacoby —, McCrindle p. 156: 10–13.

[4] Schw. frg. 56 B, p. 167: 28–168: 24, Fontes p. 150: 6–9, Jacoby —, McCrindle p. 161: 23–162: 4.

[5] verbally: "was born from a thigh".

A 10.

Διόνυσος ἐπ' Ἰνδοὺς ἐλαύνων, ἵνα δέχοιντο αἱ πόλεις αὐτόν, ὅπλοις μὲν φανεροῖς τὴν στρατιὰν οὐχ ὥπλισεν, ἐσθῆσι δὲ λεπταῖς καὶ νεβρίσι. Δόρατα ἦν κισσῷ πεπυκασμένα· ὁ θύρσος εἶχεν αἰχμήν· κυμβάλοις καὶ τυμπάνοις ἐσήμαινεν ἀντὶ σάλπιγγος, καὶ οἴνῳ τοὺς πολεμίους ἰαίνων[1] εἰς ὄρχησιν ἔτρεπεν. Καὶ ὅσα δὲ ἄλλα Βακχικὰ ὄργια[2], πάντα[3] ἦν Διονύσου στρατηγήματα, οἷς Ἰνδοὺς καὶ τὴν ἄλλην Ἀσίαν ἐδουλώσατο.[4]

Διόνυσος ἐν Ἰνδικῇ, τῆς στρατιᾶς οὐ φερούσης τὸ φλογῶδες τοῦ ἀέρος, κατέλαβε[5] τὸ τρικόρυφον ὄρος τῆς Ἰνδικῆς. Τῶν δὲ κορυφῶν ἡ μὲν κληΐζεται[6] Κορασιβίη, ἡ δὲ Κονδάσκη[7], τὴν δὲ τρίτην αὐτὸς ἐκάλεσε Μηρόν, τῆς αὐτοῦ[8] γενέσεως ὑπόμνημα. Ἐνταῦθα πηγαὶ πολλαὶ ἡδεῖαι πιεῖν[9], θῆραι περισσαί, ὀπῶραι ἄφθονοι, χιόνες ἀναψύχουσαι. Ἐν τούτοις ἡ στρατιὰ διαιτωμένη τοῖς ἐν τῷ πεδίῳ βαρβάροις ἐξαίφνης ἐπεφαίνετο, καὶ ἀπὸ τῶν ὑψηλῶν καὶ ὑπερδεξίων ἀκοντίζοντες τοὺς πολεμίους ῥᾳδίως[10] ἐτρέποντο.

[Διόνυσος Ἰνδοὺς ἑλών, αὐτούς τε Ἰνδοὺς καὶ Ἀμαζόνας ἄγων συμμάχους, εἰς τὴν Βακτρίων ἐνέβαλεν· ὁρίζει δὲ τὴν Βακτρίαν ποταμὸς Σαράγγης. Οἱ Βάκτριοι[11] τὰ ὄρη κατέλαβον τὰ ὑπὲρ τὸν ποταμόν, ὡς Διονύσῳ διαβαίνοντι ἄνωθεν ἐπιθησόμενοι. ὁ δὲ στρατοπεδεύσας παρὰ τὸν ποταμὸν τὰς Ἀμαζόνας καὶ τὰς Βάκχας διαβαίνειν ἔταξεν, ἵνα οἱ Βάκτριοι καταφρονήσαντες γυναικῶν κατέλθοιεν ἀπὸ τῶν ὀρῶν. Αἱ μὲν δὴ διέβαινον, οἱ δὲ κατέβαινον καὶ τῷ ῥεύματι ἐπιβαίνοντες[12] ἀνακόπτειν αὐτὰς ἐπειρῶντο. Αἱ δὲ ἀνεχώρουν ἐπὶ πόδα. Βάκτριοι μέχρι τῆς ὄχθης ἐδίωκον. Τότε Διόνυσος μετὰ τῶν ἀνδρῶν ἐκβοηθήσας, πεπεδημένους τῷ ῥεύματι τοὺς Βακτρίους κτείνων[13], διέβη τὸν ποταμὸν ἀκινδύνως.][14]

B 1.

τόν τε[15] Ἡρακλέα φασὶ παρ' αὐτοῖς γεγενῆσθαι, καὶ παραπλησίως τοῖς Ἕλλησι τό τε ῥόπαλον καὶ τὴν λεοντῆν αὐτῷ προσάπτουσι. τῇ δὲ τοῦ σώματος ῥώμῃ καὶ ἀλκῇ πολλῷ τῶν ἄλλων ἀνθρώπων διενεγκεῖν, καὶ καθαρὰν ποιῆσαι τῶν θηρίων γῆν τε καὶ θάλατταν. γαμήσαντα[16] δὲ πλείους γυναῖκας υἱοὺς μὲν πολλούς, θυγατέρα δὲ μίαν γεννῆσαι, καὶ τούτων ἐνηλίκων γενομένων πᾶσαν τὴν Ἰνδικὴν διελόμενον εἰς ἴσας τοῖς τέκνοις μερίδας ἅπαντας τοῖς τόποις ἀποδεῖξαι βασιλέας[17]. μίαν δὲ θυγατέρα θρέψαντα καὶ ταύτην βασίλισσαν ἀποδεῖξαι.

---

[1] Fontes: οἴνου τοὺς πολεμίους γεύων: by giving his enemies wine to drink.

[2] Fontes: καὶ ... ὄργια put to the preceding meaning: he diverted their thoughts from war to dancing and all other Bacchic orgies. All this was ...

[3] Fontes: πάντα δὲ. [4] Fontes: ἐχειρώσατο. [5] Fontes: κατελάβετο τρικόρυφον.

[6] Fontes: τῶν κορύφων (N.B.) κληΐξεται δὲ ἡ μέν. [7] Fontes: Κονδάσβη.

[8] Fontes: αὐτοῦ. [9] Fontes: ἴδαι πυκναί: immense forests.

[10] Fontes: ῥᾳδίως. [11] Fontes: — οἱ. [12] Fontes: ἐμβαίνοντες. [13] Fontes: κτείνας.

[14] Schw.: (Διόνυσος line 14–ἀκινδύνως line 22) in brackets.

[15] Fr. G. H.: τὸν δὲ. [16] Fontes and Fr. G. H.: γήμαντα.

[17] Fontes and Fr. G. H.: μερίδας, ἅπαντας τοὺς υἱοὺς ἀποδεῖξαι βασιλέας.

A 10. Polyaenus: Strateg. I: 1: 1–3[1]

Dionysos, in his expedition against the Indians, in order that the cities might receive him willingly, disguised the arms with which he had equipped his troops, and made them wear soft raiment and fawnskins. The spears were wrapped round with ivy, and the thyrsus had a sharp point. He gave the signal for battle by cymbals and drums instead of the trumpet, and by regaling the enemy with wine diverted their thoughts from war to dancing. These and all other Bacchic orgies were employed in the system of warfare by which he subjugated the Indians and all the rest of Asia. Dionysos, in the course of his Indian campaign, seeing that his army could not endure the fiery heat of the air, took forcible possession of the three-peaked mountain of India. Of these peaks one is called Korasibiê, another Kondaskê, but to the third he himself gave the name of Mêros, in remembrance of his birth. Thereon were many fountains of water sweet to drink, game in great plenty, tree-fruits in unsparing profusion, and snows which gave new vigour to the frame. The troops quartered there made a sudden descent upon the barbarians of the plain, whom they easily routed, since they attacked them with missiles from a commanding position on the heights above.

[(Dionysos, after conquering the Indians, invaded Baktria, taking with him as auxiliaries the Indians and Amazons. That country has for its boundary the river Sarangês. The Baktrians seized the mountains overhanging that river with a view to attack Dionysos, in crossing it, from a post of advantage. He, however, having encamped along the river, ordered the Amazons and the Bakkhai to cross it, in order that the Baktrians, in their contempt for women, might be induced to come down from the heights. The women then assayed to cross the stream, and the enemy came downhill, and advancing to the river endeavoured to beat them back. The women then retreated, and the Baktrians pursued them as far as the bank; then Dionysos, coming to the rescue with his men, slew the Baktrians, who were impeded from fighting by the current, and he crossed the river in safety.)]

B 1. Diodorus Siculus: Bibl. Hist. II: 39: 1–4[2]

They further assert that Heracles also was born among them. They assign to him, like the Greeks, the club and the lion's skin. He far surpassed other men in personal strength and prowess, and cleared sea and land of evil beasts. Marrying many wives he begot many sons, but one daughter only. The sons having reached man's estate, he divided all India into equal portions for his children, whom he made kings in different parts of his dominions. He provided similarly for his only daughter, whom he reared up and made a queen. He was the founder, also, of no small number of cities, the most renowned and greatest of which he called Palibothra. He built therein many sumptuous palaces,

---

[1] Schw. frg. 57, p. 168: 13–169: 19, Fontes p. 95: 20–96: 16, Jacoby —, McCrindle p. 162: 12–163: 24.

[2] Schw. frg. I: 34–38, p. 90: 16–91: 13, Fontes frg. 1, p. 18: 31–19: 15, Jacoby 3 C 2, p. 609: 8–22, McCrindle p. 37: 2–38: 2. This frg. forms the continuation of frg. A 1.

κτίστην τε πόλεων οὐκ ὀλίγων γενέσθαι, καὶ τούτων τὴν ἐπιφανεστάτην καὶ μεγίστην προσαγορεῦσαι Παλίβοθρα. κατασκευάσαι δ' ἐν αὐτῇ καὶ βασίλεια πολυτελῆ καὶ πλῆθος οἰκητόρων καθιδρῦσαι· τήν τε πόλιν ὀχυρῶσαι τάφροις ἀξιολόγοις ποταμίοις ὕδασι πληρουμέναις. καὶ τὸν μὲν Ἡρακλέα τὴν ἐξ ἀνθρώπων μετάστασιν ποιησάμενον ἀθανάτου τυχεῖν τιμῆς, τοὺς δ' ἀπογόνους αὐτοῦ βασιλεύσαντας ἐπὶ πολλὰς γενεὰς καὶ πράξεις ἀξιολόγους μεταχειρισαμένους, μήτε στρατείαν ὑπερόριον ποιήσασθαι, μήτε ἀποικίαν εἰς ἄλλο ἔθνος[1] ἀποστεῖλαι. ὕστερον δὲ πολλοῖς ἔτεσι τὰς πλείστας μὲν τῶν πόλεων δημοκρατηθῆναι, τινῶν δ' ἐθνῶν τὰς βασιλείας διαμεῖναι μέχρι τῆς Ἀλεξάνδρου διαβάσεως.

B 2.

τοὺς δὲ πεδιασίους τὸν Ἡρακλέα τιμᾶν.

B 3.

[Ἄορνον δέ τινα πέτραν, ἧς τὰς ῥίζας ὁ Ἰνδὸς ὑποῤῥεῖ πλησίον τῶν πηγῶν, Ἀλεξάνδρου κατὰ μίαν προσβολὴν ἑλόντος, σεμνύνοντες ἔφασαν τὸν Ἡρακλέα τρὶς μὲν προσβαλεῖν τῇ πέτρᾳ ταύτῃ, τρὶς δ' ἀποκρουσθῆναι. Τῶν δὲ κοινωνησάντων αὐτῷ τῆς στρατείας ἀπογόνους εἶναι τοὺς Σίβας, σύμβολα τοῦ γένους σώζοντας τό τε δορὰς ἀμπέχεσθαι καθάπερ τὸν Ἡρακλέα καὶ τὸ σκυταληφορεῖν καὶ ἐπικεκαῦσθαι βουσὶ καὶ ἡμιόνοις ῥόπαλον. Βεβαιοῦνται δὲ τὸν μῦθον τοῦτον καὶ ἐκ τῶν περὶ τόν Καύκασον καὶ τὸν Προμηθέα· καὶ γὰρ ταῦτα μετενηνόχασιν ἐκ τοῦ Πόντου δεῦρο ἀπὸ μικρᾶς προφάσεως, ἰδόντες σπήλαιον ἐν τοῖς Παροπαμισάδαις ἱερόν· τοῦτο γὰρ ἐνεδείξαντο Προμηθέως δεσμωτήριον, καὶ δεῦρο ἀφιγμένον τὸν Ἡρακλέα ἐπὶ τὴν ἐλευθέρωσιν τοῦ Προμηθέως, καὶ τοῦτον εἶναι τὸν Καύκασον, ὃν Ἕλληνες Προμηθέως δεσμωτήριον ἀπέφηναν.][2]

B 4.

Ἡρακλέους[3] δὲ οὐ πολλὰ ὑπομνήματα. Ἀλλὰ τὴν Ἄορνον γὰρ πέτρην, ἥντινα Ἀλέξανδρος βίῃ ἐχειρώσατο, ὅτι Ἡρακλέης οὐ δυνατὸς ἐγένετο ἐξελεῖν, Μακεδονικὸν δοκέει μοι τὸ[4] κόμπασμα, καταπερῶν[5] καὶ τὸν Παραπάμισον Καύκασον ἐκάλεον Μακεδόνες, οὐδέν τι προσήκοντα τοῦτον τῷ Καυκάσῳ. Καὶ τι καὶ ἄντρον ἐπιφρασθέντες ἐν Παραπαμισάδεσι[6], τοῦτο ἔφρασαν[7] ἐκεῖνο εἶναι τοῦ Προμηθέως τοῦ Τιτῆνος τὸ ἄντρον, ἐν ὅτῳ ἐκρέματο ἐπὶ τῇ κλοπῇ τοῦ πυρός. Καὶ δὴ καὶ ἐν Σίβαισιν, Ἰνδικῷ γένει, ὅτι δορὰς ἀμπεχομένους εἶδον τοὺς Σίβας, ἀπὸ τῆς Ἡρακλέους στρατηλασίης ἔφασκον τοὺς ὑπολειφθέντας εἶναι τοὺς Σίβας· καὶ γὰρ καὶ σκυτάλην φερουσί[8] τε οἱ Σίβαι, καὶ τοῖς[9] βουσὶν

[1] Fontes and Fr. G. H.: ἀλλοεθνεῖς.

[2] (Ἄορνον line 11–ἀπέφηναν line 21): Schw. in brackets, Fontes under Strabo, Fr. G. H. under "Anhang". Fontes and Fr. G. H.: ἀπέφηναν.

[3] Fontes: Ἡρακλέος. [4] Fontes: μοί τι. [5] Fontes: κατάπερ ὤν.

[6] Fontes: Παραπαμισάδαισι. [7] Fontes: ἔφασαν. [8] Fontes: φορέουσί. [9] Fontes: τῇσι.

and settled within its walls a numerous population. The city he fortified with trenches of notable dimensions, which were filled with water introduced from the river. Heracles, accordingly, after his removal from among men, obtained immortal honour; and his descendants, having reigned for many generations and signalized themselves by great achievements, neither made any expedition beyond the confines of India, nor sent out any colony abroad. At last, however, after many years had gone, most of the cities adopted the democratic form of government, though some retained the kingly until the invasion of the country by Alexander.

B 2. Strabo: Geograph. XV: 1: 58[1]

But [the philosophers] who live on the plains worship Heracles

B 3. Strabo: Geograph. XV: 1: 8b[2]

[(Again, when Alexander had captured at the first assault the rock called Aornos, the base of which is washed by the Indus near its source, his followers, magnifying the affair, affirmed that Heracles had thrice assaulted the same rock and had been thrice repulsed. They said also that the *Sibae* were descended from those who accompanied Heracles on his expedition, and that they preserved badges of their descent, for they wore skins like Heracles, and carried clubs, and branded the mark of a cudgel on their oxen and mules. In support of this story they turn to account the legends regarding Kaukasos and Promêtheus by transferring them hither from Pontos, which they did on the slight pretext that they had seen a sacred cave among the Paropamisadae. This they declared was the prison of Promêtheus, whither Heracles had come to effect his deliverance, and that this was the Kaukasus, to which the Greeks represent Promêtheus as having been bound.)]

B 4. Flavius Arrianus: Indika V: 10–13[3]

On the other hand, there are but few memorials of Heracles, [and it may be doubted whether even these are genuine:] for the assertion that Heracles was not able to take the rock Aornos, which Alexander seized by force of arms, seems to me all a Makedonian vaunt, quite of a piece with their calling Parapamisos-Kaukasus, though it had no connexion at all with Kaukasus. In the same spirit, when they noticed a cave in the dominions of the Parapamisadai, they asserted that it was the cave of Prometheus the Titan, in which he had been suspended for stealing the fire. So also when they came among the Sibai, an Indian tribe, and noticed that they wore skins, they declared that the Sibai were descended from those who belonged to the expedition of Heracles and had been left behind: for, besides being dressed in skins,

[1] Schw. frg. 41, p. 135: 30, Fontes frg. 40, p. 27: 15–16, Jacoby 3 C 2, p. 636: 8–9, McCrindle p. 97: 18–19. This frg. forms the continuation of frg. A 3.

[2] Schw. frg. 46: 9–10, p. 144: 5–145: 3, Fontes p. 49: 10–25, Jacoby 3 C 2, p. 657: 28–658: 5, McCrindle p. 111: 13–112: 14. This frg. forms the continuation of frg. A 4.

[3] Schw. frg. 47: 8–9, p. 144: 21–34, Fontes p. 20: 29–21: 12, Jacoby —, McCrindle p. 201: 18–202: 12. This frg. forms the continuation of frg. A 6.

αὐτῶν ῥόπαλον ἐπικέκαυται· καὶ τοῦτο ἐς μνήμην ἀνέφερον τοῦ ῥοπάλου τοῦ Ἡρακλέους. [εἰ δέ τῳ πιστὰ ταῦτα, ἄλλος ἂν οὗτος Ἡρακλέης εἴη, οὐχ ὁ Θηβαῖος ἢ ὁ Τύριος [οὗτος] ἢ ὁ Αἰγύπτιος, ἤ τις καὶ κατὰ τὴν ἄνω χώρην οὐ πόρρω τῆς Ἰνδῶν γῆς ᾠκισμένος μέγας βασιλεύς.][1]

B 5.

Συμφωνεῖ καὶ Μεγασθένης ἐν τῇ τετάρτῃ τῶν Ἰνδικῶν, δι' ἧς ἀποφαίνειν πειρᾶται τὸν προειρημένον βασιλέα τῶν Βαβυλωνίων (i. e. Ναβουχοδονόσορον) Ἡρακλέους ἀνδρείᾳ καὶ μεγέθει πράξεων διενηνοχέναι· καταστρέψασθαι γὰρ αὐτόν φησι καὶ Ἰβηρίαν.[2]

B 6.

[Ἐν δὲ τοῖς βασιλείοις τούτοις ἀναλήμματα λίθινα ἀνῳκοδόμησε (scil. ὁ Ναβουχοδονόσορος), τὴν ὄψιν ἀποδοὺς ὁμοιοτάτην τοῖς ὄρεσι, καὶ καταφυτεύσας δένδρεσι παντοδαποῖς ἐξειργάσατο, διὰ τὸ τὴν γυναῖκα αὐτοῦ ἐπιθυμεῖν τῆς οἰκείας διαθέσεως ὡς τεθραμμένην ἐν τοῖς κατὰ Μηδίαν τόποις.][3] Καὶ Μεγασθένης δὲ ἐν τῇ τετάρτῃ τῶν Ἰνδικῶν μνημονεύει αὐτῶν, δι' ἧς ἀποφαίνειν πειρᾶται τοῦτον τὸν βασιλέα τῇ ἀνδρείᾳ καὶ τῷ μεγέθει τῶν πράξεων ὑπερβεβηκότα τὸν Ἡρακλέα· καταστρέψασθαι γὰρ αὐτόν φησι Λιβύης τὴν πολλὴν καὶ Ἰβηρίαν.

B 7.

Τὸν Ναβουχοδονόσορ ὁ Μεγασθένης ἐν τῇ δ' τῶν Ἰνδικῶν Ἡρακλέους ἀλκιμώτερον ἀποφαίνει, ὃς ἀνδρείᾳ μεγάλῃ Λιβύης τὸ πλεῖστον καὶ Ἰβηρίας κατεστρέψατο.

B 8.

Μεγασθένης δέ φησι, Ναβουκοδρόσορον[4] Ἡρακλέους[5] ἀλκιμώτερον γεγονότα ἐπί τε Λιβύην καὶ Ἰβηρίην στρατεῦσαι· ταύτας δὲ χειρωσάμενον ἀπόδασμον αὐτέων εἰς τὰ δεξιὰ τοῦ Πόντου κατοικίσαι.

---

[1] Schw.: — (εἰ δέ τῳ line 2–βασιλεύς line 4).
[2] Fr. G. H.: Λιβύης τὴν πολλὴν καὶ Ἰβηρίαν.
[3] (Ἐν δὲ line 9–τόποις line 12): Schw.: in brackets, Fontes and Fr. G. H.: —
[4] Fr. G. H.: Ναβοκοδρόσορον.
[5] Fr. G. H.: Ἡρακλέος.

the Sibai carry a cudgel, and brand on [the backs of] their oxen the representation of a club, wherein the Makedonians recognized a memorial of the club of Heracles. [(But if any one believes all this, then this must be another Heracles,—not the Theban, but either the Tyrian or the Egyptian, or even some great king who belonged to the upper country which lies not far from India.)]

B 5. Flavius Josephus: Contra Apion. I: 20: 144[1]

Megasthenês also expresses the same opinion in the 4th book of his Indika, where he endeavours to show that the aforesaid king of the Babylonians (Nabouchodonosor) surpassed Heracles in courage and the greatness of his achievements, by telling us that he conquered even Ibêria.

B 6. Flavius Josephus: Antiquitates Iudaicae X: 2: 1 (= X: 227)[2]

[(In this place[3] (Nabouchodonosor) erected also of stone elevated places for walking about on, which had to the eye the appearance of mountains, and were so contrived that they were planted with all sorts of trees, because his wife, who had been bred up in the land of Media, wished her surroundings to be like those of her early home.)] Megasthenês also, in the 4th book of his Indika, makes mention of these things, and thereby endeavours to show that this king surpassed Heracles in courage and the greatness of his achievements, for he says that he conquered Libya and a great part of Ibêria.[4]

B 7. Georgius Syncellus: Chronograph. ad mundi a 4888[5] T. I. p. 419 ed. Bonn.

Megasthenês, in his fourth book of the Indika, represents Nabouchodonosor as mightier than Heracles, because with great courage and enterprise he conquered the greater part of Libya and Ibêria.

B 8. Abydenus apud Eusebium Pamphili: Praep. evang. IX: 41[6]

Megasthenês says that Nabouchodrosor, who was mightier than Heracles, undertook an expedition against Libya and Ibêria, and that having conquered them he planted a colony of these people in the parts lying to the right of Pontos.[7]

---

[1] Schw. frg. 48, p. 145: 8–12, Fontes —, Jacoby 3 C 1, p. 391: 14–17, McCrindle p. 113: 8–13.

[2] Schw. frg. 48 B, p. 145: 15–146: 2, Fontes frg. 22, p. 21: 14–18, Jacoby 3 C 2, p. 605: 1–4, McCrindle p. 113: 16–114: 6.

[3] Correct: "In these palaces."

[4] Correct: "... a great part of Libya and Ibêria".

[5] Schw. frg. 48 D, p. 146: 11–13, Fontes —, Jacoby —, McCrindle p. 114: 15–18.

[6] Schw. frg. 49, p. 146: 19–22, Fontes —, Jacoby 3 C 1, p. 407: 2–9, McCrindle p. 114: 23–27.

[7] The meaning of this expression is not clear. In Arabic and in Sanskrit the words for "right" (Jemen) and (Dakshiṇā = Dekkan) are used for "south", because one

B 9.

Ἡρακλέα δέ, ὅντινα ἐς Ἰνδοὺς ἀφικέσθαι λόγος κατέχει, παρ' αὐτοῖσιν Ἰνδοῖσι γηγενέα λέγεσθαι. Τοῦτον τὸν Ἡρακλέα μάλιστα πρὸς Σουρασηνῶν γεραίρεσθαι Ἰνδικοῦ ἔθνεος, ἵνα δύο πόλιες[1] μεγάλαι Μέθορά τε καὶ Κλεισόβορα, καὶ ποταμὸς Ἰωβάρης[2] πλωτὸς διαῤῥεῖ τὴν χώρην αὐτῶν. Τὴν σκευὴν δὲ οὗτος ὁ Ἡρακλέης ἥντινα ἐφόρεε, Μεγασθένης λέγει ὅτι ὁμοίην[3] τῷ Θηβαίῳ Ἡρακλεῖ, ὡς αὐτοὶ Ἰνδοὶ ἀπηγέονται· καὶ τούτῳ ἄρσενας μὲν παῖδας πολλοὺς κάρτα γενέσθαι ἐν τῇ Ἰνδῶν γῇ, (πολλῇσι γὰρ δὴ γυναιξὶν ἐς γάμον ἐλθεῖν καὶ τοῦτον τὸν Ἡρακλέα,) θυγατέρα δὲ μουνογενέην· οὔνομα δὲ εἶναι τῇ παιδὶ Πανδαίην· καὶ τὴν χώρην ἵνα τε ἐγένετο καὶ ἧστινος ἐπέτρεψεν αὐτὴν[4] ἄρχειν Ἡρακλέης, Πανδαίην[5], τῆς παιδὸς ἐπώνυμον· καὶ ταύτῃ ἐλέφαντας μὲν γενέσθαι ἐκ τοῦ πατρὸς ἐς πεντακοσίους, ἵππον[6] δὲ ἐς τετρακισχιλίην, πεζῶν δὲ ἐς τὰς τρεῖς καὶ δέκα μυριάδας. καὶ τάδε μετεξέτεροι Ἰνδῶν περὶ Ἡρακλέους λέγουσιν· ἐπελθόντα αὐτὸν πᾶσαν γῆν καὶ θάλασσαν καὶ καθάραντα[7] ὅ τι περ κακὸν κίναδος[8], ἐξευρεῖν ἐν τῇ θαλάσσῃ κόσμον γυναικήϊον[9]. [ὅντινα καὶ εἰς τοῦτο ἔτι οἵ τε ἐξ Ἰνδῶν τῆς χώρης τὰ ἀγώγιμα παρ' ἡμέας ἀγινέοντες σπουδῇ ὠνεόμενοι ἐκκομίζουσι· καὶ Ἑλλήνων δὲ πάλαι καὶ Ῥωμαίων νῦν ὅσοι πολυκτέανοι καὶ εὐδαίμονες, μέζονι ἔτι σπουδῇ ὠνέονται·] τὸν μαργαρίτην δὴ τὸν θαλάσσιον, οὕτω τῇ Ἰνδῶν γλώσσῃ καλεόμενον· τὸν γὰρ Ἡρακλέα, ὡς καλόν οἱ ἐφάνη τὸ φόρημα, ἐκ πάσης τῆς θαλάσσης ἐς τὴν Ἰνδῶν γῆν συναγινέειν τὸν μαργαρίτην δὴ τοῦτον, τῇ θυγατρὶ τῇ ἑωυτοῦ εἶναι κόσμον.

⟦Καὶ λέγει Μεγαστένης, θηρεύεσθαι τὴν κόγχην αὐτοῦ δικτύοισι, νέμεσθαι δ' ἐν τῇ θαλάσσῃ κατ' αὐτὸ[10] πολλὰς κόγχας, καθάπερ τὰς μελίσσας· καὶ εἶναι γὰρ καὶ τοῖσι μαργαρίτῃσι βασιλέα ἢ βασίλισσαν, ὡς τῇσι μελισσίῃσι[11]. Καὶ ὅστις μὲν ἐκεῖνον κατ' ἐπιτυχίην συλλάβοι, τοῦτον δὲ εὐπετέως περιβάλλειν καὶ τὸ ἄλλο σμῆνος τῶν μαργαριτῶν· εἰ δὲ διαφύγοι σφᾶς ὁ βασιλεύς, τούτῳ δὲ οὐκέτι θηρατοὺς εἶναι τοὺς ἄλλους· τοὺς ἁλόντας[12] δὲ περιορᾷν[13] κατασαπῆναί σφισι τὴν σάρκα, τῷ δὲ ὀστέῳ ἐς κόσμον χρῆσθαι· Καὶ εἶναι γὰρ καὶ παρ' Ἰνδοῖσι τὸν μαργαρίτην τριστάσιον κατὰ τιμὴν πρὸς χρυσίον τὸ ἄπεφθον, καὶ τοῦτο ἐν τῇ Ἰνδῶν γῇ ὀρυσσόμενον.⟧[14]

Ἐν δὲ τῇ χώρῃ ταύτῃ, ἵνα ἐβασίλευσεν ἡ θυγάτηρ τοῦ Ἡρακλέους[15], τὰς μὲν γυναῖκας ἑπταετεῖς[16] ἐούσας ἐς ὥρην γάμου ἰέναι, τοὺς δὲ ἄνδρας τεσσαράκοντα

[1] Fontes and Fr. G. H.: πόληες. [2] Fontes and Fr. G. H.: Ἰωμανης.

[3] Fr. G. H.: ὁμοίη. [4] Fontes and Fr. G. H.: αὐτῇ. [5] Fr. G. H.: +καλεῖσθαι.

[6] Fontes: ἵππων. [7] Fontes and Fr. G. H.: καθήραντα.

[8] Fontes and Fr. G. H.: ὅ τι περ κακόν, καινὸν εἶδος: whatever evil, [he found] a new form [of ornament for women].

[9] Fontes and Fr. G. H.: κόσμου γυναικηίου. [10] Fr. G. H.: κατὰ ταὐτὸ.

[11] Fr. G. H.: μελίσσῃσι. [12] Fr. G. H.: ἑλόντας. [13] Fr. G. H.: περιορᾶν.

[14] Fontes: — (Καὶ λέγει l. 21–ὀρυσσόμενον l. 29).

[15] Fontes and Fr. G. H.: Ἡρακλέος. [16] Fontes and Fr. G. H.: ἑπταέτεις.

B 9. Flavius Arrianus: Indika VIII: 4–IX: 12[1]

Heracles, however, who is currently reported to have come [as a stranger] into the country, is said to have been in reality a native of India. This Heracles is held in especial honour by the Sourasenoi, an Indian tribe who possess two large cities, *Methora* and *Cleisobora*, and through whose country flows a navigable river called the Iobares. But the dress which this Heracles wore, Megasthenês tells us, resembled that of the Theban Heracles, as the Indians themselves admit. It is further said that he had a very numerous progeny of male children born to him in India (for, [like his Theban namesake,] he married many wives), but that he had only one daughter. The name of this child was Pandaia, and the land in which she was born, and with the sovereignty of which Heracles entrusted her, was called after her name, Pandaia, and she received from the hands of her father 500 elephants, a force of cavalry 4000 strong, and another of infantry consisting of about 130,000 men. Some Indian [writers] say further of Heracles that when he was going over the world and ridding land and sea of whatever evil monsters infested them, he found in the sea an ornament for women, [(which even to this day the Indian traders who bring us their wares eagerly buy up and carry away to foreign markets, while it is even more eagerly bought up by the wealthy Romans of to-day, as it was wont to be by the wealthy Greeks long ago)]. This article is the sea-pearl, called in the Indian tongue margarita. But Heracles, it is said, appreciating its beauty as a wearing ornament, caused it to be brought from all the sea into India, that he might adorn with it the person of his daughter.

[(Megasthenês informs us that the oyster which yields this pearl is there fished for with nets, and that in these same parts the oysters live in the sea in shoals like bee-swarms: for oysters, like bees, have a king or a queen, and if any one is lucky enough to catch the king he readily encloses in the net all the rest of the shoal, but if the king makes his escape there is no chance that the others can be caught. The fishermen allow the fleshy parts of such as they catch to rot away, and keep the bone, which forms the ornament: for the pearl in India is worth thrice its weight in refined gold, gold being a product of the Indian mines.)]

IX. Now in that part of the country where the daughter of Heracles reigned as a queen, it is said that the women when seven years old are of marriageable age, and that the men live at most forty years, and that on this subject there is a tradition current among the Indians to the effect that Heracles, whose daughter was born to him late in life, when he saw that his end was near, and he knew no man his equal in rank to whom he could give her in marriage, had incestuous

---

faced the rising sun. While the Roman seer faced the sun at noon, and so got the West at his right, the Greek seer faced the north, and so got the East at his right. "To the right of Pontos" can mean "to the East of Pontos" according to this. But as Ibêria is situated in this direction, and Libya in the opposite direction, the meaning "to the South of Pontos" seems to be correct.

[1] Schw. frg. 50: 13–27, p. 148: 20–152: 9, Fontes frg. 23, p. 22: 21–24: 3, Jacoby 3 C 2, p. 617: 22–620: 8, McCrindle p. 206: 4–209: 12.

ἔτεα τὰ πλεῖστα βιώσκεσθαι. Καὶ ὑπὲρ τούτου λεγόμενον λόγον εἶναι παρ' Ἰνδοῖσιν· Ἡρακλέα, ὀψιγόνου οἱ γενομένης τῆς παιδός, ἐπεί τε δὴ ἐγγὺς ἔμαθεν ἑαυτῷ ἐοῦσαν τὴν τελευτήν, οὐκ ἔχοντα ὅτῳ ἀνδρὶ ἐκδῷ τὴν παῖδα ἑωυτοῦ ἐπαξίῳ, αὐτὸν μιγῆναι τῇ παιδὶ ἑπταέτεϊ ἐούσῃ, ὡς γένος ἐξ οὗ τε κἀκείνης ὑπολείπεσθαι Ἰνδῶν βασιλέας. Ποιῆσαι ὦν αὐτὴν Ἡρακλέα ὡραίην γάμου· καὶ ἐκ τοῦδε ἅπαν τὸ γένος τοῦτο ὅτου ἡ Πανδαίη ἐπῆρξε, ταὐτὸ[1] τοῦτο γέρας ἔχειν παρὰ Ἡρακλέους. [Ἐμοὶ δὲ δοκεῖ, εἴπερ ὦν τὰ ἐς τοσόνδε ἄτοπα Ἡρακλέης οἷός τε ἦν ἐξεργάζεσθαι, καὶ αὐτὸν[2] ἀποφῆναι μακροβιώτερον, ὡς ὡραίῃ μιγῆναι τῇ παιδί. [[Ἀλλὰ γὰρ εἰ ταῦτα ὑπὲρ τῆς ὥρης τῶν ταύτῃ παίδων ἀτρεκέα ἐστίν, ἐς ταὐτὸν φέρειν δοκεῖ ἔμοιγε ἐς ὅ τι περ καὶ ὑπὲρ τῶν ἀνδρῶν τῆς ἡλικίης ὅτι τεσσαρακοντούτεες ἀποθνήσκουσιν οἱ πρεσβύτατοι αὐτῶν. Οἷς γὰρ τό τε γῆρας τοσῷδε ταχύτερον ἐπέρχεται καὶ ὁ θάνατος ὁμοῦ τῷ γήρᾳ, πάντως που καὶ ἡ ἀκμὴ πρὸς λόγον τοῦ τέλεος ταχυτέρη ἐπανθέει· ὥστε τριακοντούτεες μὲν ὠμογέροντες ἄν που εἶεν αὐτοῖσιν οἱ ἄνδρες, εἴκοσι δὲ ἔτεα γεγονότες οἱ ἔξω ἥβης νεανίσκοι· ἡ δὲ ἀκροτάτη ἥβη ἀμφὶ τὰ πεντεκαίδεκα ἔτεα· καὶ τῇσι γυναιξὶν ὥρη τοῦ γάμου κατὰ λόγον ἂν οὕτω ἐς τὰ ἑπτὰ ἔτεα συμβαίνοι.] Καὶ γὰρ τοὺς καρποὺς ἐν ταύτῃ τῇ χώρῃ πεπαίνεσθαί τε ταχύτερον μὲν τῆς ἄλλης, αὐτὸς οὗτος Μεγασθένης ἀνέγραψε[3] καὶ φθίνειν ταχύτερον.]][4]

Ἀπὸ μὲν δὴ Διονύσου βασιλέας ἠρίθμεον Ἰνδοὶ ἐς Σανδράκοτταν[5] τρεῖς καὶ πεντήκοντα καὶ ἑκατόν· ἔτεα δὲ δύο καὶ τεσσαράκοντα καὶ ἑξακισχίλια· ἐν δὲ τούτοισι τρὶς τὸ πᾶν εἰς ἐλευθερίην ... τὴν δὲ καὶ ἐς τριακόσια· τὴν δὲ εἴκοσί[6] τε ἐτέων καὶ ἑκατόν· πρεσβύτερόν τε Διόνυσον Ἡρακλέεους[7] δέκα καὶ πέντε γενεῇσιν Ἰνδοὶ λέγουσιν· ἄλλον δὲ οὐδένα ἐμβαλεῖν ἐς γῆν τῶν[8] Ἰνδῶν ἐπὶ πολέμῳ· οὐδὲ Κῦρον [τὸν Καμβύσεω καίτοι ἐπὶ Σκύθας ἐλάσαντα καὶ τἄλλα πολυπραγμονέστατον δὴ τῶν κατὰ τὴν Ἀσίην[9] βασιλέων γενόμενον τὸν Κῦρον. Ἀλλὰ Ἀλέξανδρον γὰρ ἐλθεῖν τε καὶ κρατῆσαι πάντων τοῖς ὅπλοις, ὅσους γε δὴ ἐπῆλθε· καὶ ἂν καὶ πάντων κρατῆσαι, εἰ ἡ στρατιὴ ἤθελεν. Οὐ μὲν δὴ οὐδὲ Ἰνδῶν τινα ἔξω τῆς οἰκείης σταλῆναι ἐπὶ πολέμῳ διὰ δικαιότητα.][10]

B 9 b.

Μεγασθένης φησὶν[11] τὰς ἐν Πανδαίᾳ κατοικούσας γυναῖκας ἑξαετεῖς γενομένας τίκτειν.

---

[1] Fontes and Fr. G. H.: ταὐτόν. [2] Fontes: κἂν αὐτὸν. [3] Fr. G. H.: ἀνέγραψεν.
[4] Schw.: (Ἐμοὶ δὲ line 7–συμβαίνοι line 17) in brackets; Fontes: (Ἐμοὶ δὲ line 7–παιδί line 9) in brackets, (Ἀλλὰ line 9–ταχύτερον line 18) lacking.
[5] Fontes and Fr. G. H.: Σανδρόκοττον. [6] Fontes and Fr. G. H.: εἰκοσίν.
[7] Fontes and Fr. G. H.: Ἡρακλέος. [8] Fr. G. H.: τήν.
[9] Fr. G. H.: Ἀσίαν.
[10] Fontes: — (τὸν Καμβύσεω line 24–δικαιότητα line 28).
[11] Fontes and Fr. G. H.: δὲ φησιν.

intercourse with the girl when she was seven years of age, in order that a race of kings sprung from their common blood might be left to rule over India; that Heracles therefore made her of suitable age for marriage, and that in consequence the whole nation over which Pandaia reigned obtained this same privilege from her father.[1] [(Now to me it seems that, even if Heracles could have done a thing so marvellous, he could also have made himself longer-lived, in order to have intercourse with his daughter when she was of mature age. [[But in fact, if the age at which the women there are marriageable is correctly stated, this is quite consistent, it seems to me, with what is said of the men's age,—that those who live longest die at forty; for men who come so much sooner to old age, and with old age to death, must of course flower into full manhood as much earlier as their life ends earlier, It follows hence that men of thirty would be in their green old age, and young men would at twenty be past puberty, while the stage of full puberty would be reached about fifteen. And, quite compatibly with this, the women might be marriageable at the age of seven.)] And why not, when Megasthenês declares that the very fruits of the country ripen faster than fruits elsewhere, and decay faster?]]

From the time of *Dionysos* to Sandrakottos the Indians counted 153 kings and a period of 6042 years, but among these a republic was thrice established —+—+—+— and another to 300 years, and another to 120 years. The Indians also tell us that Dionysos was earlier than Heracles by fifteen generations, and that except him no one made a hostile invasion of India,—not even Kyros [(the son of Kambysês, although he undertook an expedition against the Skythians, and otherwise showed himself the most enterprising monarch in all Asia; but that Alexander indeed came and overthrew in war all whom he attacked, and would even have conquered the whole world had his army been willing [to follow him]. On the other hand, a sense of justice, they say, prevented any Indian king from attempting conquest beyond the limits of India.)]

B 9b. Phlegon. mirab. 33[2]

Megasthenês says, that the women of the Pandaian realm bear children when they are six years of age.

---

[1] Or: "that in consequence the whole race which was progeny of Pandaia (of which she was the head)".

[2] Schw. frg. 51, p. 150: 27–28, Fontes frg. 24 a, p. 24: 5–7, Jacoby 3 C 2, p. 618: 30–32, McCrindle p. 115: 22–23.

B 10.

Ab iis[1] gens Pandae, sola Indorum regnata feminis. Unam Herculi sexus eius genitam ferunt, ob idque gratiorem, praecipuo regno donatam.

B 11.

Pandaea gens a feminis regitur, cui reginam primam assignant Herculis filiam.

B 12.

Ἡρακλῆς ἐν Ἰνδικῇ θυγατέρα ἐποιήσατο, ἥν ἐκάλεσε Πανδαίην. Ταύτῃ νείμας μοῖραν τῆν[2] Ἰνδικῆς πρὸς μεσημβρίαν καθήκουσαν εἰς θάλασσαν, διένειμε τοὺς ἀρχομένους εἰς κώμας τριακοσίας ἑξήκοντα πέντε, προστάξας καθ' ἑκάστην ἡμέραν μίαν κώμην ἀναφέρειν τὸν βασίλειον φόρον, ἵνα τοὺς διδόντας[3] ἔχοι συμμάχους ἡ βασιλεύουσα, καταπονοῦσα[4] ἀεὶ τοὺς δοῦναι ὀφείλοντας.

---

[1] Fontes: his, Fr. G. H.: —.

[2] Fontes: τῆς.

[3] Fontes: τοὺς ἤδη δόντας: [so that the queen might have the assistance of] those men who had already paid their tribute.

[4] Fontes: κατανοοῦσα: [always] seeing [those who were defaulters ...].

B 10. C. Plinius Secundus maior: Nat. Hist. VI: 23: 6 (= VI: 76)[1]

Next come the Pandæ, the only race in India ruled by women. They say that Hercules having but one daughter, who was on that account all the more beloved, endowed her with a noble kingdom.

B 11. C. Iulius Solinus: Coll. rer. mem. 52: 15[2]

The Pandæan nation is governed by females, and their first queen is said to have been the daughter of Hercules.

B 12. Polyænus: Strateg. I: 3: 4[3]

Heracles begot a daughter in India whom he called Pandaia. To her he assigned that portion of India which lies to southward and extends to the sea, while he distributed the people subject to her rule into 365 villages, giving orders that one village should each day bring to the treasury the royal tribute, so that the queen might always have the assistance of those men whose turn it was to pay the tribute in coercing those who for the time being were defaulters in their payments.[4]

---

[1] Schw. frg. 56: 23, p. 166: 13–15, Fontes p. 62: 13–15, Jacoby 3 C 2, p. 617: 28–618: 3, McCrindle p. 150: 11–151: 3.

[2] Schw. frg. 56 b: 23, p. 166: 27–167: 28, Fontes p. 150: 5–6, Jacoby —, McCrindle p. 161: 21–23.

[3] Schw. frg. 58, p. 169: 24–30, Fontes frg. 24 b, p. 24: 7–13, Jacoby —, McCrindle p. 163: 29–164: 8.

[4] More correct: "... the queen might always have the assistance of those men who used to pay the tribute in coercing those ...".

PART TWO

Megasthenes on Heracles

SUMMARY OF PASSAGES

1. *Historical passages*

a. Heracles was born in India, or possibly migrated into India. In the latter case he would have been the leader of the second of the two invasions to have occurred in Indian history.

b. This would have taken place at some time in Antiquity, 15 generations after Dionysos and 138 generations before Candragupta.

c. In addition to many wives, he had

d. Many sons, but

e. Only one daughter.

f. He set his children on the thrones of India.

g. His daughter's kingdom lay in the south.

h. It was called Pandaiē, like his daughter.

i. In order to ensure the succession from Pandaiē, Heracles committed incest with his daughter when she was only seven years old.

j. The women in Pandaiē therefore become sexually mature at the age of seven.

k. The reason for Heracles' incest was that he felt his end approaching.

l. The descendants of Heracles were peaceful kings for many generations after Pandaiē, the first queen of Pandaiē, and after his sons in the other kingdoms; even to the coming of Alexander in some. Elsewhere republics had been set up.

2. *Geographical passages*

a. *Aornos:* the name of a rock hard by the sources of the Indus, which Heracles found difficulty in capturing. He was repulsed three times.

b. *Iōmanēs* (possibly Iōbarēs): evidently Yamunā (now Jumna), a river flowing through the part of the country in which Heracles was especially worshipped.

c. *Caucasus:* connected with the myth of Prometheus.

d. *Kleisobora:* one of the towns called 'great' and fortified in the area of Heracles' worship.

e. *Methora:* evidently Mathurā, now Muttra; mentioned as the other 'great' town.

f. *Palibothra:* Pāṭaliputra, now Patna; founded by Heracles.

g. *Pandaiē:* a land in the south, by the sea, the royal dynasty of which was begun by the incest of Heracles and his daughter Pandaiē, the first queen of the country.

h. *Parapamisos:* the site of the cave in which Prometheus lay bound, and was freed by Heracles.

i. *Śibi:* an Indian people, distinguished by their carrying of clubs and wearing animal skins, like Heracles; they branded their cattle with the mark of a club, and are supposed to be descended from the survivors of Heracles' campaigns.

j *Śūrasena.* a people living around Mathurā and Yamunā, supposed to have been devoted worshippers of Heracles.

3. *Heracles' Characteristics*

a. He had wandered through all the earth and the sea,

b. And had rid them of monsters.

c. He had divided all India among his children.

d. He had found a woman's jewel in the sea, and had given it to his daughter.

e. He founded many towns, and Pāṭaliputra in particular, where he allowed the people to settle.

f. He surrounded the town with a moat.

g. He built precious palaces there,

h. But he left few memorials.

i. Heracles and his worshippers are characterized by the club,

j. By the mark of the club, with which they branded their cattle,

k. By the skins of animals, particularly the lion, in which they dressed.

l. Heracles was further distinguished by his courage,

m. And by his bodily strength.

n. After his death the Indians deified him on account of all the good he had done.

o. He was worshipped in particular by the dwellers on the plains.

WHO IS HERACLES?

— *Earlier interpretations and criticism*

1. In his book *Coins of Ancient India*, Cunningham identifies Heracles with Śiva,[1] and this identification is accepted by Kennedy, in *J.R.A.S.* (1907), p. 967, for the following reasons:

a. Heracles was worshipped by the Śibi; Śibi is so like Śiva that the connection cannot be doubted.

b. Śiva wears animal skins: tiger-skin or elephant-hide.

c. Śiva also carries a club, and is therefore called *inter alia* Śiva Lakulīśa —the Lord with the club.

d. Śiva's *śakti* has the double function of wife and daughter.

On these arguments we may say:

a. The words Śibi and Śiva cannot be philologically connected with any certainty: similarity of form is no guarantee of etymological relationship. Were the two words originally related, that does not mean to say that they were connected at the time with which we are concerned, ca. 300 B.C. The force of this objection will perhaps be clearer if we point out that the Kushāna king Vāsudeva, whose name automatically leads one's thought to Kṛishṇa, was in point of fact a worshipper of Śiva. In short, it is impossible, on a basis of the similarity of two names, to assume the existence of closer links at some period chosen at random. This is not to say that there might not be a link; but the mere similarity of the names is not a valid basis for such an assumption.

b. Śiva's animal skin was of the wrong kind.[2] This may seem to be a weak objection, particularly since both Strabo and Arrianus are not specific as to the type of skin, but Diodorus states definitely that it was a lion skin that Heracles wore. If, however, Diodorus be regarded as an unreliable witness on this point, then Śiva's animal skin must be accepted as a positive argument.

---

[1] *Op. cit.*, pp. vii–viii.

[2] Cf. however Ruben, *Eisenschmiede*, p. 191, and Gopinatha Rao, *Elements in Hindu Iconography*, App. 36, pp. 229 and 235, where Śiva is said to kill lions and tigers and dress himself in their skins.

c. It is true that Śiva carried a club. But the way in which Kennedy uses this argument works against Śiva, rather than for him. He can produce no evidence for Śiva's club earlier than the *1st century A.D.* His argument is as follows: "The identification of the Indian Heracles is fairly easy. The Greek Heracles figures on the Indo-Scythic coins of Kadphises I, and is replaced by the Indian Śiva on coins of Kadphises II. Under the name Oesho, and with various attributes including the club, Śiva figures on coins of Kanishka, Huvishka, and Vāsudeva. Mr. D. R. Bhāṇḍārkar has shown that the incarnation of Śiva as Lakulīśa, 'the lord who bears the club, goes back to this very period."[1] This rather implies that Śiva was *not* equipped with his club before the date in question, i.e. not before ca. 75 B.C. The dating of the kings mentioned above has given rise to considerable difficulties, and results have diverged sharply. But the earliest alternative ever proposed is not before 58 B.C.; this was put forward by Fleet, in the same volume of *J.R.A.S.*, in which Kennedy proposed his theory. According to *The History and Culture of the Indian People* II, this theory is not favoured by modern scholars. However Kanishka is to be placed, there seems to me to be no reason to suppose that Kennedy's argument has proved Śiva to have carried a club at the time of Megasthenes.

Another piece of evidence, of an entirely different order, seems to be much more worthy of our attention. TS I.8.6.12 is addressed to Rudra: "With loosened bow, with a club in thy hand, clad in skin" (*avatatadhanvā pinākahastaḥ kṛitivāsāḥ*).[2] There can be no doubt that this passage is earlier than Megasthenes, and it therefore follows that Rudra is described as carrying a club before the time of Megasthenes if the translation *pināka*—club be accepted. However, as early as the RV the epithet "vajra-carrier" is applied to Rudra (II.33.3). On the subject of this passage, Arbman says that such an epithet ought not to be given too much importance, since it is shared by Agni, Varuṇa and Dyaus.[3] It is, then, no more than an empty epithet. Such transference of epithet from one god to another is in fact not unusual. Thus when we find in TS that the club is an attribute of Rudra this need not—indeed must not—be accounted of decisive importance; it follows that the clubs of Heracles and Śiva respectively cannot be accepted as positive evidence of identification.

d. Śiva's *śakti* cannot be proved to be both wife and daughter. Kennedy says: "Lastly, Heracles' daughter, Pandaiē, recalls the kingdom of Pandion

---

[1] Kennedy, *op. cit., ibid.*

[2] The translation is that of Keith. But *pināka* is not "club" but "bow" or "staff".

[3] *Rudra*, p. 13.

or Pāṇḍya, a famous kingdom of Southern India, while we infer from the 'Periplūs', that Kumārī was especially worshipped at Cape Comorin. Now, the Dravidians of this region are still noted for their devotion to Śiva, and Kumārī is at once his *śakti*, his daughter, and his wife."[1] On this statement there is little more to be said except that Kennedy has not proved his case. We know that the various gods' *śakti* were considered to be their wives: Indra's *śakti*, for example, was called Indrāṇī. It is thus natural to think of a god's wife when the word *śakti* is mentioned. But we read: "When Paraśurāma created the land (kshetra) of Malaiyālam, he installed a *śivaśakti* and worshipped it. This *śakti* practised mortification (*tavam* = *tapam*), meaning to marry Śiva's manifestation (*śivamukti*). Since he did not marry her, this is the place in which she is eternally a virgin."[2] This contradicts Kennedy's thesis flatly. It is true that the expression *kumārī* occurs, but only in the meaning of "girl" and not "daughter". This need not however be decisive evidence. What in the last resort renders Kennedy's thesis untenable is that it is so far from Śiva's nature to commit incest, that it is he who punishes Prajāpati for his sin of incest.[3] The general view of Śiva is that he was not one who would have been capable of incest. Thus Ruben, in his *Eisenschmiede*, again and again emphasizes Śiva's absolute faithfulness to his one wife.[4] And when Ruben can use an expression like "the motives of self-castration and incest belong here, as having to do with Śiva's bisexual character", he is referring to something entirely other than Kennedy and Megasthenes.[5] I cannot find the least support for Kennedy's statement, and consider, therefore, that we must reckon this among the objections to the equation of Śiva with Heracles.

Of the four reasons advanced by Kennedy for his identification of the two gods, we thus see that three are invalid. But may there not be other characteristics of Heracles which fit in with Śiva? When reading through the above summary, we find not only that there is little, apart from the name Śibi and possibly the club and animal skin, to suggest Śiva. But this is not all; there are a number of passages which make it impossible to establish a link with Śiva. Some of the objections are as follows:

---

[1] *Op. cit., ibid.*

[2] Mutaliyar, *Apitana Cintamani*, s.v. *kanyā-kumārī*.

[3] Ś. Br. I.7.4. Cf. Megasthenes' statement on Heracles' incest when he felt his end near with the Purāṇas' statement that Śiva after the creation of the world had castrated himself and planting his virile member as a pillar beside himself dedicated himself to asceticism. For references, see Dikshitar, *Purāṇa Index*, s.v. *Śiva*.

[4] *Op. cit.*, pp. 211, 213.

[5] *Op. cit.*, p. 213.

a. According to Megasthenes Heracles was worshipped on the plain, according to e.g. the Yajur Veda, Śiva was worshipped in the hills. TS IV.5.1 addresses Rudra: "Thou who dwellest in the mountains, thou who watchest over the mountains, thou who livest in the mountains." This, remember, is the same document as we quoted above in connection with Śiva's club.[1]

b. Heracles had many wives; Śiva, remarkably enough, had only one, to whom he was absolutely faithful. But she had many names. Does this notice so fit in with Śiva?

c. Heracles had many sons; Śiva had not many sons. Even though there are a number of traditions stating that Śiva had one or several sons, this is insufficient to establish his identity with Heracles.[2]

d. The incest tradition is unknown in Indian tradition as combined with Śiva. As we have already pointed out, it is incompatible with Śiva's character.[3]

e. There are no traditions which speak of Śiva's coming into India at the head of an army.

f. Śiva, unlike Heracles, was not a king.[4]

g. Nor was Śiva a warrior. He seems to have been of a passive type.[5]

h. What is perhaps most typical of Śiva is missing from Heracles' character: his meditative aspect as a *yogi*, his aspect of terror, his consuming third eye, etc.

---

[1] Note the important distinction between the statement "*Rudra* dwells in the mountains" (according to TS) and "*the worshippers of Dionysos* dwelt in the mountains, the *worshippers* of Heracles on the plain" (according to Megasthenes).

[2] Ruben, *op. cit.*, p. 212: "Er hat keine Ahnen ... und keine Söhne, denn Gaṇeśa ... sind in Wirklichkeit nicht von ihm gezeugt ..." Whence has Ruben got this statement? Cf. the following note.

[3] Above, pp. 75. Remark his emblem *linga* and some myths of sexual character; see Dikshitar, *Purāṇa Index,* s.v. *Śiva.* Cf. also, besides the Purāṇa tradition, mentioned p. 75, n. 3, the epithets of Śiva in Mbh. XIII 17:46: "You are a Brahmacārin without having ever neglected the rigid vow of celibacy. You are famous for your sexual continence."

[4] The validity of this statement cannot be challenged, despite the fact that Dikshitar, in his *Purāṇa Index* (s.v. *Mahādeva*) represents Śiva (?) as having been anointed king and as the father of Budha, 1050 years before Parīkshit ..., for this is not one of the essential attributes of Śiva; and further, it is not certain that *Mahādeva* in the *VP* refers to Śiva.

[5] Ruben, *op. cit.*, p. 212: "Er hatte keine Taten ausser seiner Hochzeit." Cf. Gonda, *Die Religionen Indiens,* p. 259, where it is stressed that Śiva does not perform any deeds: He acts like a power of nature. See Dikshitar, *Purāṇa Index,* s.v. *Śiva:* "He fought with Kṛishṇa, cut off Daksha's head, killed Asuras, attacked successfully Tripura."

To summarize:

1. What is told of Heracles is not told of Śiva.
2. What is told of Śiva is not told of Heracles.

2. As we have already pointed out, most scholars accept the view that Megasthenes' Heracles was in fact Kṛishṇa. On the first occasion on which this identification was put forward,[1] it was motivated in the following way:

a. Heracles was worshipped mainly by the Sūrasenes in the towns of Methora and Klisobora. (We note that Methora provides argument 1; i.e. Mathurā was Lassen's first clue in his quest for identification.)

b. He had many wives.

c. He had only one daughter, Pandaiē, to whom he bequeathed the country with the same name. This detail is *not* found in the Indian tradition, but may be deduced therefrom. Arjuna, son of Pāṇḍu, married the sister of Kṛishṇa, who bore him Abhimanyu, whose son Parīkshit obtained power in Hāstinapura, when all the kings died in the war between the Kauravas and the Pāṇḍavas.

d. He had wandered through the earth and sea and destroyed all monsters; he found a jewel in the sea (the pearl-shell). Lassen refers here to the Vishṇu Purāṇa, to the legend that Kṛishṇa killed the giant Pañcajana, who dwelled in the sea in the guise of an shell. Kṛishṇa made his shell from the bones of Pañcajana.

These four arguments in favour of the identification of Heracles with Kṛishṇa have seemed adequate to most scholars. Thus Schwanbeck, for example, was able in his edition of Megasthenes to include the name Kṛishṇa in his index; this conveys the impression that he at least considered the proposed argument proven. There is, however, some doubt as to whether Lassen himself was entirely satisfied with his own arguments, since on the next occasion he discussed the identification of Heracles, he repeats only two of them, omitting the two which the reader is tempted to regard as suspect. In *Indische Altertumskunde* I, p. 796 ff., he says: "(That it is Kṛishṇa who is referred to under the name of Heracles is clear from the facts ...)"

a. ... that he is worshipped by the Śūrasenes in particular; on a basis of this passage we may therefore conclude that in Megasthenes' day Kṛishṇa was worshipped as one of the highest gods, having the character of Vishṇu: the god who incarnates himself when sin threatens to take the upper hand in the world, and destroys it. (N.B. that this is essentially the same as the

[1] Lassen, *Bemerkungen* ... in *Zeitschrift für die Kunde des Morgenlandes* V, 1844, p. 252.

Mathurā proof, though the name of Mathurā is never mentioned. N.B. also that this is given prominence as the first argument.)

b. ... that many wives and sons are attributed to Kr̥ishṇa.

(The two following points, c. and d. are excluded from this passage.)

e. When Megasthenes describes him as carrying a club, he thereby reveals his extensive knowledge of the Indian religious situation; for Vishṇu also carries a club. (Note 3: "Hence his lesser by-name gadādhara. This club was given him by Varuṇa, the god of the sea, and was called Kaumodī or Kaumodakī ...")

f. According to Lassen, the name Pandaiē is connected with Pāṇḍava, "particularly if the form Pāṇḍavya be brought into the comparison".

Against these six arguments must be weighed two factors which Lassen himself admits to be difficult:

a. The lion-skin, which is not found in any Indian text; the author explains this by saying that Megasthenes wished in this way to make his identification of the Indian Heracles and the Hellenic more convincing. "It may be that Megasthenes has a dim recollection that the Sanskrit word for 'lion' is used to denote outstanding qualities in men. and in warriors in particular."

b. Palibothra, i.e. Pāṭaliputra, which *de facto* had another founder, and moreover one which cannot be considered for purposes of identification. But Kr̥ishṇa did found a town, Dvārakā, which was his capital, but which is never mentioned by Megasthenes.

This topic was not examined critically until about a century after Lassen first identified Heracles with Kr̥ishṇa, when Walter Ruben published his monograph *Kr̥ishṇa, Konkordanz und Kommentar der Motive seines Heldenlebens.*[1] Ruben finds six passages which agree with the identification of Kr̥ishṇa, but no less than twelve which seem to him to be dubious, not only as regards Kr̥ishṇa, but also factually. We shall first of all summarize the six positive points which, despite their paucity, are regarded as being sufficient proof of the correctness of Lassen's identification. We shall also set out in parallel columns Lassen's two groups of proofs.

Lassen in Zeitschr.	*Lassen in Ind. Alt.-K.*	*Ruben in Kr̥ishṇa*
1. 1. Heracles was worshipped mainly by the Śūrasenes, who lived in and around Mathurā and Kleisobora (the Mathurā proof).		
2.	2. H. carries a club.	

---

[1] *Op. cit.*, pp. 278–281.

3.			3. H. was stronger than others, and killed monsters.
4.	2. He had many	(3) wives and many	(4) sons ...
5.	3. He had one daughter	(4) called Pandaiē.	
6.	4. He found a jewel in the sea.		
7.			5. Generations of his descendants kings in India.
8.			6. H. was worshipped on the plain.

We see from this table that there are eight arguments in favour of Lassen's identification. Points 1 and 8 are in fact identical, or rather: 8 includes 1. Furthermore, points 3 and 6 belong together; Ruben limits himself to point 3, while Lassen pays particular attention to the jewel found by Heracles on his expedition. Neither scholar refers to what seems to be the most important factor for Megasthenes, that Heracles gave this jewel to his daughter. In our introduction, above, we quoted another passage from *Ind. Alt.-K.*, in which Lassen made particular use of the contents of point 3.[1] But since points 3 and 6 strictly belong together, we find that the total number of arguments is no more than six. Of these, only two recur in all three proof-collections: point 1, dealing with Heracles' worship among the Śūrasenes and in Mathurā, and point 4, on Heracles' many wives and sons.

We shall now examine these positive arguments, to see whether they can be regarded as decisive proof.

1. Point 1 is the only one which recurs in all three lists; it is virtually the only one which has stood through every attempt to prove Heracles' identity, and definitely the only one to have held through every examination of Lassen's position. We have also seen, above p. 20, how Heracles' link with Mathurā was regarded as being decisive. It is clear, therefore, that it was this argument which inspired Lassen's position, and this argument which has been the bulwark against all objections to Lassen's theory. The whole burden of proof rests here, as is plain from the regularity with which it recurs; no other argument has the same force, except perhaps the fourth, on Kṛishṇa's many wives and sons. We shall however return to the validity of this latter argument in due course.

In the Introduction, we subjected Lassen's procedure with this Mathurā-proof to some criticism. We cannot start from the statement that Heracles was worshipped in Mathurā in Megasthenes' day, and then come to the

[1] Above, p. 20.

otherwise improbable conclusion that it was Kr̥ishṇa who was worshipped at that time (cf. Introduction pp. 10f.). But such is Lassen's conclusion. We encounter the same process of reasoning in Ruben; but their logical inconsistencies are not so glaring, since their surprise is formally at the 'fact' that as early as Megasthenes' day, Kr̥ishṇa was the *only* great god alongside Śiva—though according to Ruben, as well as Lassen, he had been a lesser god for centuries. Strangely enough, we are forced to the conclusion that the point which emphasizes Heracles' connection with Mathurā must be rejected, mainly because of the enormous burden of evidence which is laid upon it. We might put it this way: Had it been possible to have produced twenty parallels, the name of Mathurā being missing from them all, this would have been suspicious and surprising. Had the name of Mathurā occurred among the twenty, the name as such might have been of importance. But we have already pointed out that in the last resort, the name is the sole proof on which the entire burden of identification rests. We have also stated in our Introduction that, by using the same reasoning, it is possible to 'prove' that Christ was worshipped in Rome in 300 B.C.; the system evidently stands condemned. When dealing with Kr̥ishṇa, the illogicality of the process is perhaps not so marked, since our factual knowledge about Kr̥ishṇa is not comparable with what we know about Christ at the same period. Our conclusion must therefore be, that this piece of evidence, despite the frequency with which it has been put forward, must be dismissed as untenable.

2. There is no doubt that Heracles' club is an emblem which can be demonstrated to have belonged also to Kr̥ishṇa. But we note that in his first discussion of the subject, Lassen passes over this point in silence. Why? The explanation may conceivably be, that the learned Indologist had not noticed that Kr̥ishṇa carried a club! On other points Lassen draws attention to details which concern Kr̥ishṇa, and not Vishṇu; on this point, however, Vishṇu is named, and not Kr̥ishṇa. For the sake of consistency, it ought to be Kr̥ishṇa's, as is the case in Ruben[1], and not Vishṇu's club which is brought into the picture. Should it be the case that Lassen has failed to notice Kr̥ishṇa's club, this is not altogether surprising, since it is mentioned so seldom. The Mahābhārata has the following references:

a. In I.227, which is an account of why and how he obtained the club, Kr̥ishṇa was given his club by Varuṇa at the same time as Agni gave him his discus; both were to help him in his fight with the god Indra.

b. in V.130 Those occasions on which Kr̥ishṇa reveals himself in all

---

[1] *Kr̥ishṇa*, p. 281.

c. in VI.35 his glory to various individuals.

d. in XIV.57

e. in XVI.3, which tells of the preparations for the death of Kṛishṇa. It tells how all his attributes went before him to Indra's heaven. Immediately afterward is related how the Erakā grass is transformed into an iron club in his hand; with this club he slew all those members of the clan who had survived the fight following the drinking bout.

These are, as far as I have been able to ascertain, the only passages in which Kṛishṇa's club is mentioned: five in all. He receives it, loses it, and carries it when revealing his divine nature. But on no occasion does he use it. This is strange, particularly in view of what is related under e. above—how on one occasion in his life he uses a club: not his own, which he has carried for many years without ever using, but a temporary replacement in lieu of the club he has lost. On all other occasions Kṛishṇa uses his discus. How, then, are we to understand the lack of agreement between the story of the Erakā grass and the rest of Kṛishṇa's life? The reader has a peculiar feeling that the story of the Erakā grass is a gloss, and that no attempt has been made to bring it into line with the rest of the epic. One cannot help thinking that this story originally had to do with another god, and that it has been transferred to Kṛishṇa at a later date.[1]

The club occupies a prominent position in Lassen's second discussion of the problem. He considers it to be a witness of Megasthenes' familiarity with the Indian situation. Can this be interpreted to mean that Lassen, as we have just suggested, despite his profound knowledge of things Indian, had not noticed that Kṛishṇa also carried a club? It is clear from his formulation that Lassen does not consider Kṛishṇa's club to be of any particular importance. "Detailed knowledge of things Indian" is required in order to be aware of the existence of Kṛishṇa's (or Vishṇu's) club at all. Had the club been an essential attribute of Kṛishṇa, it is hardly likely that Lassen would have expressed himself in this way. It is true that Ruben regards the club as an aid to identification, but he is unable to conceal his doubt and uncertainty about the same club in some of the other passages: "It is not strictly correct that the club is stressed as being Kṛishṇa's weapon. Vishṇu-Kṛishṇa has of course the club as his emblem but it is not employed in the battles recorded in our texts ... his discus, on the other hand, is in continual use. Is it possible that Kṛishṇa has been confused with Balarāma, the club-fighter?"[2] Can a greater contrast be imagined than between this statement

[1] We have no occasion to take up the question of the connection between Kṛishṇa in this episode and Vāsudeva in the Ghaṭajātaka. See e.g. Ruben, *Kṛishṇa*, pp. 248 ff.

[2] *Op. cit.*, p. 281.

by the leading Kṛishṇa specialist of today and that which we quoted from Lassen (above, p. 78 e.)? We are forced to the conclusion that the club is by no means certain proof of the identification of Kṛishṇa as the Heracles of whom Megasthenes wrote. We are rather tempted to think that it should be some god who carried no other weapon than the club.

3. Heracles was stronger than other men, and cleansed sea and land from monsters. Ruben is satisfied with this bare statement. Lassen regards it as a virtually exhaustive definition of Vishṇu, quoting it in his polemic against Weber, which we cited in full above, p. 20 (Intr.). He does not however make use of it in his more detailed considerations of Megasthenes. In *Zeitschr.* he discussed only the continuation, here treated separately as point 6.

That Kṛishṇa is reputed to have been enormously strong cannot be denied—if we may be allowed to quote later texts, and the Purāṇas in particular.[1] These may possibly be made up of more ancient material, which may be earlier than Megasthenes, but we have no positive evidence that such was in fact the case. In no circumstance is it possible to decide whether any individual narrative passage is so old. Were we to try and build our identification of Heracles on texts whose age cannot be determined, we should rapidly be involved in a vicious circle of reasoning. It is however possible to date certain portions of the Mahābhārata, for philological reasons, to the time of Megasthenes, while the epic continued its process of gradual growth until about the same date A.D. But we see nothing in the Mahābhārata told of Kṛishṇa which fits in with Megasthenes' verdict that Heracles was of outstanding strength. On the contrary, Kṛishṇa's victories over his allies' enemies are won by cunning, and even by treachery. There are of course many remarkable exploits which he is supposed to have carried out, but these are entirely different in character from the "miracles" worked by Kṛishṇa in the real narrative of the epic. One might be tempted for this reason to regard these exploits as later additions to the text. Nothing, however, can be said with any certainty, owing to the extreme complexity of the figure of Kṛishṇa in the Mahābhārata, which makes it extremely difficult to come to an adequate estimation of him. In short, the "Kṛishṇa" of the Mbh. is a number of different persons, having different characters: a normal man—a king, but with no outstanding qualities; a cunning, near-daemonic helper to the five brothers, whose help often causes their indignation; a moral teacher of exalted purity, whose teachings are still read today with admiration and profit in the Bhagavadgītā. And finally, he is

[1] On the age of the Purāṇas, see below, p. 92 n. 1.

a divine being who seems to lack all human qualities. In addition to all these types of personality presented to us in the epic, there are those which we encounter in the Harivaṁśa and in the Purāṇas: the child, the small boy who runs into all manner of adventures. But although some of these may be amusing, their most striking factor is the supernatural character attributed to Kṛishṇa. For example: On one occasion Kṛishṇa was charged by a mad bull. The bull was so large that its hump was partly hidden by the clouds, and so angry that it tore up the earth with its horns, making great trenches. But Kṛishṇa stood there, calm and collected, and annoyed the bull even more by clapping his hands. When the bull charged, Kṛishṇa grasped one horn and threw the bull to the ground without the least effort; the bull, on the other hand, was panting and sweating from every pore![1]

It goes without saying that this Kṛishṇa is of uncommon strength; but is his strength *capable of allowing a defeat*—or at least strain—like that mentioned in the story of Aornos? The actual "type" of strength and courage which we find in Megasthenes' Heracles is not to be found in Kṛishṇa—particularly when we remember that the most outstanding characteristic of Vishṇu-Kṛishṇa is *passivity*: a passivity to some extent abandoned by the Purāṇas. For this reason I regard this proof of identification to be dubious; there are others whom this characteristic fits much better.

4. He had many wives and many sons. This point is to be found in all three columns, a distinction which it shares only with point 1. The agreement between Heracles and Kṛishṇa on this point is incontestable. But the same may equally well be said of many oriental kings, that they had many wives and sons. It is not necessary to go to the lengths of 16,000 wives and 180,000 sons in order to justify the term "many wives and many sons". The same conditions apply to the pantheon as to the world of men. We do not always hear the names of the gods' wives: often enough we hear many names applied to one goddess. But there is another point to consider: It is by no means certain that Megasthenes or his informants were fastidious in their definitions. "Wives" may refer equally well to concubines and "sons" to their children.

After these marginal notes, I should like to express the value of this particular proof in this way: that it is a definite point in favour of the Kṛishṇa interpretation, provided that other, more convincing reasons can be found to support it. Otherwise, if it stands as an isolated proof, it is entirely worthless, since it fits in with so many others.

---

[1] Bh.P. X.35; cf. Ruben, *Kṛishṇa*, p. 114 (sarga 8d).

5. He had a daughter, called Pandaiē. Lassen is the only one who sees a reference to Kṛishṇa here. He understands the word "daughter" to be a *lapsus*; what is meant is "sister". In that case, the name Pandaiē is easily linked with Pāṇḍava, and with Pāṇḍya. This solution is certainly ingenious. Kṛishṇa's sister Subhadrā was married to Arjuna and was thus linked to the Pāṇḍavas, which makes Pāṇḍavī a possible appellation of her. Unfortunately, the whole of this hypothesis falls down on a number of contradictory factors: No mention is made of any incest story between Kṛishṇa and this sister; Arjuna was related to the Pāṇḍya royal house through another wife; all texts witness to the fact that the name Pāṇḍya existed in the time of Arjuna; Kṛishṇa had nothing to do with this family relationship; Kṛishṇa's sister fills an entirely different function from Heracles' daughter Pandaiē: Heracles committed incest with her because he felt his end approaching, and had no one to whom to give her. This had certain consequences: first, that the difference in their ages was so great as to rule out the possibility of their being brother and sister; secondly, Heracles was approaching the end of his life, and not, as in the story of Subhadrā and Arjuna, preparing himself for life and history; thirdly, there is no room for incest in the Mbh. narrative, since nothing is said about a Subhadrā child from the time before marriage, and she—fourthly and lastly—became the lawful wedded wife of Arjuna, in her relative youth, and with the express consent of Kṛishṇa. This makes it necessary to dismiss this argument as unsound.

6. He found a jewel in the sea. This is also used only by Lassen, as we have pointed out. It is to be seen in conjunction with point 3. But when Lassen discusses the point, he discusses only part of it, referring to a narrative in the Vishṇu Purāṇa, which tells how Kṛishṇa killed a giant, Pañcajana, who had dwelt in the sea in the guise of an oyster. From his bones Kṛishṇa made his own shell, his *śaṅkha*, which he called Pāñcajanya, after its originator. Apart from the fact that it is impossible to date this narrative, since we can know nothing with any certainty about the age of the text, we can nevertheless state with confidence that the actual point of the Megasthenes passage is missed by Lassen—that Heracles gave the jewel to his daughter. Kṛishṇa, on the other hand, did not gain a jewel, but one of his characteristic emblems; incidentally, Megasthenes makes no mention of this emblem. This proof of identification ought therefore to be deleted.

7. Many generations of his descendants were kings in India. This point is used by Ruben, but not by Lassen. A hint as to the connection with the royal house of India is given by Lassen, in connection with point 5 above.

The grandchildren of Arjuna (!) are, through the sister of Kṛishṇa, the source of the royal dynasties of India. But in point of fact, the Mbh. also names a grandson of Kṛishṇa, called Vajra, who is proclaimed king in Indraprastha by Yudhishṭhira and Arjuna after the death of the majority of the heroes. According to the Mbh., Kṛishṇa installed none of his many sons on any throne: a striking contrast to Megasthenes' Heracles. The hero's sons play hardly any active part in the epic. One has the impression that the story of Kṛishṇa's grandson Vajra does not fit into the pattern at all; the name Vajra suggests a connection with Indra, as does Indraprastha, the town founded by Yudhishṭhira. The motive appears to have been taken from Indra; these passages, at least in so far as the names are concerned, point to Indra. And a factual difficulty in connection with Vajra is that no mention is made of his parents or grandparents. He breaks into the narrative of the epic abruptly, and since the epic concludes immediately afterward, we hear nothing about his later history. He seems to have been the sole survivor of the entire Kṛishṇa family, but he was not a grandson of Kṛishṇa's *daughter*, but of his *son*. We hear nothing more of the history of the family—not unnaturally. The entire contents of the epic are said in the introduction to have been told to king Janamejaya, great-grandson to Arjuna and Subhadrā and a contemporary of King Vajra.

But it seems to me that Ruben puts his finger on a point which is of much greater importance for our examination, when he concludes his consideration of Kṛishṇa in the Mbh. in the following words: "Kṛishṇa was a shepherd-hero, and the shepherd caste of Ahir alone is descended from Kṛishṇa; *no Indian royal house.*"[1] The real importance of Kṛishṇa does not lie in the fact that he was a king and the founder of a royal dynasty, whereas we have every reason for saying that Megasthenes regarded this as being the main function of Heracles.

We have earlier had occasion to question Lassen's references to the later literature, the Harivaṁśa and the Purāṇas; on this occasion we have no other alternative. This later literature is the only source on which we can rely since, as we have pointed out, the Mbh. ends just at the critical moment. To be sure, the later literature does not mention Kṛishṇa's descendants, either. But it shows instead with much greater clarity that Kṛishṇa in the eyes of its authors and readers is not mainly a king but a shepherd, a cunning and successful hero of many utterly fantastic adventures. If he is a king at all, the fact is pushed completely into the background. Our conclusion must therefore be that Megasthenes' picture of Heracles as the

[1] *Op. cit.*, p. 247.

founder of a royal dynasty does not agree in the slightest with the picture of Kṛishṇa given us in the later literature. And turning to the Mbh., it is true, that the epic allows for the possibility of Kṛishṇa's family continuing to rule on any one of the many thrones of India, but the fact—if it is a fact—is never emphasized as to Kṛishṇa, as is the case with Heracles. Megasthenes' emphasis on Heracles' incest with his daughter Pandaiē in order to secure the succession seems to indicate that Heracles as a type is entirely different from Kṛishṇa as a type. One is a warrior king, the other a shepherd hero (who is not unacquainted with cunning and treachery). We are therefore compelled to state that this point conflicts with the accepted identification.

8. He was worshipped on the plain. We have already suggested that this point contains nothing new, and that its main substance is to be found in point 1. Ruben, who is alone in paying this point particular attention, says simply: "It is for the most part perfectly correct that Śiva was worshipped in the hills, and Kṛishṇa on the plain."[1] The only conclusion which can be drawn from this statement is that it is obvious that Heracles cannot be the same as Śiva. And a further conclusion suggests itself: that Heracles must be Kṛishṇa—if there are only two gods to choose from. But we are not in the situation of having an Indian pantheon limited to only two gods. For that reason we are unable to draw any positive conclusion whatever from this statement, with the possible exception that it does not imply that Kṛishṇa can be dismissed altogether, i.e. that this point is not evidence against Kṛishṇa. But it is not evidence for him, either, unless it is given overwhelmingly powerful support from a large number of other passages, having much better defined information.

To summarize, in our examination of the arguments provided by Lassen and Ruben for that interpretation which they share with most scholars, we have found a. that only one point is positively in favour of Kṛishṇa: point 4, which refers to Heracles' many wives and sons; b. that one point is against Kṛishṇa: point 7, which states that Heracles' descendants were kings, while we know that Kṛishṇa's descendants were shepherds; c. that one point has a negative tendency: point 2, on Heracles' club; Kṛishṇa's club has by no means the same prominent function in his life as that borne by Heracles; d. that the remaining five arguments are neither for nor

[1] Cf. above, p. 76 n. 1, which stresses the difference between what Megasthenes has to say about the *worshippers* of Dionysos as dwellers in the mountains and the view of the Indian literature, that *Rudra* dwelt in the hills and forests, far from the dwellings of men. This diminishes the value of the passage in question as an argument for the identification with *Kṛishṇa*.

against Kṛishṇa. These five are of two kinds: i. those which may well apply to others, such as point 3, referring to Heracles' strength, and point 8, referring to his worship on the plain; ii. those whose application to Kṛishṇa is doubtful: points 1, referring to his worship in Mathurā, 5, on his daughter Pandaiē and 6, on the jewel in the sea.

We shall not however pay more detailed attention to these "positive" arguments at this point, but will instead concentrate on others of Kṛishṇa's characteristics which are missing from Megasthenes' account:

1. Megasthenes relates that Heracles carried a club and wore a lion-skin (or animal-skin). But he says nothing whatever which might indicate that Heracles carried a discus. It is common knowledge among those who are at all familiar with the Indian Kṛishṇa-literature that the weapon used in battle by Kṛishṇa was a discus, cakra, called "Vajranābha". Any one setting out to talk about Kṛishṇa, and to describe him with only one emblem could scarcely avoid mentioning this *cakra,* this discus.

2. Were it necessary to mention any emblem other than this discus, not only his *gadā*, his club, must be mentioned, but it is equally important to mention his *padma*, his lotus, and his *śaṅkha*, shell, apart from which his club is never mentioned. A further attribute, and one which is particularly mentioned in the Purāṇas, is his flute. Kṛishṇa's shell, or snail, should, according to Lassen's understanding of the description in question, have provided a good subject for Megasthenes; but he never mentions it. On the contrary, he mentions the jewel given by Heracles to his daughter—and this can have nothing to do with Kṛishṇa. But why does Megasthenes not mention Heracles' snail or shell here, if he is really thinking of Kṛishṇa? The question is answered as soon as asked. Megasthenes was not thinking of Kṛishṇa.

3. Further, Megasthenes mentions on the one hand, the two large towns Mathurā and Kleisobora in the land of the Śūrasenes where Heracles was worshipped and, on the other, Palibothra, which was founded by Heracles—three towns, two of which are never mentioned in connection with Kṛishṇa! But why does he not mention Indraprastha, now Delhi, which Kṛishṇa often visited, and which was founded by Yudhishṭhira, or Dvārakā, which according to the epic was founded by none other than Kṛishṇa himself, and which was his capital?

But this must suffice. What we have said is quite sufficient to show i. that there is nothing which can be said to establish Kṛishṇa without any doubt as the god in question. There is nothing which one might have expected to find, had Kṛishṇa been the subject of Megasthenes' description; there is nothing typical of him, such things as the name Kṛishṇa brings into the mind of any reader, whether his acquaintance with Kṛishṇa be superficial or extensive, ii. The evidence produced in support of the established interpretation is for the most part of such a character that it must be forced into the pattern. In short, all that is told of Kṛishṇa is not told of Heracles, and vice versa.

I have not attempted to examine the extent to which those elements in Megasthenes' description of Heracles which have not been produced as positive arguments may possibly fit in with Kṛishṇa. Such a procedure must be entirely superfluous, since what we have already said shows that the arguments upon which such great reliance has been placed have proved to be so doubtful.[1]

The course of our argument so far should have proved beyond any shadow of a doubt that Heracles cannot possibly be Kṛishṇa. But in that case, who is he?

3. *Heracles is Indra.* This assertion may be verified in a number of ways. We must however begin by stating that it is not Lassen's fault that he failed to observe this fact, since a great deal of the material which nowadays can be produced to support this identification was more or less unknown in Lassen's day. For one thing, the comparative study of Indo-European religion was on a decidedly different level from what it is now. The archaeology of India had not had time to win that degree of knowledge about the country which we now possess. And the general conception of Indian literature was in a number of important respects quite different from our view. (The following paragraphs are no more than a rough outline of the subject.)

a. On the subject of the comparative study of religion, in 1915 Leopold von Schroeder undertook to compare Heracles and Indra; his result, despite certain shortcomings, was extremely thought-provoking and convincing.[2]

---

[1] Among those which Ruben reckons as "zweifelhafte Nachrichten" are some which are doubtful because of the wrong identification of Heracles as Kṛishṇa. But though factually wrong, a great deal can be rendered mythologically correct by a re-identification of Heracles.

[2] *Herakles und Indra.* Eine mythenvergleichende Untersuchung. Wien 1915. In this excellent study, it seems to me, Schroeder has quite convincingly pointed out that Indra and Heracles are originally one and the same person. Schroeder too has discussed the problem which occupies us here and says: "An Indra selbst konnte er (Megasthenes) unmöglich denken, da dieser sich ja klar und deutlich als Gott des Gewitters präsentierte, also naturgemäss und ganz mit Recht von dem Griechen vielmehr dem regenbringenden Zeus gleichgesetzt wurde." (p. 22.) How are we to know for sure that this opinion is correct? I think we have first to investigate the notices of Megasthenes before we can exclude Indra. I believe we can not prescribe which deity the Greeks

These shortcomings were pointed out by Bernhard Schweitzer in a study of Heracles which seems to state, remarkably enough, that von Schroeder had by sheer chance stumbled upon the correct result, despite the superficiality of his method.[1] Von Schroeder's work had been based on a random choice of a number of characteristics in the two figures, which were isolated and compared; they showed a considerable measure of agreement. Those characteristics of the Greek Heracles which had no Indian counterpart had quite simply been passed over in silence. Schweitzer considered himself justified in pointing out and criticizing the random aspect of this method. But Schweitzer finds, by means of a method of archaeological and textual examination of the age of the various elements which go to make up the Greek Heracles, that some of his characteristics are older than others. It is precisely those characteristics which this method proved to be the most ancient, which von Schroeder had drawn upon in his comparison of Heracles and Indra; what he had not done was to demonstrate their antiquity or their greater value, compared with those many characteristics which did not agree with the figure of Indra. Intuitively he had reached the right result: but the burden of proof had been provided by another. In the same year as Schweitzer's book was published, Herman Güntert had incorporated Schweitzer's results into his own interesting and valuable study, *Der arische Weltkönig und Heiland*.[2] This work contains an estimation of Indra which differs essentially from that which the previous century had regarded as the norm. I quote: "But I must also express my doubt of the methods of scholars who are still ... preoccupied with the storm-myths in the Vṛitra-battle ... Indra has far too much resemblance it seems to me, to Donar-Thor among the Germans, Indra's Vajra to Thor's hammer, the thunderbolt ... but we must not fall into the temptation, however unpleasant it may be, to come to the conclusion: in the Rig Veda itself the rivers are of course real rivers, but they 'really' meant something else, they 'mean' the thunderstorm. Indra is never said to cause thunder or rain; this is rather the task of Parjanya; nor may we associate the vajra only with the 'thunderbolt'; the descriptions of the terrible weapon are not unanimous: it is sometimes made of iron, sometimes of gold, sometimes of stone. To judge by the Avestan

---

ought to combine and identify with which foreign deity. We only have to state facts. Cf. also our introductory remark p. 30 f. concerning the intimate relation between Alexander the Great and Heracles, which must have been of importance for the Macedonians' choice of name, when identifying the head-god of the Indians with a Greek counterpart.

[1] *Herakles*, Tübingen 1922.

[2] *Der arische Weltkönig und Heiland*, Halle 1923.

vazrō, "club", the word is genuinely Aryan; in New-Persian, the word "gurz", derived from the Avestan, also means 'club'."[1] We see that the god we encounter in this new view is entirely other than the ancient thunder-god Indra, and is perhaps not yet fully accepted by everyone. But we notice a tendency in modern research to dismiss those ideas concerning Indra which excluded him in Lassen's day from any possibility of being considered as Megasthenes' Heracles: his club—vajra—lightning, his relation to the waters, heavenly or earthly.

b. We can summarize the results of archaeological research under two points. On the one hand, it has been stated, somewhat surprisingly, that the most ancient discoveries witnessing to the Kṛishṇa cult are comparatively late; they are fifty years younger than the oldest Buddhist discoveries.[2] We need not concern ourselves with the question of whether they in fact bear clear witness to Kṛishṇa.[3] On the other hand, there have been discovered representations of Indra dating from a period much later than that in which, according to older ideas, he should have disappeared. Such discoveries seem to confirm that he by no means lost his position, as has often been supposed.[4] It is possible that a process of change is taking place in

---

[1] *Op. cit.*, p. 19 f., partly quotation from Oldenberg, *Die Religionen Indiens.*

[2] Cf. Ramaprasad Chanda, *Archaeology and Vaishnava Tradition*, p. 173.

[3] See below, p. 166 f., for a discussion of the oldest known archaeological evidence for the cult of Vishṇu-Kṛishṇa.

[4] So e.g. Ruben, *Eisenschmiede*, p. 3 f.: "Heute aber sehen wir dass Indra, der grösste Gott der Ārya des Punjab bis etwa 1000 v. Chr., bereits um 600 v. Chr. im Gangestal ein kleiner Regengott geworden war." We may also quote an extended passage from Eliot, *Hinduism and Buddhism* II, p. 137 f.: "*The Pali Piṭakas* frequently introduce popular deities, but *give no prominence to Vishṇu and Śiva.* They are apparently mentioned under the names of Veṇhu and Isâna, but are not differentiated from a host of spirits now forgotten. The Piṭakas have no prejudices in the matter of deities and *their object is to represent the most powerful of them as admitting their inferiority to Buddha. If Śiva and Vishṇu are not put forward in the same way as Brahmā and Indra, the inference seems clear: it had not occurred to anyone that they were particularly important.*—The suttas of the Dīgha Nikāya in which these lists of deities occur were perhaps composed before 300 B.C. About that date Megasthenes, the Greek envoy at Pāṭaliputra, describes two Indian deities under the names of *Dionysos and Heracles.* They *are generally identified with Kṛishṇa and Śiva. It might be difficult to deduce this identity from an analysis of each description* and different authorities have identified both Śiva and Kṛishṇa with Dionysos, but the fact remains that a somewhat superficial foreign observer was impressed with the idea that the Hindus worshipped two great gods. He would hardly have derived this idea from the Vedic pantheon, and it is not clear to what gods he can refer if not to Śiva and Vishṇu." Note that Eliot stresses the important position occupied by Brahmā and Indra (not Śiva and Vishṇu) in Buddhist literature. But in the Greek ambassador's description of India it is Śiva and

the view of what we might term Indra's persistent greatness. But in Lassen's day it was understood that Indra had been crowded out by Brahmā, Vishṇu and Śiva, some centuries earlier, at the time of Megasthenes. Since the *oldest* discoveries date from the time of Aśoka, some fifty years after the time of Megasthenes, and since Indra is pictured either alone or together with the Buddha on no less than four occasions in Vogel's collection,[1] whilst Kṛishṇa does not occur on a single occasion—at least in that particular collection, it seems as though the archaeological material confirms Indra as the dominant deity in Megasthenes' day, and that Indra was the god mentioned by Megasthenes under the name of Heracles. We know that he was a great god before the time of Megasthenes, and he still seems after Aśoka's day, to be prominent.[2] What, then, could be more natural than to suppose that ca. 300 B.C. he was also an important god, who might be expected to be mentioned in a description of the religious life of India? Naturally enough, these are considerations which would have seemed to Lassen to be irreconcileable with the knowledge then possessed of ancient India.

These considerations may perhaps appear uncertain. The mere fact that Indra is represented in Buddhist art need not mean that his position outside Buddhism at this late date was still assured. Such evidence would only mean that he had a prominent position in the Buddha's day, and having once been brought into the Buddhist context, he kept his position, despite

Kṛishṇa who are assumed to dominate, despite the fact that the descriptions he gives do not fit. Here is a sharp contradiction between Megasthenes and the Buddhist texts—which Eliot seems to have felt. He was in fact on the verge of the truth, recognizing that Megasthenes' descriptions of Heracles and Dionysos do not point to either Śiva or Kṛishṇa, but was unable to take the final step toward a more correct identification.

[1] Vogel, *La sculpture de Mathurā*, pl. 51 B and 53 B *et al.*

[2] We may quote the following as evidence of the importance of Indra in Indian religion even after the time of Megasthenes: "In spite of Kṛishṇa's protest against the worship of Indra, it was still existing in the 7th to the 10th centuries of the Christian era. The Śilappadigāram has a chapter describing how the annual festival of Indra was celebrated in Kāvirippūm-paṭṭinam, the metropolis of the Chōḷas: it states that the festival began on the Paurṇimā of the solar month Vaiśākha and was continued for twenty-eight days. The date of this work has been determined to be the middle of the eighth century A.D. ... The Vedic deity plays also an important part in the Buddhist and Jaina religious lore." (Rao: *Elements in Hindu Iconography* II: 2, p. 517 f.)

According to Dikshitar, *Studies in Tamil Literature and History*, p. 136, the late Tamil work *Tiruvalluvamālai* also has "references to Indra". "Again, the cult of Indra-worship (sic!) is again common to all sects of Hinduism ..." Thurston, in *Castes and Tribes* I, p. 284, writes that Indra is still invoked in South India in connection with the marriage of Brahmans—not only in verses from the RV and Sūtras, but in more recent formulae and prayers; cf. Diehl, *Instrument and Purpose*, p. 149 f.: "Finally the sacrificial altar of Indra is worshipped." See also p. 140.

the fact that he had long lost it among his former worshippers. But there is serious question whether the traditions of the visit of the king of the gods to the Buddha do not necessarily belong to the period *after* the death of the Buddha. Remembering the Buddha's attitude to the world of the Vedic gods, it seems to me improbable that legends exalting the Buddha by representing the main Vedic divinities in humble worship around him could have proceeded from the great teacher's closest circle of disciples. My own personal inclination is to see in these legends the reflection of the situation which arose as a result of Aśoka's conversion to Buddhism and his missionary activity. It is naturally impossible to prove this, but I have no wish to attempt such a proof. The fact that Indra's worship lived on need not be proved with the help of Buddist literature and archaeological discoveries. The material we quoted in note 2 on the previous page is perfectly clear. The treatment accorded to Indra in the two epics points in the same direction. In both he has a position of remarkable importance; this may of course be interpreted to mean no more than that he was an important god at the time when the Mahābhārata and the Rāmāyaṇa were first set out. But these works both played an important part in the religious history of India, and they must also have had a powerful effect on the ideas current within those circles in which they lived on; as a result their hearers kept Indra in his old position, though his powers had waned.

c. The situation is somewhat different when we come to discuss the third view, of Indian literature. It strikes the reader, when studying Lassen's advocacy of Kṛishṇa, how the author repeatedly refers to the Vishṇu Purāṇa. We have already had occasion to point out that we are unable to date the Purāṇas with any degree of certainty.[1] Indian literature was originally extant during centuries of oral tradition, during which time it was altered and edited in many ways, before being written down at a much later date; for this reason it is as well, when considering the question of dates,

---

[1] Dikshitar, in his *Purāṇa Index*, attempts to date the five Purāṇas which form his material. The Vishṇu-Purāṇa he dates, on what appear to be dubious grounds, to 600–300 B.C.; this fits in with Lassen's view. But he mentions that Pargiter is unwilling to place this work earlier than 400 A.D. (*op. cit.*, p. xxv), and this puts us on our guard. We stress that Lassen's own comparisons between Megasthenes and the Purāṇa traditions of the reigns of the kings show important discrepancies: it follows that these were not Megasthenes' source. Lassen's comparison is to be found in *Zeitschrift für die Kunde des Morgenlandes* V, pp. 258 ff.

Rajendra Chandra Hazra, in an article *Purāṇas in the History of Smṛiti*, attempts to show that quotations from the Purāṇas are to be found in the Āpastamba–Dharma–Sūtra and elsewhere, thus demonstrating their antiquity. He seems to have overlooked the possibility of the quotations having taken place in the reverse direction.

not to rely too much on its antiquity. It is much more natural, in these circumstances, to begin at the other end and examine whether a passage to be dated is to be found in the oldest literature, in the Rig Veda and other Vedas, the Brāhmaṇas, etc. Had this method been applied by Lassen to Megasthenes' description of Heracles, his results might have been different. We are well aware that the reputation of the Vedas has been great in all ages, and we therefore have every hope that Megasthenes would have made at least some acquaintance with the world of the Vedas. *Why, then, we might ask, ignore a literature which is known to have been authoritative in Megasthenes' day, and instead turn exclusively to a literature which is not even known with certainty to have existed at that time?*

This concludes our introductory remarks. We shall now proceed, point by point, to consider Megasthenes' Heracles passages as we have set them out on pp. 71 f.

MEGASTHENES' HERACLES PASSAGES IN THE LIGHT OF THE OLDER INDIAN LITERATURE ON INDRA

1. *Historical passages*

a. Heracles was born in India,[1] or possibly migrated into India.[2] In the latter case he would have been the leader of the second of the two invasions to have occurred in Indian history.

Megasthenes' uncertainty as to Heracles' origins fits in precisely with what we know of Indra.

I. The following verse from the Rig Veda refers to Indra's migration into India:

yá ánayat parāvátaḥ súnītī turváśaṃ yádum
índraḥ sá no yúvā sákhā

He who from afar brought hither successfully, Turvaśa and Yadu,
He, Indra, is our young friend. (VI.45.1)

This verse is commonly taken to mean that Indra brought back his friends, the kings Turvaśa and Yadu, from a successful campaign.[3] But there is nothing in the text which justifies such an interpretation. Had that been its meaning, the text would have contained the words *punar* and *astam*: "back" and "home". Since these are missing, the most natural translation

---

[1] Frg. B 1 and 9. Prefatory remark. In the following pages the reader may get the impression that on every point I have tried at any cost to prove Megasthenes' reliability. On the other hand if may seem as though I presuppose his reliability. This impression rises because my Swedish manuscript has been translated into English, and the translation has not always followed my intentions. Therefore I am anxious to stress the fact that I have tried to avoid every form of prejudice. Previous scholars have held that Megasthenes must be wrong in his treatment of Indian religion. I have not regarded him as either right or wrong. I have only investigated whether there exist any beliefs or facts in *Indian* tradition and texts, corresponding to his observations. In some cases there are, in others there are not, at least not exactly similar. My task has been merely to investigate and compare, nothing else.

[2] Frg. B 1.

[3] See Griffith's translation of the Sāma Veda, SV I.21.4.3, with commentary.

is that which we have given; we have followed the interpretation given by Raychaudhuri, in *Studies in Indian Antiquities*, p. 47, that it is Indra who has conducted the two peoples from their former home to their new home in safety.[1]

The same idea seems to be behind VII.33.3:

evén nú kaṁ síndhum ebhis tatāra
evén nú kam bhedám ebhir jaghāna

Thus indeed he crossed with them now the Indus,
Thus indeed he fought with them now the Bheda.

The crossing of the Indus is not defined. Was it just a chance crossing: one among many? Or was it a decisive crossing, undertaken in the course of a migration, when Indra brought his people into India against the opposition of enemy tribes? The text itself does not help us on this point. Unlike VI.45.1, there is no alternative formulation which might have been expected, had the former meaning been intended. But what is important is that it is undeniable that its meaning can very well be that expressed in Megasthenes' description of Heracles, without doing violence to the text.

Heracles is described in such a way that he can be considered as the captain of a host. Is there any passage in the Rig Veda which agrees with this aspect of Indra? In VII.20.5 we read:

vṛishā jajāna vṛishaṇaṁ ráṇāya tám u cin nấrī náryaṁ sasūva
prá yáḥ senānír ádha nṛíbhyo ásti ináḥ sátvā gavéshaṇaḥ sá dhṛishṇúḥ

The bull has begotten a bull to the fight; he, the man, is born of woman.
He *who as a general leads the men* is a mighty warrior, *desirous of combat*, courageous.

This verse refers to Indra; he is said expressly to be *senānī́*, "leader of the host". The Rig Veda thus bears witness that the Indians of Megasthenes' day could have understood Indra to be the leader of a host, who crossed the Indus at the head of the Yadu and Turvaśa (here understood as tribes), crushed all opposition and led them to their new homes.

I understand Yadu and Turvaśa to mean tribes, but mentioned the idea that they may have been ancient kings. On this point we may quote Law, *Tribes in Ancient India*, where we read, under the heading of *The Śūrasenas*: "Śūrasenas claimed descent from Yadu, a hero whose people are repeatedly

---

[1] "Indian tradition preserves distinct memories of an earlier home of the Aryans. Thus in the Rig Veda I 30.9, a worshipper invokes from his 'ancient dwelling place' the god Indra whom his father formerly invoked. We are also told that Yadu and Turvaśa were brought by Indra from a distant land ..." (*Op. cit., ibid.*)

referred to in the Rig Veda; and it is probable that the Śūrasenas were included among the Rigvedic Yadus."[1] Every map of Ancient India agrees with this: Yadu and Turvaśa (or Turvasu) are placed in the same area as the Śūrasenas: the district around Yamunā and Mathurā. This is of the greatest interest for the subject of our investigation. The Rig Veda has many references to the remarkably close connection between Indra and the two peoples (or kings) Yadu and Turvaśa. We shall however return to this topic later.[2]

II. Another tradition which agrees for the most part with what we have said here is to be found in the Mahābhārata. There, Yadu and Turvasu are said to be sons of Yayāti, born in Pratishṭhāna, among the Kāśī (Mbh. I.83.9). It is true that this does not refer to Indra, but to his friends, but it is perfectly evident that it speaks of the same persons, with irreconcileable basic ideas: one having come from the far side of the Indus, from the west; the other having been born in the east of India, where his descendants lived on under the name of the Śūrasenas. We do not need to take up the detailed question of Indra's special relations to the Yadu and Turvasu mentioned in the Mbh. What we have already said is sufficient to show that Megasthenes' statements that Heracles was a migrant, a leader and possibly, that he was born in India, are all perfectly capable of being applied to Indra.

b. Heracles' invasion would have taken place at some time in Antiquity. 15 generations after Dionysos and 138 generations before Sandrakottos (Candragupta).[3] Expressed in years, Dionysos lived 6,042 years before Candragupta.

This is of no help to us in our identification of Heracles, and in this connection we can safely ignore it; it is however of considerable help in the identification of Dionysos. We may point out, though, that we can read between the lines, and deduce from the above passage that Heracles was a king. The same applies to Indra; it is seldom expressly stated that he was a king, but it is always implied.

índraṃ vā́ṇīr ánuttamanyum evá satrā́ rā́jānaṁ dadhire sahadhyai
háryaśvāya barhayā sám āpín

Indra of the invincible wrath has been acclaimed by voices unanimously
As king to victory. I will join friends with him who possesses bay horses.
(VII.31.12)

rā́jābhavo jágataś carṣhaṇīnā́ṁ sākáṁ sū́ryam janáyan dyā́m ushā́sam

[1] *Op. cit.*, p. 39

[2] Pp. 144 ff.

[3] Frg. B 9.

Thou didst become king of the world and the peoples,
when thou didst beget the sun, the heaven and the dawn. (VI.30.5)

índro yātó avasitasya rā́ja śámasya ca śr̥iñgíṇo vájrabāhuḥ
séd u rā́jā kshayati carshaṇīnā́m arā́n ná nemíḥ pári tā́ babhūva

Indra, bearer of the club, is now king of those who travel and settle, of tame and horned animal.
He is the king of the farmers; as the felloe compasses the wheel, so compasses he the people. (1.32.15)

We encounter the same conception of Indra as the king in the Atharva Veda:

1. *índro jayāti na párā jayātā adhirājo rā́jasu rājayātai*
2. *carkr̥itya īḍyo vándyaśca upasádyo namásyo bhaveha*
3. *tvám indra adhirājáḥ śravasyus tvám bhūrabhíbhūtirjánānām*
4. *tvám daivīrvíśa imā vi rā́jā ā́yushmatkshatramajáraṁ te astu*
5. *prā́cyā diśastvám-indrāsi rājotódīcyā diśó vr̥itrahaṁ śatrúho'ś i*
6. *yatra yánti srotyāstajjitáṁ te dakshiṇató vr̥ishabhá eshi hávyaḥ*

1. May Indra conquer, may he never be conquered, may he rule as king over all kings.
2. Receive our praise, receive our honour and worship, receive our reverence and homage!
3. Thou, Indra, jealous ruler, thou art over all the lords of the peoples.
4. Be king over the clans of the gods, long live thy power, may it never grow old!
5. Thou art king in the east, O Indra; thou doest also smite thine enemies in the north, Vr̥itrahan.
6. Where the currents flow, there is thy victory; thou goest in the south, a bull, worthy of praise. (VI.98)

It is often said that Indra is king over the gods. In these quotations it is evident that Indra was also king over men, and that is a further support of the identification of Heracles and Indra.

c. In addition to many wives[1] he had
d. Many sons,[2] but
e. Only one daughter.[3]

At first sight, Indra's family relations seem to place difficulties in our way. It is commonly accepted that he had only one wife, Śacī, but unlike Śiva, he was anything but faithful. Is it possible that Megasthenes was in-

[1] Frg. B 1, 9.
[2] Frg. B 1, 9.
[3] Frg. B 1, 9, 10, 11, 12.

dulging in a little euphemism? The resemblance between Indra's and Zeus' attitude to women is striking.[1] But I should like to draw attention to a hymn in the Rig Veda, which bears the heading "A woman's hymn of triumph", and which according to Anukramaṇī has Indra's wife Śacī as *ṛishi* (or speaker) and divinity. Śacī says:

1. *úd asaú sū́ryo agād úd ayám māmakó bhágaḥ*
ahám tád vidvalā́ pátim abhy àsākshi vishāsahíḥ
2. *ahám ketúr ahám mūrdhā́ ahám ugrā́ vivā́canī*
máméd ánu krátum pátiḥ sehānā́yā upā́caret
3. *máma putrā́ḥ śatruháṇó átho me duhitā́ virā́ṭ*
utā́hám asmi saṁjayā́ pátyau me ślóka uttamáḥ
4. *yénéndro havíshā kṛitvy ábhavad dyumny úttamáḥ*
idám tád akri devā asapatnā́ kílābhuvam
5. *asapatnā́ sapatnaghnī́ jáyanty abhibhū́varī*
ā́vṛiksham anyā́sām várco rā́dho ástheyasām iva
6. *sám ajaisham imā́ ahám sapátnīr abhibhū́varī*
yáthāhám asyá vīrásya virā́jāni jánasya ca

1. Yonder the sun has risen, here has risen my happiness.
In my wisdom I have compelled, won over my husband.
2. I am the banner, the head, the strong one, whose words are obeyed.
I command, irresistible, and my husband obeys.
3. My sons kill their enemies, and my daughter is a ruler,
And I am victorious, revered by my husband.
4. The sacrifice which made Indra the highest one, the shining one,
Have I now performed, O gods, and all my rivals are gone.
5. Without a rival, superior and victorious, since I crushed them,
I have got their brilliance, the gift of the unsteady.
6. All these my rivals have I beaten down,
That I may rule over this man, and over his people. (X 159)

There are a number of observations which we must make on the subject of this hymn:

1. According to the tradition, supported by Anukramaṇī, it is Śacī who is speaking. This same tradition may have been familiar to Megasthenes.

---

[1] Here we may put the question: "If Indra is meant, why then has not the name Zeus been used instead?" The answer contains two points: First we point out that this identification between Indra and Heracles was made not by Megasthenes but by Alexander the Great and his company, for whom Heracles was more important than Zeus; Alexander was in point of fact searching for the traces of Heracles. Cf. above p. 30 ff. Secondly, as will be seen below, p. 102, there is an interesting correspondence between Zeus-Dyaus and Heracles–Indra.

2. Śacī confesses that she has rivals. One is led to think of a situation in which these rivals are in fact Indra's harem, otherwise never mentioned. That the hymn is attributed to Śacī seems to indicate that there existed a tradition according to which Indra kept a harem.

3. Śacī talks about her sons (plural), which is not particularly remarkable.

4. But at the same time she speaks of her daughter (singular): this is all the more remarkable, in that it is precisely the same situation as we encounter in Megasthenes.

It may be objected, with some justification, that this hymn refers only to Śacī as the mother of many (?) sons and one daughter, but says nothing about Indra being the father of only one daughter, even though the passage about the many wives and many sons certainly appears to be substantiated here.

But if we turn to the Mahābhārata, we find that Holtzmann, in his excellent article *Indra nach den Vorstellungen des Mahābhārata*, points out that a daughter of Indra is named in the comparisons in IV.2368.[1]

Thurston, in his *Castes and Tribes of Southern India*,[2] states that Indra's daughter was given to a certain Murdaka Pālakulu, the patriarch of one of the castes of South India, by whom she had 54 sons. This suggests a point which we shall take up later: Heracles' daughter in the south.

We are now in a position to state, by way of summary, that as far as Indra's family is concerned, we have no clear proof of identification on this

[1] Misprint. What is meant? Indra's daughter is a concept which immediately suggests Strindberg's "*A Dream-play*" (*Ett drömspel*). Literary critics tend to regard this figure as a product of the writer's imagination (Martin Lamm, *Strindbergs dramer*, part II, p. 325); this may not be quite correct. In a letter from Strindberg, quoted by Taub in *Strindberg als Traumdichter*, p. 119, the playwright says that he has been reading widely in Buddhist literature, and that from this source he had taken the motif of his dream-play, evidently the character "Indra's daughter". Strindberg may well have found the idea in Buddhism. I do not know whether she plays any particular role in that religion or in its literature, and my investigations on the subject have not as yet brought any conclusive result. But Indra's daughter may well lie hidden in literature, together with a number of other characteristics of Indra, which are mentioned only in passing. *The History and Culture of the Indian People* II, p. 470, mentions that in Buddhist literature Śrī is called the daughter of Śakra, together with Āśā, Śraddhā and Hrī. Gonda also stresses, in *Aspects of Early Vishnuism*, pp. 223–225, the remarkable relationship between Indra and Śrī, which almost seems to suggest that they were married: born on the earth as Draupadī, she was to be the wife of the five Indra-Pāṇḍavas. The two are however never said to be husband and wife.

[2] *Op. cit.*, VII, p. 364, s.v. *Vellāla*.

point, but that we have found evidence of traditions about Indra which are perhaps not dominant, but which seem to be congruent with Megasthenes' description of Heracles.

f. He set his children on the thrones of India.[1]

g. His daughter's kingdom lay in the south.[2]

h. It was called Pandaiē, like his daughter.[3]

i. In order to ensure the succession from Pandaiē, Heracles committed incest with his daughter when she was only seven years old.[3]

The tradition that Heracles established his sons and his daughter as rulers leads naturally to the well-known description of Indra as "highest Lord over the kings of the earth" (Rapson, *Ancient India*, p. 72). We have already discussed Indra as king;[4] now we have the further description of Heracles as the one who establishes the kings. There is a hymn in the Rig Veda, bearing the heading "Coronation of Kings", which reads:

3. *imám índro adīdharad dhruvám̐ dhruvéṇa havíshā*

Indra has established him firmly by a firm sacrifice;

6. *átho ta índraḥ kévalīr víśo balihṛ́tas karat*

And now Indra shall make all the clans pay thee tribute.

(X. 173)

In this way, Indra's absolute power over the kings is further emphasized; the king's or the queen's power is derived from Indra. The latter quotation is strikingly like Megasthenes' words about Heracles and Pandaiē: "Heracles laid down that the villages should pay tribute to the queen, each on its own day in the year."[5]

We have already dealt with RV X.159.3, in which Śacī, according to tradition, says: *me duhitā́ virā́ṭ*, "my daughter is a ruler". The word *virāj* in fact means a queen, even though it may have the more indefinite meaning. The Rig Veda tradition thus agrees very well with Megasthenes, without any necessity for distorting the text. No more can be said.

But is there no information in the Rig Veda about this daughter's place of residence? According to Megasthenes she lived in the south. The only hint of the daughter's home in the south which I have been able to find in the RV is most uncertain, and I should like to make this fact perfectly clear

[1] Frg. B 1.

[2] Frg. B 11, 12.

[3] Frg. B 9.

[4] Above, p. 96 f.

[5] Frg. B 12.

But it also involves us in the intricate problem of Heracles' incest, a question which compels us to concern ourselves with some of the most obscure and unpleasant of all the texts in the RV.

5. *práthishṭa yásya vīrákarmam ishṇád*
ánushṭhitam núnáryo ápauhat
púnas tád á vṛihati yát kanáyā
duhitúr á ánubhṛitam anarvá
6. *madhyá yát kártvam ábhavad abhíke*
kámaṁ kṛiṇvāṇé pitári yuvatyám
manānág réto jahatur viyántā
sánau níshiktaṁ sukṛitásya yónau
7. *pitá yát svám duhitáram adhishkán*
kshmayá rétaḥ saṁjagmānó ní shiñcat
svādhyo'janayan bráhma devá
vástosh pátiṁ vratapáṁ hír atakshan
8. *sá īṁ vṛíshā ná phénam asyad ājaú*
smád á párā aid ápa dabhrácetāḥ
sárat padá ná dákshiṇā parāvṛíñ
ná tá nú me pṛiśanyò jagṛibhre
9. *makshú ná váhniḥ prajáyā upabdír*
agníṁ ná nagná úpasīdad údhaḥ
sánitedhmáṁ sánitotá vájaṁ
sá dhartá jajñe sáhasā yavīyút
10. *Makshú kanáyāḥ sakhyáṁ návagvā*
ṛitáṁ vádanta ṛitáyuktim agman
dvibárhaso yá úpa gopám águr
adakshiṇáso ácyutā dudukshan

5. He whose swollen limb had poured out seed withdrew, sated. From his young daughter the irresistible one drew out that which he had pressed into her.
6. In the full course of their coming together, as the father lusted himself on the maiden, when they separated from their deed, a drop of seed fell to the ground.
7. As the father lay and joined with his daughter, he poured seed on the ground. The friendly gods created *brahma*; from it they made the upholder of the law Vastoshpati.
8. He foamed like a bull in battle, and rocked back and forth like a madman. She fled to the south like an outlaw. "She has not been captivated by my tenderness."
9. Suddenly, like a beast of burden, came the cry of the offspring, which sought the breast like a naked seeks the fire. He was born as one who seeks fuel and reward, he who sustains and battles powerfully.

10. Suddenly, came Navagva seeking the maid's friendship, those who speak aright seeking a legal pact. They came to the watcher over the great rock and, having no present with them, wished to milk the rocks.

(X. 61.5–10)

There are two elements in this hymn which are reminiscent of Heracles and his daughter: i. the incest story, which is told without any individual being named, and ii. the girl's flight to the south.

On the subject of the act of incest, exegetes of the Rig Veda assume that the parties concerned are Dyaus Pitar, the heavens, and Ushas, the dawn. This need not be taken to mean that it is impossible that Megasthenes is referring to this very incest, but with Indra as the male.[1] For the position taken by Indra in the RV and in the piety and religious speculation of a later age, brings us very close to pure monotheism—despite the many names of the gods and their involved relationships.[2] If a pure monotheistic tendency is to be seen anywhere in the RV, it is just in the figure of Indra that the one God is to be discerned. Of the 1028 hymns in the Rig Veda Indra alone is the subject of 245, and he appears together with other gods in many more. It is therefore understandable that Geldner translates the frequently-recurring phrase *deva eka*, as applied to Indra, by "the one God" It is perhaps better, grammatically speaking, to translate these words by "God alone"—at least on a number of occasions. But if Indra is the most usual name for the emergent single deity in the RV, then we may well suppose that Megasthenes might have assumed Indra to be the one responsible for the incest referred to above, there being no name mentioned.

But this is not the only reason for supposing Indra to have been the male party. In v. 5 the father is said to be *anarvan*, irresistible, impregnable, impervious, unconquerable—an idea which at once suggests Indra. This word occurs on nineteen occasions in the RV, and of these six are clear references to Indra—including v. 13 of this hymn—while two are to Bṛihaspati, and one each to Agni, the Maruts, Pūshan, Savitar and the gods generally; there are five other examples in various contexts.[3] It is thus a much commoner epithet of Indra than of any other god; further, it is used

[1] Note in this connection Bréal's representation of Indra as the god who in India took over the function of Dyaus Pitar, as Heracles in Greece took over the function of Zeus. (*Hercule et Cacus*, pp. 153–155.)

[2] "Another important feature of the Vedic religion is the tendency towards monotheism ..." according to the review of *An Advanced History of India* in *Man in India* XXIX, 1949, p. 212.

[3] *Anarvan*, referring to Indra, is found in the following passages of the RV: IV.17.20, VII.20.3, VIII.92.8, X.65.3 and X.99.3, as well as X.61.13.

once more of Indra in the same hymn. But of Prajāpati and Dyaus Pitar it is never used.

It is clear that Megasthenes believed Indian religion to have been monotheistic. He wrote that the dwellers on the plain were monotheists who worshipped Heracles, while the dwellers in the hills were monotheists who worshipped Dionysos. But we cannot reasonably be expected to limit ourselves to a search for possible monotheism or a tendency in that direction in our oldest source, the Rig Veda. What seems in the RV tó be no more than a tendency has in the Atharva Veda become a fact. We prefer not to commit ourselves on the subject of whether it has already become a fact in RV VIII.1.1. The verse reads:

Má cid anyád ví śaṁsata sákhāyo má rishaṇyata
índram ít stotā vṛíshaṇaṃ sácā suté múhur ukthá ca śaṃsata

In Griffith's translation of the Sāma Veda this verse (SV II.6.1.5.1) is given a content not very far removed from the commandment "Thou shalt have none other gods but me":

"Glorify naught besides, O friends;
So shall no sorrow trouble you.
Praise only mighty Indra when
The juice is shed, and say your lauds repeatedly."

It seems to me that Geldner's version is rather weaker:

"Traget nur nichts anderes vor; ihr Freunde, versehet euch nicht. Preiset nur Indra, den Bullen, beim Soma, und traget immer wieder Loblieder vor."

This impression may have to do with the fact that Griffith's translation, unlike Geldner's, is in verse. But however the verse in question is to be interpreted, there is no doubt that the Atharva Veda has come a long way further towards monotheism:

2. *raśmíbhirnábha ābhṛitáṁ mahendrá etyávṛitaḥ*
4. *só 'ryamā sá váruṇaḥ sá rudráḥ sá mahádeváḥ*
5. *só agníḥ sá u sū́ryaḥ sá u evá mahā́yamáḥ*
12. *támidaṁ nígataṁ sáhaḥ sá eshá éka ékavṛídéka evá*
13. *eté asmíndevá ekavṛíto bhavanti*
15. *yá etáṁ devámekavṛítaṁ véda*
20. *támidaṁ nígataṁ sáhaḥ sá eshá éka ékavṛídéka evá*
21. *sárve asmíndevá ekavṛíto bhavanti*

2. Beam-born to the clouds he goes, hidden, being great Indra.
4. He is Aryaman, he Varuṇa; he Rudra, he Mahādeva.
5. He Agni, he is also the sun. He, too, is verily great Yama.

12. This power has entered into him; he is but one, alone, with none other.
13. These gods in him are but one together.
15. He who knows that this god is but one.
20. This power has entered into him; he is but one, alone, with none other.
21. All gods in him are but one together. (Av XIII 4.)

Monotheism could not be expressed more clearly. What is of particular importance to us is, however, that it is Indra who is the name and the god embracing the entire pantheon. In AV XIII.4.46 we read:

bhū́yānindra namurā́dbhūyānindrāsi mṛityúbhyaḥ

Indra is greater than Namura; Thou, Indra, art greater than the deaths.

This particular hymn is actually not an Indra hymn at all, as will be clear from what we have already quoted. Whitney, commenting on this verse in his translation of the Atharva Veda, says: "It is surprising to find Indra brought in here at the end for address, instead of the sun; there is nothing to show that the two remaining paryāyas are not for him. (Note, however, the praise of the sun under the names of Indra and Vishṇu, so prominent in book XVII., below ...)."

It seems therefore to be justifiable to talk of Indra as a collective term for the whole of the pantheon, on those occasions on which a monotheistic tendency puts in an appearance. We have already suggested that such a situation was revealed to Megasthenes, when he remarked on the monotheism of the plain-dwellers and the hill-men respectively. We must of course beware of pressing this hypothesis too far. If the Indian texts bear witness to the existence of a particularly crowded pantheon, we cannot dismiss the company of the gods on the evidence of Megasthenes alone. But when these same Indian texts, in the midst of their evident polytheism, give such prominence to one particular god that we can begin to talk about a monotheistic tendency, then Megasthenes can be said to have got a support—and by a most eloquent witness, too.

Although there is an evident tendency in Indra to absorb all other gods into himself, he nevertheless contrives to maintain his own personality unaltered.[1]

[1] Note Law's statement in *Tribes of Ancient India*, p. 317: "The Buddhist books show further that the Vedic gods, Indra and Prajāpati or Brahmā, were popular deities in the regions where the Buddha preached; while Kauṭilyas Arthaśāstra speaks of many gods popularly worshipped besides the Vedic divinities." It may be that we catch a glimpse of a particular connection between Indra and Prajāpati in Taittirīya Brāhmaṇa II.2.7.2, quoted by Buschardt, *Vṛitra*, p. 61: "Prajāpati created the gods and the asuras. He did not create them together with Indra. The gods therefore said: 'Create Indra for us.' He saw Indra as his own Self. He created him."

We have until now been working on the assumption that Megasthenes' action in attributing incest to Indra was a mistake on his part—an understandable error, but an error nevertheless. The suggestion that Indra could have been associated with that particular form of criminal behaviour has never been seriously put forward—despite the fact that he achieved a certain notoriety on account of his exploits with the opposite sex, and was known as "the sinner among the gods".[1] But I should like at this point to ask a most emphatic question: May it not be the case that Megasthenes, in relating the incest story, has thrown new light on this aspect of Indian mythology—an aspect which was very much alive, but which was consciously suppressed in the texts? We have at least one further example. RV III.31 is an Indra hymn, concerned exclusively with Indra. It begins in these words:

Ś́ásad váhnir duhitúr naptyàṁ gād vidvā́ṅ ṛitásya dī́dhitiṁ saparyár
pitā́ yátra duhitúḥ sékam ṛiñján sáṁ śagmyèna mánasā dadhanvé

The sacrificer came, chastising the daughter's daughter, learned in the law, revering the majesty of the law, to where the father, emptying his seed into his daughter, had hastened with a glad mind.

It is not said, either here or in any of the following verses, who the father is. But we have already said that this is an Indra hymn; its nucleus is the myth of Vala. Is it, then, quite out of the question to suppose that Indra may be the father, who comes when invoked by the sacrificer? The exegetes have never asked this question, since there is no evidence elsewhere of incest by Indra with any daughter of his. But there is another detail here which can, it is true, be found in other passages, but which takes on extra significance in this situation. In v. 15 we read:

máhi kshétram purú śćandráṁ vividvā́n
ā́d ít sákhibhyaś caráthaṁ sám airat
índro nṛíbhir ajanad dī́dyānaḥ sākáṁ sū́ryam ushásaṁ gātúm agním

He found a great and shining land; all that moves he joined with friends. Honoured by heroes Indra begot the Sun, the Dawn, the passage of Time and Fire together. (RV III.31.15)

What strikes us here is the expression "Indra begot ... the Dawn". This theme, that Indra begot Ushas, the Dawn, recurs frequently in the RV; we have encountered it once already, p. 96 f, in RV VI.30.5. But it is common knowledge that the notorious father–daughter incest mentioned in the RV and in later texts is supposed to have taken place between Father

[1] Rodhe, *Deliver us from Evil*, p. 145.

Heaven and his daughter the Dawn, Ushas.[1] In this case Ushas is involved in incest with her father, who is sometimes said to be Dyaus, and sometimes Indra. If we now find that this incest is mentioned at the start of an Indra hymn, whose sole subject is Indra, and which even names Ushas as Indra's daughter, is it stretching the imagination too far to suppose that there was a living tradition which named Indra in this particular context, but that a special effort had been made to keep the names of those involved a secret? The RV mentions the name of the father on only one occasion, in I.71.5:

mahé yát pitrá ím rásaṁ divé kár áva tsarat pṛiśanyàś cikitvā́n
sṛijád ástā dhṛishatā́ didyúm asmai svā́yāṁ devó duhitári tvíshiṁ dhāt

When he had prepared the life-fluid for the great father Heaven, he came, seeing tenderness. Boldly the archer loosed at him his arrow; the god laid his energy in his own daughter.

In this passage "the great father" is expressly mentioned. Another passage which seems indirectly to name the male partner is RV V.42.13:

prá sū́ mahé suśaraṇā́ya medhā́ṁ gíram bhare návyasīṁ jā́yamānām
yá āhanā́ duhitúr vakshá́ṇāsu rūpā́ minānó ákṛiṇod idáṁ naḥ

To the great one, our sure refuge, I bring the new-born wisdom as words of praise: he who, changing shape, has created this our form, lustful in the body of his daughter.

[1] Another incest mentioned in the texts is that of Brahmā and his daughter Sarasvatī, also called Vāc. As to Ushas Brandes has studied her in his *Ushas og Ushashymnerne i Rigveda*, København 1879, where the incest however is never mentioned and no positive relation between Indra and Ushas is stressed. On the contrary the author only notices the fact that Indra crushes the cart of Ushas, RV II 15: 6, X 73: 6; *op. cit.*, p. 66 f.

Now Ushas is often used in plural. Brandes says, p. 20: "There are several passages in the RV, where the plural form is used without there being thought of anything else than the phenomenon of a single morning." Thus, according to Brandes, the plural form has the same meaning as the singular form.

RV VI 12: 4 reads: "*... usráḥ pitéva jārayā́yi*", "... as the father of Ushas became a paramour". And RV X 138: 1: "*Táva tyá indra sakhyéshu váhnaya ṛitám manvānā́ vy àdardirur valám / yátrā daśasyánn usháso ṛiṇánn apáḥ kútsāya mánmann ahyàś ca daṅsáyaḥ*", "The conveyers of oblations in thy friendship, o Indra, truth-minded have opened the cave, where (or: when) thou didst favour to Ushas, madest the waters flow, [renderedst assistance] to Kutsa in his intentions and destroyed the dragons." RV X 10: 9 the word *daśasya* is used in evidently erotical meaning: to do favour to (referring to a woman doing favour to a man). In the last context the word is constructed with dative, whereas in the first passage *usháso* is either genitive singular or accusative plural. In the later language genitive is often used for dative, but perhaps not in RV. I only want to suggest that in RV there are passages which may possibly mean or may be interpreted to mean that Indra was the paramour of Ushas.

No name is mentioned here; but the hint that he changed shape at once suggests Śatapatha-Brāhmaṇa II.2.4, XI.1.6 and XIV (= Bṛihad-Āraṇyaka Upanishad I.4.1 f.), in which the creation of the world is described in terms of a series of reproductive acts, in the course of which Prajāpati-Ātman was constantly changing shape: from man to cow to horse, etc.

Are these obscure hints in the RV, despite their lack of unanimity, sufficient, when combined with the Śatapatha-Brāhmaṇa's three variants, to enable us to draw the conclusion that no fixed tradition existed—or at least had won general recognition? Should this be so, then there is clearly a possibility that certain groups among the castes and tribes may well have considered Indra to have been the male partner in the act of incest so often referred to.

My object in this general examination has been to show that it is not entirely out of the question for the incest tradition to have been connected with Indra. It must nevertheless be stated clearly that this point has certain intrinsic difficulties, and that it cannot be regarded as giving unqualified support to the identification of Heracles with Indra. But if the proposed identification be accepted on other grounds, then our examination may have disposed of that element of doubt at ascribing the incest story to Indra, when it is not mentioned elsewhere in the literature. I am personally inclined to believe that Megasthenes has on this occasion increased our knowledge of the Indo-Aryans' Indra mythology. I consider that the tradition is hinted at in the RV as having to do with Indra. But when the passages in question are as obscure as these have proved to be, it is quite impossible to regard them as conclusive evidence, one way or the other.

2. We have now spent some time on the consideration of the incest tradition, and must now pass on to consider a related happening: that according to RV X.61, the act affected the girl's mind, with the result that she fled to the south. No mention is however made of exactly who it was that "hurried to the lands in the south"—to translate word for word—and there is thus a certain lack of clarity. But I have followed Geldner's translation here, as well as on the matter of who it is that is speaking in the last stanza. The extreme obscurity of this verse makes it impossible to base any definite theory upon it, and if we are to demonstrate any link between Indra's daughter and the south, this can only be with the help of other sayings.

In a comprehensive series of articles in *Man in India* XVII (1937), entitled *Caste, Race and Religion,* Roy quotes, on p. 229, the Tamil document *Manimekhalai*: "The king of this country claimed to be a descendant of Indra." The country referred to was situated to the east of Ceylon—whatever that may mean. The passage nevertheless shows that such traditions existed, even though they may not be very well known. Iyengar, in his *Dravidian India*, writes: "In the same way, it appears that several Purāṇas, the Vāyu, Matsya, Agni, and Brahma, claim an Aryan descent for the southern races by making their progenitors or eponyms Pāṇḍya, Karṇata, Chola, Kerala to be descendants of Dushyanta, the adopted son of Turvasu, a prince of the Lunar line of the Kshatriyas. Turvasu, the Purāṇas say, was appointed by his father to rule over the south-east. Thus the Harivaṁśa relates, 'Yayāti', son of Nahusha, having conquered the earth with its seven continents and oceans, divided it into five portions for his sons. This wise king placed Turvasu over the south-east region."[1]

If we ignore the fact that this gives us a definite tradition as to the origins of the South Indian peoples which conflicts with what Megasthenes has to say about the country being named after Heracles' daughter Pandaiē, we find one important field of agreement: that the northern Purāṇas reckon these peoples as being Aryans; this is entirely in accordance with our thesis, that Heracles is Indra and his worshippers Aryans.

This may perhaps appear surprising. It can be proved that the people of South India are not Aryans. But we must remember two things: (i) that in all probability Megasthenes relied not on South Indian traditions, but on traditions which were vital in North India, and (ii) that times have changed.

1. In the first place, we know that the commonest South Indian traditions are definitely not in agreement with Megasthenes' description of the situation. Such a tradition is quoted by Nilakantha Śastri, in *A History of South India*: "... of the divine line of Pāṇḍyan rulers, the descendants of Śiva and Pārvatī who condescended to become the first king and queen of this celebrated line."[2]

It is quite natural that this tradition should be prominent in South India, since the population worships Śiva. But have the peoples of South India always been Śiva-worshippers? This question leads us to the second point.

2. Times change, and conditions change. That is a truism. Sircar, in *The Dravidian Problem*, considers that Aryans ruled in the Deccan before the time of the Buddha. I do not wish to commit myself on this matter, but it may be confirmed by this passage, from Fürer-Haimendorf, *Problems and Prospects of Indian Anthropology:* "We have evidence that a neolithic culture of no great elaboration persisted in South India until about 300 B.C., when a megalithic people with a fully developed iron age culture suddenly

---

[1] *Op. cit.*, p. 22.

[2] *Op. cit.*, p. 71.

overlaid the earlier civilization. The persistence of a stone age culture until so late a date compels us to revise to some extent our ideas of India's early history. Right up to the time of the Aśokan empire large parts of Peninsular India must have been inhabited by populations comparable to the more primitive of the present aboriginal tribes ..."[1] What both these passages have in common is that those peoples who speak Dravidian languages, and are now devoted worshippers of Śiva, did not live in South India before the time of Megasthenes. A change took place just at that time, as a result of which the present situation arose. We can do little more than guess at the cultural level, race, religion and language of these pre-Dravidians. They were most probably not Aryans. But a non-Aryan people may be under Aryan rule or Aryan cultural influence, at least to some extent. We cannot therefore exclude the possibility that they may have worshipped Indra, though they were non-Aryans.

This hypothesis, of Indra-worship in South India before the time of Megasthenes, may appear to be irresponsible and, what is more, unnecessary. But later in this present study we shall produce a number of proofs of the existence of Indra-worship in South India before the coming of the present religion.[2] We shall therefore leave the question for the time being, pausing first to remark that Pāṇḍya had a queen, and not a king; Iyengar, in *Dravidian India*, points out that the queen did not wear a crown unless she had inherited the kingdom in her own right.[3] A further witness to the fact that the succession followed the female line is the information that the son of Arjuna and Citrāṅgadā, the Pāṇḍya princess, succeeded to the throne of his mother's father, the Pāṇḍya king.[4] But these questions have nothing to do with the identification of Heracles, unless they may be taken as evidence against Kṛishṇa[5]; we shall therefore not spend more time on this matter.

To return to our original problem, Megasthenes stated that the villages were to pay tribute, each on its appropriate day in the year. Again, this does not help in our attempt to identify Heracles, but it does help to elucidate the matter of Megasthenes' reliability. We may compare this passage with certain verses from Manusmṛiti:

yāni rājapradeyāni pratyahaṁ grāmavāsibhiḥ
annapānendhanādīni grāmikastānyavāpnuyāt

---

[1] *Op. cit.*, p. 152.

[2] Below, under heading *Pandaiē*, point 2g, pp. 138 ff.

[3] *Op. cit.*, p. 222.

[4] Iyengar, *History of the Tamils*, p. 461.

[5] See particularly above, p. 84.

That which shall be given per day by the villagers to the king,
Food, drink, fuel and other things, shall be received by the village head man. (Manu VII.118)

The most natural interpretation of *pratyaham*, day by day, is to connect it, as Jha does, with the villagers' action before their elders: everything is to be collected in the village day by day. How it is to be conveyed to the king is another matter, which does not concern us here. But the position of *pratyaham* is such, that either Megasthenes or his informant may well have connected it with the previous word, *rājapradeyāni*, which would indicate that the tribute was to be paid to the king day by day. We mention this only as a curiosity; it has no significance for our purposes. But this little detail spotlights Megasthenes' remarkable conscientiousness. If what he says is wrong, this is due to the obscurity of the text, since the material incorporated into the text can be interpreted in either of two ways. The very unlikelihood of what Megasthenes tells us, coupled with this verse of Manu, suggests that this is one of Megasthenes' sources.

The identical idea—of tax paid successively—is also expressed in these verses, taken from the same source:

yathālpālpamadantyādyaṃ vāryokovatsashaṭpadāḥ
tathālpālpo grahītavyo rāshṭrādrājñābdikaḥ karaḥ

As the leech, the calf, the bee take their food a little at a time
So the king receives his people's annual tribute a little at a time.
(Manu VII.128)

Kārukān śilpinaścaiva śūdrāṅścātmapajīvimaḥ
ekaikaṁ kātayetkarma māsi māsi mahīpatiḥ

The craftsman, worker and labouring śūdra
Shall by the lord be taxed one day's work per month. (Manu VII.138)

I mention this, although it is not strictly part of our subject, because what Megasthenes tells us, judged from our modern presuppositions, seems at first sight to be strange and unlikely.

In the context at present under consideration there is only one point remaining to be taken up—that the kingdom was called Pandaiē, like the girl.

The two related concepts incorporated into this statement have, as far as I can see, no support in any *written* Indian tradition which has survived. There can be little doubt that the country so described must be Pāṇḍya, but there is no woman's name with which this country may be associated. There is however a man's name which occurs in this context, in an interesting way. Thus Iyengar writes, in *Dravidian India:* "A large mound near Chingleput is surrounded by a number of Megalithic graves, and believed to have been inhabited by a bearded race of Pandayar."[1] He goes on to say that the graves are known as Pandu houses, which he considers to indicate their origin in pre-Brahmanic times and in a pre-Brahmanic faith; the very fact of their existence stands in direct conflict with Brahmanic rites and concepts, as M. J. Walhouse has pointed out.[2] Wilson, in his *Historical Sketch of the Kingdom of Pāṇḍya*, says that an adventurer of the Vellalar caste named Pāṇḍya was the first to settle there, and that the country was called after him; this happened in the last *yuga*, and he was followed by 72 princes.[3] Most of the sources quoted mention some 70 kings, but one has the figure 357. Wilson points out that all the kings have Sanskrit names, which seems to indicate that they are later fabrications.[4] However, this conclusion may not be warranted, in the light of what we have said above.[5]

Is there, then, no possible connection between the daughter of Heracles-Indra and the name Pandaiē-Pāṇḍya?

We may approach this problem from two directions: from the name of the country and from the name of the woman. If we take the first alternative, we find that the form Pāṇḍya is mentioned by Pāṇini's commentator Kātyāyana in his *vārttika* on *sūtra* IV.1.171, as being derived from Pāṇḍu, with shortened root. This is absolutely unique in Sanskrit, where as the procedure of shortening the root on the addition of a suffix is quite normal in Tamil. But the form of the suffix, *-ya*, is not Tamil; and Kātyāyana's explanation cannot be accepted.

Proceeding from the Greek form of the name, we notice at once that although Pandaiē resembles Pāṇḍya, it is not identical. We may mention in passing that Pliny uses the name Pandion, which is even more like the Sanskrit form. But it must be obvious that, formally, Pandaiē could perfectly well be a Greek word meaning "all-consuming" or something similar. But a thorough check of all Sanskrit words having the same meaning which occur as women's names gave no practical result. We therefore pass on to take up the problem from the other side.

We came to the conclusion that the name of the girl involved in the incest tradition must have been Ushas, the Dawn. We found that the Rig Veda gave clear evidence of Ushas' having been Indra's daughter. But

---

[1] *Op. cit.*, p. 49.

[2] *Megalithic Monuments of the Coimbatore District* (in *J.R.A.S.* 1875).

[3] *Op. cit.*, p. 201

[4] *Op. cit.*, p. 202.

[5] Above, p. 109.

what has this name to do with Pandaiē? From the Indian point of view, nothing. But is it quite out of the question to assume that Megasthenes knew enough Sanskrit to connect the name Ushas with the $\sqrt{\text{ush}}$, vas, to burn, grow bright? This may seem at first sight to be an anachronism and unreasonable to boot; but it is nevertheless the only solution which suggests itself. It is evident that the name of the country, Pāṇḍya, has remained unaltered; it is equally evident that such is not the case with the name of Heracles' daughter. The whole discussion, as carried on by Lassen and Ruben, was based on the assumption that *her* name was more or less correctly reproduced, phonetically at least. On no occasion did Mégasthenes as much as hint at Heracles' and Dionysos' Indian names. But it has been assumed that his version of Heracles' daughter's name is identical with the Indian form. I know of no goddess or other figure from mythology whose name means "burning" or "all-burning". Ushas is the name which in its basic meaning lies nearest, and it is precisely here that we encounter the incest tradition. It is of course a moot point, whether these considerations are sufficient to prove the point, but I must confess that I am constantly being forced back to this solution as the only reasonable one, even though it seems to depend on such dubious premisses: that Megasthenes noticed the etymological connection between the name Ushas and the verb *oshati*, and that he mingled Sanskrit and Greek words in this confusing way. The latter objection has very little force; there is no more improbability in Megasthenes' procedure than in the known linguistic contortions of 16th and 17th century scholars! Megasthenes' value as a source of information about the religious and secular history of India is hardly likely to decrease just because he is suspected of having perpetrated a linguistic combination which makes a modern philologist shudder. Incidentally, have not similar mistakes been made in other connections? One recalls the supposition that there was some link between the hill Meru (Indian word) and the birth of Dionysos from his father's thigh (μηρός).[1]

Summarizing the points connected with Heracles' sons' kingdoms, his daughter's country and its name, and Heracles' incest with his daughter, we have shown that all four may be connected with Indra. None can be connected with either Kṛishṇa or Śiva.

i. (In order to ensure the succession from Pandaiē, Heracles committed incest with his daughter) when she was only seven years old.[2]

j. The women in Pandaiē therefore become sexually mature at the age of seven.[2]

k. The reason for Heracles' incest was that he felt his end approaching.[2]

[1] See frg. A 1. [2] Frg. B 9.

1. The descendants of Heracles were peaceful kings for many generations after Pandaiē, the first queen of Pandaiē, and after his sons in the other kingdoms; even to the coming of Alexander in some. Elsewhere republics had been set up.[1]

None of these passages give us any help toward solving the problem of who Heracles was. But we shall examine them nevertheless, since they throw light on another interesting aspect of our problem.

1. It is perfectly obvious that the entire tradition of Heracles' incest with his seven-year-old daughter is no more than an aitiological myth. But what is the myth attempting to explain? We can approach the problems of early sexual maturity and child marriage in two ways: by examining the Law of Manu, and by enlisting the help of relatively modern works on this particular subject as it applies to South India.

bālye piturvaśe tishṭhet pāṇigrāhasya yauvane
putrāṇāṃ bhartcri prete na bhajetstrī svatantratām

As a child she is subject to her father, in her youth to her husband,
After the husband's death to her sons; a woman is never independent.
(Manu V.146)

It may appear to be the case here that a woman must have reached puberty before being married. But that is not what is meant, as we see from Manu IX.93:

pitre na dadyācchulkaṁ tu kanyāmṛitumatīṁ haran
sa ca svāmyādatikrāmedṛitūnāṁ pratirodhanāt

The father shall receive no dowry for the girl who is mature, since having disappointed her maturity, he has no right to her.

It is clear from this verse that a father is considered to have wronged his daughter if he fails to marry her off *before* she reaches puberty. He has no further right to his child. If the girl is not married within three years of reaching puberty, she may then take steps to find herself a husband. This is expressly laid down in Manu IX.90:

trīṇi varshāṇyudīksheta kumāryṛitumatī satī
ūrdhvaṁ tu kālādetasmādvindeta sadṛiśaṁ patim

A girl who has reached maturity may wait three years more,
But then, after that time, she may seek a suitable man.

[1] Frg. B 1.

According to Indian ideas, the most suitable age for a girl's marriage is eight years: this is stated, *inter alia* in Medhātithi's *Bhāshya* on IX.4, but may also be deduced from Manu's text, IX.94.

triṁśadvarsho vahetkanyāṁ hṛidyāṁ dvādaśavārshikīm
tryashṭavarsho 'shṭavarshāṁ vā dharme sīdati satvaraḥ

A thirty-year-old man may take a pleasant girl of twelve;
If he is twenty-four, she may be eight or, if duty calls, younger.

It seems from these passages of Manu as though child marriage were an ancient institution in North India. Ruben lays particular emphasis on the information given by Megasthenes as to the early maturing of women, and their youthful marriages, in South India. One wonders whether the reason which led Megasthenes to pay attention to this situation in South India was that the conditions in North India were entirely different.[1] But such a conclusion is not justifiable. Apte writes, unfortunately without quoting his sources: "In the early period, girls were married when they were fit for consummation almost immediately after marriage whereas later on, the rule that the marriage must take place while the girl is a *Nagnikā* came gradually to have a binding force as the rules in the Dharma-sūtras show."[2] So much for North India.

In South India, according to Thurston, was carried out a candle-lighting ceremony (vilakkidu kaliyāṇam) for girls of from seven to nine years; possibly later, but always before marriage. They are given new clothes and fine jewels, which they continue to wear after the wedding (the jewel is called *kodachimani*: a jewel with a hook).[3] This is evidently a puberty ceremony, or something of the kind, since it has to be carried out before marriage. But on the other hand the girls concerned are so young that we cannot help but recall Megasthenes' words about the early sexual maturity of girls in South India.

According to Tolkāppiyam a boy should be ready for marriage at sixteen: a girl at twelve.[4] How are we to interpret this? Tolkāppiyam is an old South Indian work, a sort of copy of Pāṇini's *Ashṭādhyāyī*, but treating the

---

[1] The question of marriage and the position of women has been taken up by R. G. Bhandarkar, in the following articles: *Social History of India; A note on the age of marriage and its consummation according to Hindu religious law;* and *History of Child Marriage.* These are to be found in *Collected Works of Sir R. G. Bhandarkar* II, pp. 443–470, 538–583 and 584–602.

[2] *Social and Religious Life*, p. 36 f.

[3] Transcription following Thurston (*Castes and Tribes*, VII, p. 380).

[4] Iyengar, *Dravidian India*, p. 181.

Dravidian Tamil language; and here it advocates relatively high ages for marriage, suggestive of what we have quoted of Apte on the earlier period. May this possibly indicate that the rule in Tolkāppiyam goes back to the time before Megasthenes? One thing is certain, that the different texts bear witness to different practices. As Risley says: "The later the treatise, the earlier is the age which it prescribes. Manu 30/12 resp. 24/8; later writers 30/10,8, resp. 24/7,6,4."[1]

At this point we may pose a fascinating question—without, however, committing ourselves as to the answer: May Megasthenes be of assistance here in fixing the dates of the Manu-smṛiti and Tolkāppiyam? When Manu talks about a twelve-year-old girl who has still not reached puberty, we appreciate to the full the difference between the North Indian Manu and the South Indian situation to which Megasthenes bears witness. Megasthenes was not, as Ruben supposed, talking about child marriage in this context. Were we free to extend the meaning of his words to cover the social pattern, of which child marriage was a part, then we might draw extensive conclusions indeed. The lack of agreement between Tolkāppiyam and Megasthenes would force us to the conclusion that the Tamil document must be older than Megasthenes. But have we any right to draw such a conclusion?

First it must be proved that Tolkāppiyam does *not* demand that a girl must be married *before* puberty. For if it required a girl to be *nagnikā*, as did the later Sanskrit works, and at the same time that twelve years was a suitable age for marriage, then it would follow that puberty came later; this would also disprove Megasthenes conclusively. But if Megasthenes were correct, as Arrian attempted to prove, it follows that Tolkāppiyam makes no such demand, and that the work agrees in its rules with those laid down in an earlier period of Sanskrit literature. Is it then possible to use Megasthenes as proof that Tolkāppiyam is linked in time with the older Sanskrit literature?

We may place this question against the background fact that child marriage was accepted, even much later, in both North and South India. *Indian Antiquities* for 1874 (p. 32) contains a description of a strange *śūdra* custom. The father of a young boy marries his son to a sexually mature girl, who bears the father a number of children, who in their turn call the boy 'father'. This gave rise to a peculiar situation in which a boy who has just reached puberty and is to marry, already has a marriageable daughter! This custom

---

[1] *The People of India*, p. 189.

is confined to one caste; Megasthenes' explanation of the exceptionally early puberty of girls in Pāṇḍya is supposed to apply to the whole of the people. But I have found no proof of Megasthenes' statement: only references to child marriage, which he never mentions—assuming that Ruben was wrong in seeing references to child marriage in what Megasthenes says about Pandaiē. Has Megasthenes misunderstood the situation, supposing that girls married at the age of seven really were sexually mature? We must leave the matter here, with a number of questions unanswered.

2. Heracles felt his end approaching. A number of considerations are suggested by this statement. We wonder in the first place whether this is really what the Indians believed, or whether it is Megasthenes' own idea. We recall that Megasthenes was a contemporary of Euhemeros, whose views on the gods achieved considerable currency. He propagated the view that the gods were no more than ordinary men whose unusual achievements won them worship and a place in the pantheon. We might mention in passing that Megasthenes depicts Dionysos, as well as Heracles, as an ordinary mortal. For this reason we cannot quote Heracles' death as an argument for his identity with Kṛishṇa, though the latter certainly died, god or no god. It is clear that Heracles' approaching end fits in better with Kṛishṇa than with any other god in India. But we must go on to draw further consequences. If this *Heracles* passage contributes to the identification of Heracles with Kṛishṇa, the same passage, applied to *Dionysos*, must compel the conclusion that Dionysos and Śiva cannot possibly be identical. Where else in Indian mythology do we hear about a dying god?

The literature contains a number of clear references to dying gods—but perhaps not exactly in the direction we might have expected.

First, the Yajur Veda. TS II.3.2.1 tells us that the gods were afraid of death, but received immortality from Prajāpati in return for their sacrifice. TS VIII.4.2.1 goes on to say "As men are, so were the gods from the beginning. They desired: 'Let us abolish the accident, the evil of death, and reach the congregation of the gods'." The Greek author evidently had no need to euhemerize the Indian pantheon. The passage referring to Heracles' approaching death fits in perfectly well with the Indian way of thought—and not only about Kṛishṇa, but about other gods as well. We find evidence of the same view in the Mbh; in the words of Holtzmann (*Indra nach den Vorstellungen des Mbh*): "The most important characteristic of the gods is their immortality. But the gods have not always been immortal ... Another, more common, view sees immortality, which is neither original nor absolute, as connected with their use of *amṛita*, the gods' food of life. But *amṛita* was not always there, and so there was a time when the gods were mortal ..."[1] Holtzmann goes on to mention a fact of no little importance: "Later theology did not consider Indra to be eternal; there had already been many Indras, and even the present Indra, the king of the gods, will disappear in time. That Indra is subject to the ravages of time, that he arises and is destroyed, is expressly stated in XIII.55."[2]

Thus the possibility of Indra's death is not merely deduced from the general postulate of the mortality of all the gods: it is laid down expressly in the literature—a fact which has not always been noticed. Our conclusion on this point must therefore be that instead of the expected contradiction, what we find is a confirmation of the identity of Megasthenes' Heracles and the Indra of Indian tradition.

But Megasthenes has one piece of information which is not easily verified. He says that most men reached the age of forty. Reading between the lines, this would imply that Heracles was some forty years old when he sensed the approach of death. There is an enormous discrepancy here between Heracles and the Kṛishṇa of the epic. Kṛishṇa was 125 years old when he died—or at least 105.[3] We have no corresponding figures for Indra; all that we know is that he is often addressed and referred to as "the young".[4]

The Manu-smṛiti shows us how expectation of life has changed through the ages.

arogāḥ sarvasiddhārtāścaturvarshaśatāyushaḥ
kṛite tretādishu hyeshāṁ vayo hrasati pādaśaḥ

Healthy, reaching every goal, they lived four hundred years
in *kṛita*; in the following, life became shorter by centuries. (Manu I.83)

Since the figure "four hundred" is quoted as applying to *kṛita*, may not this lie behind Megasthenes' "forty years"? It is evident that Megasthenes was speaking of days long gone by, when man's expectation of life was no more than forty years. Manu is also referring to the distant past. But his expression "caturvarshaśatāyushaḥ", meaning "with life which lasts for four centuries", might conceivably have been misunderstood as "caturvarshadaśāyushaḥ", meaning "with life which lasts for four decades". This Manu passage may possibly account for what Megasthenes has to say on the subject of Heracles' age. But we need not go so far. The Sanskrit words for "forty" and "four hundred" are so similar that it would be easy to

[1] *Op. cit.*, p. 300 f.

[2] *Ibid.*

[3] Cf. e.g. Ruben, *Kṛishṇa*, p. 245.

[4] Cf. e.g. RV VI.45.1, quoted above, p. 94. In the Mbh he is always 25 years old, according to Gonda, *Die Religionen Indiens*, p. 228.

mis-read them: "catvārimśat" for "catvāri śatāni". But the long composite form "caturvarshaśatāyushaḥ" in Manu would be particularly easily misunderstood.

We therefore find that what Megasthenes tells us about the normal life-span of a man is dependent upon an understandable mistake in the reading of *inter alia* a passage from the Law of Manu. But we have not succeeded in coupling it with Indra.

3. Heracles' descendants were kings and queens of India in the matriarchal Pāṇḍya.

We have already touched upon this question, on pp. 100 and 108 ff, but now, when we come once more to consider Indra's relation to the kingship, it may be well to mention the view which we find in the Mbh. Holtzmann describes it in the following words: "Mention is also made of a special Indra festival, dedicated to the memory of how Indra gave a staff of bamboo to King Uparicara or Vasu, as a token of kingship; in addition, it is said that Uparicara and his descendants always celebrated the anniversary of this gift; the festival, called Indramaha, still takes place annually, as Uparicara had established it at the command of Indra after the capture of Cedi. It was a joyful festival, and was meant as an expression of the idea that the royal dignity is derived from Indra."[1]

So far, so good. According to certain Mbh. passages the king owes his dignity to Indra. But this is not the same thing as a royal dynasty. There is a tendency among modern scholars to pay undue attention to the royal genealogies of the Purāṇas. An accessible version of these is to be found in the first volume of *The History and Culture of the Indian People* (*The Vedic Age*), pp. 318–319, which has all the relevant material in appendices. Appendix I has the name of Manu Vaivasvata at the head of the list of kings; under him are a number of sons as parallel heads of kingdoms, each with only one name under him—the name of a people, There is only one exception to this latter rule: his daughter Iḷā, whose son was the famous Purūravas, on whom the whole of the following genealogy is based. We may draw attention to Manu's notorious incest with his daughter after the "flood". According to ŚB I.8.1.10, the daughter was produced from clarified butter, sour milk, whey and curds. It may be that it was this incest which Megasthenes described, since Iḷā certainly became mother of a royal line and Manu was considered to be the *Urvater* of the royal house. This applies to the "sun dynasty"; Atri was the originator of the "moon dynasty".

---

[1] Cf. below, p. 135.

But Manu was not a god, and was never worshipped as was Megasthenes' Heracles, the only one worshipped on the plain. And it was not Purūravas, the coming founder of a royal dynasty, who resulted from Manu's incest with his daughter. On the contrary, there are two versions of the story, in which Purūravas was born of either Budha or Iḷa (the latter also functioning as father). Otherwise, nothing in the Manu tradition fits in with Megasthenes' Heracles; nor is there any reference to Heracles which suggests Manu, apart from the incest tradition and the origin of the royal dynasty. Manu, like Heracles, had many sons and daughters; but this is of little account compared with what is told of Indra, who was really a known, recognized and worshipped god. As far as I know, Manu and his daughter had no particular connection with South India.

Manu, then, cannot be Heracles. But it is quite feasible that the stories of Heracles' incest and founding of a dynasty have been borrowed from Manu and attributed to Heracles. Irrespective of who Heracles may have been, I have great difficulty in imagining how Manu could have been identified with any conceivable Indian god—whether Indra or any other—who might correspond with Megasthenes' description, except possibly through RV IV.26.1, where Indra says:

ahám mánur abhavaṁ sū́ryaś cāhám kakshī́vāñ ṛishir asmi vípraḥ

I was Manu, and I was the sun also; I am the wise seer Kakshīvān.

But can Indra's identification of himself and Manu in this connection be adequate reason to ascribe to him a myth which is known to have had to do with Manu? We have already quoted (above, p. 107) the tradition of a king in South India—or wherever his kingdom may have been—who claimed to be descended from Indra. But traditions of this kind are far too sparse and far too obscure to be reckoned as sources for what Megasthenes has to tell us. My own conviction is that on the subject of the origins of the royal dynasties, our Greek author has made a mistake—though his ultimate responsibility may well lie with his informant. Or perhaps Megasthenes has nothing to do with it at all? Diodorus is the only author to have mentioned this detail, and as we have said, he never credits Megasthenes with originating what he quotes. But Arrian's version seems to be based on the same idea: that Heracles, through his incest with his seven-year-old daughter, became the father of the Indian royal house. But Arrian is the only one to mention the incest tradition; this, too, has given rise to certain problems, but we have found it possible to connect Indra with the incest story mentioned in the RV. May it not be possible that someone in the long chain of tradition—Indian story-tellers, Megasthenes himself or his reporters—has confused the two notorious occurrences, with the result that Indra, who committed incest with his daughter Ushas, driving her away to the south, has become confused with Manu, who committed the same act with his daughter Iḷā, who in her turn founded the Indian royal dynasty? And this confusion was all the more understandable, since according to Indian theory, Indra was the origin of the royal dignity.

2. *Geographical Passages*

a. *Aornos:* the name of a rock hard by the sources of the Indus, which Heracles found difficulty in capturing. He was repulsed three times.[1]

Before proceeding to discuss this point in more detail, I should like to draw attention to one obscurity. The reason why the rock, Aornos, is mentioned at all is that Alexander the Great is reputed to have captured it in a single attack. But Alexander was never anywhere near the sources of the Indus![2] It is important that we should bear this in mind, since every attempt to identify this particular rock has been based on Alexander's campaigns, which can be traced with a fair degree of accuracy. Aornos was situated by the Indus; this implies that Heracles was involved in a battle near the Indus. Of only one Indian god is this predicated, and that god is Indra. As to the name we state that the word Aornos *per se* might well mean "free from birds".[3] But it may well be an Indian word with Greek termination, too.

---

[1] Frg. B 3 and 4.

[2] On the Greeks' views on the situation of the sources of the Indus, see Lassen, *Indische Altertumskunde* II², p. 50 n. 1, which refers to Darda who according to Ptolemaios VII.1 lived ὑπὸ τὰς τοῦ Ἰνδοῦ (πηγάς). On the other hand the *Indians* mention Meru and Kailāsa, which all maps place in the vicinity of the true sources of the Indus. The question is, whether this corresponds to the views held by the ancient Indians. According to the map in Law's *Historical Geography* Darada lived by the knee of the Indus, at the place where the river, after having flowed in a north-westerly direction from its source, turns sharply to the south-west.

[3] On proposed identifications, see *The History and Culture of the Indian People* II, p. 47 n. 1: "The great controversy over the identification of Aornos, a solitary rock about 7000 feet high washed by the Sindhu, has been set at rest by Sir Aurel Stein. He has proved by local investigation that it corresponded to Pir Sar range (*On Alexander's Track to the Indus*, p. 104). For a detailed account of the fort and its siege and the different theories on its identification, cf. *E.H.I.* 2nd Edition Appendix D, 3rd Edition pp. 56–58."

We may quote the following from Sir Aurel Stein's book (p. 115): "I heard for the first time the name of Mount Ūṇa mentioned. It was believed by all people to be the highest peak on the range that stretches from the pass of Upal to the Indus ... It did

As an example of the kind of linguistic speculation which has been carried on we may mention Spiegel's article *Varena* in ZDMG XXXII (1878), p. 716. The author refers to the four occasions on which the word appears in the Avesta—all suggesting that what is meant is the land where Thraetaona lived, and conquered Azi Dahaka. This country had four corners. Spiegel goes on to point out the often proposed connection between Varuṇa and Ouranós. But then, by comparing all Avestan words ending in -ena with the corresponding Sanskrit words, he takes the step of linking "varena" with the Sanskrit "varṇa", meaning originally "covering". His final step is to take up the word "Aornos", which he refers back to the Sanskrit "āvaraṇa", following Lassen. Last of all he mentions the name of a river, "varṇu", which occurs in Pāṇini IV.2.103, and which he takes to refer to a river and its basin, probably in the Himalaya.

---

not take long for my philological subconsciousness to realize that Ūṇa would be the direct phonetic derivative to be expected, according to strict linguistic evidence, from the Dardic or Sanskrit name that Greek tongues had endeavoured to reproduce by Aornos." P. 152: "There is not the least reason to doubt that Aornos was meant to render a genuine local name and was not a freely invented Greek designation. That the name Ūṇa has a wider local application can safely be inferred from the fact that the appellation Ūṇa-sar, 'head of Ūṇa', and not merely Ūṇa, is used for the highest portion of the massif."

Stephani, *Thesaurus Graecae Linguae*, reckons up the occurrence of this word *Aornos* in Greek and Latin authors. This does not however go beyond Pauly-Wissowa, and gives us no clue as to the identification of Heracles. It is clear, following Stein (supra) that the Greek name must be based on a native word. We therefore have no occasion to examine other occurrences of the name Aornos along Alexander's route. It cannot be denied that the Greeks may have been given certain associations when the word was mentioned, or have had certain definite ideas: i.e. that the hill was so high that no man could reach the top, and that it was the dwelling-place of the gods. This is outside the scope of our investigation. Similarly with the interesting suggestion, that it may have to do with the Iranian *Upairisaena*, "over the falcon"—i.e. the hill that is so high that no falcon can fly over it. Here we have a connection between Greek and Iranian thought, but this idea does not seem to be present in Indian literature. The name Aornos might provide a fruitful field of study from the point of view of Greco-Iranian links.

On the subject of Aornos we read in Pauly-Wissowa, *Realenzyclopädie der classischen Altertumswissenschaft*: "1. Stadt in Bactrien: Sie lag am nördlichen Ausgang der Hindukusch-Pässe und lässt sich nicht genauer bestimmen ... 2. Eine für uneinnehmbar gehaltene Bergfeste am westlichen Ufer des Indus nördlich von der Einmündung des Kophes ... der Name ἄορνος, den Vögeln unerreichbar, giebt volksetymologisch skr. *āvárana*, Schutzwehr wieder."

The idea, that the Greek name reproduces a Sanskrit form, is also expressed in Lübker's *Reallexikon des klassischen Altertums*: "Die Griechen etymologisierten diesen Namen ebenso töricht wie den des Avernersees: wohin kein Vogel fliegt." (Reference to Kaerst, *Geschichte des hellenistischen Zeitalters* I, p. 362.)

After Spiegel had thus shown the close connection between the Avestan word "varena" and Thraetaona and his battle with Azi Dahaka on one hand, and Aornos on the other, it is a little surprising that no one has attempted to find similar Indian words, which may be combined with Indra (Thraetaona's main Indian counterpart) and with Vṛitra (Azi Dahaka). There is in fact such a word, but it has evidently been neglected hitherto. I refer to the word Aurṇavābha, which occurs in the RV as follows:

Dhishvā́ śávaḥ śūra yéna vṛitrám avābhinad dā́num aurṇavābhám
ápāvṛiṇor jyótir ā́ryāya ní savyatáḥ sādi dásyur indra

O hero, take the strength wherewith thou didst crush Vṛitra, Dānu Aurṇavābha.
Thou didst shine freely for the Aryans—on the left lay Dasyu thrown down, Indra.((RV II.11.18)

áhan vṛitrám ṛicīshama aurṇavābhám ahīśúvam himénāvidhyad árbudam

He pushed Vṛitra into the "*ṛicīshama*", Aurṇavābham Ahīśuva; he defeated Arbuda with snow. (RV VIII.32.26)

Ād īṁ śavasi àbravīd aurṇavābhám ahīśúvam té putra santu nishṭúraḥ

Then Śavasī said to him, 'Aurṇavābha, Ahīśuva, they will overthrow thee, my son'. (RV VIII.77.2.)

This is the sum total of the occasions on which Aurṇavābha is mentioned in the RV. We are given no clear picture of the figures concerned. It may well be thought, in the first of these verses, that Vṛitra and Aurṇavābha are synonymous.[1] The latter word is derived grammatically from *Ūrṇavābha*, son of the "woolweaver". Nor is there anything in the other two passages to rule out the possibility of the two being identical. The only thing we can state categorically is that Aurṇavābha and Ahīśuva are different persons, since the verb of which they are the subject is in the plural (, though we should have expected the dual).[2] But we have the distinct impression that even if Vṛitra and Aurṇavābha are not actually identical, they must be closely connected; this is clear from the first quoted verse.

We note that Indra's mother Śavasī warned her son that this Aurṇavābha would conquer him. We also recall that on three occasions Heracles was repulsed by or at the rock Aornos—Heracles, who was of uncommon strength and unaccustomed to the taste of defeat. But one wonders: What

---

[1] This view is shared by Renou and Buschardt: *Vṛitra et Vṛthragna*, p. 164, *Vṛitra*, p. 49.

[2] This grammatical peculiarity is of no importance in this connection.

sort of rock is this, which is able to repulse an assailant?[1] It is perfectly obvious that what we are dealing with here is no ordinary block of stone. But the unusual aspect disappears when compared with what the RV says about Indra's enemy Vr̥itra, on whom we must continue to concentrate, since such a lot is said about him. We have already reviewed what is said about Aurṇavābha, and it seems justifiable to bring in the Vr̥itra references by way of complement, as it can be demonstrated that the two are closely connected, and possibly identical.[2]

The most frequently quoted of all the hymns of the RV begins with these words:

índrasya nú vīryā̀ṇi prá vocam yā́ni cakā́ra prathamā́ni vajrī́
áhann áhim ánv apás tatarda prá vakshánā abhinat párvatānām

I will proclaim the heroic deeds of Indra, the first carried out by the vajra-bearer. He slew the dragon, loosed the waters, and shattered the heart of the mountains. (RV I.32.1)

RV IV.16.8 is worded as follows:

apó yád ádrim puruhūta dárdar avír bhuvat sarámā pūrvyáṁ te
sá no netā́ vā́jam ā́ darshi bhū́riṁ gotrā́ rujánn áṅgirobhir gr̥iṇānáḥ

When thou who is often invoked didst tear up the rock, there Saramā appeared before thee: Thou, our leader, mayest take rich spoils and destroy the byre, called by Angiras!

---

[1] The Aornos discussion has assumed the phenomenon to be a fortress. But is it reasonable to make this assumption of a rock? There is no honour in capturing an inaccessible rock, by whose defenders earlier assailants have been driven back. In the expression ἀποκρουσθῆναι there is activity. It is quite another thing to say: "He was not successful in capturing the rock" than to say: "He was driven back." There seems to be a dichotomy in the Greek description of Aornos: rock and warrior—corresponding remarkably well to Vr̥itra in the Indian texts.

On Vr̥itra's activity, see Benveniste–Renou, *Vr̥itra et Vr̥thragna*, p. 127: "Une seule fois le poète indique que Vr̥itra 'avait provoqué' son adversaire, *ā́ hí juhvé* I 32: 6; une fois aussi qu'il 's'élance' sur Indra, *úpa hī́m ádudrot* II 30: 3; ailleurs c'est Indra qui 'attaque', *abhikrámya* I 80: 5. Ces indications, dont il n'est tiré aucun parti, peuvent être déduites des formules usuelles plutôt qu'elles ne représentent des moments authentiques du drame." We read in a footnote: "En sanskrit postrigvédique, tantôt Indra 'fond sur' V., *abhyā́ dudrāva* ŚB I 6,3: 16; Bh. Pur. VI 10: 15; tantôt V. sur I., Bh. Pur. VI 11: 9; 12: 1."

[2] Both Renou and Buschardt regard the identity between Vr̥itra and Aurṇavābha as self-evident (see above, p. 122 n. 1); Grassmann regards Aurṇavābha as an epithet of Ahīśuva (*Wörterbuch zum RV*, s.v.). We have pointed out (above, p. 122) that the identity of the two is impossible, since RV VIII.77.2 has the names of only these two as the subject of a verb in the plural. Strangely enough, Buschardt seems to have the same view when he calls Aurṇavābha "an extra name which seems to have been transferred from the demon Ahīśuva".

It is not difficult to collect examples of the way in which Vṛitra is described as either a rock or resting upon a rock. Expressed more carefully, Indra's deed is sometimes described as the crushing of a rock, and sometimes as the crushing of Vṛitra. We may compare Benveniste-Renou, *Vṛitra et Vṛthragna*, "Le terme en soi fort banal *ví-yā-* dans (*márutaḥ*) *ví vṛitrám parvaśó yayur ví párvatān* VIII 7: 23 'ils sont passés à travers V., membre à membre, à travers les montagnes' montre excellemment le contact entre Vṛitra personnel et le mythe des montagnes bloquant les eaux, qui est à la base des luttes ṛigvédiques Indra-Vṛitra."[1] ŚB III.1.3.12 says that "when Indra slew Vṛitra, he transformed his eye into the mountain Trikakud". Other passages which may be quoted in this context are RV VII.104.19 (Indra armed with a stone, which he throws from heaven, crushing the rock). VIII.45,30 (split the mountain), VIII.64.5 (Indra broke apart the mountain), 69.14 (Indra split the mountain), 70.11 (the enemy's friend the mountain), X.67.12 (Indra split the head of Arṇava).

But there is another important point. When we read that the rock Aornos was situated so that it might be said: "... A rock, at the foot of which flows the Indus, near its source," we are tempted to wonder whether the RV provides any evidence that the place at which the myth of Vṛitra was played out was near the source of the Indus. As a matter of fact, this is possible, if we may interpret the following verse of the RV as I am inclined to do.

---

[1] In note 1, the same page, we read: "Même contact *ádrim* ... *valám* ... *darayah* 'tu as fait éclater la montagne, Vala' I 62: 4; et *apó yád ádrim* ... *dárdaḥ* 'quand tu fendis avec force les eaux, le rocher' IV 16: 8: raccourci de *apó vṛitráṁ vavrivā́ṁsam* ... *dardaḥ* (cf. vers 7) qui montre l'inutilité, dans ces formules d'un Vṛitra personnel." P. 102, note from the preceding page, is discussed the meaning of the word *Vṛitra*: "Le sens de 'montagne' de quelques lexiques (BR.) doit reposer sur l'équivalence *vṛitrá-*: *girí-* MS IV 5, 1: 62, 15, qui elle-même s'explique aisément dans le cadre de la narration du RV.; de même, le sens de 'pierre' (cité dans pw.) sur des allusions du ŚB. III 4, 3: 13; 9, 4: 2; IV 2, 5: 15." P. 145 we read: "... c'est la résistance manifestée ailleurs par un Vṛitra personnel que vise certainement la formule interrogative de IV 18: 6 *káṁ ápo ádrim paridhíṁ rujanti* "quelle montagne comme obstacle les eaux brisent-elles?" P. 147 mentions "l'équation *girir vai vṛitráḥ*", and a note: "La juxtaposition de la mort de V. et de la brisure des montagnes est attestée I 32: 1; le thème des montagnes fendues intervient I 57: 6 à l'endroit précis où l'on attend celui de V. (analogue IV 17: 3): Hillebrandt, 162, rejette à tort, semble-t-il, l'intention vṛitraique du vers, cf Geldner. Un rapport moins direct entre V. et *girí-* est indiqué ŚB. III 4, 3: 13 = 9, 4: 2 = IV 2, 5: 15." The last mentioned passage reads: "... Soma was indeed Vṛitra his body is the same as the mountains and the rocks", *vṛitro vai soma āsīt tasyaitacharīraṁ yad girayo yadaśmānas* ...

sódañcaṁ síndhum ariṇān mahitvā́ vájreṇána ushásaḥ sám pipesha
ajaváso javínībhir vivṛiścán sómasya tā́ máda índraś cakāra

He made the Indus flow northward by his power; with the vajra he crushed the car of Ushas. He cut down the slow with the swift—Indra did all this intoxicated by soma. (RV II.15.6)

"He made the Indus flow northward by his power"; the Indus of course flows south-west.[1] But if we trace the course of the river back to its source we find that it takes a long curve to the north of the point where Alexander the Great crossed the river. Continuing upstream, we find it flowing north-west. But its highest reaches, by the actual source, flow directly northward! Thus the events described in RV II.15.6 seem to have taken place hard by the source of the Indus.[2] But was this the same as the subject of the Vṛitra myth? There may well be doubts as to whether Indra carried out the same deed on a number of occasions. But this much is certain, that the result of his conquest of Vṛitra is described in RV I.32.2 in these words:

áhann áhim párvate śiśriyāṇáṁ tváshṭāsmai vájraṁ svaryàṁ tataksha
vāśrā iva dhenávaḥ syándamānā áñjaḥ samudrám áva jagmur ā́paḥ

He slew the dragon, encamped there upon the mountain; Tvashṭar made the whining club for him. Like cows who, calling, run to their calves, so the water streamed downward to the sea. (R I.32.2)

Thus the Indra hymn *par excellence,* which deals with Indra's battle with Vṛitra, says that the battle resulted in the waters streaming to the sea, as we read later in the same hymn. In other words, the result is identical with that mentioned in II.15.6. It may well be the same event with which both

---

[1] The objection that this may not refer to the Indus at all falls when we recall that the Indus is the only North Indian river that flows northward, with a couple of a minor tributaries as unimportant exceptions. We cannot neglect the possibility that the verse may only refer to a temporary change of Indus' course.

[2] Cf. Benveniste–Renou, *Vṛitra et Vṛthragna*, p. 148: "La mention des eaux pour séjour de Vṛitra est évidemment celle qui découle le plus directement des conditions générales du mythe. Elle figure sous des aspects assez nombreux, mais qui ne portent aucune réelle innovation: ... *síndhum āśáyānam* II 11: 9." It is possible to regard Vṛitra as "laying siege to the great Indus" here. See Renou, p. 188: "A l'origine du mythe indo-iranien, qui n'est guère représenté ailleurs, et dont le développement doit tenir à l'importance particulière de l'eau dans les régions aryennes, se trouve probablement la notion d'un être fabuleux qui, comme l'hydre de Lerne, gîte auprès d'une source et tue quiconque passe à sa portée. De même Vṛitra a son repaire dans la montagne au voisinage d'une source dont il interdit l'accès. Il était facile d'imaginer qu'il retenait la source captive et empêchait en général les eaux de couler, de sorte que sa mort seule pouvait les libérer."

hymns—and a number of other hymns as well—deal. The only difference is that in II.15.6 we are told where the deed took place—and the description agrees to a remarkable degree with the description of where was situated the rock Aornos.

But where did Megasthenes get his information about the three attacks, and how Heracles was repulsed three times?

As far as I have been able to discover, this theme is entirely missing from the RV. But TS, in its Brāhmaṇa sections, says that Indra's attack on Vṛitra took place in three stages, though not because of the degree of opposition, but because Vṛitra tried to prevent his own defeat by resorting to bribery. Indra lifted his weapon to kill Vṛitra, who cried, 'Do not strike! I will give you what strength I have.' Indra accepted the offer and spared his enemy. This was repeated three times, by which time Vṛitra had exhausted his resources, and Indra was able to win without difficulty. Substantially the same story is told in TS II.4.12 and VI.5.1, but this time, Vṛitra's strength is linked with magic power derived from the sacrifice. When this is related in ŚB V.5.5 the three things gained by Indra are a. Yajush formulae, b. Rig verses and c. Sāma hymn melodies.

Proceeding to the Mbh., we find that Holtzmann, in the work from which we have already quoted a number of times, says that Indra was repulsed several times in the course of his fight with Vṛitra, at least according to some of the versions given in the epic.[1] According to Mbh III.101 Indra, vajra in hand, approached Vṛitra. The latter filled the whole of heaven and earth, and was surrounded by enormous Kālakeyas who were like mighty mountain-tops (parvata) with their lifted weapons. Kāleyas attacked the gods, who fled in terror, at which sight Purandara became deeply depressed. Purandara (i.e. Indra) ran to Nārāyaṇa, where he was given a share in his special strength. When the other gods saw this they took courage and each gave Indra some portion of his special powers; the ṛishis, too, took part, and Indra became stronger than he had ever been. Vṛitra saw what was going on and gave vent to a terrible roar; heaven and earth shook, and Indra trembled with fear. In his terror he threw away his *vajra*, which struck and laid low Vṛitra, as the hill Mandara was laid low by the hand of Vishṇu. But Indra fled in panic and hid in the water.

In Śāntiparvan we have rather a different version, which its translator, Pratāpa Chandra Rāy, considers to be much older. It is to be found in section 281, and has a somewhat unusual introduction in which Vṛitra is said to be pious, devoted to Vishṇu and familiar with the Upanishads and the

---

[1] *Indra nach den Vorstellungen des Mbh*, pp. 305 ff.

Vedānta. Vr̥itra is also called an Asura. Indra was riding along in his chariot, followed by the hosts of heaven, when he caught sight of Vr̥itra encamped in front of him like a mighty mountain. The sight terrified the gods, and Indra became crippled in his lower extremities by terror. Clubs and great rocks were among the weapons used in the ensuing scuffle. When Vr̥itra saw that they were being observed by Rishis, Gandharvas and Apsarasas, he formed a great wall of rock, darkening the sky, which he then threw at Indra. But the gods loosed their arrows and broke up the rocks in flight. Then Vr̥itra took up his second weapon, illusion, with the help of which he perplexed and numbed the chief of the gods. But Indra was brought back to consciousness by Vasishṭha by means of sāma hymns. Helped by yoga, he was then able to overcome the illusion, and to make himself fit for fight once more. But before a victory could be won, Śiva had to send a fever into Vr̥itra's body, so severe that flames spurted from his jaws, his whole body shuddered, he went pale and breathed heavily, gaping and uttering horrible noises. At this psychological moment, Indra threw his vajra at him, which took immediate effect, probably because Vishṇu was in it. But Indra fled and hid himself in a lotus, driven by guilt over the murder of a Brahman.

These two related versions in the Mbh of Indra's battle with Vr̥itra show that the actual course of events is not well defined. But they have so much in common, that Indra is first repulsed, though it is not clear how often: on one occasion he is bewitched, on another threatened by flying rocks. The first version's story of the gods' flight may possibly be combined with the same detail in Śāntiparvan; we should then have two successful counter-attacks from Vr̥itra's side; but if both may be incorporated into the actual course of events, then we have three successful counter-attacks. If we then add Indra's subsequent flight, then he was repulsed three times and more. But we cannot build on these speculations. All we can do is state that this particular myth occurs in a mass of variations in the RV, the Brāhmaṇas and Mbh. There is another version in the Mbh, in the Udyogaparvan (= V), in which the first thing which happens in the battle is that Indra is swallowed up by Vr̥itra; he is saved, though, thanks to the elder gods, who make Vr̥itra yawn, and open his mouth wide enough to allow Indra to get out.[1] As the battle proceeded, Vr̥itra is expressly stated to have taken the upper hand, and Indra to have given way. Vishṇu thereupon joined in and succeeded in persuading Vr̥itra to agree to a cease-fire, and a conditional treaty. The conditions were that he was not to be killed with wet or dry,

[1] Mbh V. 8–9.

with stone or wood, with sword or spear, by day or by night, by Indra himself or by the gods. Some time later, at sunset, Indra happened to see great masses of foam, resembling mountains; he mixed this with his vajra, and threw the mixture at Vr̥itra. Again, since Vishṇu had incorporated himself into the mixture, it had the desired effect. As in the other versions, Indra is overcome by remorse on account of his sins. Here we really have a version in which there are three elements: a. Vr̥itra devours Indra; b. Indra is liberated, the battle continues, but Vr̥itra has the upper hand; c. Indra breaks the treaty and kills Vr̥itra.

We need not summarize all the different elements which occur in all the different Mbh versions. It is perfectly clear that it is a myth which is related of Indra, though with variations, and that it fits in well with that told by Megasthenes of Heracles and the rock Aornos.

But we may summarize the points in which Heracles and Indra coincide, with respect to Aornos and Vr̥itra.

1. Heracles carried out a great deed by the Indus. Indra is the only god in India who is said to have special connections with the River Indus. It is often told, how he crossed the river, e.g. in the company of Yadu and Turvaśa (RV VII.33.3), how he caused the waters of the Indus to flow northward (RV II.15.6), etc. There is some doubt as to whether the word *sindhu* refers to the Indus or to waters in general, but this is a doubt which has assailed the Indians themselves. We can only state as a fact, that the RV text says about Indra something which may very well be taken to mean exactly what Megasthenes says about Heracles. What the text really means is of no interest to us here. What is important is that it *may* coincide with Megasthenes' version, or at least that it may have been understood in this way.

2. Heracles' experience with Aornos took place near the source of the Indus. Indra, too, judging by his feat of making the waters of the Indus flow northward, was hard by the sources of the Indus, the only place at which the waters in question flow in that direction. We must, however, add the *caveat* that the text may possibly mean something entirely different, e.g. that Indra managed to reverse the flow of the waters for a moment, or something similar. But the actual wording of the text seems to suggest that the event took place just where the river has ever since flowed northward, i.e. just by the source, or at least, at the head waters.

3. Heracles made the acquaintance of a remarkable rock, which repulsed him. We may well ask what was the nature of this rock. We are given our answer when we compare Heracles' experience with that of Indra before Vr̥itra. Vr̥itra was also said to be a rock, as we have seen. But this

Vṛitra had in fact repulsed Indra several times. The strange duality which appears in the Greek version is common to Aornos and Vṛitra.

4. Heracles was repulsed three times. This detail, too, can be combined with Vṛitra, particularly if we telescope several of the versions of the narrative. a. Once he was swallowed by Vṛitra; b. once he retreated; c. once he and all the other gods fled to Vishṇu; but we may add d. the terrible counter-attack, in which Vṛitra threw rocks and other objects at the gods, or e. the attack by Vṛitra's people on the gods = c. and f. Vṛitra's successful psychological warfare with the weapon of illusion. The figure three recurs frequently in accounts of the Indra-Vṛitra battle in "older" texts, as we have said.[1]

5. The rock which Heracles attacked, and by which he was thrown back, was called by Megasthenes Aornos. If we have succeeded in demonstrating satisfactorily that Aornos must be identical with Vṛitra, the simplest explanation of the name would seem to be that Aornos is neither a Greek translation (= the hill without birds, i.e. the hill which is so high that no bird can fly over) nor a corrupt form of *āvaraṇa* or any such word; it is purely and simply a form of Aurṇavābha, the RV epithet for Vṛitra. There is no word in Sanskrit which resembles the Greek *aornos* so closely as does Vṛitra's epithet Aurṇavābha. We have no ready-made explanation of why the word has become abbreviated in this way, except perhaps that the Greeks often revised "barbarian" words as they thought fit. Nor can we exclude the possibility that the shortened form was in existence in the Indian version, since we often meet with double forms of proper names; in such cases one is longer and the other a shortened form, containing only the first part of the word: Bhīmasena—Bhīma; Balarāma/Baladevā—Bala; Kuntibhoja—Kunti, etc. However, our texts do not contain the shortened form Aurṇa, which must be, and remain, hypothetical. The most natural explanation seems to me to be that the form Aornos actually sounds Greek and means something; the latter part of the word, on the other hand, would not only be meaningless to a Greek, but begins with a sound of which Greek has no equivalent—"v"—and might therefore be discarded. We remarked above, on p. 120 n. 3, quoting Stein, that there seems to have been a shortened version, which now exists in the form Ūṇa; Aurṇa, as we have said, is derived from Ūrṇa, and is strictly speaking the same word as that quoted by Stein.

Summing up, the name Aornos can with a little ingenuity be combined with Vṛitra. This completes the tally of passages having to do with Heracles' connection with the rock Aornos, all of which may be linked in one way or another with Indra's encounter with Vṛitra.

[1] Above, p. 126.

One final question: Why do we here encounter this name for Indra's enemy which is so seldom used in Indian texts? The answer is implied in what has gone before. The Greeks' contact with the myth of Vṛitra was linked to a definite geographical milieu, which the Indians had pointed out as the field of battle between Indra and Vṛitra, and which they called Aurṇa, or something similar.[1] In the version of the Vṛitra myth which the Greeks heard, they were told that the site lay near the source of the Indus, although we know that this was far from being accurate. One wonders, though, whether the Indians knew that at this point the Indus had already run the greater part of its course? But we cannot indulge in such speculation, however fascinating, in this context.

One has the impression that what Megasthenes says about the rock Aornos fits in remarkably well with the traditions of Indra's combat with Vṛitra, as we have reviewed them here. In other words, the evidence of the rock Aornos is strongly in favour of Heracles' being identical with Indra.

b. *Iōmanēs—Iōbarēs*—i.e. *Yamunā*, which Megasthenes named as a great and navigable river flowing through the land of the Śūrasenas.[2]

The identification of this river with the Yamunā is undoubtedly correct. Since this river figures in the Kṛishṇa tradition, it has contributed to the identification of Heracles with Kṛishṇa. But it is mentioned on three occasions in the RV: V.52.17, VII.18.19 and X.75.5. The first and third of these are of comparatively little interest to us here; the second reads:

ávad índraṁ yamúnā tṛitsavaśca

Indra received help from Yamunā and Tṛitsu. (RV VII.18.19)

There are certain grammatical difficulties in this verse, since Yamunā (sing.) and Tṛitsu (pl.) form the subject of *ávat* (sing.). But we need not go into this problem, since it is at all events clear that Yamunā is placed alongside Indra, as his helper. Kṛishṇa is then not the only one who can be connected with the sacred river.

The Yamunā is also mentioned in the AV IV.9.10, where a particular form of anointing is said to derive its name from the sacred waters. But we cannot draw any extensive conclusions from this; it is sufficient to point out that the Yamunā did not derive its sacredness from Kṛishṇa, nor is it to be found only in that literature dominated by the divine figure of Kṛishṇa. It follows that the name as such cannot be used, explicitly or implicitly,

[1] In the same way, according to Prof. S. Wikander, the inhabitants of Urartu are still able to point to the mountain near which they live as the landing place of Noah's ark.

[2] Frg. B 9.

as an argument for the identification of Heracles with Kṛishṇa. It has no value whatever as an argument for identification, and cannot be used for or against either Kṛishṇa or Indra. We shall therefore pass on to the next point.

c. *Caucasus* and the myth of Prometheus are mentioned in a context which makes it virtually impossible to reckon them among the means of identification of Heracles.[1] The only thing we learn from the occurrence of this name is that the Greeks seemed to regard the Indian Heracles not merely as a counterpart to the Greek god, but as identical with him in every way; thus myths told of the Greek Heracles may be incorporated into a narrative about the Indian. This does not exactly simplify matters; but since nothing is said about the role, active or passive, played by the Indian Heracles in the myth of Prometheus, we shall pass over this complex of problems.

d. *Kleisobora*, in Megasthenes' account (which we have from Arrian) was a large town in the land of the Śūrasenas;[2] it is mentioned in the same breath as the Yamunā, but we are not told whether it is supposed to have been situated on its banks. The town has never been identified. Lassen and Schwanbeck, building on the speculations of v. Bohlen, consider it to be a corruption of Kṛishṇapura,[3] but we have no evidence for the occurrence of such a name in that district. One argument in favour of this interpretation is that we encounter the name Carisobora in Pliny; this in turn convinced Cunningham that behind the Greek and Latin forms there was an Indian Kālikāvarta.[4] But if we compare Pliny's description of the site of Carisobora with Arrian's description of Kleisobora, we begin to have serious doubts as to whether it can be the same town which is meant. We have already met Arrian's expression. Pliny says: "Amnis Iomanes in Gangem per Palibothros decurrit inter oppida Methora et Carisobora"—"The River Yamunā flows down to the Ganges through Palibothra (= Pāṭaliputra) between the towns of Mathurā and Carisobora." Does this mean that these two towns were situated on opposite banks of the river? Or does it mean that Carisobora lay on the other side of the confluence of the Ganges and the Yamunā? This latter alternative makes it impossible that Carisobora and Kleisobora can have been identical. If the former be adopted, then Pliny has given us some assistance in the identification of the town. But there is more than one way of understanding Pliny. That a river flows "between" two towns may mean

[1] Frg. B 3.

[2] Frg. B 9.

[3] *Ind. Alt.* k. I² p. 648 n. 1, Schw., p. 37 f.

[4] *Ancient Geography of India*, p. 375.

that one is situated upstream, the other downstream. And a long distance between the two towns in question would make the expression even more feasible. If this is what is meant, then the phraseology indicates no more than the approximate direction in which the river flows.

We know for certain that one of the towns was Mathurā, and that the Yamunā flowed through the town; our problem, then is to follow the course of the river, and see which notable towns are passed on the way. We do not have very many to choose from. Indraprastha is the only other town on the Yamunā. And using the latter alternative for interpreting Pliny, we find that the Yamunā flows between the two towns Mathurā and Carisobora = Indraprastha. Furthermore, Indraprastha is the only town which bears any resemblance to Megasthenes' description: in the land of the Śūrasenas there are two large towns, Mathurā and Kleisobora = Indraprastha. To be sure, according to Indian ideas the town was situated in the land of the Kurus. But a foreigner giving an account of what he has himself seen may be forgiven if his grasp of Indian ethnic geography is not all that it ought to be. The territories of the two peoples were adjacent, and their limits may have been somewhat fluid. The fact that Indraprastha was the capital of the land of the Kurus does not seem to me to be a valid objection against the identification of Kleisobora with Indraprastha.[1]

It is impossible to decide how the documented forms Kleisobora/Carisobora originated. All manner of hypothesis may be put forward: it is not impossible that the last syllable -so in the first part of the word might be traced back to a Sanskrit genitive -sya; but which is the previous syllable? Has the Indian word an "a" (Cariso-) or is this provided in order to simplify the pronunciation of the Latin version? Or has the Indian word an "r" or "l"? There is so much uncertainty here that it is not worth attempting to solve these linguistic problems. Śakrasyapura = "Indra's town" would *per se* be conceivable.

But the difficulties we experience in explaining the origins of the Greek form do not constitute an argument against the proposed identification, which seems, as we shall soon see, to be very well justified.

---

[1] Shafer, *Ethnography of Ancient India*, seems on map 1 to locate Indraprastha in the area of the Śūrasena; cf. Pargiter in *J.R.A.S.* 1908: 1, p. 332 f. The former case is obviously a mistake, since Mathurā lies outside this area. In the latter, Indraprastha is placed almost exactly mid-way between the names Kuru and Śūrasena. Note that the classical authors never mention Kuru, which recurs frequently in Indian texts, including Buddhist texts. Manu and Mbh usually mention Kuru and Śūrasena together. (Law, *Tribes of Ancient India*, pp. 17–29 and *Historical Geography*, p. 42.) May this perhaps indicate that the classical authors regarded the two related peoples as one?

It is evident that Dvāravatī, Dvārakā, cannot be the town referred to, since this particular town disappeared in the depths of the sea, according to the Mbh. And when it existed, in Kṛishṇa's day, it was nowhere near the land of the Śūrasenas.

We have said that there was no town called Kṛishṇapura in that district. But it seems unreasonable to postulate some town which is not mentioned in the existing literature; Megasthenes cites the town as being large and, presumably, well known. Indraprastha is often mentioned in Indian literature as being situated on the Yamunā, as being ancient and reputable. Anderson, in *The Peoples of India*, supposes it to have been existing, like Mathurā and Kanauj, in Madhyadeśa at the time of the second Aryan invasion.[1] It has survived the ravages of time and is now known as Delhi. Its site has varied a little during the ages, as has its name, according to Law, *Historical Geography of Ancient India*, p. 86. We know the town to have been worthy of mention; we know that it was never mentioned by Megasthenes, Pliny, or anybody else, by any other name; it is, then, highly likely that it is this very town which is here called Kleisobora. A further conclusion which suggests itself is that, just as Indra's name is incorporated into the name Indraprastha, so Kleisobora may be a corrupt form of Heraclespura; this may be so, but it is of course quite impossible to verify. For that reason we shall refrain from reckoning this particular point among those which support our identification of Heracles with Indra.

e. *Mathurā* is the name[2] which formed the foundation of the discredited identification of Heracles and Kṛishṇa, which we discussed at the beginning of our examination.[3] The first occasions on which we meet with the name Mathurā in the literature are, as Law points out,[4] in Pāṇini's sūtra IV.2.82, in the Buddhist tradition, according to which the Buddha visited the town, and the Jain tradition, which says the same of Mahāvīra.

These early passages do not provide us with any detailed information about the town. Law stresses repeatedly that in Megasthenes' day Mathurā was a centre of the Vishṇu cult, Bhāgavata religion and the worship of Kṛishṇa; but he bases his argument on Lassen's circular proof, which we have already had occasion to criticize. Despite his erudition, he has been unable to produce proof that a cult of Kṛishṇa existed in Mathurā before the coming of the Buddhist and Jaina monks, between ca. 150 B.C. and ca. 300 A.D. That means that the early history of the town is shrouded in

---

[1] *Op. cit.*, p. 72.

[2] Frg. B 9.

[3] Above, p. 10 f.

[4] Law, *Tribes*, p. 41, n. 6; *Historical Geography*, p. 110.

mystery. From Hsüan Tsang we learn that there were at his time Buddhist monasteries and Deva temples, but this is of little weight, since Hsüan Tsang lived in the 7th century A.D., by which time Hinduism had begun its victory over Buddhism.[1]

The name Mathurā thus has no contribution to make to the quest for the identity of Heracles, unless we draw the conclusion from the archaeological evidence reviewed in J. Ph. Vogel's *La Sculpture de Mathurā* that while Kṛishṇa is conspicuous by his absence, Indra occurs on no less than five pictures from the Buddhist period. Vogel says in his commentary on Pl. 51: "... It may be that the ancient chief of the Vedic gods, though long dethroned by the great gods of the Hindu Trimūrti, had contrived to preserve something of his old prestige among the agricultural population of Braj."[2] Elsewhere in the same work this is explained in the words: "Apart from the Buddha, the gods reproduced are *Nāgas*, snake gods, who have an intimate connection with the fertility of the earth, and the god who sends the rain no less necessary for agriculture"—i.e. Indra.[3]

If this interpretation of the archaeological material be legitimate, then the name Mathurā is a positive piece of evidence for the identification we are attempting to establish. The occurrence of Indra on these pictures seems to be clear proof that he was by no means dethroned by the Trimūrti. I would even go so far as to suggest that Indra, the greatest of the gods, is here represented as paying homage to the Buddha, precisely in order to emphasize the Buddha's supremacy.[4] This must at least be one explanation of the presence of Indra in this particular situation.

[1] The concept of the temple is unknown in ancient Indian history and literature. P. K. Acharya, in *The Origin of the Hindu Temple*, writes: "The Śulva-sūtras which are the supplementary portions of the Kalpa-sūtras treating of the measurement and construction of the different Vedis or altars, furnish us with some interesting structural details of the Agnis, the large altars built of bricks. *The construction of these altars, which were required for the great Soma sacrifice*, seems to have been based *on sound scientific principles and was probably the beginning of religious architecture or temple-building in India.*" This applies only to the Vedic-Aryan peoples. The situation among the non-Aryans is largely unknown. We do not know just what was implied by the term "a *deva* temple".

[2] *Op. cit.*, p. 59 f.

[3] *Op. cit.*, p. 47.

[4] The greater the adoring, the greater the adored. Cf. Eliot, *Hinduism and Buddhism* II, p. 137 (quoted above in another context, p. 90, n. 4): "*The Pali Piṭakas* frequently introduce popular deities, but *give no prominence to Vishṇu and Śiva* ... The Piṭakas have no prejudices in the matter of deities and *their object is to represent the most powerful of them as admitting their inferiority to the Buddha.* If *Śiva and Vishṇu are not put forward in the same way as Brahmā and Indra*, the inference seems clear: *it had not occurred to anyone that they were particularly important.*"

f. *Palibothra*, i.e. Pāṭaliputra, now Patna, was said in Megasthenes' account to have been founded by Heracles, who surrounded the town with moats and built palaces there.[1] We know from Buddhist and Jain texts where, and by whom, the town was built. In his *Historical Geography*, p. 250, Law tells us that a contemporary of the Buddha, the Magadha prince Ajātaśatru, founded the town,[2] but the same author, in his *Tribes in Ancient India*, quotes another tradition to the effect that the son and heir of Ajātaśatru, Udāyi Bhadda, founded the town in the fourth year of his rule and made it his capital. It appears to have been founded and made capital ca. 500–450 B.C. Megasthenes is at fault here, if he is in fact responsible for the information provided. We read about it in Diodorus Siculus, but he never mentions the name of Megasthenes. In his preface to his edition of Megasthenes, Schwanbeck justified (on p. 57, n. 49) his inclusion of Diodorus by saying that "Diodorus seems to have copied Megasthenes; of that there is no doubt, since we can compare almost every separate part of his description with other Megasthenes fragments". Our conclusion must be that if Megasthenes claimed Heracles to be the founder of Pāṭaliputra he is not quite the reliable authority we claimed him to be in our introduction.

In his account of India, the Chinese traveller Fa Hien (5th century A.D.) described a great Buddhist procession in Pāṭaliputra. It is certain that the town's festivities through the ages were not limited to this kind of procession.[3] Its character as capital suggests that it must have seen festivals celebrating the inauguration of the kingship and the founding of the town itself. Here an interesting narrative from the Mbh suggests itself, viz. the story of the establishing of the Indramaha festival.[4] Indra presented a bamboo staff to King Uparicara (Vasu) of Cedi as a symbol of the royal position which Indra had helped him to attain. A year later the king planted the staff and thus worshipped Indra who had bestowed it. "After that, the kings have to this day planted a staff, as this king began to do." It is understood that this takes place to the glory of Indra. When Indra saw Vasu worshipping him, he was delighted, and said, "Those men and kings who celebrate my festival joyfully and do as the King of Cedi, shall win honour and their kingdoms shall conquer." The King of Cedi continued to celebrate Indra's feast, and therefore continued to stand high in the favour of the

---

[1] Frg. B 1.

[2] Cf. *The History and Culture of the Indian People*, pp. 24–26.

[3] Law, *Tribes*, p. 218, considers that festivals were usual in the capital of Magadha in the time of the Buddha.

[4] Mbh I.63; cf. above, p. 118.

king of the gods. He had five sons, of immeasurable strength. These he appointed to rule over various provinces, among them Mahāratha, or Bṛihadratha, in Magadha. And this passage of the history of Vasu ends by telling that these five founded kingdoms and towns in their own names, and their own dynasties, ever after.

In this context, the name Magadha is of the greatest interest, for Pāṭaliputra was the capital of the Magadha kingdom. Further, it seems from the formula *adya api*, "to this day", that the Indra festival must have continued to be celebrated for many years—to the time at which the epic came into existence. That means in other words that it should still have been occurring in Megasthenes' day, if Hopkins and others are correct in dating the origin of the epic to ca. 300 B.C.–300 A.D.: a dating which is supported *inter alia* by the fact that Pāṇini has nothing to say on its many peculiarities, grammatical or otherwise.[1] Megasthenes mentions no particular festival which he saw in Pāṭaliputra. Shortly before Megasthenes' arrival in India, there occurred a change of dynasty in the great kingdom of Magadha. Candragupta, at whose court Megasthenes was ambassador, had with the help of his famous minister Kauṭilya overthrown the ruling Nanda dynasty and assumed power. It is uncertain in such conditions whether a usurper will be prepared to go on observing ancient traditions of this kind. Incidentally, it was not the first time a usurper had taken the throne of Magadha. But in all probability the new ruler would be concerned to establish his claim to the throne by observing the old traditions—particularly the Indramaha which, as Holtzmann pointed out, expressed the derivation of his dignity from Indra.[2] The fact that the capital had been transferred elsewhere is of little importance. It is likely that there was some part of the festival which aimed at demonstrating the links of various capitals with Indra. As far as I am aware, no information on this point is to be found in India. But at all events, a theory such as this helps us to understand Megasthenes' mistaken information as to the founding of Pāṭaliputra.

Passages describing the town are of no interest to us, but are naturally

---

[1] Böhtlingk, in the introduction to his edition of Pāṇini's *Ashṭādhyāyī*. We stress that the dating applies to the epic in its present form. Wikander's studies in Indo-European epics have shown that at least the kernel of such epics among the various Indo-European peoples goes back to the time of the presumptive "original" language; similarly with certain themes (war between two related royal families), *Indo-Eupopean Eschatology in Myth and Epic.*

[2] *Indra nach den Vorstellungen des Mbh*, p. 326. Cf. above, p. 118.

reliable, particularly since they are confirmed by the Chinese traveller Fa-Hien.[1]

Finally on this point, Megasthenes was in fact mistaken, but his attitude can be fairly well understood on a basis of Indian myths and traditions on the subject of Indra. Kṛishṇa, on the other hand, is entirely excluded.[2]

g. *Pandaiē* is stated to be the name both of a girl and a country.[3] We can only state that no such personal name is known in India. But as the name of a country we have the well-known South Indian Pāṇḍya, which fits Megasthenes' description perfectly: it is southerly, by the sea, rich in pearl-shells, etc. There can be no doubt whatever that it is this land which is referred to by the Greek name Pandaiē. But how reliable is Megasthenes' information on its government and the origins of its royal dynasty? We shall first give some account of these traditions, after which we shall endeavour to solve the problem raised by the two identical names.[4]

1. Iyengar, in *Dravidian India*, has a great deal of valuable information on this first problem. Thus we read: "In the same way, it appears that several Purāṇas, the Vāyu, Matsya, Agni and Brahma, claim an Āryan descent for the southern races by making their progenitors or eponyms Pāṇḍya, Karṇata, Chola, Kerala to be descendants of Dushyanta, the adopted son of Turvasu, a prince of the Lunar line of the Kshatriyas. Turvasu, the Purāṇas say, was appointed by his father to rule over the south-east. Thus the Harivaṁśa relates, 'Yayāti', son of Nahusha, having conquered the earth with its seven continents and oceans, divided it into five portions for his sons. This wise king placed Turvasu over the south-east region."[5] We are also interested to note this observation, by the same author: "A large mound near Chingleput is surrounded by a number of megalithic graves, and believed to have been inhabited by a bearded race of 'Pandayar'."[6] The proper name is particularly interesting, bearing as it does such close resemblance to Megasthenes' Greek form. Iyengar is extremely cautious in his dating of the earliest dynasty in Pāṇḍya. He quotes

---

[1] Law, *Historical Geography*, p. 250. S. K. Bose, in an article *Pāṭaliputra in the time of Patanjali*, has combined information from Megasthenes and from Patanjali, and has come to the conclusion that the town was at that time mainly situated on the river Śon, and not on the Ganges. Further, there is said to have been "a very valuable guide-book to the capital", containing, in Bose's view, descriptions of temples and palaces. Cf. also H. C. Chakladar, *Pāṭaliputra*.

[2] On Vishṇu's relation to Kingship, see D. R. Bhandarkar, *Lectures*, pp. 125–128.

[3] Frg. B 9, 10, 11, 12.

[4] This has to some extent been dealt with above, pp. 110–112.

[5] *Op. cit.*, p. 22.

[6] *Op. cit.*, p. 49. Cf. above, p. 110 f.

the Rāmāyaṇa, the Mahābhārata, the Edict of Aśoka and other works telling of flourishing monarchies in South India. But when he comes to Pāṇḍya, he will say no more than that the first dynasty, if the Skanda Purāṇa and other writings are to be believed, arose earlier than 400 B.C.[1]

When the Pāṇḍiyas had become Arianised, there grew up the legend that they belonged to the Lunar dynasty, and the son of Arjuna and the Pāṇḍya princess Citrāṅgadā succeeded her father on the throne.[2] There is thus an incontestable link between Arjuna and the royal house of Pāṇḍya. But Kṛishṇa, who was Arjuna's contemporary, has no place in the picture. On the contrary, the Pāṇḍya dynasty seems from this tradition to have already been in existence in Kṛishṇa's day. Nor in this context does Arjuna appear as the founder of a dynasty, since his son succeeded on the throne of his maternal grandfather. If this tradition is of any value at all, it must be as a witness against the identification of Heracles with Kṛishṇa.

In addition, Iyengar has taken up the question of this identification, though only in passing.[3] He considers that the tradition of Kṛishṇa's daughter Pandaiē, who became queen of a country with the same name, is proof positive of Megasthenes' unreliability. He also remarks that Kṛishṇa's flute and Heracles' club are irreconcileable, and that this and other mistakes from Megasthenes only demonstrate that he is not worth discussing. Needless to say, he fails to see that Heracles might have been identified wrongly.

What we have so far quoted has not touched on the subject of the Pāṇḍya rulers. We have however mentioned the topic above, on p. 108, where we quoted Nilakantha Śastri: "... the divine line of Pāṇḍyan rulers, the descendants of Śiva and Pārvatī who condescended to become the first king and queen of this celebrated line."[4]

On that occasion we mentioned that this quotation has to do with South Indian traditions, whilst Megasthenes presumably, living in North India, reproduced North Indian traditions. The great difference is that in South India Śiva has long been the most prominent god, a position which he has not always held in North India. But there is one comment which must be made: It is possible that Śiva was not always dominant in South India, either. A certain amount of material has come to light which places our problem in a new perspective.

The Mbh mentions a holy place, a *tīrtha*, consecrated to Indra, which

[1] *Op. cit.*, p. 185.

[2] Iyengar, *History of the Tamils*, p. 461.

[3] *Op. cit.*, p. 137 f.

[4] *History of South India*, p. 71.

had formerly been consecrated to another god;[1] incidentally, this shows that gods might change, but that their sanctuary remained holy. We do not know where this particular *tīrtha* was situated; it is unfortunately impossible to work out its situation from the list of *tīrthas* given in the Mbh. For as Iyengar says, referring to the famous centre of pilgrimage, Cape Comorin: "The places which Arjuna visited in his pilgrimage are mentioned without any regard to geographical sequence, in quite as confused a manner as Sugrīva directed his soldiers to go in search of Sītā."[2]

Some pages later, he writes: "In the list of the Nārītīrthas occurs the first mention of the sea at the Cape Comorin, as a sacred bathing place, called the Kumārī-tīrtha, in the country of the Pāṇḍyas.—This tīrtha is also called Kanyā tīrtha. Thus the legend of Kumārī waiting for Śiva at the southernmost corner of India had been evolved in this age; but the Tamils had nothing to do with this legend or with the idea of Cape Comorin being a holy spot, for there is no Tamil name for the Cape."[3]

Apart from this, Iyengar has no explanation of how the name might have originated; but we have enough to be able to draw certain conclusions. I have no wish to state categorically that this was Indra's tīrtha as mentioned in the Mbh. But we have reason to suspect that it had certain connections with Indra.

Those who held Cape Comorin to be a holy site were not Tamils or Dravidians in general, but Aryans, since the names in the area are Sanskrit names, though the only language spoken is Tamil. Today—and obviously for hundreds of years past—Śiva is worshipped there by a population largely Dravidian. But the evidence of Periplūs, our oldest source (1st century A.D.), leads us to believe that Śiva was also worshipped on that spot by non-Dravidians: "To Cape Comorin came those men who wish to consecrate themselves for the rest of their lives, and bathe and dwell in celibacy; and women also did the same, for it is told that a Goddess once dwelt here and bathed."

"We now learn from the Periplus that, as now, even in the I century A.D. Sādhus and Sanyāsīs travelled to Cape Comorin to bathe in the sea, and that, at this early date, had arisen the legend of some (probably mortal) maiden waiting for Śiva to marry her at Cape Comorin, where her effigy still stands patiently. Perhaps this legend existed from the days of the Mahābhārata. But yet the Śiva-worshippers of the North do not seem to

---

[1] Mbh III 5023.

[2] *History of the Tamils*, p. 90.

[3] *Op. cit.*, p. 95.

have actively attempted to spread the Aryan cult of Śiva in the Tamil country, for the bulk of the Tamil people continued to live in the I century A.D., unattracted by the desperate anxiety of the Āryas to seek by devotion to Śiva, means of escape from the ills that flesh is heir to."[1]

From what we have quoted here we gain the distinct impression that we are dealing with a cult which may be traced back to Pārvatī. But Lassen says, "The Pāṇḍyas are familiar with the holy virgins, Kumārī ... It is thus not the goddess Pārvatī, but the Apsarasas, which have given Cape Comorin its name."[2] The Apsarasas have nothing whatever to do with Śiva—but with Indra! He is called *Apsaraḥ-pati*, lord of the Apsarasas.

We have here three important points: i. Those who regarded this site, in Dravidian territory, as being a sacred *tīrtha* were not Dravidians, but Aryans; ii. but since the Dravidians themselves did not regard it as a sacred spot, it follows that the god worshipped there was not Dravidian, but Aryan; iii. everything we know of the Dravidians is in favour of their always having been Śiva-worshippers, but as Indra is the only Aryan/Vedic god who can be shown to have had a cult in the area, it seems highly likely that it was Indra, and some goddess, who were worshipped at that shrine.

But we have anticipated something here for which we have yet to produce evidence. It is still possible today in South India to come across traces of an earlier Indra cult—indistinct traces of Indra in popular religion and of Indra in a situation which presupposes that he must at one time have been the leading god. I quote: "Finally the sacrificial altar of Indra is worshipped. The altar is placed in front of the shrine of the goddess. There is no such altar near the shrine of Comacuntarar, because Śiva and Indra are not friends. During the annual Kāmānpaṇṭikai, which is being celebrated in Mathurai in Feb.–March, Indra, riding on a white elephant, leads his army of Kaḷḷar in an attack on Śiva."[3] A foot-note to this passage reads: "Indra was the first to benefit from Mathurai's holiness, when he had slain (Vṛitra). The guilt of killing followed him like a shadow till he worshipped Śiva in this holy place ... A study of the relationship between Indra and Śiva is desirable. We cannot pursue the matter further after having noticed a connection between Indra and the goddess and an estrangement between Indra and Śiva."

---

[1] *Op. cit.*, p. 78, quoted by Iyengar, *History of the Tamils*, p. 309 f.

[2] *Indische Altertumskunde* I², p. 678, n. 2. Cf. 1st ed., p. 564, n. 2, containing a correction of the statement, p. 158, n. 1, that Kumārī should be Pārvatī.

[3] Diehl, *Instrument and Purpose*, p. 149 f., partic. 150 n. 3; cf. Dikshitar, *Studies in Tamil Literature*, pp. 305 ff., for the festival of Indra in South India; cf. also Iyengar, *Dravidian India*, p. 202.

By way of summary we must first of all point out that our knowledge of the situation in South India at this particular time, ca. 300 B.C., is not very extensive. But what we do know, and what we can deduce from Sanskrit and Tamil texts, and from the present-day situation, is enough to establish that Indra was not unknown in this part of India. It is not possible to state dogmatically just how strong his position was, but we would appear to be justified in saying that, apart from Śiva, no god had a more prominent position in Pāṇḍya, of which Mathurai is the capital. But we cannot be sure whether or not in Megasthenes' day Indra was the main god in Pāṇḍya, later to be ousted by Śiva. It is not impossible. It seems most probable that it is Śiva, the newcomer, who drove out the earlier lord, who now only lives on in those myths and rites celebrating Śiva's triumph. Were Indra the usurper, who lost in the first round of the contest, it would be difficult to understand how those myths we have quoted from Diehl could stress Śiva's victory as they do. The victory of a great leader is only celebrated by posterity if his opponent was a worthy foe.[1]

There may well have been a time when Indra was of some importance in the myths describing the origins of the Pāṇḍya royal house, myths which were transferred to Śiva when he took the sceptre of the pantheon from Indra. The name Pāṇḍya-Pandaiē is of no direct relevance as an argument for the identification of Heracles. But should the identification be regarded as proven on other grounds, then this point need not stand in the way, since it fits in reasonably well with Indra, who was an important god in Pāṇḍya from time to time.

2. Secondly, on the problem of the connection between the country Pāṇḍya and the women's name Pandaiē, we may refer to our more detailed consideration above, on pp. 111 f. We there put forward positive reasons for the proposed combination and took up some of the most significant objections. The two main points are: i. that it is possible, without considerable doubt, to identify the name of the country, Pandaiē, with the phonetically similar Pāṇḍya; ii. that Pandaiē, as the name of a woman, cannot be combined with any known Indian name, as long as we concentrate on phonetic resemblances.

Lassen's attempt to connect Pandaiē and Pāṇḍavas fails in that it leaves no room for any Indian god—least of all Kr̥ishṇa, who did not stand in the same relationship to the Pāṇḍavas and one or other of their wives as Heracles did to his daughter Pandaiē. And despite the exercise of much imagi-

---

[1] On the subject of Aryan rule in the Deccan and changing conditions, see above, p. 108 f.

nation, I have not been able to find any woman's name which may be connected phonetically with Pandaiē. The one remaining alternative is to assume Pandaiē to be the translation of some Indian name; and the only name which seems to fit is Ushas, for the following reasons: 1. The name is etymologically connected with a word having the same meaning as that which may be given Pandaiē. 2. Ushas is the name of Indra's daughter. 3. Indra has many other characteristics which are postulated of Heracles. 4. Ushas is connected in Indian tradition with an incest story; this motif is not told about many others.

These four points, when taken together, suggest that this is the only possible combination of names. We have no need to go over the objections again. It may of course be felt that this is a blot on Megasthenes' reputation for reliability, but this linguistic *faux pas*—by no means unique—should not be allowed to detract from his worth as an eye-witness and historical source.

Once more we must say that this point is not positively in favour of our identification of Heracles as Indra. But nor is it entirely negative, others being positive; this is of some importance, since earlier proposed identifications have tended to founder on this rock.[1] While Lassen provides an astute explanation, built on the assumption that Megasthenes had confused Kr̥shṇa's sister with his daughter, Ruben casts doubt on the entire passage. As we have it, the passage cannot possibly be reconciled with Kr̥shṇa or with Śiva. But Indra fits into the picture, as we have said, without distortion or undue speculation; the only condition being that Megasthenes must be assumed to have practised a little popular etymology on the way—which, as we said, is by no means unique.

h. *Parapamisos—Paropamisadē* is said by Strabo and Arrian to be the place where Prometheus was held captive, and where Heracles came to set him free.[2] There is nothing to suggest that this myth was told of the Indian Heracles; the only reason why we note this point at all is the interesting passage telling how the Greeks "shifted the Caucasus from Pontus to Paropamisadē". This reveals something which may help us to understand an otherwise obscure situation. The myths have been localized by their tellers and hearers. The same myth has been told many times; but even though the *dramatis personae* have not been changed, the scene has. This is expressly stated to be true of the Prometheus–Heracles myth. Why should not this also apply in other situations, e.g. to the myth of Aornos?

---

[1] Cf. above, pp. 76, 84, 112.

[2] Frg. B 3, 4.

This is so obvious that, once pointed out and emphasized, we need not discuss the matter further.

i. *Śibi*—an Indian tribe, characterized by their clubs, animal skins, and their practice of branding their cattle with the mark of the club, were mentioned by Arrian and Strabo, and were supposed to be descended from the survivors of Heracles' campaigns.[1] It is understandable that their name has been coupled with that of the god Śiva. But it is always hazardous to deduce relationship from nominal resemblance, and on this occasion we are given no help from older Indian texts. In his *Tribes in Ancient India*, pp. 82 ff., Law quoted RV VII.18.7 as the oldest relevant passage, in which the tribe is referred to by the name Śivas. But this is most uncertain. Geldner, following Pargiter,[2] allows the possibility of a pun on the ethnic name, but translates the word adjectivally: "friendly". Grassman's *Wörterbuch zum Rigveda* does not mention Śibi, not even under the form Śiva. It is thus impossible to make any use of this passage from the RV. But as long as there is a possibility of the ethnic name being referred to in some form here, it may be of interest to examine the verse in question.

á pakthā́so bhalānā́so bhananta álināso vihāṇinaḥ śivā́saḥ

Pakthas, Bhalānas, Alinas and Vishāṇin called themselves (Indra's) good friends (= Śivas). (RV VII.18.7)

The verse is practically untranslateable, and this interpretation is based on Geldner's version. It is thus Geldner who couples Śibi with Indra. But the extreme obscurity of the verse prevents us from drawing any conclusions therefrom.

This is, however, not the only occasion on which Indra and Śibi are brought together; there are others, of considerably greater interest.

First the RV: RV X.179 is said to have been composed by a rishi called Śibi Auśīnara. The hymn is addressed to Indra, and is the only one in the RV with which is coupled the name of Śibi.

The name occurs in the Mbh. on a number of occasions—as the name of one of Indra's sons; a tribe descended from a person of the same name; even a name of Indra, in the fourth Manvantara (this latter in the Vishṇu Purāṇa). We have no reason to undertake a complete account of all its occurrences, but we may point out that in the texts it is never connected with the name of the god Śiva; it is, though, often coupled with Indra. We must conclude that if this evidence is to be allowed at all (which is far from certain) then it must be taken as being rather in Indra's favour than other-

[1] *Ibid.*

[2] *J.R.A.S.* 1910, p. 49.

wise. (We shall return in due course to the question of the weapons and clothing of the Śibi.[1])

j. *Śūrasena*, a people living in and around Mathurā on the Yamunā, who were particularly devoted to Heracles, are mentioned only by Arrian in connection with Heracles.[2] Their location in Mathurā and by the Yamunā makes it convenient to connect them with Kṛishṇa, but if we consider the matter more closely we shall find their true connection to be not with Kṛishṇa, but with Indra.

The first time we come across the name Śūrasena in Indian literature is, according to Law,[3] in Manu and the Mbh. Manu II.19 enumerates a number of countries, including the country of the Śūrasenas; it is referred to in the following verse.

etaddeśaprasūtasya sakāśādagrajanmanaḥ
svaṁ svaṁ caritraṁ śiksheran pṛithivyāṁ sarvamānavāḥ

Every man on earth shall learn his duty directly from a Brahman who was born in that land. (Manu II.19)

The Brahmans among the Śūrasena were evidently held in high esteem. Remembering Manu's emphasis on the Veda as the foundation of all dharma, this seems to indicate that the Veda occupied a particularly strong position in this area just at the time when the Law of Manu was compiled—i.e. the centuries around the beginning of the Christian era. (We may mention in passing that Kṛishṇa is never mentioned in Manu, but that Indra and the other Vedic gods are.) The honour accorded by Manu to the Śūrasena is thus an indirect witness to their Vedic orthodoxy and their Indra cult. Is it, one wonders, feasible, that Kṛishṇa could have avoided mention in Manu, had he been a great god in the country of the Śūrasenas just at this crucial time, as Lassen and Ruben believe? Manu's warm testimony to the Śūrasena makes this question all the more pressing.

The other passage of Manu which we can quote, may point in the same direction. This is VII.193, in which the king is advised to place the Śūrasena, and others, in the front rank, on account of their skill in battle, their size and their courage. It is generally stated that the RV only refers to the N–W of the country and the Punjab; but we find Rapson, in *Ancient India*, p. 47, describing how the Yajur Veda marks an Aryan migration from the north-west to Kurukshetra, the great plain around the Sutlej, Yamunā and Ganges—hard by what was later to become the district of the Śūrasena. At

[1] 3 i., p. 152, j., p. 155 and k., p. 157.

[2] Frg. B 9.

[3] *Tribes in Ancient India*, p. 39.

the time when Megasthenes wrote, the Aryan invasion had long been a fait accompli.

But who are these people, and who do they consider themselves to be? Law gives us the answer, already quoted: "They claimed descent from Yadu, a hero whose people are repeatedly referred to in the Rigveda; and it is probable that the Śūrasenas were included among the Rigvedic Yadus."[1]

But this brings us into immediate contact with Indra. The Yadu are a tribe which is often said to be closely connected with Indra. For the sake of simplicity we quote from the index of names in Geldner's excellent translation, under "Yadu":

Yadu, name of a king, usually mentioned with Turva(śa)
Turvaśa and Yadu made famous by Indra X.49.8
Turvaśa and Yadu saved by Indra IX.61.2
Indra will strike down Turvaśa, the Yadu king VII.19.8
Turvaśa and Yadu, Indra's favourites I.54.6, 174.9, IV.30.17, V.31.8
Turvaśa and Yadu, the Maruts' favourites VIII.7.18

On each occasion but one, when they are mentioned (either as kings or as tribes), they are closely linked with, and helped by, Indra. This is a consistent impression provided by a thorough reading of the RV. We see that Maṇḍalas I, IV, V, VIII, IX and X contain material which stresses that Indra and Yadu-Turvaśa are friends; only Maṇḍala VII provides the exception which proves the rule. But Geldner's index of names is incomplete. We find a valuable complement under "Turvaśa".

Turvaśa, the name of a king, the Aśvins with I.47.7
  Indra's friend VI.27.7
  Indra will strike him down, the Yadu king VII.19.8
  Indra with him VIII.4.1
  the enemy of Sudā VII.18.6

Indra and Agni with Yadu and Turvaśa I.108.8
The Aśvins with Yadu and Turvaśa VIII.10.5
Their sacrifices prepared for the Aśvins VIII.9.14
Indra's favourites I.36.18, VI.45.1, VIII.45.27

The result of this review is to confirm our earlier impression of the remarkably close relationship existing between these and Indra. Again, only one case of enmity has been brought to our notice; again it is from Maṇḍala VII, where Sudā is depicted as Indra's confederate. Their alliance is seen

[1] Cf. above p. 95 f., *Tribes in Ancient India*, p. 39.

to be a theme which recurs, not only in the above-mentioned Maṇḍalas, but even in Maṇḍala VI. We must note at this point that the relationship between Indra and these two kings (or peoples) is not merely in the nature of a non-aggression pact, but a warm friendship: Indra helps them to cross the river (IV.30.17); he conducts them in safety to their new homes (VI.45.1), etc.

The word Śūrasena means (the people) whose army is made up of heroes. May this not originally have been an epithet of that people which stood closely related to Indra, that people which the RV calls Yadu and Turvaśa? The question becomes even more important when we recall that the Law of Manu laid great store by the fighting capabilities of the Śūrasena. Be that as it may; the words of Manu cannot but emphasize the particular links of this people with the god of war.

The name Śūrasena therefore seems to be positively in favour of our proposed identification of Heracles with Indra, for three reasons: i. The Śūrasena seem to be identical with Indra's particular friends the Yadu. ii. In Manu's day the Śūrasena were regarded as Vedic experts, and this implies the existence of an Indra cult, excluding an heretical Kṛishṇa-worship; iii. Manu stated that the Śūrasena were particularly gifted in war, which again suggests Indra. Additional evidence is provided by archaeological discoveries, which show Indra, either alone or in homage to the Buddha, from the Śūrasena district at a time later than Megasthenes.[1]

3. *Heracles' Exploits*

a. Heracles had wandered through all the earth and sea,[2]
b. And had rid them of monsters.[3]

It is unnecessary to produce examples showing that this description agrees perfectly with Indra. The correspondence could not be more striking. In the myth of Vṛitra, Indra's enemies are said to have been two in number, mother and son, and they are aptly described as "monsters". The same is true of Viśvarūpa, Tvashṭar's three-headed son, whom Indra slew. We have no need to draw up a list of all those defeated by Indra, according to the RV and later texts. The point agrees with the character of Indra, and it is something of a mystery how Lassen could make it refer primarily to Vishṇu, whose character is extremely passive. But the Vishṇu of the Purāṇas is not

---

[1] See Vogel, *La sculpture de Mathurā*, according to quotation above, pp. 91 and 134.
[2] Frg. B 9.
[3] Frg. B 1, 9.

the same as the Vishṇu of the Mbh and older texts. His radical change, from passivity to legendary heroism, makes his identification as Heracles extremely dubious; Indra, on the other hand, has never been other than active and powerful—an admirable counterpart to the Heracles of Greece.

c. Heracles divided the whole of India among his children.[1]

This is not expressly said of Indra, nor of Kṛishṇa. But we must make two observations, which show that it is at least possible to couple Indra with what is said here.

i. RV IV.26.1 and 2 place these words in Indra's mouth:

1. *ahám mánur abhavaṁ sū́ryaś cāhám kakshī́vāṅ ṛíshir asmi vípraḥ*
   ahám kútsam ārjuneyám ny ṛiñje 'hám kavír uśánā páśyatā mā
2. *ahám bhū́mim adadām ā́ryāyāhám vṛishṭíṁ dāśúshe mártyāya*
   ahám apó anayaṁ vāvaśānā́ máma devā́so ánu kḗtam āyan

1. I was Manu, and I was the sun also: I am the wise seer Kakshīvān. I have conquered Kutsa, son of Arjuna; I am the Kavi Uśana: give heed to me!
2. I have given land to the Aryans: I have given rain to mortal sacrificers; I have directed the obedient waters: the gods observed my will.

May the meaning of the second of these verses not be identical with what Megasthenes has to say about Heracles?—I have given land to the Aryans—Heracles divided the land of India among his children

ii. We have said that Indra was believed to have originated the kingship in India.[2] This may possibly provide the solution of our problem.

The identity of Indra and Manu, as demonstrated from the RV, seems to be the only possible link between Indra and the royal dynasties of India, which are said to have been descended, via Iḷā and Purūravas, from Manu. But this is an obscure point, and we shall not attempt to make use of it as proof.

d. Heracles had found a jewel in the sea, which he gave as an ornament to his daughter.[3]

It is extremely difficult to demonstrate the accuracy of this point by producing evidence drawn from Indian literature. The difficulty is not confined to Indra, but has to do with the very nature of the information we are given. The passage has two elements, and we may begin with the first, that Heracles found a jewel in the sea—the sea pearl.

i. "Treasure" or "pearl" is mentioned in the RV in the following contexts:

---

[1] Frg. B 1.

[2] See above, pp. 100 and 118 f.

[3] Frg. B 9.

ávindad divó níhitaṁ gúhā nidhíṁ vér ná gárbham párivītam áśmany anantḗ antár áśmani

He found the treasure of heaven, which had been hidden away, like the bird's fruit, enclosed in the mountain, in the endless rock ... (RV I.130.3)

ā́ devó dade budhnyā́ vásūni vaiśvānará úditā sū́ryasya
ā́ samudrā́d ávarād ā́ párasmād ā́ agnír dade divá ā́ pṛithivyā́ḥ

The god Vaiśvānara has taken to himself the treasures of the ocean at the dawn; Agni took them from the nearer and the further ocean, from heaven and earth.(RV VII.6.7.)

eshá víprair abhíshṭuto apó devó ví gāhate dádhad rátnāni dāśúshe

Praised by wise men, this god dives deep to bring from the water pearls for the sacrificer. (RV IX.3.6)

rāyáḥ samudrā́ṅś catúro asmábhyaṁ soma viśvátaḥ ā́ pavasva sahasríṇaḥ

O Soma, purify thousandfold riches, the four seas full, to us, on all sides, (RV IX.33.6)

In RV X.5.1 is mentioned *ékaḥ samudró dharuṇo rayīṇā́m:* the one sea which bears riches. May this possibly have to do with the myth told by Megasthenes about Heracles, who had gathered pearls from the sea to enrich his daughter's country?

dhṛitávrato dhanadā́ḥ sómavṛiddhaḥ sá hí vāmásya vásunaḥ purukshúḥ
sáṃ jagmire pathyā́ rā́yo asmin samudré ná síndhavo yā́damānāḥ

He who gives effect to the law, riches, strengthened by soma—for he bestows good gifts liberally—in him combine the ways of riches, as the rivers flow together in the sea (or: as the rivers join themselves to the sea: cf. III.36.7). (RV VI.19.5)

1. *satrā́ mádāsas táva viśvájanyāḥ satrā́ rā́yó 'dha yé pā́rthivāsaḥ*
   satrā́ vā́jānām abhavo vibhaktā́ yád devéshu dhāráyathā asuryàm
4. *sá rāyás khā́m úpa sṛijā gṛiṇānáḥ puruścandrásya tvám indra vásvaḥ*
   pátir babhūthā́samo jánānām éko víśvasya bhúvanasya rā́jā

1. Thine are all the peoples' intoxicating drinks, thine all the riches of earth; thou didst apportion prosperity, exercising *asurya* among the *devas* (*asurya* = the authority of an *asura* [Geldner], or divine fulness of life [Grassmann].)
4. Cause, praised, to overflow the spring of riches, of that good thing which is called gold, O Indra! Thou didst become a matchless lord among the peoples, alone king over the whole world. (RV VI.36.1.4)

These examples, dealing with riches and bounty, show that it is Indra in particular who is considered to bestow these gifts—emphasized by the epithet *maghavān*, the generous one, bestower of gifts. But our search for "pearls" in the RV is practically in vain. In later usage, *ratna* is a technical term for "pearl, jewel", but both Grassmann and Monier-Williams are of the opinion that *ratna* in the RV means no more that "gift, riches" in general. Geldner's translation renders "*ratna*" by "pearl" in III.3.1 and X.74.3; cf. also IX.3.6 (p. 148 above). Otherwise "pearl" reproduces *kṛiśana* (four times, two of which are metaphorical) or *maṇi* (twice only). A common word in later literature, *muktā*, evidently derived from the root *muc*, "to loose", is said by Iyengar (*The History of the Tamils*, p. 23 f.)[1] to be of Dravidian origin, but the view is not substantiated. So much is however clear: that nothing is said about a god, whether Indra or any other, giving a pearl to anyone.

Proceeding to the later literature, we find this interesting passage in the Atharva Veda:

5. *samudrājjāto maṇirvṛitrājjāto divākaraḥ*
so asmāntsarvataḥ pātu hetyā devāsurebhyaḥ

7. *devānāmasthi kṛiśanam babhūva tadātmanvaccaratyapsvantaḥ*
tatte badhnāmyāyushe varcase balāya dīrghāyutvāya śataśāradāya karśanastvābhi rakshatu[2]

5. The ocean-born jewel, born of Vṛitra, creator of the day, protect us on all hands from the arrows of the asuras and devas.
6. The gods' bones became a pearl; with a soul it wanders the waters. I bind it upon you to life and honour, to strength and long life up to a hundred autumns; may this jewel protect you. (AV IV.10.5.7)

The most interesting thing about this text seems to me to be the fact that the jewel is said to be "born of Vṛitra", or of the gods. This brings us immediately into the same territory as that occupied by Megasthenes in his description of how Heracles found the pearl in the ocean, after having cleansed earth and sea from monsters. It is all the more remarkable that Lassen linked this Megasthenes passage with the legend of how Kṛishṇa obtained his conch from the bones of the vanquished giant Pañcajana.[3] Lassen quotes the Vishṇu Purāṇa, but this has nothing to say on the subject of a jewel being given away. But here we first learn that the pearl originated with Vṛitra—which immediately suggests Indra—and then that

---

[1] Iyengar, *Dravidian India*, p. 137, expresses the same opinion.

[2] For *karśanas* ... read *kṛiśanas*.

[3] See above, p. 84.

it is made to benefit some other person. Is it possible, strictly speaking, to come any closer? At all events, these AV verses seem to approximate more closely to the Megasthenes passage than the text quoted by Lassen from the Vishṇu Purāṇa.

Mbh V.55.55 describes the way in which Indra steals Karṇa's earrings as a present for his wife Śacī. It is true that we have no reference here to the sea, but another passage, I.17.12, tells how Nārāyaṇa advises the gods and demons together to churn the sea with the mountain Mandara, "for the ocean contains the juice of all precious stones and all healing herbs". They do so, with the result that there appears *inter alia* the jewel "Kaustubha", which is destined to adorn the breast of Nārāyaṇa. Here we have the motif of the sea, but no gift made to a wife or daughter. Nor was Indra responsible for producing the jewel; it was found by the combined efforts of all supernatural beings. We may add the passage from the Matsya Purāṇa, quoted by Dowson in *A Classical Dictionary of Hindu Mythology*, p. 3 (under "Aditi"), which tells how Indra gives earrings to his mother Aditi. Dikshitar, in his *Purāṇa Index*, p. 192 (art. "Indra"), expresses himself in more general terms—"gifts of elephants and gems pleasing to ..."—and quotes in support Matsya Purāṇa 47.114–122, 171–9; 266.62.

It is thus possible to establish a definite link between Indra and the woman's pearl in the Indian literature. Indra is similarly said to have given away the jewel.

ii. But one factor is missing: the daughter. The text we quoted from the AV says nothing about the person addressed, and on whom the jewel is fastened. This is never so much as mentioned in the hymn, which has exclusively to do with the pearl, born in the water, which can by its mere presence lengthen a person's life. Here we must leave the question.

The conclusion which may be drawn from the evidence we have put forward on this point is that it is not impossible for Indra to have found the pearl in the course of his battle with Vṛitra, since it is said to have proceeded from Vṛitra. Further, Indra is the owner of all riches, inclusive of the pearls of the sea, and is the generous one, who bestows liberally. The point is thus capable of being applied to Indra, although we are unable to point to any particular text stating that he gave the pearl to his daughter. Of the three gods, Kṛishṇa, Śiva and Indra, there is only one—Indra—who can really be linked with the pearl motif. The only other divinities commonly associated with riches and pearls are Agni and Soma.

e. Heracles founded many towns, and in particular Pāṭaliputra, where he allowed the people to settle.[1]

[1] Frg. B 1.

f. He surrounded the town with moats,[1]

g. And built costly palaces,[1] but

h. Left few memorials.[2]

We have already touched upon the possibility of Indra's having connections with Pāṭaliputra,[3] even as regards the detail of the moats. We have no intention of reversing the negative result arrived at on that occasion—that Indra did not build Pāṭaliputra, its moats and palaces. But the actual passage could to some extent be understood as having to do with Indra, so long as we confined ourselves to Pāṭaliputra; there is no such possibility with regard to other towns. But since the passage cannot be combined with Indra, we are led to ask whether it is altogether certain that Megasthenes was the originator of the passage in question. The points e.–g. above are to be found only in Diodorus, and as we have said on a number of occasions previously, Diodorus never mentions the name of Megasthenes.[4] In point of fact we do not know from whence Diodorus obtained his information. May it be the case that Diodorus has read, and misunderstood, Megasthenes' account of the land of the Śūrasena, in which there were two great towns,[5] and reproduced it in such a way as to make Heracles the founder of these towns? I believe this to have been the case. At all events, there is nothing in the other writers who quote Megasthenes to indicate that Heracles founded any towns; nor is there any evidence in Indian literature to show that Indra did so.

Although this passage—or rather these passages—must be rejected as probably spurious and having no connection with Indra, so much cannot be said about the last passage, which fits Indra very well indeed. It is found in Arrian, in a passage beginning: "This Megasthenes says that the Indians neither waged war on any other people ..."[6] When Megasthenes comes to deal with the memorials connected with Heracles, he mentions neither the mountain Govardhana, nor Gadāvasāna, where Jarāsandha's club, *gadā*, fell when hurled against Kṛishṇa and his town Mathurā, nor to any other memorial which conjures up the name of Kṛishṇa. He tells us only of the rock Aornos, which Kṛishṇa seems never to have visited, so far as we can see from the texts. The paucity of memorials thus favours Indra rather

[1] Frg. B 1.

[2] Frg. B 4.

[3] Above, p. 135 f.

[4] See e.g. above, pp. 29, 119, 135.

[5] Quoted by Arrian, frg. B 9 here.

[6] Frg. A 5 here.

than Kṛishṇa, whose name was in fact connected with a number of places never mentioned.

While on the general subject of moats and palaces, we may quote these verses from Manu VII:

70. *dhanurdurgam mahīdurgamabdurgaṁ vārkshameva vā*
nṛidurgaṁ giridurgaṁ vā samāśritya vasetpuram

76. *tasya madhye suparyāptaṁ kārayedgṛihamātmanaḥ*
guptaṁ sarvartukaṁ śubhraṁ jalavṛikshasamanvitam

70. Let him taking his refuge dwell in a town, making for his safety a fortress, protected by bows, earth, water, trees, men or a hill.

76. Let him cause to be built for himself, in the centre of it, a spacious palace, (well) protected, habitable in every season, resplendent (with white-wash), supplied with water and trees.

It need hardly be said that the particular book of the Laws of Manu from which these verses are taken deals with the duties of the king. Were such verses as these to be found in a book which seems to have been one of Megasthenes' principal sources, it is quite understandable that the imaginative reader would draw the conclusion that the king *par excellence*, Indra, did just that. Mention is made of both palace and moats (*abdurgam*: cut off by water). The only thing that is missing is a passage saying that Indra—or any other god, for that matter—ever undertook any such building project.

i. Heracles and his worshippers were distinguished by their club.[1]

We here only are discussing Heracles' distinguishing features. We can therefore safely ignore the matter of the Śibi's club, which is never mentioned in the available Indian texts, and is in any case irrelevant.

Heracles is said to carry a club. What is remarkable here is that this club is the god's sole attribute; the lion- or animal-skin is, as we shall see, a different kind of attribute. The skin garment belongs to the necessities of life: such is not the case with the club. In the same way Kṛishṇa's clothes are never mentioned, though it is perfectly evident that he wore them; his discus, his lotus, his conch, his club and his flute, on the other hand, are mentioned repeatedly, though not one of them can strictly be called a necessity. So none of the texts have anything to say about Indra's clothing, but his *vajra* is mentioned almost as frequently as Indra himself. But no other emblem or attribute is ever brought into the picture.[2]

---

[1] Frg. B I, 3, 4.

[2] As to Indra's bow, see below, p. 154 n. 2.

We must now ask whether Heracles' club can possibly be coupled with Indra's *vajra*. And we are forced to the conclusion that there is no possible alternative.

1. Etymologically, the Sanskrit *vajra* is identical with the Avestan *vazra*, meaning "club"; from this is derived the New Persian *gurz*, still with the same meaning.

2. Proceeding to the RV and its description of the *vajra*, we find what Buschardt expressed in these words: "In the RV itself there is no concrete example of the *vajra* being identified with the lightning (*vidyut*), a phenomenon which is linked with the Maruts, and which does not occur in any other connection."[1] Güntert, in a passage which we have earlier had occasion to quote,[2] says, "*Vajra* is not the lightning, and the liberated waters are not the rain-clouds, but the actual rivers, Yamunā, Indus, etc., whose waters have been dammed and imprisoned by some demon at their sources among the hills."[3] Buschardt also points out that RV I.33.4 has a word *ghana*, meaning "cudgel" or "club", referring to Indra's weapon in his battle with the demons.

Geldner's translation of the RV, when compared with that of Ludwig, proves to have replaced Ludwig's "Keil" for *vajra*—by "Keule".[4] In the face of such evidence as this it seems almost superfluous to have to quote Apte's short but relevant article *Vajra in the Rigveda*. However, we quote: "The *vajra* in the Rigveda is no thunderbolt![5] The Rigveda has a different word, '*vidyut*', for the lightning-stroke, which alone (not *vajra*) is associated with Parjanya, *the proper and only raingod of the Rigveda* ...

The '*vajra*' is a weapon and a *weapon* in no abstract or figurative sense of the term. It is a '*vadha*'—a deadly weapon, of the nature of a '*ghana*' i.e., a club, mallet or hammer. It is made of '*ayas*'—a metal, either iron or a kind of bronze. It is a weapon that is *wrought*, *forged* or *fashioned* by Tvashṭṛ, the artificer-god ..."[6]

Such was the picture in former times; RV exegesis has shown Indra's *vajra* to have been undoubtedly a club. How does this compare with later ideas?

---

[1] *Vṛitra*, p. 148.

[2] Above, p. 89.

[3] *Der arische Weltkönig und Heiland*, p. 19 f.

[4] Bréal has throughout the word "*massue*", "club" for *vajra* (*Hercule et Cacus*, pp. 80–84).

[5] That *vajra* in the RV was not considered to be identical with the lightning is clear from the fact that the sound of Indra's *vajra* is compared to the thunder of heaven in RV I.100.13.

[6] *Op. cit.*, p. 292–295.

The Śatapatha Brāhmaṇa I.2.4.6 describes it in these words: "The thousand-spiked, hundred-edged! he adds, for a thousand spikes and a hundred edges had that *vajra* which he hurled at Vṛitra: he thereby makes it to be that (*vajra*)." In III.4.4.8 we read: "He takes eight times in the *juhū* and four times in the *upabhṛit*. He thereby makes the *vajra* heavy in front, and with that *vajra* heavy in front he cleaves these worlds, and conquers these worlds." III.7.1.25 is also of interest in this context: "That (sacrificial stake) he sets up on the fore-part (of the altar); for the stake is a *vajra*, as the club (*daṇḍa*) is a *vajra*." It does not say that the *vajra* is a club, but that the club is a *vajra*; but the mere fact of their being connected in this way shows that they can be combined in the Brāhmaṇas. This fact must not be carried too far, since in these texts virtually anything can be *vajra*: clarified butter, water, a sword, a spade, a bow, a knife, and even the ritual cry and the sacrificial horse. But a *vajra* which is heavy in front and a *vajra* with a thousand spikes and a hundred edges may well suggest a club.

Other later texts contain no detailed description of the *vajra* which contradict the RV. For instance, we read in Mbh. III.100 how the gods approach the pious Dadhīca and ask for his bones, from which they can make a *vajra* to be used on Vṛitra. The pious man proves to be fully co-operative: smiling, he expires on the spot. Tvashṭar then makes his *vajra*, which thus in the Mbh version, too, is not like the lightning, but a fatal weapon.

3. The evidence we have from the texts is supported with unexpected force by the archaeological evidence. Although Gopinatha Rao, in his *Elements of Hindu Iconography*, takes account of nothing but the "lightning" element of the *vajra*, Banerjea points out in *The Development of Hindu Iconography* that *vajra* can be presented in two ways: as a thunderbolt or as a club, narrow in the middle and broader at the ends.[1] There is no doubt that this important discovery has been made since Lassen's day, and it is therefore unreasonable to expect Lassen to have connected the figure of Heracles carrying a club with Indra. The situation today is entirely different. There is no difficulty in linking the club with Indra's *vajra*; and more than this, we can even go so far as to say that since Indra is the only god in Indian religion having only one attribute[2]—a club—and since

[1] *Op. cit.*, p. 301 f.

[2] Both the Greek Heracles and Indra had bow and arrows, too. With Heracles this sort of weapon dominated much more than with Indra. See v. Schroeder, *Herakles und Indra*, p. 15. It is an interesting fact that Arjuna in Mbh. is exclusively a bowman instead of club-bearer, though evidently he represents Indra. Cf. Dumézil, *Remarques sur les armes des Dieux de "Troisième Fonction" chez divers peuples Indo-Européens*, p. 7. To explain this incongruity is not the task of our investigation.

Heracles was also distinguished by the identical attribute, no other god can reasonably be brought into the picture.

j. Heracles' worshippers, the Śibi, were characterized by the fact that they branded their cattle with the mark of the club.[1]

Here there are at least two important elements: 1. a connection between Heracles and the cattle; and 2. the actual branding of the cattle.

1. It is common knowledge that the RV provides evidence of a close bond between Indra and cattle: RV I.51.3, 32.12, 84.10 f., 101.4; II.12.7; III.31.4; IV.23.9, 32.18; VI.35; VII.18.1; X.89.7, 103.6 f., etc. Indra is often said to liberate imprisoned cattle; in VI.28 he is said to take care of them, protecting them from being stolen, going astray, or other harm. This hymn also has the heading, "The Cattle and Indra".[2] We have no need to spend more time on this point, and can thus proceed to

2. The branding of the cattle. There appears to be only one mention of this custom in the whole of the RV:

índreṇa yujā́ níḥ sṛijanta vāgháto vrajáṁ gómantam aśvínam
sahásram me dádato ashṭakarṇyàḥ śrávo devéshu akrata

Allied with Indra the singers emptied the meadow of cattle and horses.
They who give me thousand ear-marked cows, have won praise among the gods. (RV X.62.7)

The custom of branding cattle is also mentioned in the later literature; *vide* Apte, *Social and Religious Life*, p. 114: "Another interesting feature of cattle-keeping is the making of marks on the cattle. Thus according to Gobhila, ..., he makes marks ... with a sword of udumbara wood."

The object here is to ensure that the cattle thrive and multiply. The same custom is mentioned in the Śāṅkhāyana-Gṛihya Sūtra.[3] This may be evidence of the relative importance of domestic animals. Apte has also pointed out that the most important source of income in Vedic times was cattle-keeping[4] and it is therefore not surprising that every reasonable step was taken to protect them.

[1] Frg. B 3, 4.

[2] A number of passages in the Yajur Veda express the connection between Indra and cattle. E.g. II.2.7.1: "He who wishes for cattle is to offer to Indra, for cattle belong to Indra."

[3] III.10.2: (He brands the animal) with (the words): "You are the world, blossoming a thousandfold; may you be given to Indra by use (?). You are untouched, unhurt, drink, food, protection ..." Despite the obscurity of the verse, it seems clear that the import is that the animal is dedicated to Indra. Nothing is said about the mark set upon the animal, though our thoughts are naturally led to Indra's *vajra* in this connection.

[4] *Op. cit.*, p. 103.

The practice of ear-marking seems here to have had a function other than simply denoting ownership; it acted like an amulet to protect the animal. It is only natural in such circumstances to turn for protection to a god whose particular interests were known to lie in this direction, viz. Indra. The mark of his club, *vajra*, on the animal's ear must have been a potent protection, for it was with the *vajra* he defeated the demons who held the cattle prisoner, and liberated them, thus the RV. That the *vajra* could protect is seen *inter alia* in ŚB I.7.1.20: "He then covers it over by a vessel, with the hollow part upwards and containing water, 'lest the evil spirits, the Rakshas, should touch it from above'; for water, indeed, is a *vajra*; hence he thus drives away from it the evil spirits, the Rakshas, with a *vajra* ..."[1]

I have not been able to find direct evidence in favour of Megasthenes' passage in Indian literature. But the construction I have sketched here seems to fit in remarkably well with the ancient tradition of Indra as the liberator and protector of cattle. This does not however mask the fact that our failure to produce evidence of the club in this context is a serious one. AV VI.141 in fact has evidence to the contrary. We read: "May Vāyu gather them, may Tvashtar stand fast for their protection, may Indra bless them, may Rudra guard their number. Go, take the copper knife and make a pair on their ears; the Aśvins have made the mark, may their offspring multiply." Whitney, in his commentary on this passage, states that the mark made was like the genitals (*strīpuṁsātmakaṁ cihnam* as the Indian commentary on *mithunám* says). The club (*vajra*) and phallus do however frequently correspond,[2] and Whitney's explanation is by no means excluding the vajra; on the contrary, it may well be one and the same picture, interpreted by one observer as a club and by another as a phallus.[3]

[1] The same idea seems to be expressed in the formula "untouched, unhurt ... protect". Does this not express the identical thought as "May Indra protect you"?

[2] See e.g. Gonda, *Aspects of Early Vishnuism*, pp. 32–55.

[3] Crooke, in *Religion and Folklore of Northern India*, p. 94, mentions that cattle have in modern times been branded with Śiva's *Triśūla* and Vishṇu's *Cakra*. This is of no help for our identification, since Megasthenes says that it was Heracles' *club* which was the brand mark used. This excludes both the *cakra*, a wheel, and the *triśūla*, a trident. A sort of change has taken place in the intervening time. It is hardly likely that *Śiva*'s *club* was exchanged for his *trident*; or that *Vishṇu*'s *club* for his *discus*, since the club has never been a more important emblem with these two gods than the trident and discus respectively. We conclude that the change must have to do with the *god*, whose emblem before the change was a club. The god who was favoured after the change did not have the club as emblem: Śiva and Vishṇu. This tends to exclude these two gods as Heracles. Dare we suggest that the fact of Heracles' club being branded upon cattle might reflect a situation which existed before the victory of Hinduism,

k. Heracles and his worshippers dressed in the skins of animals,[1] particularly the lion.[2]

We have said that this piece of information suggests Śiva; not Kṛishṇa, and—as far as we can see—not Indra either. When discussing Śiva we pointed out that Diodorus alone has anything to say about the lion skin; this means that the passage as such is suspect in the extreme, and may well not have originated with Megasthenes at all.

We have also drawn a distinction between the club as an "unnecessary" attribute and the dress as "necessary". Essentials obviously run the risk of being overlooked, and were we to find that Indra's clothing is never mentioned, this would not imply that he went unclothed. He may, then, have worn a lion-skin or the skin of some other animal without it ever being mentioned in the texts.

There are however two verses in the RV which may perhaps be taken as proof that Indra wore an animal skin—possibly even a lion-skin. We must however emphasize that this particular interpretation of these verses is by no means certain.

ādhréṇa cit tád v ékaṁ cakāra siṁhyàṁ cit pétvenā jaghāna

He has accomplished one deed through the weak; he has killed the lioness with the help of the buck. (RV VII.18.17)

mahīva kṛ́ttiḥ śaraṇā́ ta indra prá te sumnā́ no aśnavan

Let thy pleasure come to us, o Indra, as thou art covered by the great skin. (RV VIII.90.6)

When we read the first of these verses, telling us how Indra slew the lioness, we are reminded of our quotation from Rao, above, p. 73 n. 2: "Śiva slays tigers and lions and dresses in their skins." If the RV text really refers to Indra's having killed a lioness with a buck, it is by no means

---

i.e. before Śiva and Vishṇu came to power. The detail recorded by Crooke suggests that the change in religion took place *after* the time of Megasthenes.

Stein, in his book *On Alexander's Track to the Indus*, notes that the area covered by Alexander is now Muhammedan, and rich in archaeological evidence of the rule of Buddhism before the coming of Islam.

We may note, finally, that A. Christensen, *Smeden Kavāh og det gamle persiske rigsbanner*, p. 16, quotes an Iranian expression *gurz-i-gāvsār*, corresponding to Skr. *vajra go śiras*, "the club with the bull's head". The implications of this we cannot go into, but it is interesting to see the connection in Iran between the *vajra*, the club, and the bull. The Śibi lived near the Afghanistan border.

[1] Frg. B 3, 4.

[2] Frg. B 1.

out of the question that he celebrated his victory by draping himself in the lion-skin, like Heracles. Further, an illustration in Vogel's book, which is not for a certainty interpreted, represents a man fighting with a lion.[1] The picture has been taken to be a representation of the Greek Heracles. May it not be the case, in view of the RV verse we have quoted, that it is in fact "the Indian Heracles"—Indra—who is pictured?

The interpretation of the second of these RV verses is even more uncertain. It *can* mean, literally, "May thy goodwill come to us like a great protecting skin, o Indra." In other words, it is no more than a figure of speech, without direct reference to Indra's dress. The first mentioned translation resembles Geldner's interpretation: "Thou dost bear as it were a great protecting skin, o Indra. May thy grace come to us." Personally, I am inclined to reject Geldner's interpretation, though it would have been a useful support for my thesis; it seems to me that the skin is no more than a picture of Indra's grace. But is it possible that Megasthenes' picture was derived from both these verses? If such be the case, then it is understandable that he applied it to Indra, particularly since he would have sought, more or less unconsciously, for links with the Heracles of his own country.

Lassen's attempt to apply this piece of information to Kṛishṇa forced him to take into account an entirely pointless transfer from the Greek Heracles to Kṛishṇa.[2] But we have shown that it is possible to corroborate it in Indian sacred texts; and although we have interpreted these texts in a more dubious way, at no point have we had to do violence to the texts themselves.

The Atharva Veda makes express mention of disturbances caused in the forest by people dressed in animal skins and dancing like eunuchs, and says that such people are to be driven away.[3] Here we have a form of behaviour which is out of the ordinary run of things, and which is even anti-social. The identity of these dancers provides an interesting subject for speculation, but we cannot go into it here.

The following quotation from the Śatapatha Brāhmaṇa may be of greater relevance for our investigation of the identity of Heracles. In V.3.5.3 we read: "He spreads a tiger-skin in front of the Maitra-Varuṇa's hearth, with, 'Thou art Soma's beauty.' For because when Soma flowed through Indra he (Indra) thereupon became a tiger, therefore he is Soma's beauty ..."

We may also quote from *The History and Culture of the Indian People* I,

---

[1] *La sculpture de Mathurā*, fig. 47b., according to Vogel "Hercule étranglant le lion de Némée", according to Foucher Kṛishṇa.

[2] Cf. above, p. 78.

[3] AV VIII.6.11.

p. 410: "The hymn AV IV.8 also refers to the custom of treading on a tiger-skin at a coronation: 4. As a tiger on a tiger-skin stride unto the great quarters; let all the people and heavenly waters rich in milk desire you."

The material which we have assembled here shows that Indra can very well be combined with Megasthenes' Heracles on the matter of animal-skins —whether the animal in question be lion, tiger or some other.

l. Heracles was also renowned for his courage[1] and

m. his physical strength.[2]

n. He was deified after his death by the Indians for all the good he had done them.[3]

o. He was worshipped particularly by dwellers on the plains.[4]

The first two of these four points can be applied directly to Indra; this is common knowledge, and need scarcely be corroborated by means of textual evidence. We shall produce evidence nevertheless to show the great emphasis placed on Indra's strength and courage. Indeed, this emphasis is greater than expected. That his exploits are mentioned and described would have been sufficient, but it is explicitly stated that his strength is unsurpassed—an appropriate attribute of Megasthenes' Heracles. The Indian texts' description of Kr̥ishṇa, on the other hand, allows the exploits to speak for themselves. We begin with RV I.80.15:

nahí nú yád adhīmási índraṁ kó vīryā̀ paráḥ
tásmin nr̥imṇám utá krátuṁ devā́ ójāṅsi sáṁ dadhur
árcann ánu svarā́jyam

For as far as we know Indra has no superior in strength. In him the gods have combined courage, good sense and strength, praising his sovereignty. (RV I.80.15)

tvám indrābhibhū́r asi víśvā jātā́ny ójasā sá víśvā bhúva ā́bhavaḥ

Thou, Indra, art superior in strength to all beings. Thou didst reach to all worlds. (RV X.153.5)

We have quoted only one verse from the latter hymn, although the entire hymn has to do with the same subject, Indra's infinite strength. He is born of strength, of incomparable strength; in strength has he raised up the heavens—and so on. Nothing similar is ever said about either Śiva or Kr̥ishṇa; but it is Indra's one great attribute, which he seems to have shared with Megasthenes' Heracles.

1 Frg. B 1, 5, 6.
2 Frg. B 1, 7, 8.
3 Frg. B 1.
4 Frg. B 2, 9.

Nor does the RV provide the last mention of Indra's strength; the theme is carried on and developed in the AV and in the Brāhmaṇas. We quote a number of passages from the Śatapatha Brāhmaṇa:

i. I.2.4.6

"He murmurs: 'Thou art Indra's right arm!' for Indra's right arm no doubt is the most powerful one ..."

ii. IV.3.3.17–18

"And again, why he draws the Māhendra cup. Before the slaughter of Vṛitra, he was indeed Indra; but when he had slain Vṛitra, he became the Great Indra, even as one who has conquered all countries around, becomes a Great King: therefore he draws the Māhendra cup. And, moreover, he forsooth makes him great for the slaughter of Vṛitra: therefore also he draws the Māhendra cup. He draws it in the Śukra vessel, for bright and great indeed is he (the sun) that burns yonder: therefore he draws it in the Śukra vessel.

He thus draws it from that, with, 'Great is Indra and hero-like, gladdening the people, of double stature and unimpaired in power. For our sake he waxed strong for heroic deed,—great and broad was he, and well-shapen by the shapers ..."

iii. IV.6.4.6

"O Viśvakarman, with strengthening libation madest thou Indra an invincible champion: to him did the people bow down of old, because he, the mighty, is worthy of adoration."

iv. IV.6.6.4

"They said to Indra, 'Verily, thou art the strongest of us ...'"

And according to the Aitareya Brāhmaṇa VIII.4.12 the gods, led by Prajāpati, said to one another: "This is the strongest and most courageous of all the gods ..."

These quotations should suffice. It may be possible to produce similar expressions taken from the later literature, though there is much truth in Buschardt's saying that in the later literature Indra is little more than an adventurer.[1] Such late stories about him have no contact with the cultus, as a result of which an important aspect of his enormous strength disappears—the fact that he is never addressed directly. Be that as it may, the fact remains that express mention is made in the texts of Indra's strength and courage, thus providing a further vital resemblance between Heracles and Indra.

Indra's strength enabled him to become a great benefactor of the Indians.

---

[1] *Vṛitra*, p. 20 f.

This can of course be said equally well of a mortal man as of a god, and when Megasthenes explains that Heracles was deified after his death, the reader tends to interpret this as proof of Megasthenes' own euhemerism—of which there is, naturally enough, no evidence in the texts. Our first observation must be that it is nowhere stated that Indra was first a man, and was then posthumously given divine attributes. But this does not exhaust the subject. Renou, in his study of Vṛitra, has come to the conclusion that Indra was originally a hero, and that he was later elevated to the pantheon by being combined with the Indo-Iranian god Vṛitrahan,[1] on account of his work as a ḍemon-slayer. Renou's conclusions have not gone unopposed; it is nevertheless interesting that modern scientific scholarship has made exactly the same assertions about Indra as Megasthenes put forward about his Heracles! If we examine the process of Renou's argument more closely, we find that these views are *not* based on the primary thesis of his work. His conclusions about Indra having originally been a hero, and his later deification, are entirely independent of this thesis. We may summarize Renou's argument as follows:

Indra is a hero, primarily on account of his name, which Renou explains as meaning "the masculine principle *par excellence*"; with it are combined the epithets *indriyá-*, *nárya-* and *mánusha-*. The descriptions of his birth and his appearance depict a man, as do certain of his characteristics: his appetite, his drunkenness, etc. "One also recalls Heracles at Admete's banquet." His physical strength qualifies him to be king over men; his conquest of Vṛitra to be king over the gods. But the gods are unwilling to recognize his claims, and he has to use force to gain his rightful place. Renou, in a footnote, complements this argument by pointing out that his mother was to all appearance a human mother, and that the waters he liberated were real earthly waters—the great rivers. He concludes that these facts witness against Indra's divine origin.

Has Renou proved his case? The question is far from simple. We might add one more fact to those advanced by Renou: that Indra, unlike the rest of the pantheon, is consistently called "friend" (*sakhi*).[2] This might be taken to indicate a closer degree of relationship between Indra and mankind than that usual between gods and men. In point of fact, practically every element in the Indra myths can be shown to be Indo-Iranian, if not Indo-European. Benveniste and Renou have evidently overlooked the fact that Bréal had earlier established a tentative connection between Indra and

[1] *Vṛitra et Vṛthragna*, pp. 189–192.

[2] I thank Professor Widengren for drawing my attention to this point.

Heracles, and had shown that Vṛitra is to be found in Greek mythology under the name of Ὄρθρος, which deprives the absence of Vṛitra from Iranian mythology of much of its significance.[1] If the myth is as ancient as this would appear to indicate, then we should require indisputable evidence before depriving Indra of his divinity. Or are we to accept Heracles' character as a hero as evidence that Indra must also have been a hero at some time, the inference being that the original Indo-European religion had both gods and heroes?[2] We cannot in this context attempt to answer these questions, which have arisen as a result of our exclusive preoccupation with the Greek religion as comparative material. If we turn for a moment to the Scandinavian Tor, whose resemblance to Indra cannot be called in question, we find once more that we are dealing with a god having all the characteristics which motivated Renou's conclusion that Indra was originally mortal. Although Renou's hypothesis is an attractive one, this brief comparison with Tor is sufficient to demonstrate its inadequacy.

We are thus reluctantly compelled to reject Renou's thesis, which would have been of such value in the present context; but that does not mean to say that we are not in a position to be able to make use of his argument. If

---

[1] *Hercule et Cacus*, p. 95, quoted by Lassen, in *Ind. Alt.-k.* I, p. 940. There is an etymological connection between the two; the factual connection, on the other hand, is more doubtful.

[2] Indra's humanity has been stressed by a number of scholars. Barnett, *Hindu Gods and Heroes*, is quoted with approval by Charpentier, Art. *Indra* in *Le Monde Oriental*, 1931, Vol. XXV, pp. 1–28, partic. pp. 18 f. See also the work of Bréal and Bhupendra Nath Datta. Bréal, in his *Hercule et Cacus*, has made a number of interesting comparisons. E.g. the words Hercules and Heracles have nothing in common etymologically (p. 48). Hercules is a shepherd (p. 55). The name Hercules is an epithet of Jupiter, who is also called Sancus and Recaranus (p. 57). Heracles is a parallel on the earthly level to Zeus on the divine level (p. 64). The same pair, a god and a corresponding hero, is to be found in India, in Dyaus and Indra (p. 92). This means that Bréal was the first to couple Heracles and Indra. Bhupendra Nath Datta writes in *Vedic Funeral Customs and Indus Valley Culture*, p. 11: "... when a set of thinkers began to be sceptics about their (the Vedic hymns') meanings. Thus in the idea advanced by these sceptics that the Vedic gods were deified kings or mighty men, an important ethnological information seems to be hidden. Again, the Mahābhārata corroborates this idea. It says, "Bhaga, Amśa ... Indra, and Vishṇu—these twelve suns (Āditya) are the sons of Mahātmā Kāśyapa (a Rishi) ... Formerly, they were reputed to be the Devas and Pitṛis ... (Śāntiparvan 208). Thus, the Mahābhārata conceives the gods as deified men." P. 12: "Dr. Girinrasekhar Basu says, 'As different gods appear on this earth as men, likewise the best of men in the reverse process are transformed into gods ... *Indra was at first a man, then he became a god,* and later became the Sun. The exploits of Indra as a man, a god and the Sun have been described in the Veda ... Kṛishṇa was a man, the Nārāyaṇa and the Sun ...'"

a modern scholar is able to draw such conclusions from the Indian texts, what is there to prevent an ancient Greek, viewing them as an outsider, from having drawn precisely the same conclusions from the same material? There is a distinct element in the texts which seems to indicate that Indra was not 100 % divine. We conclude, therefore, that this particular piece of information from Megasthenes compels us to identify Heracles as Indra and no other. Śiva is quite out of the question. So is Kŗishņa, although as Garbe pointed out, the occurrence of Euhemerism in connection with Kŗishņa is a fact. But we are not dealing with plain facts here; nor was Megasthenes, for whom they were presumably largely unknown. We are concerned with the Indians' views, as demonstrated in the texts. And the Indians' view of Kŗishņa was anything but euhemeristic; Kŗishņa for them was a *real* god, who became man for the salvation of the world. The texts tell us that he was worshipped during his life on earth, and not only after his death.

Since the final point in this group—Heracles' worship on the plains—coincides with what we have already said about Mathurā and the Śūrasena, we have no need to go over it again. This therefore completes our examination of Megasthenes' "Heracles" passages.

SUMMARY OF RESULTS AND CONCLUSIONS

As there was one point—the animal-skins—in support of the identification of Heracles with Śiva, and one point—Heracles' many wives and sons—in support of the identification of Heracles with Kṛishṇa, we have found no less than seventeen which fit Indra[1]; six additional points[2] may be connected with Indra, though with some uncertainty: twenty-three points in all.

We were able to produce a large number of objections against the identification of Heracles with Śiva and with Kṛishṇa respectively; only one of the items of information was not directly applicable to Indra, on a basis of the Indian texts: his royal descendants[3]. Of the other passages, one—dealing with his founding of towns[4]—may not have originated with Megasthenes at all, and may be based upon a misunderstanding. But even this can be understood on a basis of the general view of the kingship and of Indra. Other passages have no direct relevance to our quest for identification, though they may to some extent be understood from the Indra traditions.

In the course of our examination we have from time to time been compelled by the nature of the material to use a certain amount of speculation. In this present summary we have naturally included such features among the more uncertain points, where they have been reckoned on the positive side of the balance.

Our brief investigation of the proposed identification of Heracles with Śiva and Kṛishṇa respectively brought us to the conclusion that what is told of Heracles is not told of Śiva or Kṛishṇa, while what is told of Śiva or Kṛishṇa is not told of Heracles. On the subject of Indra, our account cannot be held to be complete before we have undertaken a summary of the evidence in the opposite direction, beginning with what is told of Indra, and seeing whether or not this is related of Heracles.

---

[1] Viz. 1a, b, f, g, h. i, k, 2a, e, i, j, 3a, b, h, i, l, m, n, o. It is difficult to reckon the number of points exactly, since 2e, j, and 3o are identical; in other cases one point can have two or more parts: e.g. 1a, 2a, etc.

[2] Viz. 1c, d, e, 2f, 3d, k.

[3] Point 1l.

[4] Point 3e.

A description of the character and attributes of Indra might be expected to contain the following features:

1. The myth of Vṛitra.
2. The *vajra*.
3. The rivers which he liberated.
4. These are called cows; Indra is therefore called Govid too, a link with cattle being thereby established.
5. Indra's closest friends were the kings (or tribes) Yadu and Turvaśa.
6. His main activity had to do with the Indus.
7. He loved to drink *soma*.
8. He was peculiarly attracted to women, not least to other men's wives.
9. He was strong: a mighty warrior, a king and the leader of an army.

We find that every detail of importance which is attributed to Indra in the RV and other Indian texts is to be found in Megasthenes, with the sole exception of his addiction to *soma*. This is all the more remarkable, since Dionysos is described as having introduced the use of wine, and the drinking of wine formed part of his cult. There seems to be no reasonable explanation of why this element, so essential to Indra, should be missing here.[1]

I had long been puzzled by the rock Aornos. At the same time, I was surprised that Megasthenes had never mentioned the myth of Vṛitra, which forms such a vital part of the Indra complex. However, a comparison of the two proved most profitable, and it became clear that virtually everything told about Heracles is also told about Indra, and the essential elements of the Indra narrative are also linked with the name of Heracles.

What conclusions may be drawn from this? *First*, that Indra was the great god as late as in Megasthenes' day; this has not hitherto been capable

---

[1] May the answer perhaps lie in the actual word *soma*—Gk. σῶμα, which means 'body, corpse'? Is it possible that the animal-skins mentioned by Megasthenes are due to a misunderstanding of the Sanskrit word *soma*? The idea seems far-fetched, but we must account for the animal-skins, as well as explain the absence of Indra's favourite drink. And if a Greek-speaking Indian were to use the Indian word *soma*, a misunderstanding might well arise; this possibility is increased by the fact that the drink was obsolete by this time, and that the Śibi wore animal-skins, and were seen to do so. Further, in the Indian texts and the Greek description of Heracles the club is associated with *soma* and with animal-skins. Indra was drunk with *soma* when he killed Vṛitra with the *vajra*. In RV I.32.2, Tvashṭar is said to have made the *vajra* for him, and in the following verse, that he chose *soma* like a bull. Just as Megasthenes' description of Heracles is characterized by the closely-associated club and animal-skins, so Indra is characterized by the closely-associated *vajra* and *soma*. This is however only a suggestion; it gives rise to considerable difficulties.

of proof, but archaeological and other evidence point in the same direction.[1] *Secondly*, it is not possible to quote Megasthenes as a witness to the extreme antiquity of Kṛishṇa as a great god, or even as a minor god. *Thirdly*, the problem of the relation between Christianity and Krishnaism is now placed on a new footing, since the only witness of the Kṛishṇa cult as early as 300 before Christ is now removed. *Fourthly*, the question of Kṛishṇa as an *avatar* of Vishṇu must be reconsidered. There is no doubt that the *avatar* concept as such is of great antiquity. But if we compare Vishṇu's many *avatars*, we find that Kṛishṇa is the only one who was born, who lived through all the ages of men, and then died. Vishṇu's *avatars* are normally regarded as being unrepeatable, coming to pass for a definite and limited purpose. If Kṛishṇa be regarded as the one great exception, and if no evidence of his existence as an *avatar* of Vishṇu can be produced dating from the period before the birth of Christ, then the question once more forces itself upon us with undiminished force: May not Kṛishṇa, despite everything that has been said on the subject, be a result of Christian influence?

It is no part of our intention to provide an answer to this question; we wish only to take the necessary step of asking the question once more. It is necessary because all the witnesses which have been produced in order to corroborate the pre-Christian existence of the Kṛishṇa cult have proved to be unreliable in the extreme. These are: 1. Pāṇini; ii. Megasthenes; iii. Patañjali; iv. Two inscriptions; and v. Buddhist texts.

i. *Pāṇini's Vāsudeva Sūtra*. We have discussed this *sūtra* above, and have found that it was talking about something entirely other than Kṛishṇa-bhakti.[2]

ii. *Megasthenes* was not referring to Kṛishṇa, but to Indra, and the cult of Kṛishṇa was in opposition to that of Indra.

iii. *Patañjali* has not been dealt with in the course of this investigation, and I do not regard myself as qualified to express a definite opinion as to his worth as a witness. To judge from the work of such authors as Garbe and Bhāṇḍārkar, however, Patañjali's *Mahābhāshya* seems to provide no clear evidence of Kṛishṇa's divinity.

iv. *Two inscriptions*, dating from ca. 150 B.C. and ca. 100 B.C. respectively, are stated by Ramaprasad Chanda in *Archaeology and Vaishnava Tradition* to be Vaishnava memorials. The first is said to be the oldest

---

[1] Cf. Rao, *Elements of Hindu Iconography* II.2, p. 517: "In spite of Kṛishṇa's protest against the worship of Indra, it was still existing in the 7th to the 10th centuries of the Christian era." Cf. above, p. 91 n. 2.

[2] Introduction, pp. 23–26.

Vaishnava memorial which can be dated. It reads: "This Garuḍa column (*Garuḍadhvaje*) of Vāsudeva the god of gods (*devadeva*) was erected here by Heliodorus, a Bhāgavata, the son of Dion, and an inhabitant of Taxila, who came as Greek ambassador from Mahārāja Antialkidas to king Kāsiputra Bhāgabhadra." The other reads: "This Garuḍa column of the excellent temple of the Bhagavat was erected by Gautamī-putra, ... a Bhāgavata, in the twelfth year after the installation of Mahārāja Bhāgavata."

These inscriptions are generally interpreted as evidences of Vishṇu-Kṛishṇa *bhakti*, because of the occurrence of the words Vāsudeva and Bhāgavata-Bhagavān. But Heliodorus is said to have been from Taxila, a district where at this time—the middle of the second century B.C.—Buddhism was the dominant religion. And it is common knowledge that the Buddha is called "Bhagavān", although his followers are not normally spoken of as "Bhāgavata". But is such a practice entirely impossible? We ask this question because, although there are at this time many traces of Buddhism in Taxila, there is no trace of the Vishṇu-Kṛishṇa cult.[1] Vāsudeva, as we pointed out in our discussion of the Pāṇini *sūtra*, need not refer to Vishṇu-Kṛishṇa.

I do not wish by this to suggest that the accepted interpretation is wrong; only that it is open to doubt. It is built i. on an interpretation of the word Vāsudeva for which there is no evidence in the older texts, ii. on a similar interpretation of the word Bhāgavata, and iii. on the assumption that there existed a cult of Vishṇu-Kṛishṇa, for which there is no evidence, either textual or archaeological. As against these difficulties we have to take these factors into consideration: i. the Buddha is called Bhagavān, of which the grammatical derivation is Bhāgavata; ii. the dominant religion in Taxila during the centuries around the beginning of the Christian era was Buddhism, and Heliodorus might very well be supposed to be a Buddhist; iii. the second pillar was erected by Gautamī-putra, a name which immediately suggests the Buddha; iv. Vāsudeva, like *devadeva*, calls to mind Indra, who occupied a prominent position in Buddhism.

For these reasons, it is impossible to accept this as definitive evidence for the existence of a Vishṇu-Kṛishṇa cult. With these words I only have wanted to show the necessity of a radical investigation of these inscriptions and their bearing, before important conclusions are drawn from them.

5. *Buddhist texts* have been used by Sénart in his excellent book *Essai sur la légende du Buddha* to show how the Kṛishṇa cult must be implied in

[1] Cf. Tarn, *The Greeks in Bactria and India*, p. 391–393. As to the discussion on "a quotation" from Bh. G., p. 380 f., I do not feel competent to express any opinion. I only ask: "Is it considerably different from Aśoka's Edicts?"

the rise of the Buddha legend. Nowadays, however, it can no longer be accepted as proof, since it works on the basis of a view which has been rejected by scholars. The following quotations and notes will perhaps demonstrate this:

"This is one of the few occasions on which we find a mention of Kṛishṇa, the divine hero, in a Buddhist document. At that moment, when Siddhārtha is lost in meditation, five *rishis* pass through the air over the trees which are sheltering him. Suddenly they are halted by a mysterious power; they soon recognize the radiance spread around by the young prince; surprised, they ask: 'Who is that person sitting there?' 'Is it Vaiśrāvaṇa, lord of riches? Or is it Māra, the lord of pleasures, the ruler of the snakes? Or Indra, the thunderbolt-wielder? Or Rudra, the prince of Kumbhāṇḍa? Or Kṛishṇa with his irresistible strength? Candra, son of the gods? Or Sūrya with his thousand rays?' (Lal. Vist. 148.14 f.)"[1]

On p. 303 we read that "... a number of characteristics show that this episode belonged first to the legend of Kṛishṇa, before being incorporated into the life of Śākya: it is infinitely better motivated in the former than in the latter; it is there explained as one of the god's victories over the *asura* of many forms; on the other hand the situation of the two brothers demands that they fight and that each takes his due share of the spoils; transferred to the Buddhist version and reflected in the threefold action of Devadatta, Nanda and Siddhārta, this has no longer any *raison d'être*; on the contrary, the legend has sought a new trace of enmity which tradition claims to have existed between Devadatta and Śākyamuni ... Such affinities as these explain Śākya's grudge against their family's honoured descendant; or, better expressed, their faithless ignorance of his superiority. These considerations, which are clearly opposed to the overall content of the narrative, gain unexpected significance; they call to mind the special conditions under which Kṛishṇa grew up. Forgotten and hidden among the shepherds, a stranger to the tribe of Yadu, he is compelled to show his suspect powers. He has to draw the supernatural bow, in order to slay the mad elephant and to conquer the warriors sent against him by his own relative Kaṁsa, in an outburst of treachery soon to be punished."

And on p. 307: "On the other hand it is quite certain that if the origins of the two legends are to be compared and connected, it is the Kṛishṇa legend which proves to be the elder. Not only that the presence of the 'shepherdesses' is much better motivated in his story than in Śākyamuni's; these names, and even these traditions, have arisen out of naturalistic sources. They could never have been connected with the name of a perso-

[1] *Op. cit.*, p. 298.

nality like that of the Buddha, who is not at all mythological, other than through a secondary connection of elements already fully accepted as belonging together."

To this we need add little more than that Sénart points, on pp. 314 f., 318, etc., to closely related myths from the RV dealing with Indra. Why, then, did he not consider the possibility that the original (Indian) myth was applied to Indra, from whom it was transferred, with a number of variations to the Buddha and finally to Kṛishṇa? It is only natural—as well as being generally recognized—that Indra was the dominant personality in the mythological background of Buddhist thought. And on the other side, there is no doubt that Buddhism also exercised influence on Hinduism. In these circumstances it is not really necessary to assume *Krishnaism* to have been the source of elements which can be demonstrated to have existed in the RV in connection with Indra.

A further question which may be directed to Sénart is as follows: In what way is Kṛishṇa more mythological than the Buddha? The two share the same situation: a historical figure (as far as we can ascertain) with whom have subsequently been connected complete cycles of myth and isolated mythological motives respectively. The mere fact that a Buddhist text, Lal. Vist., mentions the name of Kṛishṇa tells us nothing about the divinity of Kṛishṇa in the Buddha's day. Theoretically the five *rishis* could equally well have said Christ, or Moses, or Muhammed, if the author of Lal. Vist. had been acquainted with their names. He did not ask whether the personalities actually mentioned lived before or after the Buddha—which we may perhaps be permitted to point out, since the historical perspective is conspicuous by its absence. We cannot undertake in this context a thoroughgoing criticism of Sénart's work; this would be altogether beyond the bounds of this study. Our brief comments are intended only to be a means of asking whether in fact Sénart has provided the only possible solution of an intricate problem. He seems not to have done so, when we examine some of his arguments for Kṛishṇa worship in pre-Buddhist times, but it must not be thought that we have given a definitive answer to the problem, either. But it is at least worthy of reconsideration in the light of the views we have put forward.

This brings us to another question, which is also deserving of closer examination, viz. the relation between Indra and Kṛishṇa. We may perhaps provide a number of points of contact, which seem to be symptomatic of Kṛishṇa's development from Indra:

1. Both were worshipped in Mathurā (according to our results and the Govardhana episode).

2. Both bore the epithet Gopati.

3. Both bore the epithet Govinda·Govid.[1]

4. Kṛishṇa is a herdsman; Indra liberates cattle. (Cf. Bréal, *Hercule et Cacus*, p. 85: "Indra est le berger d'un troupeau de vaches célestes de couleur éclatante.")

5. In the epic the friend of Kṛishṇa is called Arjuna, as is Indra himself in the Rigveda and other texts.

6. Kṛishṇa is called Vāsudeva; Indra Vāsava. Indra is *de facto* Vasudeva, i.e. god-king of Vasu.

7. The horses of Indra are called Hari as is Kṛishṇa, too. Indra is therefore known as Harivān: the one with the yellow horses.

8. Kṛishṇa is called Bhagavān; Indra *is* Bhagavān—"the one who controls and apportions good fortune"; Indra is called Maghavān.

9. Indra carries his *vajra*, which is a club; Kṛishṇa also carries a club, *gadā*.

10. Both have a peculiar relationship to the snakes: Indra fights the snake Vṛitra-Ahi; Kṛishṇa the snake Kāliya-Nāga.

11. Later, both bring about a reconciliation with the snakes.

12. Kṛishṇa had a number of lawful wives, apart from his many herdmaidens; Indra had an extensive and promiscuous love-life.

Despite the undoubted attractions of continuing here and now, this meditation on the subject of the undoubted correspondences between the two, we shall content ourselves with only one more point:

13. The decisive difference between Indra and Vishṇu is that Indra is active, while Vishṇu remains passive. Nevertheless Indra would be utterly lost without Vishṇu. We observe in the Mbh that Kṛishṇa fulfils the same auxiliary function for the five Pāṇḍava brothers, and Arjuna in particular, who, without Kṛishṇa, would be quite helpless. But in the Purāṇas it is Kṛishṇa who is active; it is Kṛishṇa who has become a hero in precisely the same sense as Indra has been hitherto. The passive Vishṇu has disappeared, and one is led to wonder whether Kṛishṇa may not be a continuation of the Vedic Indra prototype. Should this be the case, then the way would seem to go *via* Vāsudeva, who can be taken in Pāṇini and other older writers to be a form of either Indra or Kṛishṇa.[2] This is another of the

---

[1] Bhandarkar, *Vaishnavism, Śaivism* ..., p. 35, considers Govinda to have originally been Govid: the Indra epithet which was given Kṛishṇa when he became identical with Indra. See also Gonda, *Aspects*, pp. 107, 109, for the relationship between Indra and Kṛishṇa.

[2] This idea seems to be supported by this passage from Eliot's *Hinduism and Buddhism* II, p. 194: "Kṛishṇa belonged to Sāttvata and it is probable that *his name*

questions which must be asked when the basic revision of our ideas on the origins of Krishnaism is finally undertaken. It is of course quite conceivable that Kṛishṇa may be an ancient god; we cannot base our ideas on arguments *e silentio.* But the more numerous the sources of our knowledge of Indian religion, the more remarkable is their persistent silence on the subject. There is no word in Buddhist, Jainist or Brahmanic texts, no trace in archaeology, no hint in Manu which can be taken without more ado to refer to the hero-god Kṛishṇa.

Another subject requiring detailed examination is that of Kṛishṇa's relation to Vishṇu. If Kṛishṇa cannot be shown to have existed before the birth of Christ, then he can hardly be the cause of the growth of popular reverence for Vishṇu. On the other hand it is clear that Vishṇu underwent, shall we say, a development from relative unimportance to a position of dominance. The different aspects of Vishṇu have been studied by Gonda, in his *Aspects of Early Vishnuism* which we have already quoted on a number of occasions, and by M. S. Gladstone in a brief work entitled *Vishṇu in the Rig Veda and after until the Epic Period.* The latter work systematically examines text after text, in chronological order, and comes to the remarkable result that there is no point of contact between the various portrayals of Vishṇu in the different writings.[1] A new consideration of this same

---

Vāsudeva was not originally a patronymic but *the name of a deity worshipped by it.* The hero Kṛishṇa was identified with this god and subsequently when the Brahmans wished to bring this powerful sect within the pale of orthodoxy both were identified with Vishṇu." We have no reason at present to follow this thought further. What we have already said is sufficient to show that this is a reasonable assumption: Indra is the god who ought by rights to be called Vasudeva—Vāsudeva; Indra was worshipped in Kṛishṇa's country by his people: *vide* the Govardhana episode etc.

[1] This work is not printed; we may therefore summarize: "We have seen several Vishṇus so different that they have scarcely anything in common: let us consider what connection there is between them.—First there is the Vishṇu of the Rigveda: remote ... he is a creative spirit, a kindly spirit, a redeeming spirit ... He is always 'the friend': of Indra, of the Maruts, of mankind ... But his remoteness, his mystery, is held in reverence always.—Secondly there is the Vishṇu of the Brāhmaṇa period. All the characteristics of the former Vishṇu ... beauty of form, relationship with humanity ..., have vanished: but the essential Mystery remains and has increased tremendously. It is now interwoven with the great mystery of the Sacrifice and the second mystery has exceeded the first ... If this be so, we find here the trace of Vishṇu, the Kinsman, the Friend ...—Thirdly there is the chaotic, kaleidoscopic Vishṇu of the Mahābhārata, side by side with the elegant, theatrical Vishṇu of the Rāmāyaṇa. In the Mahābhārata, one takes one's choice of a wilderness of Vishṇu's among which to speculate. Vishṇu the Creator, with his lotus and his demons: Vishṇu the Vedantic *sac-cid-ananda*: Vishṇu the incarnate friend of the Pāṇḍavas, warlike and unscrupulous: the theistic Vishṇu of the Gītā, the immanent Vishṇu, the pantheistic Vishṇu." Note that the authoress has on

material, concentrating on points of contact with the later figure of Kṛishṇa might however open a new perspective. It would be of particular interest to attempt to incorporate this enigmatical figure into its Indo-European, and not only its Indo-Iranian, context.[1] Just as Indra was assisted by Vishṇu, Heracles was helped by Jolaos and Tor by Loke. But can the parallel be extended any further? Have these "assistants" anything in common? Such questions lie outside the bounds of our investigation, and require the expenditure of a great deal of time and trouble; we leave them, therefore, with a bare mention.

The result of our work has thus been to pose a number of problems, some new, some old, which must be examined in detail. Two matters more:

1. If our proposed identification of Heracles and Indra be accepted, it follows that we must to some extent use Megasthenes as a foreign witness to living ideas of which Indian literature bears little or no trace. This is a bold concept. But we must allow that there may have been myths, historical legends, and the like, which were never incorporated into Indian literature, and which have happened to be preserved for posterity through the work of a Greek. For example, the Aornos episode in Megasthenes' version; or the legend of the act of incest; or the whole story of Heracles' daughter Pandaiē and the gifts given her—soldiers, elephants, horses, jewels. This may well have been common currency in Indian tradition, though we are condemned to seek in vain for traces of it in the written sources.

2. Hesychius mentions the name of Δορσάνης as being the Indian Heracles. The question of how this is to be interpreted has been taken up by Sylvain Lévi in *Journal Asiatique* IX, 9, p. 37; by Lüders in *KZ* 1905 (= 38), pp. 433 f., and by L. H. Gray and M. Schuyler in *AJPh* XXII, pp. 195 ff. In an attempt to couple this name with Kṛishṇa, it has been assumed that an error of transcription has taken place—the original word being κορσάνης; Charpentier is the only one who has retained the form as given, coupling

---

p. 49 strongly emphasized the spiritual nature of Vishṇu as a necessary complement to the physical strength of Indra. Some few pages earlier she wrote of Vishṇu: "He is purely spiritual. He represents Life and Liberty and Eternity. He is in fact the Holy Ghost of the Rigveda, mysterious, inspiring, aiding, life-giving. He is the complement of Indra, the god of battles, the representative of physical strength. It is Indra who gives practical expression to Vishṇu, the Spirit. It is Vishṇu who is made active by and for the sake of Indra."

[1] Dumézil, in *Vishṇu et les Marút à travers la Réforme zoroastrienne*, p. 11 f., *Journal Asiatique*, 1953, has combined Vishṇu with Rashṇu in Iran. He has also attempted, in his book *Loki*, to demonstrate the connection between the Nordic Loke and a trickster belonging to the Ossetes, a North Iranian people. This need not exclude the possibility of the combination we have proposed.

it with Kṛishṇa's epithet Daśārha. He points out (*KZ* 45, p. 91) that the word in Hesychius comes between δόρχελοι and δοτάδης; this indicates the possibility of a further error: Δοσσάνης. It is evident that scholars have been prepared to maltreat the text in many ways in order to be able to couple the name with Kṛishṇa. But if Hesychius was referring to Indra—of which there is no direct proof—the epithet *dhṛishṇu*, "bold", suggests itself, particularly since in the RV the word refers to Indra on twenty-two occasions of the sixty on which it occurs. I must however point out that Hesychius is dated as late as 500 A.D., and that we have not the slightest indication as to where he obtained the word. It is not improbable that it may have been derived from some author of later date than Megasthenes, perhaps post-Christian, in which case Kṛishṇa may of course be the god indicated. But the suggestion here proposed seems a good deal less forced than many of those hitherto put forward. We cannot reach any definite conclusion, since we do not even know whether Hesychius' informant was referring to a known god.

As a final indication of the possibilities available, we may point out that the Koṭa of South India have a hero called Durčn, of whom Emeneau informs us that he is a particular favourite of the women, and the men contemplate killing him. In forms which resemble the accounts of the Purāṇas of Kṛishṇa, he liberates the people from a great bird.[1] "How great a man of heroic deeds just this man must be ... Therefore we from today must go on thinking, considering this man equal to a god."[2] The same story is told of Durčn as that related concerning King Śibi and Dharma and the falcon, though on this occasion the god is a hunter instead of a bird of prey.[3]

At this point we must call a halt to the enumeration of our conclusions. We shall complement what we have set down here with a number of interesting results when we have analysed and identified the god whom Megasthenes calls Dionysos.[4]

---

[1] Emeneau, *Kota Texts*, p. 165 f.

[2] *Op. cit.*, p. 167.

[3] *Op. cit.*, p. 171.

[4] For the discussion on the origin of the Kṛishṇa-cult and related matters see Gonda, *Die Religionen Indiens*, p. 237–244.

PART THREE

Dionysos in the Work of Megasthenes

SUMMARY OF RELEVANT PASSAGES

1. "*Historical*" *passages*

a. Dionysos was born from his father's thigh and nursed in a cave.

b. He came in prehistoric times from the west; or, to be more precise, 6451 years before Alexander the Great or 154 kings before Sandrakottos, i.e. Candragupta.

c. A divergent tradition suggests that he may have had his origin among the Indians.

d. His arrival seems to be described by Megasthenes as being in the company of a great army, including women. With this he is said to have marched through the whole world and conquered not only all India but all Asia.

e. He either reigned over the whole of India for fifty-two years; or, again according to a variant account, as king he set one of his men, Spartemba, on the throne, and Spartemba reigned for fifty-two years, the kingdom passing on to his family in succession. The first version also described the monarchy as hereditary; when there was no son to succeed to the throne, then a king was to be chosen.

f. Dionysos may have left India again and attacked and captured Bactria. Be that as it may, Megasthenes describes Dionysos as dying at a great age.

2. "*Functional*" *passages: Dionysos as culture-hero*

I. *Dionysos' "social" contribution*

a. He cured the sick army by leading it up into the mountains.

b. He gave the Indians weapons (possibly also tools).

c. He built towns.

d. He passed laws and set up courts.

II. *Dionysos' "agricultural" contribution*

e. He passed on all manner of inventions.

f. He made the Indians into cultivators (they had previously lived on raw meat).

g. He introduced the custom of ploughing with oxen.

h. He gave the Indians the seeds of domestic plants.

i. He taught them to cultivate the soil and grow crops. Among the plants he introduced may be mentioned:

j. Ivy,

k. Laurel,

l. Myrtle,

m. Box-wood,

n. Fig,

o. All manner of fruits, which he taught the Indians to grow, gather and store, particularly

p. Grapes, which he taught them to plant, pick, press, and make into wine and drink.

q. He is therefore called "Lēnaios".

III. *Dionysos' "religious" contribution*

r. He founded a religious cult.

s. He was regarded as a god (even before his death).

t. He was worshipped by the inhabitants of the mountain areas. His cultus included, and Dionysos was regarded to be the originator of:

u. Dancing,

v. Processions,

w. Music played on the cymbals,

y. Kettledrums, and

z. Side-drums;

aa. Fine linen clothes, which were spotted,

bb. Bright, and

cc. Colourful;

dd. A girdle (or possibly turban),

ee. Long hair,

ff. A carefully combed beard;

gg. He is therefore also called "Katapōgōn";

hh. And perfumes (sweet-smelling oils).

3. "*Geographical*" *passages, etc.*

a. According to one tradition, Dionysos was three separate persons, who lived and did their good deeds at different times. The first of these "persons" is said to have been

b. Indus; the other two have been mentioned already, viz.

c. Lēnaios (see above, 2q.) and

d. Katapōgōn (see above, 2gg.).

e. When Dionysos' army was on the point of perishing from the plague which came in the hot weather, Dionysos saved them on a hill with three peaks:

f. Kondaskē,

g. Korasibiē and

h. Mēros.

i. One of the towns founded by Dionysos himself (cf. above, 2c.) was called Nysa.

j. The Oxydrakai were believed to be descended from Dionysos and his men.

k. A tree used by the Indians already before the coming of Dionysos was called "tala".

THE IDENTITY OF DIONYSOS IN EARLIER INTERPRETATIONS. MOTIVATIONS AND CRITICISM

1. The earliest identification of Dionysos which has come to my notice is that proposed by Cunningham in his *Coins of Ancient India*,[1] in which he identifies Dionysos with Sūryadeva, but without any motivation. The theory has however won no support; only Kennedy, in *J.R.A.S* (1907), p. 969 n. 2 mentions it in passing. Remarkably enough, he makes no attempt to refute the theory. though his own view differs radically from that held by Cunningham.

2. Another view of respectable antiquity is that expressed by Growse in his *Mathurā*.[2] Growse sees traces of the Holi Festival in Megasthenes' description of the Dionysos cult.[3] Note, however, that he makes no attempt

[1] Preface, pp. vii–viii.

[2] P. 94.

[3] Cf. Basu, *The Spring Festival of India*, p. 135: "A festival similar to the Holi also occurs in different parts of the european continent. Among the ancient Roman festivals, there were two which were held on the 15th and the 17th of March. *The former was celebrated with drinking, dancing, singing and vulgar speech*, while the latter with burnt offerings to the god Bacchus. The use of burnt offerings was said to have originated after the conquest of India and the East by Bacchus. (J.R.A.S. 1848 p. 105 ff.) This fragmentary account shows the latter festival at least to have been related to the Holi of Northern India, in which also fruits, corn, and cooked food are thrown into the fire or parched in the flames and *there is drinking, singing and the unrestricted use of vulgar language*." On pp. 128–133 Basu demonstrates the non-Aryan origin of the festival by pointing out that non-Hinduised tribes with mutual linguistic or cultural relations have festivals with approximately the same content. The tribes mentioned by name are the Kandh, Goṇḍ, and "hill-tribes of Assam", Oraon and Nāgas. The author says nothing about the racial, cultural and linguistic connections of these tribes. It seems that the common element is Muṇḍa, though the Oraon, Kandh and Gond tribes speak Dravidian languages and the Nāgas are of Mongolian race and speak a Tibeto-Burman language. Muṇḍa tribes also have spring festivals of a similar character. The Hindi names of these need not imply that they are taken over from Hinduism. One such festival is described by Roy in *The Savaras of Orissa*, p. 315: "The Savaras were a rude forest tribe and knew nothing of music, vocal or instrumental. The goddess told them to go to Śiva in Kailās who would supply them with musical instrument necessary for the occasion. The Savaras went up to Śiva in Kailās and requested him to supply a musical instrument for their dance. Śiva received them kindly and gave them

to go more deeply into the matter. He mentions only the cultus; he has nothing to say about the god, nor does he attempt to connect him with any member of the Indian pantheon. For that reason, since it is our object to find the Indian counterpart to the god whom Megasthenes calls Dionysos, we need pay no further attention to Growse's theory.

3. When Kennedy attempts to motivate his interpretation of Dionysos and Kṛishṇa, he does not, strangely enough, support his theory by referring to Megasthenes' description of Dionysos; he turns instead to archaeological and *kulturgeschichtliche* evidence which seems on the surface to be irrelevant. But since the theory has been launched, we must give it due consideration, particularly as certain general factors appear to weigh in its favour.

When we consider the figure of Vishṇu in the Rig Veda, we cannot but notice that this god is characterized by a general air of benevolence. He is the indispensable helper of Indra in the battle against evil for the benefit of men. This characteristic becomes more and more marked in the later literature. Vishṇu's *avatars* express precisely this: that the god comes down to earth in various incarnations in order to liberate men from real or threatened evil. This benevolent aspect of Vishṇu may well be associated with Dionysos' "heroic" quality, particularly since Kṛishṇa is the primary representative of Vishṇu's benevolence.

1. When we read that Dionysos is conceived of as three distinct persons, who lived and worked at different times, our thoughts are naturally drawn to Vishṇu and his *avatars* (cf. points 3a.–d. above).

2. The point drawing attention to the long hair of the worshippers of Dionysos may possibly be connected with two of the names of Kṛishṇa:

---

a Ghumura, which is an earthen jar open on one side and closed on the other with leather. Śiva said that it would serve the purposes of a stringed and a leather covered musical instrument. The Saurs in great joy came back to their forest homes and since then they have been worshipping Banadurga every year on Gamāpurrnimā day with *dance and song.*" P. 318: "*The dance is accompanied with beatings of Ghumura*, a kind of tomtom. There are at least three distinct varieties of the dance, viz. the peacock dance, the cock dance and the bear dance. It appears that the Saurs try to reproduce the amorous movements of these animals when they are courting their males. The males ... beat the Ghumura ...; women dancers form two groups ... *The song that swells with the dance is full of obscene allusions*, which are made palpable by gestures and postures. Young women on this occasion do not feel the least delicacy in singing obscene songs in the presence of their (p. 319) husbands and other male relations. *The dance does not begin before the entire party is tipsy with wine.*" It is not possible to say anything about the origins of this festival; the practices described are found practically all over India. J. J. Meyer, *Trilogie altindischer Mächte und Feste der Vegetation* (who refers constantly to Mannhardt, *Wald- und Feldkulte*), regards the context as Indo-European.

Keśava and Hṛishīkeśa, which mean "he of the long locks or the long-haired one" and "he of the upswept hair" respectively (cf. point 2ee. above).

3. Similarly the passage drawing attention to the girdle worn by the worshippers of Dionysos (point 2dd. above) may suggest Kṛishṇa's name Dāmodara, "he who has a band around his waist". This has been interpreted by scholars as one of many indications of the connection between Kṛishṇa and the life of the herdsman and shepherd.[1]

4. The story of Govardhana represents Kṛishṇa, like Dionysos, not only as the founder of a cult (point 2r. above), but

5. also as a man, who became an object of worship during his lifetime (point 2s. above).

6. There are certain less important characteristics shared by Dionysos and Kṛishṇa. Kṛishṇa died at the age of 125, and this corresponds to the statement that Dionysos died a very old man (point 1f. above).[2]

7. Dionysos built towns. So did Kṛishṇa–Dvārakā (point 2c. above).

8. We may complete the list of direct correspondences between Dionysos and Kṛishṇa by quoting a strange passage from Diodorus Siculus (frg. A 2): "Among Indians there is still shown today both the place where the god was born (ἐν ᾧ συνέβη γενέσθαι τὸν θεόν) and the names of the towns called after him in the dialect of the people; and there have been preserved many other important proofs of his origin among the Indians (τῆς παρ' Ἰνδοῖς γενέσεως), which we have no time to write down." This passage fits Kṛishṇa very well indeed, at least as far as the place of his birth goes. But against it we have a piece of information quoted by the same Diodorus in the same work (frg. A 1): "They (the most learned among the Indians) say that Dionysos came from the west with a great army long ago ..." The description that follows leaves us in no doubt that we are dealing with a conqueror from outside the national boundaries. In the same way Megasthenes stresses, as we can see from a large number of fragments, that India was invaded by only two military leaders, Dionysos and Heracles. The passage about the birthplace of Dionysos evidently does not fit in with the rest of the account.

Here we have no less than eight points connecting Dionysos with Kṛishṇa. Nor have we had to do violence to any of the passages as they stand in order to identify Dionysos with the god in question. But do they amount to a definite and incontestable identification?

We may conveniently begin by examining the alleged resemblances. First of all, we must dismiss points 2. and 3. They have to do in the first

[1] See e.g. *The History and Culture of the Indian People* II, p. 434.

[2] Cf. above, under Heracles, Part II, p. 116.

place with the emblems of the worshippers of Dionysos, and in the second place with the names of Kṛishṇa, neither of which can be allowed as characteristics of either him, his equipment, or his worshippers or their equipment. Point 8. must also be rejected, since it has to do with a very weakly supported passage concerning Dionysos. It is true that it fits in with the only existing tradition concerning Kṛishṇa and his birthplace, but the most common tradition, of Dionysos as an immigrant from the west, cannot be reconciled with Kṛishṇa. Of the original eight points, there thus remain only five.

Point 7. is doubtful. Kṛishṇa built only one town: Dionysos is said to have built towns. The points of correspondence have been reduced drastically. Do the remainder suffice as an adequate basis of identification between Dionysos and Kṛishna?

The remaining four points must be accepted as important areas of agreement between the two gods in question: 1. Vishṇu's *avatars* and Dionysos' three persons—though the names Indus, Lēnaios and Katapōgōn do not appear to bear much resemblance to any of the *avatars* of Vishṇu; 4. and 5. Kṛishṇa as the founder of a cult, and Kṛishṇa teaching the shepherds in the Govardhana episode to worship himself agree fully with the description of Dionysos, that he "taught (them) to worship gods ... primarily himself ...";[1] 6. Both died at an advanced age.

When examining the possibility that it may be Kṛishṇa who is referred to under the name Dionysos, it is of course illegitimate to pick out at random certain points of agreement. We must see, on the one hand, whether the main mass of material dealing with Dionysos agrees with or can be connected with Kṛishṇa, and on the other, whether the basic essentials in the character of Kṛishṇa are included in the description of Dionysos.

Here we may limit ourselves to straightforward statement. The main mass of the Dionysos material does *not* in any way suggest Kṛishṇa. Dionysos is said to have been a pioneer in teaching the Indians to cultivate the ground; Kṛishṇa in the Govardhana episode, to have opposed the cultivators. Kṛishṇa is a shepherd and a friend of shepherds; this is never said of Dionysos. The whole of the complex of material dealing with Dionysos as a "culture-hero" is entirely disconnected from Vishṇu-Kṛishṇa, and it is just there we find most of the Dionysos material. The benevolence which we have advanced as a possible typological link between Vishṇu and Dionysos expressed itself in two entirely divergent ways: Kṛishṇa is a hero, it is true; but he is not a "culture-hero". Dionysos is said to have been the

---

[1] Arrian, frg. A 6.

one who *first* taught the Indians to build towns ("when the people of India still lived in villages ..."); Kṛishṇa, on the other hand, was born in a town Incidentally, it may appear a little strange that although the town Mathurā is mentioned in other contexts, Dionysos' birthplace is never mentioned by name! The cult of Dionysos was celebrated with the help of drums and cymbals, while Kṛishṇa's instrument was the flute. The worshippers of Dionysos lived in the mountains: the worshippers of Kṛishṇa on the plains around Mathurā.

If we reverse the comparison, and examine the most essential characteristics of Kṛishṇa, seeing whether they are incorporated into the description of Dionysos, we come to exactly the same result. We can state without doubt that it is not the Kṛishṇa of the Purāṇas who is described by Megasthenes as Dionysos. The herdsman, playing with the other herdsmen and maidens, is not so much as hinted at by Megasthenes. Nor is there any mention of Kṛishṇa's dealing with his uncle Kaṁsa; nor of his relation to the snakes; nor of his friendship with the Pāṇḍavas.

The result of this investigation must therefore be that everything that is essential in the description of Dionysos is unknown in connection with Kṛishṇa; and vice versa, that the essentials of the character of Kṛishṇa, as described in Indian literature, are missing from the description of Dionysos. This means that there can be no question of an identification between Dionysos and Kṛishṇa, despite the four admitted points of contact.

4. Stein[1] thinks that Dionysos is Manu on account of the three similarities: a. Both originated the royal dynasties, b. both were law-givers, c. both were "Kultur-bringer".

There are no other similarities, but above all: "Has Manu anywhere or ever had the position of a god, or even more of the only god or the most dominating god?" It seems to me that this question shows the impossibility of the proposed identification.[2]

5. This brings us to the identification which had won the almost unanimous approval of scholars: Dionysos is Śiva. This view is motivated largely by the Bacchic character of the cultus as described. But no detailed motivation has been presented, either by Lassen in *Zeitschrift* or *Indische Altertumskunde*, by Schwanbeck in his edition of Megasthenes, or by any other scholar. Nevertheless most scholars have been content to accept the identification, though with the exceptions of which we have given an account. Eliot, in his *Hinduism and Buddhism* II, pp. 137 f., has ventured

---

[1] *Megasthenes*, in Pauly-Wissowa, Bd 15.

[2] Cf. above, p. 118 ff.

the general suggestion that the identification of Heracles as Kṛishṇa and Dionysos as Śiva may not be entirely satisfactory, but he is prepared to accept it until such time as a better suggestion has been put forward.[1] He also explains why these identifications have taken place. There are two gods mentioned; two gods have played a particularly prominent part in the religion of India—Vishṇu and Śiva. If Heracles is Kṛishṇa, then Dionysos must be Śiva, and vice versa. However, this method of identification can hardly be called satisfactory, much less convincing.

The first thing to be said here is that the link between Dionysos and Śiva is not confined to Megasthenes and his narrative. Kirfel, in a suggestive article entitled *Śiva and Dionysos*,[2] has attempted to prove the existence of an original connection between the two. His point is not that Śiva has been borrowed from Greece, but that the Dravidians came to India from the Mediterranean area, bringing with them their god Śiva, who many years later was still being worshipped in their original area under the name of Dionysos.[3] We cannot here go into the complex question of the origin of the Dravidians, the Dravidian origin of Śiva and the anthropological situation of India. We shall return to the latter point in due course, and we shall see that this particular field of studies leaves a great deal of room for the exercise of the imagination. The first of these questions is dependent upon the last. At present there is too much uncertainty on the subject of Indian anthropology for there to be much hope of reaching reliable conclusions on the origin of the Dravidians and other matters connected with this topic. Our investigation may nevertheless perhaps contribute to the final solution of this problem. Before proceeding, I should however like to touch upon the meaning of the name Śiva, and upon a view which is tending to gain ground among Indologists.

The old view was that the name Śiva was a Sanskrit word meaning "mild, gracious"; this, the only conceivable view, was of course a euphemism, the god in question being anything but mild and gracious. In recent years there has been a tendency to interpret the word Śiva as being instead a Dravidian word, meaning "red". One reason why this view has become so widely accepted is that the name Rudra can also mean "red". How this is to

---

[1] The passage in question is quoted above, p. 90 n. 4.

[2] In *Zeitschrift für Ethnologie*, Band 78, Heft i, pp. 83–90

[3] Chowdhury, *Prototypes of Śiva in Western Asia*, stresses "certain common features in the religious beliefs of the ancient peoples of Anatolia, Mesopotamia and India which may serve to elucidate certain points in the history of the mythological beliefs associated with the worship of Śiva and the great Devī in the Vedic, Epic and Puranic age". See review in *Man in India* XII, 1942, p. 81 f.

be understood is another matter. Is Śiva a Dravidian translation of the Aryan Rudra, or is the Aryan Rudra a translation of the Dravidian Śiva? Kirfel accepts the latter alternative.[1]

It has been held to be probable, on the grounds of racial group characteristics, that the Dravidians stemmed originally from the Mediterranean area. They are said to belong mainly to the Mediterranean race, with certain other racial features.

After this bare mention we can content ourselves by saying that the statement that Dionysos came from the west fits in well with the idea that Śiva was the god of the Dravidians at the time of their migration from the lands of the Mediterranean—which must have taken place before the Aryan invasions began. There is thus an important factual agreement between what Megasthenes has to say about Dionysos and Heracles on the one side and the two waves of invasion—the supposed Dravidian invasion with their god Śiva and the later Aryan invasion with their chief god Indra—on the other. This construction however collapses when we recall the fact that although there are traditions about the Aryan invasion with Indra, there are no traditions—at least traditions having written support—concerning the Dravidians' invasion with Śiva. And Megasthenes refers expressly to Indian traditions (frg. A 1, the beginning).

Of the "historical" passages in Megasthenes on the subject of Dionysos, there is only one, that which speaks of his arrival from the west (1 b. above) which shows an agreement in factual matters between the two gods. But we cannot take this into account, since there is no Indian tradition in which an invasion by Śiva and his worshippers is as much as mentioned.

We may note in passing that Śiva is said to be the founder of the royal house of Pāṇḍya; we have dealt with this on a number of occasions.[2] But agreement with point 1 e. stops there, for Śiva was never king, and unlike Dionysos did not reign for fifty-two years.

We can summarize by saying that there is not one of the "historical" Dionysos passages which is immediately capable of being linked with Śiva.

Proceeding to the "functional" passages, and examining Dionysos' "social" contribution, we find that the list commences in a more promising vein. Dionysos is said to have cured a sick army; Rudra-Śiva is the very god who is approached for protection from sickness. He heals by chasing away fog and mist, and by cleansing the air. He swallowed the *kālakūṭa*

---

[1] See Konow in *Linguistic Survey* IV, p. 279, Kirfel, *op. cit.*, Chatterji in *H.C.I.P.* I, p. 162 etc.

[2] See above, pp. 108 and 138.

poison, which came from the churning of the ocean, thus saving the world, but colouring his own neck blue.

Dionysos is said to have given the Indians weapons; it is written of Śiva that he gave Arjuna the weapon *pāśupata*, that he set Indra's armour upon him before the battle with Vṛitra, and that he gave Rāma Jamadagnya the divine weapons.

These are resemblances which can be proved. But the reader must be aware that what is told of Śiva cannot possibly form the basis for what Megasthenes has to say about Dionysos. But there is a certain area of general agreement here, though only on these two points; the other points, dealing with Śiva's building of towns, etc., cannot be demonstrated anywhere.

If we continue with Dionysos' agricultural contribution, we find it quite conceivable to point the connection between Dionysos' use of oxen in ploughing and Śiva's famous white bull Nandin, who may have been used in ploughing, or Śiva's epithet Paśupati, "lord of cattle".[1]

There is another epithet given to Śiva, "the god in the fig-tree", and an epithet "lord of the vineyard", Drākshārāmeśvara, which suggest Dionysos, who is also known as Lēnaios, and the introducer of the fig-tree and of the vine-creeper.[2]

Here we have three more points of agreement between Śiva and Dionysos; added to the two previous points, we now have five in all.

This brings us to the point which originally suggested to scholars that there might be a case for the identity of Dionysos with Śiva. The description of the Dionysos cult contains elements which are easily connected with Śiva: this is undeniable. The dancing Śiva is a familiar motive. His wife's cult included the *tāṇḍava* dance and the drinking of wine. Śiva himself carries a drum, *ḍamaru*. We might also mention his trident, *pināka*, which is easily connected with the Bacchic staff, mentioned in the last fragment, the spear wreathed in ivy. Śiva has many links with the mountains, and this has given rise to the supposition that it is this which is reflected in the statement that the worshippers of Dionysos lived in the mountains. But we have had occasion to point out in the previous section that this implies an error of reasoning. Śiva lives in the mountains, it is true, but *far from human habitation*—the direct opposite of what is said about Dionysos, that he was worshipped by dwellers in the mountainous

---

[1] Thurston, *Castes and Tribes of Southern India*, VII, p. 364. Cf. quotation below, p. 223.

[2] Iyengar, *History of the Tamils*, p. 184. Cf. however Iyengar, *Dravidian India*, p. 54, where the fig tree is said to be unknown in older Tamil literature.

regions of India. We have no evidence from the texts suggesting that Śiva's worshippers wore their hair long; we know, on the other hand, that Śiva himself is described as having long, bushy and matted hair, gathered in a knot over his forehead. It is doubtful whether this can be reckoned as an agreement with Dionysos. If we do allow it, our total of positive identifications increases from five to ten.

The third group of passages begins by representing Dionysos as three different persons on different occasions. Something similar can in fact be said of Śiva: *vīra-bhadra*, the eight Bhairavas and Khaṇḍo-bā are regarded as being different forms of Śiva. But there is no link between Śiva and Indus. He has, however, gathered up the Ganges in his knot of hair. This does not constitute an identification. Despite the resemblance between Lēnaios ("the one with the wine-press") and Drākshārāmeśvara ("the lord of the vineyard"), which we have already touched upon, the resemblance between Dionysos and Śiva on this point is extremely dubious. It is on the other hand undeniable that both have connections with the Himalaya: Śiva dwells on Kailāsa, one of the highest of the Himalayan peaks, while Dionysos led his army up a mountain with three peaks, one of which was Mēros, i.e. Meru. We cannot connect this directly with Śiva; or perhaps it would be better to say that the connection is not immediately obvious. We have nevertheless two more points of contact between Dionysos and Śiva, which brings us to a grand total of twelve points on which the two can be connected; none are however capable of carrying absolute conviction. The question now is whether the sum total of these points of contact constitutes an unquestionable identification.

We cannot answer this question until we have examined, first, the essential elements in the nature of Dionysos to see whether they correspond to the nature of Śiva and, secondly, the most prominent characteristics of Śiva to see whether they are mentioned in the description of Dionysos.

On the first point, the review on p. 177 ff. suggests that the nature of Dionysos can be expressed most simply and most adequately by the term "culture-hero". This characteristic is practically unknown in connection with Śiva. The term "culture-hero" implies that the personality in question shall be benevolent and shall demonstrate his benevolence in every possible way—exactly as Dionysos in fact does. Śiva's character provides the diametrical opposite to this. Śiva is the terrible one, who destroys, consumes and works evil with or without cause. Then according to Megasthenes Dionysos was a man who was deified as a result of his good deeds. We must suspect *a priori* that this is an element of euhemerism which has been introduced by Megasthenes himself, and which does not correspond with the facts. But when we examine the many "historical" statements made of Dionysos, we find that there is clear trace of euhemerism in the Indian tradition which Megasthenes reproduces. But this rules out Śiva altogether. Śiva is never the subject of this kind of tradition. The idea of Śiva dying is remote from the Indian tradition. He is never said to have built towns; but the Indian tradition does not lack cases of Śiva destroying towns.

If we approach the problem of the links between Śiva and Dionysos from the other direction, namely by concentrating on Śiva's most prominent characteristics, we find that the most outstanding of these—his aspect of terror—is entirely missing from Dionysos. Śiva has a third eye, with which he consumes all things upon which its gaze is turned. His capacity for arousing awe and terror is hardly lessened by his accoutrements—snakes, skulls and the like—but none of these are to be found in the description of Dionysos.[1] We must emphasize that the essential fact is not the absence of the details as such, but the absence of the whole of this complex, which may be regarded as the expression of the real nature of Śiva. Śiva's asceticism, his meditation and his *liṅga* are other essentials of the character of Śiva, but all are missing from Megasthenes' description of Dionysos.

We may summarize our result thus: The essential features of the description of Dionysos are missing from Śiva's type, while all that is inseparable from Śiva is missing from Dionysos as described here. This makes it quite impossible to accept the current identification of Dionysos as Śiva.

We must therefore turn elsewhere for an answer to the question "Who is Dionysos?"

---

[1] Rao, *Hindu Iconography* II, pp. 39–41, considers that the identity of Rudra and Agni is to be seen "throughout the Vedic period". He considers, too, that this is the view of the Mbh (p. 42); in the Purāṇas Rudra-Śiva is regarded as the supreme god, with discus, trident, club, axe and sword, as well as association with snakes. This is of course not an exhaustive description of the god in question, but it indicates the main characteristics of the type to which Śiva belongs. Megasthenes' description of Dionysos is of an entirely different type of god.

DIONYSOS IS A CULTURE-HERO BELONGING TO ONE OF THE PRIMITIVE PEOPLES OF INDIA

There are two kinds of statements made about Dionysos which seem to me to provide a clue to his identification. In the first place, both Diodorus and Strabo state explicitly that Dionysos was worshipped by the inhabitants of the Indian mountain areas. And secondly, Dionysos is described as a person who lived on earth at the dawn of history as a man, and who functioned as a culture-hero.

1. On the matter of the mountain areas, this statement is connected with two geographical details, viz. the mountain Mēros and people called Oxydrakai. We know so little about these that we are unable to derive any satisfactory information from them. But what is interesting is that Diodorus describes the mountain area in such a way as to lead our thoughts away from the attitude of the dwellers on the plains. The mountains are described in entirely positive terms, which would have been an impossibility if the information had been drawn from our usual sources on India. The Indian Sanskrit literature is constantly placing the plains and the mountains in opposition to each other. The Law of Manu states that the mountains, the Himalaya and Vindhya are the land of the Mlecchas, but that on the plains dwell the Aryans.[1] This is the same distinction between the mountains and the plains as that made by Megasthenes. We have the pattern:

Mountains—Mlecchas—worshippers of Dionysos
Plains—Aryans—worshippers of Heracles

Our previous investigation has attempted to show that Heracles is Indra, the god of the Aryans. This suggests that Dionysos may well be the god of the non-Aryans.

We found in our first section that most of the gods in the Indian pantheon were at once ruled out, since there was no reason to connect them with the object of our study; something similar applies to our examination of the Dionysos passages in Megasthenes and their connection with the mountain tribes of India. Most are ruled out, since their culture resembles that de-

[1] II.22, 24.

scribed as existing in India *before* the coming of Dionysos, or lacks all resemblance to that which Dionysos is said to have introduced. Furthermore it can be shown that their religion lacks those characteristics which are most typical of the religion of Dionysos (see above, p. 177 ff.). After having examined all the cultural and religious types represented in India, insofar as these are available in modern ethnographical works, only one possibility remained, the Muṇḍas of Chota Nagpur.[1]

2. The other observation we can make concerning Dionysos is that he is described as having lived on earth in the distant past as a man, and that he fulfilled the functions of a culture-hero.

Dionysos corresponds exactly to the "culture-hero" type. We could call him—following Jensen—"Dema" with perfect justification.[2] Jensen considers that the "dema"-type is to be found in the Aryan religion of India; it is however easier to recognize the type in Megasthenes' Dionysos and in the religious life of the Muṇḍa people.

Earlier attempts to identify Dionysos have worked on the assumption that the Indian Dionysos drew upon the Greek Dionysos for the majority of his characteristics. This is easily explained when we remember that little was known about the tribes dwelling in the mountains of India, and less about their religion. But now the deficiency has to some extent been remedied. What is perhaps of the greatest value for our investigation is that the same scholars have studied different racial types, and that it is now perfectly clear that it is by no means all the tribes in the hills of India that have a conception of a "culture-hero."[3] We encounter it among people who

[1] For literature on the comparative ethnography of India, see bibliography. Thompson–Balys, *The Oral Tales of India*, shows that the information given by Megasthenes about Dionysos can be paralleled in only one part of India: the district south of Pāṭaliputra, the area now occupied by the Muṇḍas. We quote from this index of subjects:

A 1425. Origin of seed.—Central India. Elwin (1939) 318. (Elwin, *The Baiga.*)

A 1427. Acquisition of spirituous liquors.—Central India. Elwin (1949, 1953).

A 1441. Acquisition of agriculture.—Central India. Khond: Thurston III 369; Elwin (1939) 318 f., (1949, 1953); Oraon: Roy 468.

A 1461. Acquisition of music.—Central India. Elwin (1949, 1953).

A 1462. Origin of dancing.—Central India. Elwin (1949, 1953).

We see that practically everything which Megasthenes describes as characteristic of Dionysos is found here, noted down from the Muṇḍa tribes of Central India. Other parts of India are of course represented, but not in connection with themes touched upon by Megasthenes.

[2] *Mythos and Kult bei Naturvölkern.*

[3] Some scholars have evidently not noticed the occurrence of the idea of the culture-hero among the Muṇḍas. Elwin and Fürer-Haimendorf have been largely responsible for describing the different types of religion practised by different tribes. See bibliography.

speak the Muṇḍa language, and among others who are now Dravidian-speaking, but who do not belong together with other Dravidian peoples, either racially or in terms of their culture in general. The Oraons, who live in the vicinity of the Muṇḍas, speak a Dravidian language but have no racial resemblance to the Dravidians. Culturally they bear a close resemblance to the Muṇḍas. We may follow Hutton in supposing them to have been originally a Muṇḍa tribe, particularly since they are closer, racially speaking, to the Muṇḍas than to the Dravidians.[1] Those Dravidian-speaking peoples who live in the vicinity of the Muṇḍas nowhere pose a problem as great as that provided by the Koṭas in Nīlgiri, in South India. They speak a Dravidian language but belong to a different racial group from other Dravidians. But they do not seem to belong to the Muṇḍas, who furthermore live in a different part of India. They do however have myths concerning a culture-hero—a Dema.[2]

This is all there is to say on this particular subject. When Megasthenes described a certain god as the bringer of civilization, he was not borrowing the characteristics of the Greek god Dionysos in order to clothe an Indian god. There were already traditions concerning the "culture-hero" in India, to be more precise, in the mountains, and it is these dwellers in the mountain regions whom he describes as worshippers of Dionysos.

---

[1] See Hutton, *Census of India*, 1931, p. 358, and Basu, *The Racial Affinities of the Oraons* and *The Racial Affinities of the Muṇḍas*.

[2] See Emeneau, *Koṭa Texts*; he had given mankind fire: this is not related either of the Indian Dionysos or of the Muṇḍas' culture-hero.

MEGASTHENES' DIONYSOS PASSAGES IN THE LIGHT OF ARYAN AND DRAVIDIAN LITERATURE AND THE ETHNOGRAPHY OF THE MUṆḌAS

1. *Historical passages*

a. Dionysos was born from his father's thigh[1] and nursed in a cave.[2]

The first of these two pieces of information does not seem applicable with any degree of certainty to the Indian Dionysos. Diodorus Siculus, who is the oldest and—according to Timmer—the most reliable of the textual witnesses to Megasthenes' terminology and the construction of his work, puts it thus: "That is why the Greeks related for posterity that the god Dionysos was born out of his father's thigh." This seems to mean that the myth of the supernatural birth of Dionysos was only current among the Greeks and only applied to the Greek version of the god.

But at the same time we remember that in the RV and in Manu the four castes are described as originating out of the various parts of the body of Brahmā and Purusha respectively;[3] the *vaiśyas* are described as coming from the thigh of Brahmā or Purusha. This, remembering Dionysos' function as a "culture-hero", closely connected with agriculture, suggests that there may be a connection between what Megasthenes has to say about Dionysos and a deity particularly connected with the *vaiśya* caste, in other words, between Dionysos and the Aśvins or some other god representative of the third function—the agricultural—in Dumézil's scheme.[4]

The Vishṇu Purāṇa also has a passage describing the Asuras as the first-born of Brahmā, sprung from his thigh.[5]

The second statement, that Dionysos was nursed in a cave, is so poorly supported that its genuineness may be called in question. It is mentioned only by C. Iulius Solinus, from the middle of the 3rd century A.D. He claims that it is the ancient Indians who tell that father Bacchus was nursed in a cave. Schwanbeck includes this among his *Fragmenta incerta*, and Megasthenes is never mentioned as its originator.

---

[1] Frg. A 1, 8 and 9.

[2] Frg. A 9.

[3] RV X.90.12, Manu I.31.

[4] See e.g. Dumézil, *Les dieux des Indo-Européens*.

[5] Vi.P. 1.5, 28–32 (Wilson, p. 40).

There seems to be no direct parallel in Indian literature to what is told of Dionysos. A suggestion in the same direction is however given in the tradition that the one destined by Śiva to destroy Viśvakarman was born from the bowels of the earth near the Ganges.[1] Similar stories are found in the Mbh, but are obviously irrelevant.

The Muṇḍas have a tradition about their first king Rani Mukut Rai, that he was born in the depths of a forest. His parents died soon afterward, whereupon he was protected by a great snake, Pundarika Nag.[2] The child stands in a peculiar relationship to the sun-god, Sing-Bonga, the chief god of the Muṇḍas, and is destined to become king. Although this Muṇḍa tradition may be connected with what we have been discussing, it is impossible to give it weight, since there is so much doubt concerning the authenticity of the statements in question. Had it been identical, the situation would naturally have been different, or had it been possible to demonstrate the existence of the identical tradition from elsewhere in India; such is not however the case.

b. He came in prehistoric times from the west: 6451 years before Alexander the Great or 154 kings before Sandrakottos, i.e. Candragupta.[3]

The statement that Dionysos came from the west cannot be supported anywhere in the Sanskrit literature.[4] But similar traditions are to be found in a number of places. Among those still current are the following:

Anderson, in *The Peoples of India*, states that the writer caste in Bengal claim to have come from the west; this is supported by their cranial and nasal features.[5] The Bengali Brahmans, according to the same author, make the same claim and have the same racial features in their favour.[6] But on the other hand the Chittagong Mag do not deny their Tibeto-Burman origin, either.

Iyengar, in his book *Dravidian India*, quotes Tamil traditions of a great continent in the Indian ocean, connected to South India, but later destroyed by "a huge deluge".[7] It is true that he does not quote any traditions concerning the coming of the Dravidians from the west. But he does answer a

---

[1] See Thurston, *Castes and Tribes* VII, p. 363.

[2] Roy, *The Muṇḍas and their Country*, p. 135. Cf. also below, p. 208: the story of the first couple who were saved from the "flood" in a cave on Mount Harata.

[3] Frg. A 1, 7.

[4] The actual facts are irrelevant. Gordon, *Sialk. Giyan, Hissar and the Indo-Iranian Connection*, deals with discoveries in Iran which resemble e.g. the discoveries made at Harappa. It is possible to trace the various peoples who came from the west.

[5] *Op. cit.*, pp. 17 ff.

[6] *Op. cit.*, p. 23.

[7] *Op. cit.*, p. 24.

theory put forward by Slater, that the Dravidians came to India via this lost continent.—Since Slater's work is unfortunately unobtainable, I have no way of knowing whether his theory is based on native traditions. But it appears in any case to be clear that such traditions, if they exist, have been deliberately suppressed by Iyengar. Support for this suspicion is forthcoming from Thurston, in *Castes and Tribes* VII: "In speculating on the origin of the Vellālas, Mr. J. H. Nelson ("Manual of the Madura District") states that 'tradition uniformly declares them to be the descendants of foreign immigrants, who were introduced by the Pandyans: and it appears to be extremely probable that they are and that an extensive Vellāla immigration took place at a rather remote period' ..."[1] It is the traditions that interest us here, and not the present situation of research on the origins of the various peoples, tribes and castes of India.[2] Hence we have no need to concern ourselves with Nilakantha Sastri's stimulating comparison of the Dravidians and the Mitanni, with whom he finds parallels in pronunciation, grammar and vocabulary; this he interprets as meaning that the Dravidians came from the north-west.[3] We have no idea whether this tradition just mentioned is to be interpreted as meaning that they came into India from some area outside India, or whether they came to South India from another part of the same country.

It is thus impossible to find any convincing link between Megasthenes' statement that Dionysos and his people came from the west and the Dravidian tradition (with the exception of the Brahui tradition, quoted below, n. 2). The Muṇḍa traditions are however much easier to connect with Megasthenes' Dionysos passage. Roy quotes a tradition, one which is still alive among all Muṇḍas, that they once lived as shepherds in the valleys and hills of north-west India.[4] In the *Linguistic Survey* IV, pp. 30–31, we

---

[1] *Op. cit.*, p. 369.

[2] Hutton, *Census of India*, 1931, p. 454 f.: "In either case the presence in Baluchistan of the Brahui, speaking a Dravidian language, living among remnants of a lost civilization, in a country rendered inhospitable by a change of climate, professing a skin-deep allegiance to Islam but in practice worshipping at pre-Islamic shrines and phallic stones, and using circles of stones to dance in, and (455) exorcising devils by the dancing of medicine-men like the people of the Malabar Coast, points very suggestively to speakers of Dravidian languages as the ancient inhabitants of Mohenjodaro and perhaps the givers of culture to India, while the fact that *they claim Aleppo as their place of origin* and bury their dead to face westwards, indicates their ancient connection with Mediterranean." Cf. above, p. 185.

[3] *A History of South India*, p. 57. Cf. Iyengar, *Dravidian India*, pp. 28, 39, 41 ff., in which he introduces the Sumerians into the picture.

[4] *The Muṇḍas and their Country*, pp. 43 ff. Cf. below, p. 274 f.

find mention made of a Santal tradition according to which they came from the west (north-west), together with a number of attempts to date these migrations. Risley dates them to the 14th century A.D., while Skrefsrud supposes them to have taken place in the very far distant past. According to him, they indicate that there took place an ancient immigration into India from the north-west, while Dalton interprets them as referring to an ancient migration from Assam. All the places at which they stopped on the way are enumerated at the annual initiation ceremony.[1]

The stubborn Muṇḍa tradition of a migration from the west has given scholars much food for thought, for there is no doubt that the Muṇḍa language is linked with the Austro-Asiatic group of languages, most of which are found in Polynesia and Melanesia. In point of fact the Muṇḍas are the furthest west of all the representatives of this group, and this suggests that they migrated from the *east*. But their appearance points to a western origin.[2]

We are however not primarily interested in the factual origin of this people, but in the traditions which may conceivably have formed a basis for Megasthenes' passage. It is clear that there are still living traditions among Indians concerning the coming of their forefathers in prehistoric times from the west. The great lapse of time since Megasthenes however renders this factor extremely uncertain as proof. But with this *caveat* we may nevertheless regard this point, that Dionysos and his people came to India in prehistoric times from the west, as being in favour of the Muṇḍas as the worshippers of Dionysos.

The date assigned to Dionysos, 6451 years before Alexander the Great and 154 or 153 kings before Candragupta, does not agree with that given in the Heracles section, which speaks of 6042 years and 153 kings respectively.[3]

In the former case the average length of the reign of each king is about 42 years; in the latter 39 years. This indicates that the divergence is not of the slightest importance, since the figures are quite unreasonable in any case. This is not history: it is mythology. When dealing with the ancient history of India even a modern scientific scholar cannot very well avoid discussing the existent historical facts given us in the "unhistorical"—to our eyes—Sanskrit literature. Since Megasthenes' historical statements on

---

[1] See also Bodding, *Traditions and Institutions of the Santals*, pp. 8–11, particularly p. 9 n. 21.

[2] The ethnographical picture is too complex to enable us to give an adequate picture here of the issues involved.

[3] Frg. A 7 *contra* B 9.

Dionysos and Heracles have already been compared with the royal lists preserved in the Purāṇas,[1] and since the latter have been examined with the utmost thoroughness in modern works, such as *The History and Culture of the Indian People I: The Vedic Age*, we have no real need to go into the subject more thoroughly here. Suffice it to say that Megasthenes' history can in no way be connected with that of the Purāṇas, which incidentally shows a great deal of internal discrepancy. Benfey, attempting to reconcile Megasthenes with the Purāṇas, was often forced to do violence to the information given in the texts. Lassen, in his answer, confuted Benfey's imaginative speculations factually and convincingly. One is left with the impression that Megasthenes cannot have been using the same information that is given us in the Purāṇas. In passing we may perhaps remark that this ought to have dissuaded Lassen from building his identification of Heracles with Kṛishṇa on this group of texts, which contain historical statements which are utterly irreconcileable with those made by Megasthenes. Faced with such enormous discrepancies as those between Megasthenes and the Purāṇas, one must conclude that the likelihood of Megasthenes having used the Purāṇas as source-material must be reckoned as minimal. The only natural explanation seems to be that Megasthenes knew nothing whatever of the Purāṇas or their contents, and that he drew his information from an entirely different source. What this source was, I have not been able to discover. I may perhaps be permitted to make a couple of important observations, however.

Anyone who has ever gone into Indian texts and Indian problems knows that there is a timelessness and a lack of a sense of history about India. Thus when we are faced with a collection of "historical" facts, as we have in the Purāṇas, we automatically suspect them of having little in common with the Indian way of thought. Further, when the various "traditions" diverge so sharply as these undeniably do, then our suspicions are intensified; we tend to regard them as being not ancient and living traditions, but relatively late speculations unfamiliar with the Indian mind, perhaps added long after by later editors; the royal lists themselves may well be pure fabrication. It is true that a certain proportion of the names in these lists have appeared in the archaeological evidence, but this is *per se* a poor of historicity: *vide* European attempts to write the history of the world from the creation to the present! Even if they can be shown to be accurate in respect of their own day, this is no guarantee of their accuracy over the whole of the preceding thousand years. The resemblance between the two—

---

[1] By Benfey and Lassen in *Zeitschrift für die Kunde des Morgenlandes* V, pp. 218–259.

the ancient histories of Europe and the Puranic histories—may perhaps be summed up as a *horror vacui*: an invented "fact" is better than no fact at all, irrespective of the period in question. The Purāṇas stretch back over immense periods of time; yet the historical facts supported by archaeology are limited to the centuries around the beginning of the Christian era. We may well ask whether the Purāṇas' royal chronicles existed in Megasthenes' day. We do not even know whether there existed any corresponding data among the Aryans. May not the interest in history to which they bear witness be traced back to the Greeks or to some other non-Indian people with whom the Indians came into contact as a result of Alexander's Indian campaign? Or is there a "sense of history" among the non-Aryan peoples of India?

I have not been able to trace any royal chronicle among the Dravidians, though this does not of course mean that such a chronicle has never existed

Roy, on the other hand, has said that the Muṇḍārī-speaking Muṇḍas have a living tradition according to which their first king Fani has had no more than sixty-one successors; this has enabled Roy to date Fani to the period after Christ, possibly the fourth century.[1] Elsewhere Roy has stated that the Muṇḍas came to their present dwelling as far back as ca. the seventh century B.C.—i.e. to Chota Nagpur, near Patna-Pāṭaliputra. If it is true, as we have suggested above, p. 196, that the Muṇḍas have succeeded in preserving in a cultic context the names of all the places at which they halted on their migration from the west, then they may well have preserved a similar tradition concerning the names of their kings. All we would say here is that it seems possible that the Muṇḍas provide the external conditions in which a sense of historicity may have been conserved, and which agrees with what we are told by Megasthenes about Heracles and Dionysos —a sense which is conspicuous by its absence from Sanskrit literature, the Purāṇas and the epics excepted. The Muṇḍas, reciting their stopping-places in the dawn of history, demonstrate at least a certain affinity with the attitude revealed in Megasthenes' historical passages.

Although it is not possible to establish that Megasthenes obtained his knowledge of the period of time, and the number of kings, separating Dionysos–Heracles from his own day, from the Muṇḍas, the Muṇḍa traditions seem to me to conform more closely to Megasthenes' statements than does the Puranic literature. Deserving of particular attention is Roy's statement that certain Muṇḍa tribes possess traditions of rule in pre-Dravidian India,[2] since it provides a link with what Megasthenes tells

[1] *The Muṇḍas and their Country*, p. 139. Cf. above, p. 194.

[2] *Caste, Race and Religion, M.I.* XVII, 1937, p. 172.

us about the interval of time between Dionysos and Heracles. I do not however consider this to be a positive argument in favour of the identification of the worshippers of Dionysos and the Muṇḍas.

c. A divergent tradition suggests that Dionysos may have had his origin among the Indians.[1]

"Among Indians there is still shown today both the place where the god was born and the names of the towns called after him in the dialect of the people; and there have been preserved many other important proofs of his origin among the Indians." The words are those of Diodorus Siculus, in the same work in which we read that "the most learned among the Indians say that Dionysos came from the west with a great army long ago". We have already pointed out that this tradition has the strongest support. But since the coming of Dionysos to the Indians is so well-documented, we may wonder if the actual notice is that of Megasthenes. In our textual part it is stated that the whole frg. is missing from Fr.G.H. and is placed among the Diodorus-texts in Fontes. Schw. has the same frg. in brackets. We observe also that it is never said in this frg. that it relates the traditions of the *Indians*. Nor is it said that the notice is told of the Indian Dionysos. The notice is to be regarded as that of Diodorus himself: On accunt of the different myths of different peoples on the same Dionysos, the same is to be regarded as three different persons. In the same way Cicero distinguishes five different Dionysos, as has already been mentioned.[2] The point is worthless as a help to identification, and must be excluded.

d. His arrival seems to be described by Megasthenes as being in the company of a great army, including women. With this he is said to have marched through the whole world and conquered not only all India but all Asia.[3]

That Dionysos came with a great army is a statement which is hardly capable of proof, whether from Sanskrit or from Tamil literature.

There is however an interesting piece of information in the Muṇḍa tradition, which has been quoted by Roy, in his book *The Muṇḍas and their Country*: "The Muṇḍa tradition of a compact body of twenty-one thousand Horoko (= Muṇḍas) marching up from the north-west and settling in the central portion of the modern district of Ranchi has however to be taken with a large grain of salt. We are not to suppose that the journey was effected in a brief space of time, or even in one generation."[4] There is no evidence that the tradition is one of an army.

[1] Frg. A 2. [2] Above, p. 33.

[3] Frg. A 1, 2, 5 and 10.

[4] *Op. cit.*, p. 132.

The link with the Muṇḍa tradition is however strengthened by the statement that the army included women,[1] a detail which is portrayed in particular detail in our last extract from the text. We read of Amazons who played an active part in the capture of Bactria.[2] We may compare this passage from Roy's *The Muṇḍas*: "And it is said that even females would gladly render military service to the community under the leadership of the Muṇḍa on such occasions[3] ... Taking advantage of the drunken revelry in which the Uraons were engaged in the Khadi or Sarhul festival, the enemy attacked them unawares and though at first repelled by the Amazonian Uraon women attired in masculine dress, they at length succeeded in capturing the Uraon citadel."[4] It is true that this account is negative, this tribe, the Oraons, being on the losing side.[5] But it provides proof that it was not unknown for women to fight in the Muṇḍa army. Mention is made of the same custom in Hoffmann's *Muṇḍārī Grammar*: "In this era sendera the women don the men's clothes, and carrying the men's arms raid the neighbouring villages."[6]

"With this he is said to have marched through the whole world and conquered not only all India but all Asia." This is the account we are given in fragments A 1, 2, 5 and 10. Can this tradition be connected with another tradition, related *inter alia* in the Mbh, telling of Yayāti, an ancestor of Jarāsandha, the opponent of Kṛishṇa, who divided the whole of India among his five sons, after which, ten generations after Turvasu, four brothers, Pāṇḍya, Kerala, Kola and Chola, divided the country among themselves?[7] As far as I am aware, there are no further literary or ethnographical factors to take into consideration here. Even if the tradition in question belongs in this context, it cannot be advanced in support of any particular identification. The notice of women in the army brings to mind

[1] The practice of using women as warriors is also known among the Bhils. G. Ahmed Khan, *The Bhils of Khandesh*, p. 139, writes that "at one time women excelled in tribal warfare and used slings with great effect". Referring to the same branch of the Bhils, he also writes (on p. 135): "Whatever their origin the present Bhil possesses the mixed racial characteristics of the Caucasians and the Australoids. (According to some authorities the Bhils are a branch of the Mediterranean race.)" In other words, this author considers there to be a close ethnic relationship between the Bhils and the Muṇḍas. Cf. Fürer-Haimendorf: *The Chenchus*, p. 293, and Koppers, *My Central Indian Expedition, 1938–39*, p. 179.

[2] Frg. A 1 and 10.

[3] *Op. cit.*, p. 119.

[4] *Op. cit.*, p. 126.

[5] See below, p. 225 f.

[6] *Op. cit.*, p. v. Cf. RV V 30: 8 and Mbh. III 39.

[7] See Roy, *The Muṇḍas*, p. 43 f., *Harivaṁśa* XXX.1616, XXXII.1836.

the Muṇḍa-peoples. Nowhere in India we hear of Dionysos conquering the world, which is a popular theme in Greece.[1]

e. He either reigned over the whole of India for fifty-two years; or, again according to a variant account, as king he set one of his men, Spartemba, on the throne, and Spartemba reigned for fifty-two years, the kingdom passing on to his family in succession. The first version also described the monarchy as hereditary; when there was no son to succeed to the throne, then a king was to be chosen.[2]

We have only two textual witnesses, and these contradict each other. Diodorus Siculus says that Dionysos himself reigned as king for fifty-two years; Arrian, on the other hand, says that Dionysos set Spartemba on the throne, who was succeeded by his son Boudyas and his grandson Kradevas.[3] Which is the more reliable? This is of particular interest on account of the work of Lassen, who has brought together the names mentioned by Arrian and certain names mentioned in the royal chronicles of the literary tradition. We quote Lassen: "Das Mondgeschlecht stammt nach der Indischen Sage ab von dem Planeten Merkur oder *Budha*, der mit Iḷā, der Tochter des Manu, des ersten Gesetzgebers und des Urvaters aller Königsgeschlechter, den Purūravas, den ersten menschlichen König des Mondgeschlechts,-erzeugte. Da nun der Name Budhas und Budyas derselbe ist, ist die Annahme, dass Megasthenes mit seinem zweiten Indischen König den Budha meinte, nicht abzuweisen ... Ist diese Zusammenstellung, wie ich glaube, sicher, so folgt, dass der zweite Name der des Purūravas seyn muss. Wir finden dafür κραδεύας und selbst in dieser Form darf er uns an unserer Erklärung nicht irre machen; denn wenn wir uns dafür ursprünglich πραρεύας geschrieben denken, haben wir eine Gestalt des Namens, welche der Indischen nahe genug steht und aus welcher leicht die jetzige Lesart entstehen konnte ... Es bleibt übrig zu sehen, ob der erste König der Manu der Inder seyn kann; denn diesen müssen wir an der Spitze der einen der zwei ältesten Dynastien finden, wenn wir glauben sollen, dass diese uns von Megasthenes ächt überliefert worden ist ... Sein unterscheidender Beiname

[1] See above, p. 31 f.

[2] Frg. A 1 and 6.

[3] Cf. above, p. 76 n. 4, where Mahādeva (= Śiva?) is said to be anointed as king and father of Budha. Pargiter, *Ancient Indian Historical Tradition*, identifies "the Mānava Stock or Solar race with the Dravidians" and "the Aryan or Aila stock with the Lunar race". "The Mānava (Dravidian) city of Ayodhyā is made the most ancient, and these allegations imply that civilization was so far advanced among the Mānavas as among the Ailas when the latter entered there." While South India as a whole belonged to the Mānava Dravidian family, "it is said that the ruling families in Pāṇḍya, Cola and Kerala were offshoots from the Turvasu branch of the Ailas".

ist Svāyambhuva und, wenn man berücksichtigt, dass in diesem Namen zwei Laute sind, welche die Griechische Sprache zu Megasthenes' Zeit längst nicht mehr kannte und das Alphabet nicht bezeichnen konnte, y und v, wird man kaum Bedenken tragen, ihn in Spartembas wiederzuerkennen ... Nur dieses ist klar, 'says the author at last,' *Megasthenes giebt nicht die grossen Zahlen der Inder; dagegen hat er mehr Könige von Budha auf Candragupta, als die Inder, welche nicht zwei Drittel seiner Zahl besitzen.* Ich schliesse daraus, dass wir die alten Verzeichnisse nicht unverkürzt vor uns haben."[1]

We may note that the older the text, the fewer are the kings mentioned by name; and vice versa, the more kings are named, the more recent the text seems to be. It seems that Megasthenes must have had access to sources entirely different from those known to us today, but sources which began with the same name.

On the subject of hereditary or elected monarchs, Apte, in *Social and Religious Life*, states that the witness of the RV is not clear.[2] Later, in Manu IX.323, we find a statement which without doubt favours hereditary monarchy, as does our Greek text.

datvā dhanaṁ tu viprebhyaḥ sarvadaṇḍasamutthitam
putrai rājyaṁ samāsādya kurvīta prāyaṇaṁ raṇe

Giving his wealth to the Brahmans, obtained through all sorts of tributes, and the kingdom to his son, the king draws out to battle.

If the king's family did not stand in a special situation by the hereditary transfer of power, then on the absence of the king it seems likely that someone was appointed his successor or his viceregent. Nowadays the king is represented in his absence by some other member of the royal family: his son or even his grandson. Such is the practice in lands having a hereditary monarchy. But should a president travel abroad, he is never required to be represented by a relative. This principle suggests that Manu's statement favours hereditary monarchy, as the king makes over the rule to his son when he goes out to wage war—in which anything can happen.

We have already dealt with the question of the position of hereditary monarchy in Dravidian society, and need not go over the material again.[3] But what is the situation in Muṇḍa society? We have elsewhere quoted two passages from Roy, which together answer the question. On p. 194 we have the myth of Fani Mukut Rai, the first of the Muṇḍa kings; this settles the question of the monarchy. And on p. 213 we have the question of the hered-

[1] *Bemerkungen über dieselbe Stelle des Megasthenes*, p. 253 (in *ZKM* V, 1844).

[2] *Op. cit.*, p. 49.

[3] See above, pp. 109 and 137 f.

itary status of the position of Manki—indicating a situation similar to that described by Megasthenes. But the whole of the context of the first of these passages is of interest to us here. We quote:

"We have already described the Patti or Parha system in vogue among the primitive Muṇḍas and subsequently adopted by the Uraons. *The most influential of the patriarchal heads of villages*, as we have seen, *used to be chosen by the Muṇḍas as their leaders or Mankis*, and by the Uraons as their Parha-Rajas. 'This arrangement,' as the late Mr. G. K. Webster, C. S., quondam Manager of the Chotanagpur Estate, wrote in his well-known report to the Government of Bengal, dated the 8th April 1875, '*This arrangement being found clumsy, one head Raja was chosen, whose descendants are now the possessors of the Chotanagpur Estate.*'"[1]

f. It is possible that Dionysos left India again, attacked and conquered Bactria. According to Megasthenes, he died at an advanced age.[2]

When Arrian states that Dionysos left the country of India, are we to interpret this as meaning that he died, or simply that he left India and went on his way to another country? The second alternative seems to be the more likely. Arrian does not say that Dionysos "passed on"—in other words, he does not make use of a common euphemism for "to die"; he states that Dionysos left the country of the Indians. If this is so, are we justified in drawing a parallel between this statement and that advanced by Polyaenus, that Dionysos attacked Bactria? The mere fact that Dionysos attacked Bactria need not of course imply that he had left India once and for all—any more than Alexander's Indian campaign need be interpreted as meaning that Alexander had no intention of returning to Greece. Thus even if Arrian's statement be considered free from ambiguity, the episode from Polyaenus cannot be taken as evidence of the same view. This statement is however to be modified somewhat in the light of an earlier passage in Polyaenus: "... by which he brought the Indians and the rest of Asia into subjection". We conclude therefore that on this point we have two witnesses, Arrian and Polyaenus, against one, Diodorus.[3]

---

[1] *Op. cit.*, p. 135.

[2] Frg. A 1, 6 and 10.

[3] Breloer, *Megasthenes über die indische Stadtverwaltung*, discusses Dionysos without mentioning proposed identifications. Note that he mentions (in common with Law, *Tribes*, p. 154 f.) an information about Dionysos which comes, not from Megasthenes, but from Alexander's scribes. But it is of such a nature that it rules out an identification with Śiva or with any other Indian god, since Dionysos is expressly said to have returned to Greece. These passages complicate the problem of identification considerably. Since they do not originate with Megasthenes they can in the circumstances be

It is not too difficult to reach a definite conclusion on these contradictory statements. Which Indian god is believed *by the Indians* to have conquered the whole of Asia? The question is answered as soon as asked. There is no such god in the Indian pantheon. There can be no doubt that on this point Arrian and Polyaenus—whether or not they are quoting Megasthenes—are dependent upon the Greek attitude to the gods. They assume that the Dionysos they have encountered in India and the Greek Dionysos are one and the same. Consequently they are compelled to assume that he journeyed from country to country, irrespective of whether they have come across relevant traditions in the country in question. It is frequently impossible for us to decide whether what they describe in fact originates in the country, and among the people with which they are concerned. The only course of action open to us is, first, to examine their statements to see whether the author in question says in so many words that the tradition originated with the Indians. This applies to the tradition of the coming of Dionysos from the West, but not to the point at present under discussion. And secondly, we can see whether the tradition can be demonstrated as having been known among the people in question; the coming of Dionysos from the West once more provides a case in point.

The mere fact that we cannot produce proof of a Dionysian campaign against Bactria need not of course mean that no such tradition exists or has existed. But in the circumstances this particular point can have no significance, one way or the other, for our identification of Dionysos.

We are however assailed by misgivings when we consider the possibility of a relationship between this tradition and Śiva. We know that Kṛishṇa was a warrior; so much is clear from the Mbh, even though his participation in the battles of which we have a detailed description is limited to passive observation. Śiva, on the other hand, was never involved in war. One exception only serves to prove the rule: his fight in the form of a Kirāṭa with Arjuna.[1] We hear a good deal about Śiva the destroyer, but his destructive activity has nothing to do with his prowess at arms: rather with his extra eye and its supernatural power. It seems, therefore, that this relatively unimportant point must be ruled out as even a potential identification of Dionysos with Śiva. But we must not forget the identification of Śiva and Rudra. Rudra was linked with Indra and the Maruts, none of whom were strangers to the art of war. We quote Barth: "Rudra is also

passed over in silence. In Breloer's view Megasthenes is much more reliable than these scribes—all the more reason to ignore those passages which do not derive from Megasthenes himself.

[1] Mbh. III 39.

the head of the armies, the god of the brave, of footsoldiers, and of those who fight in chariots, of all those who live by the bow, the sword and the spear."[1]

So Śiva and Rudra were far from being identical in character and habit. This suggests that the theory explaining the name Rudra as a translation of Śiva is inadequate. If the name Rudra is in fact a translation, how does he come to be credited with characteristics foreign to the character of the original, Śiva? A detailed investigation of the relationship between Rudra and Śiva would seem to be called for, in this case concentrating on the points brought up by Kirfel.[2]

Finally we are informed that Dionysos died—an unexpected piece of information, particularly in connection with a supposed member of the Indian pantheon. Our surprise is not lessened when we recall that Heracles is also said to have died. We have already discussed the "death" of Heracles,[3] and we shall return to the subject of Dionysos' end when we come to consider Megasthenes' euhemerism against the background of Indian ancestor-worship.[4] In the meantime we may state briefly that, should the death of Dionysos prove to have connections with Indian ancestor-worship, then the way is open for a consideration of any of the religions of India—Aryan, Dravidian or (especially) Muṇḍa.

This concludes our examination of the "historical" passages. Sanskrit literature has not proved particularly helpful in the matter of their elucidation. We have found no connection, whether with Kṛishṇa or Śiva, which does not have an element of doubt and ambiguity. One sole exception is the statement that Dionysos died an old man, which is substantially identical with the tradition of Kṛishṇa's death at the age of 125 (*vide* Mbh). As for the Holi festival, we can see no link with these historical (or pseudo-historical) passages.

We have however touched upon certain Dravidian and Muṇḍa traditions, and have seen that the Muṇḍa traditions alone are capable of being connected with Megasthenes' Indian traditions. This applies to those points on which the Indian origin of the traditions is placed beyond reasonable doubt:

1. The entry from the West,
2. Nourished in a cave (?),
3. A *large* army,
4. Women in the army.

---

[1] Barth, *Les Religions de l'Inde*, p. 147. Eng. ed. p. 162.

[2] Cf. above, p. 185.

[3] Above, p. 116 f.

[4] Below, p. 244 f.

Two kinds of passage have resisted connection with Muṇḍa traditions. The first class comprises such as cannot be traced with any degree of certainty back to an Indian informant, and which may not have to do with the Indian Dionysos:

1. Born from his father's thigh,
2. Originated among the Indians,
3. Left India in order to attack Bactria,
4. Campaigned over the whole world, conquering all India and even the rest of Asia.

The second class comprises traditions which are irrelevant from the point of view of identification:

5. 6451 years before Alexander, 154 kings before Sandrakottos.
6. Ruled over all India for 52 years.

The first at least of these last passages connects Alexander with Indian history in a way which appears un-Indian in the extreme. May it not possibly be based on Greek calculations which build in their turn on native lists of kings? It is on the other hand quite out of the question to suppose that the number of kings *before Candragupta* would have formed part of the Muṇḍa tradition. We must therefore assume the two statements summarized in point 5. to have been edited in some way, with a consequent diminishing in their identification value.

In short, the statements which are of value from the point of view of identification can all be connected with Muṇḍa tradition; not, however, with Sanskrit literary tradition and not with Tamil tradition, as far as it is known.

2. *Functional passages: Dionysos as culture-hero*

I. *Dionysos' "social" contribution*

a. He healed the sick army.[1]

We have previously[2] connected the tradition according to which Dionysos cured a sick army by leading it up into the cool winds of the uplands[3] with

---

[1] Frg. A 1 and 10.

[2] Above, p. 186.

[3] Crooke, *Natives of Northern India*, p. 14: "Mr. Baden-Powell remarks that in the Punjab 'the location of Mohammedan villages usually follows the river lowlands, where cultivation is less troublesome, and the crop more secure, though the climate is less healthy. The Jats and hardier agricultural races, on the other hand, follow the higher lands, where the soil is good, but the labour of raising a full crop more considerable; the climate, however, is drier and much healthier.'" A couple of unhealthy

certain facts having to do with Rudra-Śiva. Monier-Williams, in his *Sanskrit-English Dictionary*, relates how Rudra healed sickness by driving away mists, thereby purifying the air, and how Śiva drank the Kālakūṭa poison, saving the world and colouring his neck blue. A number of passages in the RV can be advanced in support of Rudra's role in the healing of sickness. For example, II.33.4, which not only mentions Rudra's medicine (this is a common theme) but states that Rudra is the doctors' best doctor.[1] The RV also mentions the wind and the waters as healing agencies: not however in connection with Rudra. We may quote RV X.137:

2. *dvā́v imaú vā́tau vāta ā́ síndhor ā́ parāvátaḥ*
dákshaṁ te anyá ā́ vātu párānyó vātu yád rápaḥ
3. *ā́ vāta vāhi bheshajáṁ ví vāta vāhi yád rápaḥ*
tváṁ hí viśvábheshajo devā́nāṁ dūtá íyase
4. *ā́ tvāgamaṁ śáṁtātibhir átho arishṭátātibhiḥ*
dákshaṁ te bhadrám ā́bhārsham párā yákshmaṁ suvāmi te

—

6. *ā́pa íd vā́ u bheshajī́r ā́po amīvacā́tanīḥ*
ā́paḥ sárvasya bheshajī́s tā́s te kṛiṇvantu bheshajám

2. May these two winds blow from yonder Indus;
one renew thy strength, one drive far thy sickness.
3. O wind, blow hither healing, O wind, blow far all sickness,
for thou, who curest all, dost bear the great gods' messages.
4. I have come to thee with healing: I have come thy medicine bearing.
I bring thee healing power; I drive away thy sickness.

—

6. The waters, they heal (thee) the waters cure (thy) sickness.
The waters heal all, bringing thee health.

Elsewhere in the RV it is the Aśvins who are the healers—not to mention the Brāhmaṇas and the Mahābhārata; many are the accounts of the miracles wrought by the twin gods. These are in fact so well-known that there is no need to do more than mention them here. They are of course irrelevant for the purposes of the identification of Dionysos: they are two and they are inseparable. Further comment is unnecessary.

---

localities are mentioned on pp. 8–9, viz. the Ganges delta and the foot of the Himalaya. Koppers, visiting the Bhils, found another on the north side of the Vindhya mountains (*Geheimnisse des Dschungels*, pp. 39 ff.). The exact situation of the Jhabua mentioned here is between 22°28′ and 23°14′ N. and between 74°20′ and 75°19′ E. Cf. also Koppers, *Die Bhil in Zentralindien*, p. 2.

[1] Other RV passages: I.43.2, 4; 114.1, 5; II.33.2, 3, 7, 12, 13; V.42.11; VI.74.2, 3; VII.36.5; 46.2, 3; VIII.29.5.

Thurston mentions this Dravidian tradition: "... when the inhabitants of the world were rude and ignorant of agriculture, a severe drought fell upon the land, and the people prayed to Bhūdevī, the goddess of the earth, for aid. She pitied them, and produced from her body a man carrying a plough, who showed them how to till the soil and support themselves. His offspring are the Vellālas, who aspire to belong to the Vaiśya-caste ..."[1] This has, it is true, nothing to do with the curing of disease, but the narrative fits in very well with Megasthenes' overall picture of Dionysos. The people suffer from heat and thirst—not however disease—and are benefited in exactly the same way as in Megasthenes' account of Dionysos: they learn cultivation and the care of the soil. But this is a South Indian *goddess*, and not a god. There can therefore be no question of a direct connection between the two, despite the fact of Dionysos' undeniable relationship with the female sex. The point of the narrative—the healing of an army—is missing, and we quote the parallel only as comparative material.

Turning to the Muṇḍas, we find that Roy describes their chief god, Sing-Bonga, as follows: "Their principal deity—Sing-Bonga (literally, the Sun God, and secondarily but in reality the Supreme Deity)—is altogether a beneficent Deity, ever intent on doing good to mankind."[2] We may compare with this account an ancient Santal myth reproduced, in a free translation, in the *Linguistic Survey* IV, p. 64: "It rained fire for seven days and seven nights; seven days and seven nights, incessantly. Where were you two then, where did you take shelter?—On the mountain Harata, in a cave there we two were, there we two took shelter." Again there is no question of identity between this myth and that told of Dionysos and his army. Instead of an army the Santal myth speaks of the parents of mankind; instead of disease a storm of fire, sent by God to destroy the human race. But in each case salvation is found in the hills. In the version of the myth reproduced by Bodding, *Traditions and Institutions of the Santals*, p. 8, it is God (here called Ṭhākur) who tells the man and the woman to seek shelter in a cave in Mount Harata. A variant speaks of "the rain of heaven" instead of a rain of fire: we thus have a "flood" myth. But whatever the detail, it is insufficient as a basis of identification.

By way of summary we may state that it is not possible to demonstrate any exact parallel to what Megasthenes says about Dionysos, that he cured a sick army in the hills, whether in Dravidian, Aryan or Muṇḍa tradition. But the passage as such is entirely in accordance with the traditions of all

---

[1] *Castes and Tribes* VII, p. 362.

[2] *The Muṇḍas and their Country*, p. 122.

three ethnic groups, both in respect of the character of a certain god and ethnic prehistory.[1]

b. Dionysos was responsible for arming the Indians.[2]

We have already examined the tradition according to which (in the Mbh) Śiva was regarded as bestowing weapons.[3] We may also recall that the Mbh represents Kṛishṇa as receiving his *gadā* from Varuṇa and his discus from Agni.[4] Evidently Śiva was not the only god who made presents of weapons. Indra also received his favourite weapon, the *vajra*, from a god, Tvashṭar.[5] It will be clear that this point is of little practical value as a source of identification.

In fragment 10 is described Dionysos' cunning in hiding his weapons in ivy. It may be of interest to recall that Manu VII.90 reads:

na kūṭairāyudhairhanyād yudhyamāno raṇe ripūn
na karṇibhirnāpi digdhair nāgnijvalitatejanaiḥ

Not with veiled weapons are the enemies to be slain in battle,
And not with poisoned, barbed nor burning arrows.

Can we trace in this sharp contrast between war as practised by Dionysos and morals as laid down in Manu a conflict of cultures? The treachery forbidden in Manu and practised by Dionysos certainly fits in remarkably well with the character of Kṛishṇa in the Mbh. Virtually everything that Kṛishṇa undertakes in the epic is characterized by an uninhibited cunning; even his friends find it difficult to accept his actions. This has been dis-

---

[1] In his paper *Some Cure Divinities* Chaudhuri names three kinds of deities worshipped in connection with sickness, among them Rudra-Śiva and Devī-Kālī; female cure deities are invoked on the occasion of cholera epidemics, etc. Female deities are in the majority. Chaudhuri does not draw a clear distinction between Hinduism and the religion of the primitive tribes. This is explained in another essay from the same author: *The Sun as a Folk-God*, in which he stresses the character of the sun-god as a curer of sickness. He mentions the Muṇḍas' Sing-bonga, but seems to regard him as having been taken over from the Aryans. The same view is met with in Sastri's *Hydro-Selenic Culture*, in which two religions are compared and contrasted: a moon-phallos-snake cult, represented in India by the Dravidians and Śivaism, and a sun cult, represented by the Aryans and Vishnuism. Since all Muṇḍas have a unified type of sun-god, quite different from e.g. the Aryans' Vishṇu or Mitra, it seems unlikely that borrowing can have taken place from this source. At all events a detailed analysis of the two types of sun-god is called for. Note the difference between Sastri's view of the opposing religions and that of Pargiter, quoted above, p. 201 n. 3. Chaudhuri shares Sastri's view.

[2] Frg. A 6.

[3] Above, p. 187.

[4] Mbh. I.227.

[5] RV I.32.2 etc.

cussed by Ruben in his book *Kṛishṇa.*[1] Emphasis is laid on the contrast between the life of Kṛishṇa in the Mbh and the exalted teaching of Kṛishṇa in the BhG.[2] Little more need be said, save that Ruben attempts to prove that Kṛishṇa was the god of one of the Muṇḍa tribes before the Aryan invasions.[3] We have no reason to discuss Ruben's theory, and may content ourselves by saying that the epics and the Purāṇas make it clear that Kṛishṇa gave no weapons, and that the point under discussion therefore cannot be applied to Kṛishṇa.

Nor did the god Murukan (= the younger, Śiva's younger son) give away weapons. But we read in Iyengar's *History of the Tamils* that he was in fact equipped with a spear, vēl, and for that reason was called Vēlan, the spearman.[4] Note that fragment 10 emphasizes that the disguised weapon was a spear. Dionysos, too, was evidently a spearman, a fact which seems to favour the proposed identification, since there is a particularly close link between Murukan and Śiva.[5]

The Muṇḍas are a peaceful people. We hardly expect to find them equipped with spears. Such is however the case.[6] Their history shows that they first came, cleared and cultivated an area of forest, that they were driven out by other tribes, and that they then moved on, repeating the process as they went. The same drama was played out with great regularity wherever they went. A peaceful people, they made little attempt to defend themselves. But it is noteworthy that their wedding ceremonies and their hunting ceremonies include the use, symbolical and actual, of the bow, arrows, hatchet, spear, shield and sword.[7] The source of these weapons is not mentioned in the traditions.[8]

---

[1] *Op. cit.*, pp. 253–263.

[2] Particularly p. 259

[3] E.g. p. 176 f.

[4] *Op. cit.*, p. 76.

[5] Cf. also Emeneau, *Koṭa Texts*, p. 39: "From that iron he made arrows, bows, knives, axes, everything, and made them to cut."

[6] See e.g. Konow's prefatory remarks to Vol. II of Bodding's *Santal Folk Tales*, Hoffmann, *Muṇḍārī Poetry, Music and Dances*, and Jørgensen, *Evangeliet blandt Santalerne.*

[7] Roy, *The Muṇḍas*, pp. 59 and 370.

[8] Thompson–Balys, *The Oral Tales of India*, A 1459 (under *Origin of weapons*): the origin of bows and arrows are the subject of aitiological myths only in the Himalaya, the Assam Hills and Nīlgiri. We noted in our section on the texts that there is more than one possible translation of the words ὅπλον and ὁπλίζειν: "weapons" and "to arm" are not the only possibilities. (See above, p. 53.) The first in fact means properly "tool", and the second "to equip (with)". If Megasthenes used the words in this sense, then the passage in question means nothing more than that Dionysos made the Indians

c. Dionysos built towns.[1]

Diodorus has the following: "Dionysos came long ago, *when the Indian people still lived in villages.* He was able to conquer the whole of India *because there was no large town* to oppose his advance." Later we read: "furthermore he built important towns by moving villages to suitable sites". Arrian notes: "Neither had the Indians towns ... but when Dionysos came and assumed lordship over the Indians, he built towns ..."

Megasthenes doubtless meant that Dionysos was Indian's first town-planner and builder. This suggests two important conclusions. First, that Kṛishṇa cannot be meant, since the texts make it quite plain that he was familiar with the towns of Mathurā, his birthplace, and Indraprastha, which he visited on a number of occasions. He built only one town, Dvārakā, and this is far from an adequate motivation for the words of the Greek text.

But secondly, this passage rules out the whole of the Indo-European pantheon. When the Aryans invaded India there were already many towns, which aroused the envy and greed of the newcomers. This is the witness of the RV as interpreted by both the author of *Dravidian India* and the author of *The Muṇḍas and their Country.*[2] This is in fact the generally accepted view of the RV. And it corresponds to history: when the Aryans entered India there were towns, and they were made to fight for them.

Although it is thus possible to demonstrate from the RV that the worshippers of Dionysos cannot have been Aryans, but must have been members of a pre-Aryan ethnic group, there is nothing in Dravidian or Muṇḍa tradition which supports Megasthenes. There were certainly cities in India before the coming of the Aryans: the Indus Valley civilization may have flourished as far back as 1000 years before the Aryan invasions. But who were the originators of this civilization? Dravidian scholars insist that they were Dravidians. Iyengar interprets the words of the RV to mean that the fortified towns which opposed the Aryans were Dravidian, and that the Dravidians had a developed civilization at the time of the Aryan invasions.[3] But it is by no means certain that North-West India was occupied by Dravidians at that time. We are not aware of the existence of any tradition

into farmers—a subject which we shall take up in due course. Farmers need tools. Should this be what is meant, then the passage must be placed in the class of "agricultural" passages. But this interpretation is not likely, since the word ὅπλοισι is qualified by ἀρηΐοισι, "warlike". Farmers do not need tools of war. But the context is agricultural, and Megasthenes may mean "tools which can be used as weapons" (in an emergency).

[1] Frg. A 1 and 6.

[2] Iyengar, *Dravidian India*, p. 116; Roy, *The Muṇḍas*, p. 59.

[3] *Ibid.*

among the Tamils attributing the introduction of towns to any specific god. But this is not to say that there has never existed such a tradition.

That the Muṇḍa traditions have nothing about a god or culture-hero teaching men to dwell in towns is not really surprising.[1] The Muṇḍas of today, as studied by the ethnographers, do not live in towns. Some Muṇḍa tribes have simply never had the chance to settle down in a town; the unfriendliness of other tribes has meant that they have far too often been forced to move on before taking root. The Santals provide a case in point. Strictly speaking we need not assume that the entire ethnic group has always lived without the fixed point provided by a town,[2] but we are given nothing in such an argument which can be used to help demonstrate that Dionysos was worshipped by the Muṇḍas. But probability seems to indicate that the choice lies between the Dravidians and the Muṇḍas. The Indus Valley civilization and certain passages in the RV make it quite plain that a city culture in fact existed in pre-Aryan India. And we know of no other people who could conceivably have supported such a civilization. There is of course always the possibility that the race in question has disappeared from the face of the earth. Or should the race have continued a precarious existence in some minority group, the disappearance of their civilization would not be unnatural. Hutton has suggested that the Brahui, who live on in the vicinity of Mohenjo-daro, are just such a splinter group. Might it not be possible to conjecture that the northern town Harappa was the seat of the highly civilized Muṇḍas, while the Dravidian people lived in and around Mohenjo-daro? We cannot of course go into this question here. The final impression which we have obtained from this investigation is that Dionysos evidently had nothing whatever to do with the Aryan invasion; but on the other hand, we have no further evidence, whether positive or negative, on this point to connect him with either the Muṇḍas or the Dravidians.

d. Dionysos made laws and set up courts in the towns.[3]

Since our previous point has shown that the traditions with which we are comparing our text make no mention of towns, we shall concentrate on the legal system as a whole. This has not the same intrinsic difficulties as point c. First then the Aryan system, in which law and order played such a prominent part, had a special deity whose task it was to safeguard just

---

[1] Thompson–Balys have no record of a myth on this subject.

[2] See Przyluski's article *Names of Indian Towns in the Geography of Ptolemy* (Bagchi, pp. 136–148), particularly pp. 145–147; can there have been a connection between the Muṇḍas and the Sumerians?

[3] Frg. A 1 and 6.

these principles: Mitra, god of the "first function", the rulers.[1] But he is nowhere said to have been a lawmaker. He is said to have guarded his people as king, and this of course implies that he punished law-breakers. Incidentally, it is difficult to distinguish between Mitra and Varuṇa in the matter of function. Varuṇa is the recipient of such Vedic hymns as speak of the sin of the singer, and the punishment that he is forced to undergo in consequence of his sin. Hence it is fully in accordance with the common Indo-European heritage in India that a hymn directed to Mitra and Varuṇa can say:

tā́ hí kshatrám ávihrutaṁ samyág asuryàm ā́śāte
ádha vratéva mā́nushaṁ svàr ṇá dhāyi darśatám

For they attained indestructible might; they became *asuras* wholly.
Bright as the sun their laws became the law of man. (RV V.66.2)

Is this to be understood as saying in a different way what is said of Dionysos, that he passed laws? Possibly, but the resemblance ends there. The same applies to the great lawgiver Manu, who is nowhere said to have been deified and worshipped, at least in the mountains.[2]

On the other hand we have no tradition concerning the origin of the legal system observed among the Muṇḍas and Dravidians, with one exception.[3]

Of course they had a respect for law and order. We quote Roy once more: "Herdsmen and farmers by occupation, these aborigines of the soil could build houses for themselves, erect castles of stone, make flint weapons fitted for all uses, and understood the benefits of law and order."[4] This may be exemplified; their society was organized as follows: "... the Manki, like the Muṇḍa (= village headman). was always looked upon as a chief among equals—a leader and not a ruler. Nor did any superior rights of property appertain to the Mankiship. As with most Oriental institutions, the offices of the Manki as well as of the Muṇḍa, gradually came to be hereditary. In the internal administration of each village, the Muṇḍa was assisted by the village Panch or council of village elders. The tribunal thus constituted, arbitrated in all disputes among the villagers inter se. Custom was the recognised law. And offences against the Code of Custom were

---

[1] See e.g. Dumézil, *Les dieux des Indo-Européens.*

[2] Cf. above, p. 118 f., where it is stressed that Heracles is represented as the only god worshipped on the plain (as Dionysos is the only god worshipped in the hills). Manu has never been worshipped in this sense. Cf. also p. 184.

[3] Thompson–Balys, *The Oral Tales of India* gives "A 1580. Origin of laws.—Nīlgiri. Koṭa: Emeneau."

[4] *The Muṇḍas*, p. 59.

punished with fines and in extreme cases with expulsion from the village community. In disputes between village and village and in cases of unusual importance of tribal interest, the Patti-Panch presided over by the Manki, was called upon to adjudicate. And even now the village-Panch and the Parha-Panch or Patti-Panch play important parts in Muṇḍa village polity. 'Sing-Bonga (= the Sun-god) on high and the Panch on earth' is the orthodox formula for an oath amongst the Muṇḍas to this day."[1] The form of this oath shows that their supreme god, Sing-Bonga, was also considered to have connections with the legal system. This does not of course mean that it was he who made the laws and set up the legal system but his interest in the system must be considered as proven. At the same time we can scarcely claim that this bears witness to the existence of fixed "god-given" laws: a clear difference between Dionysos and the Muṇḍa system. The occurrence of the name of Sing-Bonga in the oath is nevertheless of considerable interest.

It can be said of Śiva that "he was no judge".[2] May this not be an argument against the identification of Dionysos with Śiva? On the one hand we have the lawgiver Dionysos, and on the other a god, Śiva, who was largely indifferent to the processes of justice.[3] A god whose role in myth and legend has been wholly unconcerned with jurisdiction is hardly likely to have been named as the lawgiver of mankind, though a general statement of this kind cannot be taken as final proof. Our conclusion must however be that on this point there is no adequate connection between the description of Dionysos and the character of Śiva.

II. *Dionysos' "agricultural" contribution.*

e. He passed on all manner of inventions.[4]

Note that this is not a case of general benevolence to persons in need, such as we associate with the name of the Aśvins. This particular god teaches mankind something which can be of permanent benefit to them. As far as I am aware there is no god in the Indo-Aryan pantheon which can be described in this way. Certainly not either Śiva or Kṛishṇa.

None of the innumerable gods of Hinduism fits in with this description. But the tradition of education for life at the hand of a great benefactor is found among the Koṭa of Nīlgiri,[5] and among the Muṇḍa and Dravidian

[1] *Op. cit.*, p. 120 f.

[2] Ruben, *Eisenschmiede*, p. 212.

[3] Note, however that Rudra-Śiva was the one who punished Prajāpati for his incest, see above p. 75.

[4] Frg. A 1 and 2.

[5] Emeneau, *Koṭa Texts*, p. 39: "To those three persons, to his three sons, he taught and gave all the skills that he himself had learned."

tribes of Chota Nagpur. The agreement with Megasthenes' statements to the effect that it was the mountain peoples who described their Dionysos in this way, is striking. The only thing calculated to surprise us is that after more than two thousand years these peoples have succeeded in preserving, more or less intact, their own religious heritage. The process of assimilation by Hinduism seems only to have begun.

We may exemplify this general statement. Roy, speaking of Sing-Bonga, the supreme god of the Muṇḍas, says that "(Sing-Bonga) is altogether a beneficent Deity, ever intent on doing good to mankind".[1] The same attitude to a closely related god is found among members of another branch of the Muṇḍa people. Bodding, describing the religion of the Santals, writes: "Marang Buru taught the two human beings to dig out medicines, to collect and prepare the stuffs for fermenting beer, to cut trees, to sow millets, to offer the first fruits of these, to invoke the spirits of the sacred grove and other matters."[2]

This in some measure indicates that the beneficent deeds attributed to Dionysos need not have been brought from Greece and transferred from the Greek Dionysos to the Indian. They in fact form part of the character of gods still worshipped today by certain of the mountain peoples of India.

f. Dionysos made the Indians into farmers. They had previously lived on raw meat.[3]

This brings us to that statement which is perhaps most characteristic of Dionysos as described by Megasthenes: that he benefited the Indians by teaching them the art of agriculture. The first thing to be said is that this Dionysos is far removed from the Indo-European pantheon. The Aryan literature of India knows of no connection between any of the gods and farming, at least as described by Megasthenes. Apte, in his *Social and Religious Life in the Gṛihya Sūtras*, describes the situation thus: "Agriculture was an occupation of gradually increasing importance to the RV Indians."[4] One wonders, particularly in view of the statement that Dionysos taught the art of farming, whether the Aryans were agriculturists before entering India, or whether the pre-Aryan population of India was an agricultural population.

But the task of this investigation is not to give an account of facts as to the real origin of agriculture among the Indo-Europeans, but what the traditions have to say about its origin. But the references in Sanskrit

[1] *The Muṇḍas*, p. 122.

[2] *Traditions and Institutions of the Santals*, p. 18.

[3] Frg. A 6.

[4] *Op. cit.*, p. 103.

literature are sparse. We read in Chapter VI of the Vishṇu Purāṇa how the various elements of civilization—towns, villages and the like—were acquired.[1] But at the same time we find this statement in the Vishṇu Purāṇa: "... there was no cultivation, no pasture, no agriculture, no highway for merchants: all these things (*or* all civilization) originated in the reign of Pṛithu. Where the ground was made level, the king induced his subjects to take up their abode. Before his time, also, the fruits and roots which constituted the food of the people were procured with great difficulty, all vegetables having been destroyed."[2] This passage contains an undeniable factual agreement with what we are told of Dionysos. There is, however, no further connection between King Pṛithu and Dionysos: the resemblance between the two is restricted to this one point. There may be an indirect connection, though: the god Megasthenes describes may have been a prototype and an example to Pṛithu.

The second question concerned the agricultural activities of the pre-Aryan population of India. We quote: "We may picture survivors of early man in India influenced from the dawn of Neolithic time by immigrations of long heads, akin to those termed Mediterranean ... These immigrations may well have brought to India many improvements, lifting men above the merely hunting stage, and even giving *the beginnings of agriculture* ... It seems justifiable to use the hypothesis that the culture elements, which thus reached India not less than a thousand years before the coming of the Aryans, interwove themselves with the earlier achievements of the higher races among the populations already settled in India and that the Dravidian culture is the result."[3] We owe to the same author the information that the earliest works of Tamil literature describe "the physical features of the semi-pastoral Tamil people".[4] And further: "The earliest Dravidians

[1] *Op. cit.*, p. 45: "They therefore constructed places of refuge, protected by trees, by mountains, or by water; surrounded them by a ditch or a wall, and formed villages or cities."

[2] *Op. cit.*, p. 104, Dikshitar, *Purāṇa Index*, s.v. Kṛishi, writes that according to the Purāṇas agriculture was introduced by Pṛithu (not by Śiva or Kṛishṇa). Cf. Crooke, *Religion and Folklore*, p. 256: "Even the great gods take their share in the protection of the fields. Thus Kṛishṇa is closely connected with agriculture, and his title Dāmodar, 'belly-rope', which legend says was applied to him because his mother tied him up to prevent him from doing mischief, has been interpreted to imply that he was originally a sheat of wheat. The same may be said of Balarāma, brother of Kṛishṇa, called Phāla, 'ploughshare', Halabhṛit, 'plough-bearer', Lāngali and Sankarshaṇa, 'ploughman', Mūrala, 'holder of the pestle' with which rice is husked."

[3] Iyengar, *Dravidian India*, p. 31, quoting from Slater, *Dravidian Element in Indian Culture*, p. 40, quoting from Fleure (name of work not given).

[4] Iyengar, *ibid.*, p. 55.

were not primitive tribes, but tilled the ground and raised crops of various kinds, e.g. rice and sesamum. They were *agriculturists by nature*."[1] A little further on in the same book we read that "... the Dravidians were of all the great races of antiquity *the first to systematise agriculture*".[2] It is not clear to the European reader on what grounds Iyengar bases this sweeping assertion.

Concerning traditions of the origins of farming, we may refer to that tradition we quoted above, p. 208: "... when the inhabitants of the world were rude and ignorant of agriculture, a severe drought fell upon the land, and the people prayed to Bhūdevī, the goddess of the earth, for aid. She pitied them, and produced from her body a man carrying a plough, who showed them how to till the soil and support themselves."[3] The point here, according to the tradition, is that the people were once ignorant of agriculture, but were taught how to till the soil for a livelihood by means of divine intervention. Despite the obvious differences, we have here an important area of agreement. We are evidently dealing with the same group of ideas, both in the South Indian tradition and in that reproduced by Megasthenes, the content of which centres on the divine transmission of the knowledge of agriculture. Śiva is never mentioned. The same applies to the related tradition quoted by Thurston in VII, p. 364.[4]

This group of ideas is however found among the Muṇḍas too, as we have already seen in the quotation from Bodding's *Traditions and Institutions of the Santals*.[5] A passage in the *Linguistic Survey* IV, p. 65, included as a sample of Santālī, points in the same direction: "Cut timber, young man, make a plough-beam and a yoke. Then you will earn gold from the soil." This is taken from a Santālī song, but nothing is said about its origin, whether or not it may be regarded as going back to a mythical tradition. This seems to be indicated by the next sample, which strictly belongs to the section following, but which we shall place here. "Marang Buru then told the man to break in two (bullocks), and he began to do so, and when he had broken them in, Marang Buru took him away in order to cut a plough and taught him to do so. Having chipped and bored it, he began to plough and broke the highland by ploughing. Then he asked, 'Marang Buru, what shall we sow?' Marang Buru then brought an Iri (= millet) from heaven

---

[1] *Op. cit.*, p. 124.

[2] *Op. cit.*, p. 127, quoting from Hewitt, *The Pre-historic Ruling Races* (page number not given).

[3] Thurston, *Castes and Tribes* VII, p. 361 f. Cf. III, p. 369.

[4] Quoted below, p. 223.

[5] Above, p. 215.

and gave it to the man to sow. It sprouted, became a plant, and ripened, and they began to perform the ceremony of first fruits."[1] This text removes the matter beyond doubt. Agriculture was taught by Marang Buru, "the Great Mountain", the Santals' culture-hero. He is really a "bonga", i.e. a spirit, clearly distinguishable from the one god, the high god, whom Bodding tells us is called Ṭhākūr (*Traditions and Institutions of the Santals*, p. 132). Since the high god has largely lost his place in the Santal mind, his place has been taken by the Sun-god, Sing-Bonga, who is also a "spirit". On this class of beings Bodding's informant said: "In the primeval age we had no bongas. During our wanderings we have got them."[2] The description given by the Santals themselves of the origins of their Bonga-cult—if it is in fact of native origin—corresponds remarkably closely to Megasthenes' description of the origins of the Dionysos cult.[3] We are thus virtually compelled to assume a connection between the two.

Note, however, that there are Muṇḍa tribes which have still not reached the agricultural level of civilization. For example, the Birhōr. Roy writes: "And thus even though some Birhōr families now and then settle down in one place and take to some sort of agriculture, they very rarely stick to it for any length of time, but are apt, on the slightest disturbance, to revert to their old life of nomad hunters and gatherers."[4] This is contradicted by the same author in his book *The Muṇḍas and their Country*, where he states categorically that "the Muṇḍa is essentially an agriculturist".[5] But Roy in this book does not deal with the Muṇḍa people as a whole: only with its Muṇḍārī-speaking section. Nevertheless there is a remarkable contrast between Roy's account of the Muṇḍas as relatively highly civilized and Hoffmann's account, in his *Muṇḍārī Grammar*: "Hence names of trades, products, and implements belonging to a somewhat advanced culture are not to be met with in the purely Muṇḍārī vocabulary."[6] Hoffmann regards the possession of an "advanced culture", even by the Muṇḍas of today, with a certain degree of scepticism; while Roy goes so far in the opposite direction that he is prepared to claim such a cultural attainment for the Muṇḍas of the second millenary B.C., at the time of the Aryan invasions. "Herdsmen and farmers by occupation, these aborigines of the soil could ... make flint weapons fitted for all uses."[7]

[1] *Linguistic Survey* IV, p. 66.

[2] *Op. cit.*, p. 132.

[3] For Elwin's statement concerning Kittung, the god of the Saoras, see below, p. 232.

[4] *The Birhōr*, p. 543.

[5] *Op. cit.*, p. 371.

[6] *Op. cit.*, p. v.

[7] *The Muṇḍas*, p. 59.

Roy bases his judgment on his own interpretation of what the RV has to say about the tribes encountered by the invading Aryans. This interpretation gives rise to two difficulties. In the first place, current agricultural terms are of Sanskrit origin, which he interprets to imply that the Muṇḍas were not agriculturists before the coming of the Aryans.[1] And secondly, that the Muṇḍas of today stand on a lower level of civilization than that they occupied before the Aryan invasions. Roy dismisses both in one sentence: "And in that wide space of time they probably unlearnt some of the peaceful arts of civilization that they had acquired in their pre-Aryan days of peace and prosperity."[2]

"Before Dionysos came to the land of the Indians, they lived on the flesh of captured wild animals, which they ate raw."[3]

This short explanatory statement belongs in the context of this same problem: whether the Indians learned agriculture from Dionysos. It is not altogether clear whether or not Dionysos is said to have put a stop to the practice of eating flesh.[4] It may be worth mentioning that the Hindu Muṇḍas refer contemptuously to lower branches of the tribe as Urang Muṇḍas, "probably to indicate their objectionable Uraon-like habits of eating beef".[5] We may also note that Sylvain Lévi, in his article *Pre-Aryan*

---

[1] *Op. cit.*, p. 101 n.

[2] *Op. cit.*, p. 73.

[3] Frg. A 6.

[4] Cf. Emeneau, *Koṭa Texts*, p. 41: "In ancient times, when there lived a few people in the jungle (and there were no other people in the Nīlgiris) and *when they went on eating* fruit, jungle potatoes, honey, kavḷ bulbs (Cero pegia pusilla), *raw flesh*, all these things, concerning the appearance of the three gods, possession by the god came to one man in the crowd of those men." P. 39: "With that fire *they roasted raw flesh and ate it* ... In this pot *he boiled flesh and made them eat it.*" Datta, *Ethnological Notes on some of the Castes of West Bengal*, p. 218: "*The Kheṛiās eat raw flesh* (?) They live on the roots and tubers dug out in the jungles." Bhaduri, *The Kōṛwās of the Udaipur State*, p. 128: "... *eat the flesh of the animals they kill*, and, if possible, by sowing a few crops on ground prepared by burning the shrubs and jungles." Griffiths, *Folklore of the Kols*, has the following chapter headings: The Origin of the Earth (II); The Origin of Insects (III); The Origin of People (IV); The Spread of Mankind (V); The Origin of Kols (VI); The Domestication of Animals (XIII) in which is related how it became possible for men to use oxen for ploughing; Where Agriculture Started (XIV) relating how Bhagavān gave cattle, "and therefore they left living off of fruits and roots and began to grow crops".

[5] Roy, *The Muṇḍas*, p. 359 n. Cf. Elwin, *Myths of Middle India*, p. 320: "One of the earliest occurs in the Lingo legend recorded by Hislop: How did the Gonds conduct themselves? Whatever came across them they must needs kill and eat it; They made no distinction. If they saw a jackal they killed And ate it; no distinction was observed: They respected not antelope, sambhar, and the like. They made no distinction in

and Pre-Dravidian in India, writes: "The name of the Pulindas is interpreted in Tibetan (Mahāvyut., 188,15) by *gyuñ po,* "out-caste", and in Chinese by *tu-kia,* "the race which kills the beasts for their food". Ptolemy, VII,i,64, also gives to the Pulindai the epithet of *agriophagoi,* a rare term, which appears to be invented to translate an Indian original; *agrio* signifies "wild", *phagos* "eater of"; one hesitates to make a choice between "who live on wild fruits" and "who live on raw meat"."[1] Lévi regards the Pulindas as being Muṇḍas. Shafer, in his *Ethnography of Ancient India,* counts them as Dravidians; his only reason for doing so is however that Ptolemy places them among the Dravidians in his list of Indian tribes.[2] Unfortunately it is impossible to determine the ethnic and language groups to which a given tribe must be assigned, purely on a basis of their geographical location. Nor does their level of civilization provide an adequate indication. We have already mentioned the cultural differences between the Birhōrs and the Muṇḍārī-speaking Muṇḍas; there are of course also considerable differences within each group.[3] An aitiology of these differences is provided in the following tradition:

"After the destruction of all mankind, except one pair, Ṭhākūr guided this pair back to Hihiri Pipiri. Here they got children and these were divided into septs. Gradually this division proved itself to be insufficient; they could not all get proper mates. Seeing this Ṭhākūr said to Marang Buru: 'Do persuade these men to go to the Khanderae forest to hunt; otherwise they will again turn as bad as they were. As we (it might be noted that Ṭhākūr here constantly uses the inclusive plural[4]) did not call what they did good, we exterminated them, the earth became empty, and we also repented. Therefore we shall not exterminate mankind, rather we shall again separate them into many septs.' Marang Buru did this, and all men went to this forest happy in mind. He then divided each sept into twelve, and from that time they found opportunity of marrying. Marang Buru was

---

eating a sow, a quail, a pigeon, A crow, a kite, an adjutant, a vulture, A lizard, a frog, a beetle, a cow, a calf, a he- and she-buffalo, Rats, bandicoots, squirrels—all these they killed and ate. So began the Gonds to do. They devoured raw and ripe things." Elwin in this quotation does not say that this change of practice was due to the intervention of Lingo—as the matter is described by Megasthenes, referring to Dionysos and the Indians. Lingo's efforts in the direction of changing the habits of the people are however described in the following sections.

[1] *Journal Asiatique* CCIII, 1923, pp. 1–57, here quoted from Bagchi, *Pre-Aryan and Pre-Dravidian in India,* p. 91.

[2] *Op. cit.,* p. 140.

[3] Cf. Roy, *The Khāṛiās,* who points to three distinct levels of culture (p. 21 f.)

[4] The one addressed is included in "we".

again given over to mankind, and he is ruling.—Then something again occurred to Marang Buru: he said to Ṭhākūr: 'Again mankind have become very numerous; we cannot get further in the old way; therefore I think we shall make mankind into different races.' Ṭhākūr said to him: 'Very well, see to their wants, that they may live well and not be exterminated from the earth, and so that they will remember us; make them work so. Then he again acted on a thought and stirred up the mind of the men. He gathered them in a plain near a river. Here he made them cook all kinds of flesh, viz., ox-meat, buffalo-meat, the flesh of goats and sheep, of fowls and pigs, of fish and camels. He arranged all this cooked meat in twelve leaf-cups, and having selected one principal man among each of the original septs he called these aside and said to them that they should look at the leaf-cups. When they had done this he took them away as far as the length of three or four plough-furrows; then he said to them: 'Now run along from here and whichever leaf-cup any of you may like, take that and eat. Start running from here all of you at the same time, and any one who can gain on the others, let him.—They ran from there, and the man who reached there in advance, he took the leaf-cup with ox-meat and ate its contents. At this time, it is told, he separated the Santals and the Dekos.[1] They who ate ox-meat became Santals, and they who ate the flesh of goats, of sheep, and of fish became Dekos. At that time their language was also altered; they who got the Deko language were spread in all directions from there, that is to say, they emigrated hither and thither. Those who got the Santal language all stayed together."[2]

We have in this tradition two divergences from what is supposed to have been the state of India before the coming of Dionysos; these agree at the same time with what Megasthenes has to say about Dionysos' contribution. First, the Santal tradition says that meat was eaten, but not eaten raw: it was cooked first. Marang Buru taught the people to cook their meat. And secondly, the animals eaten were domestic, not wild: oxen, goats and sheep. Again it was Marang Buru who was responsible for choosing these animals. Here we appear to have a striking resemblance between the Santal tradition we have quoted and the probable meaning of the passage in Megasthenes. There is a twofold agreement with Megasthenes' Dionysos at this point, which we might express thus: both Marang Buru and Dionysos are reputed to have taught the Indians agriculture; both taught them to cook their

---

[1] *Deko* is the name used by Santals to describe non-Santals of better class, particularly Hindus; but not Muhammedans.

[2] Bodding, *Traditions and Institutions of the Santals*, p. 19.

meat instead of eating it raw; and it is possible that both taught them to eat the meat of domestic animals.

Summing up, we have no evidence that such a tradition ever existed among the Aryans; it is true that among the Dravidians agriculture was believed to have been taught by the intervention of a supernatural being, but not by a culture-hero, to whom all other benefits of civilization can also be traced. Only among the Muṇḍas do we find a tradition the contents of which prove to be virtually identical with those of the Megasthenes passage in question. Important resemblances are also to be found in the traditions of the Koṭas of South India, a Dravidian-speaking people, but a people who bear no further resemblance to the mass of Dravidian peoples.

g. Dionysos introduced the practice of harnessing oxen to the plough.[1]

As usual, we have no explanation from the Aryan traditions of the origins of the practice of ploughing with oxen. But the Aryans were well acquainted with the method. "The operation of tilling the soil," writes Apte, without however quoting his RV sources, "meant (as now) making furrows in the field with the metallic share of a plough drawn by bullocks."[2] Apte's statement may be based on a combination of e.g. I.32.7, which speaks of *vadhri*, 'the (castrated) ox', and *vṛishan*, 'the bull', and VIII.20.19, in which the ploughman (*cárkṛishat*) sings (*abhí-gā́ya*), of his bullocks (*gā́s*).

Turning to non-Aryan India, and to Mohenjo-daro, we find the following passage in Ruben's *Eisenschmiede*: "Sehr merkwürdig ist, dass der Stier unter den vier Tieren des Mohenjo Daro Siegels fehlt, der doch sonst auf unzähligen Siegeln dort erscheint; die vier Tiere sind eben wilde, der Zebustier war aber bereits gezähmt. Gerade die Zähmung des Stieres, das Kastrieren des Wildstieres zum Pflugochsen, die Notwendigkeit der Kastrierung für geordnete Zucht, zum Gewinn zahmer Packochsen, lenksamer Herden, wobei ein einzelner Stier in seiner vollen Kraft erhalten bleiben musste trotz aller seiner Gefährlichkeit, wobei sogar im Interesse der Zucht der beste, stärkste, feurigste und also gefährlichste Stier erhalten bleiben musste, das ist offenbar eine der Wurzeln des Śiva, seiner Furchtbarkeit und Fruchtbarkeit. Wie der Stier im Hinduismus das Tier des Śiva ist, so ist sicher auch der prachtvolle Stier der Mohenjo Daro-Plastik im Zusammenhang mit einem Śiva-ähnlichen Gott zu denken, aber in welchem Zusammenhang?"[3]

This indicates that there is no real connection between Dionysos and Śiva on the matter of their relationship with the bull. Śiva's was a wild

[1] Frg. A 6.

[2] Apte, *Social and Religious Life*, p. 103.

[3] *Op. cit.*, p. 192 f.

bull; Dionysos tamed the bull by means of castration, and hence Dionysos' bull is no more than a tame ox. But although Śiva and Dionysos thus seem to be entirely irreconcileable on this point, there are traditions in South India which do something at least to bring about a reconciliation. We may take these words, written by Thurston, in his *Castes and Tribes of Southern India* VII, p. 364:

"The deities bestowed on the person these three names. First Bhūmi Pālakudu or saviour of the earth, because he was produced by her. Second, Ganga Kulam or descendant of the river Ganga, by reason of having been brought forth on her banks. Third, Murdaka Pālakudu or protector of the plough, alluding to his being born with a ploughshare in his hand, and they likewise ordained that, as he had lost his diadem, he should not be eligible for sovereignty, but that he and his descendants should till the ground with this privilege, that a person of the caste should put the crown on the king's head at the coronation. They next invested him with the *yegnōpavitam* or string, and, in order that he might propagate his caste, they gave him in marriage the daughters of the gods Indra and Kubera. At this time, *the god Śiva was mounted on a white bullock* and the god Dharmarāja on a white buffalo, *which they gave him to plough the ground*, and from which circumstance the caste became surnamed Vellal Wārus or those who plough with white bullocks."[1] Note however that this is uncharacteristic of Śiva.

We have already had occasion to point out that this attribute can be paralleled in the Santals' Marang Buru,[2] and we need not repeat what we said there. But the mention of seed in this connection brings us to the next point. There is little more to be said on the point under discussion apart from once more emphasizing that we have been able to establish a link with both Dravidians and Muṇḍas, but not with Indo-Aryans.

h. Dionysos gave the Indians seed and

i. taught them to sow the land.[3]

It need scarcely be said that these complementary passages have no Aryan connections.

It seems, to judge from Thompson–Balys' *The Oral Tales of India*, that the primitive Dravidian tribes of South India have no such traditions.[4] Nor does Thurston, in his exhaustive account of the most important tradi-

---

[1] Thurston, *Castes and Tribes* VII, p. 364. Cf. also Emeneau, *Koṭa Texts*, p. 39: "He ploughed the fields with the bullock."

[2] Above, p. 217.

[3] Frg. A 6.

[4] Under heading A 1400–A 1499, *Acquisition of Culture*. See also Emeneau, *Koṭa Texts*, p. 41 (quoted below, p. 240 f.).

tions of the South Indian peoples (in *Castes and Tribes*), seem to have included any tradition dealing with the origin of the staple foods. We conclude therefore that this Megasthenes passage cannot refer to the Dravidians, and this conclusion in turn implies that Śiva must be ruled out.

We have already quoted a passage from the *Linguistic Survey* IV p. 66 in which is related how Marang Buru gave mankind seed and taught them to sow. There are large numbers of similar examples to be found in the various works of Verrier Elwin, taken from those parts of India occupied primarily by the Muṇḍas. A number of tribes in this area, as we have noted, are Dravidian-speaking, but they have been subjected to the powerful influence of their Muṇḍa neighbours; it is even possible that they may originally have spoken Muṇḍa languages. It is therefore not altogether surprising that similar traditions have been shown to exist among these tribes. But they have also been influenced by Hinduism, and we occasionally find that typical Muṇḍa myths are told of their god, who has been given one of the names of Śiva. On this subject, Elwin writes (in *Tribal Myths of Orissa*, p. 638): "MAHADEO—The Great God. One of the names of Śiva. The word is applied indiscriminately by the tribesmen to any deity who is married—the wife is then called Pārvatī—and who interfered amiably in human life. There is little connexion between the rather kindly peasant god of the tribesmen and the terrible Hindu deity." It is clear from this account that this "Śiva" has none of the essential characteristics of the Śiva of Hinduism. We must be quite clear on this point, since we have already emphasized that Megasthenes' Dionysos cannot be Śiva. When Lassen and his followers claimed that this Dionysos was identical with Śiva, they naturally meant the Śiva of Hinduism. It is hardly likely that the names and myths of the gods of the various Muṇḍa tribes—Lingo, Mahadeo, etc.—would be called to mind at the mention of the name Śiva, and vice versa.

Elwin quotes a further example from Gond: "When men were first born, they lived on berries, plums, mangoes and other fruit; they had no grain. But growing dissatisfied with this diet they went to Mahaprabhu and said, 'Give us some other food.' Mahaprabhu said, 'Be content with this for a time; presently I'll give you something else.' Mahaprabhu sought everywhere, but could find no rice-seed. There was a Raja who had a horse; the horse went daily to the jungle to graze; one day it ate a rice-plant. When it came back, it excreted and rice came from its excreta. A Ghasia saw it and picked it up. One day Mahaprabhu came to the Ghasia in his search and the Ghasia asked what he wanted. 'Grain-seed,' he said. 'What do you want with that?' Mahaprabhu said, 'I'll have fields made and the seed sown in them and when there is plenty, all will eat.' The Ghasia said, 'I have some kind of seed, but what it is I do not know.' He showed it to Mahaprabhu who cried, 'Here is every kind of food.' The Ghasia gave ten seeds to Mahaprabhu and kept five for himself, so as to have some profit. Mahaprabhu took the seed, had a field made, and sowed it. From the ten seeds ten kinds of grain were born. That year Mahaprabhu stored it all, but next year he had more fields made and soon there was a great quantity of seed and he distributed it to men."[1]

The name Mahaprabhu, which means 'great Lord, Master', is a name given to the Supreme Being. Although the Gonds are a Dravidian people, and although their supreme god has a Sanskrit name, the myth appears to be of Muṇḍa origin. The Gonds are one of the most southerly peoples investigated by Elwin, and their language is a Dravidian language; but the Hill Saoras also belong in the same area, though their language is Muṇḍa. From this source Elwin has taken the following: "In the old days there was no grain in the world, and men were few. What men there were lived on roots. Gradually more and more people were born until there were not enough roots to go round. Men got together and went to Kittung. But Tumgul Saora and his wife, who lived in Tumgulpur, did not go, for they had grain hidden in their house. Kittung said to himself, 'All men have come except Tumgul,' and he told the others, 'Go now and manage somehow or other for this year. Next year I'll give you plenty to eat.' Kittung sent his messengers to find grain. They searched everywhere without success until they came to Tumgul's house, where they found the wife husking on the veranda. When they saw her, they quietly went away. Kittung sent two of his officers to arrest Tumgul. He said to him, 'Give me the grain so that I can increase it for the sake of all men and for your sake also; for if you eat it it will soon be done.' After a lot of fuss, Tumgul gave him seven handfuls. Kittung had a field made and sowed the grain. When it was ready he reaped, threshed, winnowed it and stored it in his house. Then he called the whole world and distributed it."[2]

In his book *The Myths of Middle India* Elwin gives a sketch of "the discovery of grain", in which he says, "In Chota Nagpur the Uraon and the Kharia attribute the origin of grain to the Supreme Being."[3] Of these tribes, the Kharia are Muṇḍa-speaking. T. C. Hodson, in his introduction to S. C. Roy's book *Oraon Religion and Customs*, writes, referring to the Oraon, "They speak a language which belongs to the Dravidian family. They are

---

[1] Elwin, *Tribal Myths of Orissa*, p. 162.

[2] *Op. cit.*, p. 172.

[3] *Op. cit.*, p. 312.

settled among speakers of the Muṇḍa (Austro-Asiatic family) group of languages. They are in constant contact with Hindu and Hinduised groups. There are features in their intellectual beliefs which—apart from resemblances due to the common elements of the universal pattern—are unmistakably borrowed from their Muṇḍa or Hindu neighbours."[1] On the subject of the Kharia Elwin writes, "To this day the Kharia offer a cock to Ponomosor in their rice-fields before they cut the crop and they recall that it was this deity who taught them how and when to sow rice."[2]

These examples could easily be multiplied. What we have quoted should however suffice as a demonstration of those salient features essential to our argument: that a number of culturally closely-related peoples have preserved virtually identical myths, the only notable variation being in the name of the deity concerned. Incidentally, it is perhaps not unnatural that anyone attempting to describe the religion of a certain area containing a large number of closely related tribes, should choose a divine name having no connection with any of their deities—merely for the sake of clarity and convenience.

We hinted under 2b. above that Dionysos may have been the one who gave the Indians not only the tools of war, but the tools of peace as well, e.g. the plough. Although on purely linguistic grounds we have no evidence in support of such an assumption, the context seems to demand it (see fragment A 5). With this in mind it is of particular interest to read these words written by Elwin in his *Myths of Middle India*: "There is a general belief among most of the tribesmen that the implements of husbandry and the processes of agriculture were invented by the gods and taught by them to mankind. The practice of shifting cultivation is everywhere regarded as having been inaugurated by the original tribal hero: Lingo taught it to the Muria, Nanga Baiga to the Baiga, Rusi to the Juang, Boram Burha to the Bhuiya. The Koṭa hero, Kitur Payk, was the first to make fire and invented pottery and agriculture. 'He took black clay and made an unbaked pot and baked that and made a pot. In this pot he boiled flesh and made them eat it ... He took stones from the jungle and put them into the fire and heated them and made smelted iron. From that iron he made arrows, bows, knives, axes, everything, and made them to cut ... He caught jungle buffaloes and jungle cows and tamed them. He ploughed the fields with the bullock. He milked the female buffalo.'"[3]

This tradition has been collected from a tribe which not only speaks a

[1] *Op. cit.*, p. xii. Cf. above, p. 192 and 200.

[2] *Myths of Middle India*, p. 313.

[3] *Op. cit.*, p. 300 f.

Dravidian language, but which also lives in an area far from that occupied by the Muṇḍas: Nīlgiri in South India. Elwin nevertheless follows this tradition with one from the Garwhal Himalaya and another from the Muṇḍas. The latter, drawn from the *Encyclopaedia Mundarica*, is rather amusing. The great and mighty god is busy making a plough for man to use: man, whom he has created. But this work takes time. His wife, feeling lonely and forsaken, tries to make him come home. She creates one unpleasant animal after another to disturb him in his work. But the god is so wrapped up in what he is doing that he ignores all these interruptions, and not until, in the fulness of time, he has finished his plough does he bear it home in triumph. His wife is however not impressed, and bursts out in scorn, "What a wretched plough you have made, and what a long time you have taken over it." The god replies, "The sons of men will spend many many days making ploughs like this; they will not be able to find trees big enough to make serviceable ploughs out of."—"Throw the plough on the ground then, and we shall see what happens!" The god did so, and the plough broke. He said, "Look, my plough is broken. What are the sons of men going to plough with now?" His wife answered, "I will make another kind of plough, not a big, heavy, clumsy thing that men are unable to use, and not one that falls to pieces when it is dropped on the ground; my plough can be made quickly." She made the plough rapidly of a number of pieces which were easily put together. And it was strong, as the god found when he threw it on the ground. He said, "You have excelled me, a man, in making a plough; therefore I say, 'From now on no woman need be troubled by the making of any plough. They shall be made by men; and no woman will be allowed near them'."[1] The first part of this story is found among a number of peoples. Elwin writes, "The Juang ascribe this incident to Rusi, the Muṇḍa to Singbonga, the Santal to Chando, the Birhōr and Baiga to Mahadeo and Pārvatī."[2]

We may now turn to the plants which Dionysos is said to have introduced, and which are mentioned by name. We shall list them in tabular form, concentrating first on the author in whose works the information is to be found, secondly on the Latin name and thirdly on the Sanskrit name, where this is known.

j. ivy (κισσός, κιττός)[3]
Strabo, Arrian, Polyaenus, *Hedera helix* (Skr. name missing)

---

[1] Hoffmann–van Emelen, *Encyclopaedia Mundarica* XIII, pp. 3984 ff.

[2] *Myths of Middle India*, p. 200.

[3] Frg. A 3, 4, 5 and 10.

k. laurel (δάφνη)[1]
Strabo, ***Laurus nobilis*** **(Skr. name missing)**

l. myrtle (μυρρίνη)[1]
Strabo, ***Myrtus communis*** (Skr. name missing)

m. box (πύξος)[1]
Strabo, ***Buxus sempervirens*** (Skr. name missing)

n. fig (σῦκον)[2]
Diodorus, ***Ficus religiosa*** (***Aśvattha***), ***Ficus indica*** (*Nyagrodha*), ***Ficus glomerata*** (*Udumbara*)

o. all manner of fruits which Dionysos taught the Indians to grow, gather in and store[3]

p. principally the grapevine-(ἄμπελος, οἶνος)[4]
Diodorus, Strabo, Arrian, Polyaenus, *Vitis vinifera* (*surā*, *drākshā*, *madhu*)

The documentation here is clearly of such a quality that only in the case of the grapevine can one be reasonably certain of the authenticity of the information conveyed. Laurel, myrtle and box are mentioned only by Strabo; fig only by Diodorus. Such general terms as "fruits" and "fruit-trees" are also used freely by the latter author, thus leaving ample room for the exercise of imagination. But we must now ask whether these fruits are mentioned in the Indian literature and/or traditions.

We see from the final columns that the first four entries have no Sanskrit names. It is true that three of these are to be found in Monier-Williams' *English–Sanskrit Dictionary*, expressed by detailed descriptions of the plants concerned, but none of these are found in his *Sanskrit–English Dictionary*.

Ivy: *vṛikshâgṛihādirohī latāviśesha* (a species of clinging vine, which grows on trees, houses, etc.), *taruruhā* (= growing in trees), *tarurohiṇī* identical meaning)

Laurel: *lārelākhyo vṛikshabheda* (= a species of tree called *lārel*), *śyāmavṛikshaviśesha* (= a species of tree with a very dark colour)

Myrtle: missing

Box: *atidṛiḍho vṛikshaprabheda* (= a species of tree which is enormously strong/tenacious)

Monier-Williams himself is evidently responsible for the definitions we

[1] Frg. A 3.
[2] Frg. A 2.
[3] Frg. A 1 and 2.
[4] Frg. A 1, 2, 3, 4, 6 and 10.

have quoted. He seems to have been forced to invent these, not only because they were not previously to be found in Sanskrit, but because the plants themselves are unknown in India. The brief summary of the flora and fauna of India in *The History and Culture of the Indian People* I is of no direct help.[1] Although the author points out that the climate of India is favourable to all the world's plants, he makes no specific mention of these in which we are particularly interested.

According to Thompson–Balys' *The Oral Tales of India*, Elwin is the only writer to have collected myths and traditions about the origin of the various kinds of tree, and the field covered is thus limited to Central India. No mention is made of ivy, laurel, myrtle or box. This need not however mean that these are unknown in India. Strabo stated explicitly that they grow in Nysa and Mēros—i.e. in or near the Himalaya. Incidentally, can we without more ado assume Megasthenes to have been a sufficiently skilled botanist to identify correctly the plant *Aralia*, a species of ivy found in Southern Asia? There are a number of species of laurel in India; similarly myrtle. In the circumstances, it is wellnigh impossible for any but an expert in the flora of India to supply the correct identification of each of these plants. We shall therefore leave this particular section of our problem, pausing only to remark that it is likely that the species mentioned by name were not those which grew in India, but some closely related types, and that—more important—we do not know with any degree of certainty which of these names may be traced back to Megasthenes himself.

Two plants remain; both—the fig and the grapevine—are of the greatest interest.

In TS VII.4.12 there is a list of trees, in which the following are mentioned: the cotton tree, the rubber tree, the fig, the banyan and the udumbara. The three last-named are all varieties of the fig tree: *aśvattha*, *nyagrodha* and *udumbara*, or, to give their Latin names, *ficus religiosa*, *ficus indica* and *ficus glomerata*. The *aśvattha* is sometimes known as the *pippala* (pipal tree) and *gajabhakshaka*; the *nyagrodha* is also called *vaṭa*, and an alternative form of *udumbara* is *uḍumbara* (with lingual 'ḍ'). These three, together with *bassia latifolia*, form a group known as 'milk trees' (*kshīravṛiksha*). There are also two other species of fig tree in India, *parkaṭī* (*ficus infectoria*) and *añjīram* (*ficus oppositifolia*); the latter name is Persian: its Indian name is *uḍumbarī*.

The *aśvattha* was the most important of these trees during the Vedic period; the *nyagrodha*, on the other hand, is missing from the RV,[2] though

[1] *Op. cit.*, particularly p. 108 f.

[2] Apte, *Social and Religious Life*, p. 117.

it is mentioned in the later *saṁhitās* and in the Brāhmaṇas. It is however never connected with the name of any particular god in Aryan tradition.[1]

In South India Śiva is called the god in the fig tree.[2] But this does not seem to be applicable to elder Tamil literature, i.e. that nearer in time to Megasthenes. Iyengar, in his *Dravidian India*, claims that there is nothing in this literature which indicates acquaintance with the fig tree.[3] He also makes the same claim with respect to later living tradition. The impression we gain from Iyengar's work is that none of the plants mentioned by Megasthenes can be traced in the Tamil tradition.

J. Przyluski, in an article entitled *Un ancien peuple du Penjab: les Udumbara*, has demonstrated the Austro-Asiatic origin of the word *udumbara*.[4] And Erik Gren, discussing the possibility of identifying the bearers of the Indus civilization with the Muṇḍas, notes in passing that "when we find representations of a tree in the Harappa culture, it is usual to interpret these as being of the sacred pipal (*ficus religiosa*), a tree which also has a ritual function among the Muṇḍas. Note, however, that it is equally or more plausible to identify them as the sal-tree (*shorea robusta*), a plant sacred to the Muṇḍas".[5]

In order to stress the importance of the fig tree in Muṇḍa tradition we reproduce a passage from "The Ancestors' Story", quoted by Bodding in *Traditions and Institutions of the Santals*:

---

[1] Crooke, *Natives of Northern India*, p. 231: "The many varieties of the fig genus, again, like the Banyan and the Pipal, are regarded as sacred by all Hindus, and are found growing near many shrines. In fact, the catalogue of holy trees is enormous, and there are few trees or plants of peculiar beauty, appearance, or interest, which are not in some way utilised for the purpose of ritual."

[2] See e.g. Iyengar, *History of the Tamils*, pp. 184 ff.

[3] *Op. cit.*, p. 54: "There is nothing in Tamil to answer to the cold regions of the Asiatic table-lands, to the ice-bound polar plains, or to the vine-growing, fig-shaded Chaldean regions."

[4] *Journ. Asiat.* 1926, pp. 25–36; included in Bagchi, *Pre-Aryan and Pre-Dravidian*, pp. 149–160, particularly p. 157.

[5] Gren, *Indien*, p. 40. Cf. Roy, *Caste, Race and Religion in India* (in *Man in India* XVII, 1937, pp. 159 ff.). Hutton, *Census of India* 1931, p. 397, states that the cult of the fig tree is the Negrito contribution to the culture of India. Doubt is expressed by Roy, who points out that the Vedic Indians held the *Aśvattha* to be the holiest of all trees, and that in the Mbh (*Anuśāsana Parvan*, 149, 101) Vishṇu is called *Nyagrodha Uḍumbara Aśvattha*. "On the other hand, no special cult of the fig-tree is found among the Muṇḍa tribes of India." Mitra has written an article, *On the Cult of the Banyan and the Pipal Trees*, in which he points out that these trees are sacred. This is of course not disputed. But this is not what Megasthenes says: he claims that the fig-tree was introduced by Dionysos.

"So they lived on; living on they grew up and became big. Haram on his side was in the habit of going with the boys to hunt in one direction, and in another direction Budhi on her side was going with the girls to pluck and bring vegetables and leaves, and when it became evening they used to come together at home. One day the young men went to Khanderae forest to hunt by themselves alone, and the girls also had gone alone to Surukuc forest to pluck vegetables. When they had finished doing this, they came out at the foot of the Capakia fig tree (*ficus tmentosa*) and were playing swinging on the pendulous roots of the fig tree. Thereupon they shifted and commenced to dance *dahar* and sang: 'The ants, the ants swarm, o mother, on the lower branches of the Capakia fig tree they swarm.'—Having become tired from hunting the young men were coming out of the forest bringing a *boi bindi* deer with them. Hearing the singing of the girls they said: 'Listen you, who are singing?' Then they left the deer there and went to the girls and commenced to dance with them. Dancing along they became delighted. The eldest young man chose for himself the eldest girl and the youngest boy the youngest girl, and in this way all of them did. Thereupon the eldest young man and the eldest girl went to have a look at the deer. At that time the other ones sang: 'Along under the fig tree to the young deer, o mother, quick to see the young *boi bindi* deer.' Then all of them became pairs of their own accord. Having observed this Haram and Budhi said: 'They have found each other, we shall marry them.'"[1]

A number of myths of the origins of the trees are to be found in Elwin's *Tribal Myths of Orissa*. We quote one such, told among the Hill Saoras:

"Before the creation of the world, Kittung and his sister used to live in a gourd. When the new world was made and the gourd broke open, brother and sister came out and made their home on Kurabeli Hill. There were no trees on the earth at that time and the two had to sleep in the open under the sky. One night while they were asleep, a mountain squirrel bit off four of the fingers of Kittung's left hand. Only the third finger remained. Kittung woke with the pain and cried; his sister also awoke and cried.—When the hot weather came, the girl said, 'How can I live in this heat when there is no shade?' Kittung cut off his maimed left hand, and put it on a stone. It soon grew into a tree and gave shade beneath which Kittung's sister sheltered. This was the pipal, which has one finger in the middle of its leaves and grows on rocks in the forest."[2]

The myth immediately preceding this in the same book contains certain details strikingly reminiscent of the terms used by Megasthenes:

[1] *Op. cit.*, p. 7.

[2] *Op. cit.*, p. 132 f.

"Satiya and Nambo, two brothers, lived in the Manjul Hill. In those days there was no grain anywhere. The whole world lived on fruit and roots. But when the people increased in number, there were not enough roots to go round. Kittung came to the two brothers and said, 'There are not enough roots for all these people. If you will bring grain to birth, all will be well.' The brothers replied, 'But where are we to find grain? We have no seed.' Kittung took them to the Mandarjan Hill and showed them how to use the digging-stick. He found a flower of the wild fig tree and in this flower was every kind of grain. They sowed the seed and learnt which kind of seed was which. Since then there has been grain in the world, but no one can ever find the flower of the wild fig."[1]

It is remarkable that most of the myths of the origin of trees and plants quoted by Elwin, and particularly in his *Myths of Middle India*, do not have a deity as the *fons et origo*. Elwin himself writes, "I was surprised at the difficulty in getting from people who spend all their lives in the forest any account of how trees came into being or acquired their different characteristics. Some tribes trace the colour or shape of trees to contact with a tribal hero ..."[2] He goes on to give a number of examples, one of which tells how the Muṇḍas believe the tamarind to have obtained its leaves through the direct intervention of Singbonga and his brother. But there is no evidence of any particularly close connection between Singbonga and the fig tree, and we are unable to draw any conclusions as to the correctness of our identification. No support is forthcoming from the Saora myth of Kittung, since Kittung is not one, but a large number of beings. Elwin, writing in *The Religion of an Indian Tribe* points out: "As we see later in this chapter, there are a number of different Kittungs and the Saoras are entirely uncertain as to which of them is the Creator ... Probably the inconsistency arises from the fact that the Saoras have never been able to make up their minds whether Kittung is a supra-mundane deity or a simple cult-hero. This is why, according to some myths, he made, and, according to others, he was, the first man."[3] Do we not recognize in this strange ambivalence—creator-god and human hero at one and the same time—something of Dionysos as described by Megasthenes?

Finally, the grapevine. Here we come up against a number of difficulties.[4]

---

[1] *Op. cit.*, p. 132. Cf. frg. A 6: The Indians previously ate the bark of the trees.

[2] *Op. cit.*, p. 129.

[3] *Op. cit.*, p. 85. Cf. p. 94: "Kittung is ... an approximation to a Supreme Being."

[4] Charpentier, *Beiträge zur indischen Wortkunde*, p. 93: "Da in Indien selbst Wein aus Traubensaft überhaupt nie dargestellt worden ist ..." In *ibid.*, n. 2: "Die antiken

It is mentioned in the RV primarily under the name *surā*, but always with the connotation that the drinking of wine is morally harmful. This antipathy increases in the following period, despite the fact that *surā* is the daughter of Varuṇa.[1]

Madhu, which means 'honey' in the RV, has by the time of the Gṛihya-Sūtras come to mean 'wine'.[2] Drunkenness in India is usually connected with the names of Indra and Soma; but the *soma* plant had disappeared by the time the Gṛihya-Sūtras came to be written.[3] Thus neither *soma* nor the despicable *surā* can come into consideration as applying to the time of Megasthenes; the intoxicant favoured at that time was *madhu*.

There is however a more uncommon word for 'wine', *drākshā*. This is found in one of Śiva's epithets, Drākshārāmeśvara (= lord of the vineyard), and at once suggests Dionysos' epithet Lēnaios (= the one with the wine-press). Monier–Williams' *English–Sanskrit Dictionary* has for 'winepress' *drākshāpeshaṇayantram* or *drākshāpeshaṇī*; both appear to be translations by the lexicographer himself: descriptions in Sanskrit of the objects re-

---

Schriftsteller wussten, dass in Indien kein Wein vorhanden war; nur im Lande des Musikanus fanden sich nach Onesikritus Weinstöcke (Strabo XV 1, 22)." Ray, *Food and Drink in Ancient India*, p. 33: "Of the six kinds of liquor, *surā*, whisky, *medaka*, beer, *arishṭā*, tincture, and *madhu*, wine, appear to have been much in demand. *Maireya* and *Āsava* were liquors."

Sanjana, *Prohibition in Hinduism*, suggests that all the religions of India favour intoxicants. Even Kṛishṇa and Rāma drank wine. Not until the coming of Islam in the 14th century was there any attempt at prohibition. A hundred years later Vishnuism exercised the same influence. Cf. however our quotations in the text from Apte and Manu.

Sir Aurel Stein, writing in *Ancient Khotan*, pp. 144–166, quotes Marco Polo, who visited Khotan in 1272: "The people have vineyards and gardens and estates. They live by commerce and manufacture and are no soldiers." This quotation is taken up by Roy in his series *Caste, Race and Religion*, in *Man in India*, XVIII, 1938, p. 87, in the course of his description of the Alpine race. which he claims to be fairly unmixed racially in the Pamirs and the Hindu Kush, i.e. the areas through which Alexander the Great passed, and where he heard the people speak about their "Dionysos". He goes on to stress their great interest in literature and music, and points out that they are most numerous in Bengal.

Thurston, *Castes and Tribes in Southern India*, conveys the impression that most of these tribes are *not* in favour of intoxicants. The following castes and tribes are named as exceptions to this rule: Chakkliliyan in the Tamil area, Cheruman, Dasari (though Vaishnavites), Dōmb, Dommara, Gamalla (called "toddy-drawers"), Golla (Kṛishṇa's caste Gopāla), Haddi, Halēpaik (Vaishnavites and "toddy-drawers"), Hasala (Negroid gatherers), Holeya, Īdiga (Vaishnavites and "toddy-drawers"), etc.

[1] Apte, *Social and Religious Life*, p. 96 f. Cf. lexicon; see also RV VII.86.6.

[2] *Op. cit.*, p. 98.

[3] *Op. cit.*, p. 102.

ferred to. The first means 'a tool with which grapes are crushed'; the second, 'grape-crusher'. *Drākshā* means 'grapevine' or 'grape', but is incorporated into a number of words for 'wine': *drākshārasa, -sava, -surā* and *madyam*. There is no point in making a list of all the words for 'wine' and 'grapevine' in Monier-Williams' *English-Sanskrit Dictionary*. In this case there is nothing said about where the plant is found. Nor is the grapevine mentioned in *The History and Culture of the Indian People*, a work which is in any case not very exhaustive.[1] Wine and the grapevine are seldom mentioned in the texts. Manu makes mention of wine, adding the interesting observation that there is nothing intrinsically wrong in drinking it.[2] But a Brahman must not indulge himself; intoxicating drinks belong to the sphere of the demons, and since the Brahman offers sacrifice to the gods he must abstain. Should he drink wine, he loses his rank and sinks to the level of a śūdra.[3]

It is perfectly obvious that we cannot reconcile the positive attitude to wine which is so characteristic of Dionysos and his followers with the attitude expressed in the Aryan literature, as exemplified in the statements we have quoted. Note however that the aversion to intoxicants we find in the texts was very largely theoretical; the practice followed seems to have been far different.[4]

It is more difficult to form an opinion as to the drinking habits of the Dravidians, and their attitude to intoxicants. Thurston on the one hand seems, in his *Castes and Tribes*, to suggest that the average South Indian is sober and unfavourably inclined to strong drink. On the other hand we learn from Iyengar's *Dravidian India* that "strong-bodied *mlecchas* and Maravas get drunk with fermenting toddy ..."[5] He says nothing about the source of his information, but it seems likely that he is relying on some Aryan text. Some Dravidian authors are however liable to interpret every mention of *mlecchas* as a reference to Dravidians, and we must therefore dismiss this statement, at least for the purposes of proof.

Dikshitar, in his *Studies in Tamil Literature and History* states from Perumpāṇāṟṟuppaḍai, that drunkenness was common in most classes of society. Various kinds of drink were consumed, and he suggests that there may well have existed "wine shops". He goes on to take up the question of dancing, music and religious festivals, and combines music and the practice of religion, but has nothing to say about intoxicants in this connection.[6] This

[1] *Op. cit.*, pp. 107–112.

[2] Manu V.56.

[3] *Ibid.*, VI.94–97.

[4] Cf. above, p. 232 f. n. 4, quotation from Sanjana.

[5] *Op. cit.*, p. 193.

[6] *Op. cit.*, pp. 268 and 288–308.

detail seems to point away from any identification of Dionysos with Śiva, and from the identification of the worshippers of Dionysos with the worshippers of Śiva, despite the fact that Śiva himself is called *drākshārāmeśvara*, Lord of the vineyard, and despite the fact that the drinking of wine formed part of the worship of his consort.[1] The fact remains that wine was far from being a prime essential of the Śaivite cultus, and that the texts say nothing which can be taken to point to an unmistakeable connection between the god Śiva and the drinking of wine. The first the Greeks noted of the cult of the Indian Dionysos seems to have been the practice of wine-drinking.

This corresponds closely to what we know of the Muṇḍas and their religion. Reading Roy, we meet with passages like these time and time again: "Then, as now, the Kols appear to have taken the utmost delight in drinking and in singing."[2] "The favourite drink of the Muṇḍa is rice-beer or *ili*."[3] "It is a most remarkable fact that the majority of Hinduised Muṇḍas have given up their age-long habit of drinking."[4] "Their love of drink appears to have been almost an inborn propensity with the tribe. According to their legends, the mysterious root used in the manufacture of *ili* or rice-beer was pointed out to their first parents by Sing-bonga (the Sun-god) himself. Then, as now, the Muṇḍa, after a hard day's labour, knew no better occupation than drinking, dancing and singing up to a late hour of the night."[5]

Elwin, in his *Tribal Myths of Orissa* tells of the following tradition among the Hill Saoras about the use of wine in worship. "At first the Saoras had no gods and of course no need of priests. When the gods were born among the Saoras, Jungo and his wife Kaiti became the first shamans. They offered sacrifices but in those days they did not know how to get palm-wine, and the gods were not satisfied.—One day Kittung gave Jungo a dream and told him what to do. 'Give wine to every god.' Next day Kittung went to a palm and when his pot was full, he called the Kuramar and gave him some to drink. Kittung said to the wife, 'You drink too.' She did and was pleased. After that, they always offered wine to the gods.—When the tree dries, the Saoras offer it rice and fish and the sap flows again ..."[6]

Another tradition from the same tribe is related by Elwin: "One day,

---

[1] Above, p. 187.
[2] *The Muṇḍas*, p. 59.
[3] *Op. cit.*, p. 381.
[4] *Op. cit.*, p. 382.
[5] *Op. cit.*, p. 121.
[6] *Op. cit.*, p. 195 f.

when the number of people in the world was greatly increasing, Kittung and his wife went to a mountain and made a hut apart from the crowd. One night, Kittung was sitting by the fire in front of his hut and roasting a cob of maize. He began to eat the grains and by mistake put a live coal in his mouth. It burnt him and he spat it out. It was now black and Kittung thought, 'This thing has hurt me very much. It's no good just throwing it away. I'll make it into something.' He dug a hole in the ground in front of his house and poured some millet gruel into it. He dropped the bit of coal into the hole and covered it with earth. Daily he watered the place and in seven days a tree grew up. He carefully looked after it and it grew tall and in two years bore a spadix.—Kittung called Ramma to cut it and told him how to take out the sap and drink it and that if he did so, he would be drunk and happy. When the sap was exhausted, he should cut down the tree, remove the pith, dry it, powder it and make it into gruel. In this way the whole tree would be used and nothing wasted."[1]

The context in which this god-given intoxicant is to be viewed becomes clearer from Bodding's account, in *Traditions and Institutions of the Santals*, of how mankind became conscious of the sexual life.

"One day Lita (= Marang Buru) came to them and said to them, 'Where are you, grandchildren? How are you? I am your grandfather; I have come to pay you a visit. I see you are well; but there is one great joy that you have not tasted. Do brew beer; it has a very sweet taste.' Then he taught them to prepare the fermenting stuff. All three went to the forest. Lita showed them the roots. The two dug up and brought these. When they had brought them Lita said to Pilcu Budhi, 'Now you make the rice wet for us.' She did so. Having made it wet she pounded it into flour; they jabbed the 'medicine' (fermenting stuff), they squeezed it and kneaded the flour with the 'medicine'-juice; having kneaded it into a dough they made balls of it; having made balls they put these into a basket together with straw and put this aside. When next day came, at the time they had made the balls, at the same time they uncovered them; having done this they threw the straw away and spread (the balls) out on a winnowing-fan; spread out there the balls became dry, and they put them aside. When this was done they gathered the *sumtu bukuc* and *sama* ears and pounded them. They boiled the grain and thereupon let it cool; when cooled they kneaded the fermenting stuff into it; thereupon having assembled all they covered it up in leaves and kept it there. In five days the fermentation was complete. In the afternoon they poured water on it. Then Lita said to them, 'Now both of you

---

[1] *Op. cit.*, p. 198.

drink this after first having poured on the ground some to Marang Buru. Tomorrow I shall come again and visit you.'—Thereupon they made three leaf-cups and filled these; having done this they poured on the ground one in the name of Marang Buru; then they drank themselves. When they were drinking they commenced to toy amorously; continuing this they both drank all and also became very drunk. It became night, they lay down together.——When it became dawn Lita suddenly came. He called out to them: 'How is it, grandchildren, have you got up or not? Do come out.' When they had regained consciousness they recognized that they were both naked and felt very ashamed; therefore they answered him, 'O grandfather, how can we possibly go out? We are awfully ashamed; we are both of us naked; last night when we had become drunk from beer, we have done something bad.'—Lita then said to them, 'It does not matter.' And smiling to himself he went away. To cover their shame Pilcu Haram and Pilcu Budhi made a skirt and a loincloth for themselves of ficus-leaves."[1]

The same tradition among the Muṇḍas is related in the following version, taken from the *Encyclopaedia Mundarica*:

'The Muṇḍas' account of the origin of man says that the first man and the first woman made by Sing-bonga remained in childlike simplicity and abstained from sexual intercourse until Sing-bonga taught them the art of preparing rice-beer.—A second legend says that once upon a time Sing-bonga rained fire from heaven which destroyed all men with the exception of one boy and one girl who were brother and sister. These two had been hidden by Nageera in a cool cavern on the water-side and thus saved from death. Sing-bonga obtained them from Nageera, built a hut for them and brought them up. At sleeping time he always put a log between them and they were ignorant of sexual connection until one day he taught them how to prepare rice-beer. After they had got intoxicated and gone to sleep, he removed the log which was between them and from that time they became husband and wife and from them came all men now living.—*In this legend there is not only no restriction on the use of intoxicating liquors but its divine origin and its purpose are calculated to act rather as a commendation.*"[2]

The reason why we have quoted the two variants of this tradition may appear obvious. Some explanation is however called for.

There was a clear connection between Dionysos and wine. Mention is made of the gathering, storing and pressing of the grape. It may seem at first sight as though we have this detail to thank for the choice of the name Dionysos by the Greeks to describe the Indian god they found. But sup-

[1] Bodding, *Traditions and Institutions of the Santals*, p. 6.

[2] Hoffmann–van Emelen, *Encyclopaedia Mundarica*, s.v. *Baranda-bonga*, p. 430.

pose a group of Dionysos-worshippers should remove to a part of the world unsuitable for the cultivation of the grape vine, what then? They naturally transfer their allegiance to some other convenient intoxicant. There seems to be an important typological agreement here with the traditions on which Megasthenes' narrative is based. Marang Buru shows mankind the plant to use; he shows them what to do with it; and so on. The main difference is the name of the plant in question. But we know, *inter alia* from place-names in Western India, that some branch of the Muṇḍa people once lived there, and we suspect that in that place there were very likely similar traditions dealing with the relation between Marang Buru, Sing-bonga, Kittung and the rest, and wine. The traditions naturally became extinct, at least in this form, when the people were forced to abandon their vineyards. But they are found later, in a modified form, linked with the name of the substitute for wine they have found in their new home. The decisive factor in all this is not the name of the plant; it is the type of tradition. And it is an inescapable fact that the traditions connected with Dionysos on the one hand and the Muṇḍa culture-hero on the other are of identical type—a type unknown outside the Muṇḍa sphere, having not the slightest connection with either Kṛishṇa or Śiva. Differences in detail there may be; in form and outline they are identical.

It is not quite clear whether Megasthenes meant to suggest that the drinking of wine formed an integral part of the cult of Dionysos. It is possible that this is what is meant by Fragment A 10. This element of doubt makes it necessary to deal with the question briefly here. If Megasthenes meant that wine-drinking was a part of the cult, we may compare a quotation from Elwin's *The Religion of an Indian Tribe*. In the first place, the drinking of wine plays an important part in the daily life of the Saoras: "The men gather morning and evening in this open-air tavern; some of them fetch the wine, mixing the sap from two or more trees if possible, for this improves it."[1] "Religious drinking is made heavier by the convenient belief that the gods who gave wine to the world are as fond of it as men are. When a shaman in trance is possessed by a spirit, he becomes the spirit, and if the spirit is to drink he can only do so through the shaman's mouth. In a lengthy ceremony, in the course of which a shaman may be possessed by a score of different gods and ancestors, each clamorous for refreshment, he has to put down a considerable quantity to satisfy them all. And the assistants and onlookers too feel it their duty to drink with the divine visitants, with the result that most ceremonies conclude with everyone more than a little drunk."[2] Drinking thus forms an integral part of the life of the

[1] *Op. cit.*, pp. 184–188. [2] *Op. cit.*, p. 186.

Saoras, both in their daily round and at their religious festivals. Elwin goes on to show how wine occupies a place of honour on all the most important days in a man's life: when he is born, when he is given his name, when he marries; and it is often the only comfort when death comes.[1]

The same cannot be said of the Dravidian peoples, or of Hinduism generally; nor of the Aryans in India, as far as we can see from the texts.[2] And we find that Kṛishṇa and Krishnaism have an entirely negative attitude toward wine-drinking: in Mbh XVI Kṛishṇa forbade the practice, though he later relaxed his ban for one day only. In the orgy which followed his entire family was annihilated. Wine-drinking formed part of the cult of Śiva's consort, but that is irrelevant for our purposes, since Megasthenes was concerned only with a single god, the bearer of all the attributes we have mentioned. It might be possible to transfer attributes from one deity to another in certain circumstances, but such a procedure is not called for in this case; Megasthenes' description of Dionysos fits in so well with the Muṇḍas' culture-hero/sun-god that we have no need to seek support elsewhere.

q. Dionysos was called Lēnaios, 'the one with the winepress''.[3]

I have been unable to find support for this statement in any tradition. The nearest equivalent is Śiva's name Drākshārāmeśvara, 'lord of the vineyard', which is not quite the same thing. The age of this epithet is uncertain. There is no word in Sanskrit meaning 'winepress', and we can safely assume that no support is likely to be forthcoming from the Aryan literature. Nor is there any word in Tamil meaning 'winepress'. A word *alai*, quoted in Percival's *English–Tamil Dictionary* means, according to Bishop Bexell's *Tamil–English Dictionary*, 'a press for the pressing of sugarcane, etc.'. There is nothing meaning 'winepress' under the Tamil words for 'wine' and 'grapevine'. This suggests that the concept, if it in fact exists in South India, is either insufficiently important to require a special word, or too infrequent to warrant a special entry in the lexicon. I have had no means of checking the situation with regard to the various Muṇḍa languages. If it is true, as Charpentier suggests, that wine is never made out of the juice of grapes in India, then we have no need to prolong the discussion.[4]

---

[1] *Op. cit.*, p. 187.

[2] Dowson, *A Classical Dictionary of Hindu Mythology*, s.v. Soma, gives us information which reminds of Dionysos. The position of *soma* in the Indian cultus is prominent. But there is no myth connected with the *soma* plant which calls to mind Dionysos' contribution in teaching the Indians to grow and make use of the grape.

[3] Frg. A 2.

[4] See above, p. 232, n. 4.

III. *Dionysos' Religious Contribution*

r. Dionysos founded a religious cult.[1]

The theme of the god who encourages men to worship him is never met with in the RV. The same applies to the Aryan literature before the Govardhana story told in the Harivaṁśa and the Purāṇas of Kṛishṇa. It is quite possible to establish a connection here with Kṛishṇa.

In Mbh XII.285.125 we read that Śiva claimed to have founded the religion of Pāśupata. This is however in no way an article of faith among Śaivites. Śiva is not represented in the literature as particularly active among men. But there are variants in the representation of Śiva, and it should therefore be possible to produce concrete evidence in support of this particular statement. In Dikshitar's *Purāṇa Index* (s.v. Śiva), the god is said to have "appeared before the Pracetasas and initiated them into the Rudragītā in glory of Hari".[2] But is this sufficiently typical of Śiva to attract the attention of a foreign observer and commentator? Hardly. The question is answered as soon as asked: its omission from a list of Śiva's attributes would scarcely be noticed.

Turning to those tribes which speak Dravidian languages, I have come across this Koṭa tradition. It is to be found in Emeneau's *Koṭa Texts*:

"(The god) said: 'It is not fitting that you (pl.) live like this in the jungle like buffaloes or cows or domestic animals. Hereafter, you (pl.) acting like human beings and knowing: 'They are the ones who created us' and saying to that one who created you: 'God' and calling his name,—those gods, we (excl.) are three persons. For the one Kamatr Father-god saying another name: 'Elder Father-god and Younger Father-god and Mother-goddess', you must make the three gods. For the day when you make the god, for all these three gods there are nine tunes (*lit.* 'clarinets'). Once a year playing those tunes, and twelve times in twelve months (without making music), you must come to my entrance and all the people must bow down. To go on worshipping me at the temples, there must be two priests and three diviners. When those five men go on getting up daily at cockcrow and washing in cold water and coming to my entrance and joining their hands in salutation and bowing down, I after this will go on giving you (pl.) good gifts, giving you intelligent children and the like, watching over you. Keep me in your minds!' All the people who were on that Drug mountain believed the words that this diviner had said, and they made three temples and went on bowing down, saying: 'God!' (God speaking through the diviner) said: 'You (pl.) are human beings. If I come directly to you like a man and you see me, if

[1] Frg. A 1 and 6.

[2] Bhāgavata Purāṇa IV.24.25–68; 25.1; 29.42.

I come and stand before you, because you are sinners, all of you, having caught alight like fire and having become burnt up, will without fail be destroyed. Therefore, since it is not fitting that I come and speak advice to you directly and go on bringing you forward, whoever in this crowd goes on praying with much thought upon me, to that man a son will be born. The name of that boy, he must call the name, saying: 'Kiturpayk.' When he calls the name, when that boy has become a grown man, just he will tell you all and show and grant to you the whole way, namely: 'How must we make you act?' At that time, I will make so that your condition of being jungle men will cease to be and so that after that you will go on acting like people, building a village, keeping a village, making crops and seeds, keeping buffaloes and cows, wearing cloaks (i.e., clothes). After that, after Kiturpayk has been born and has shown and granted to you this whole way, I will go taking you from this mountain to a good place and will make you enter it and I will go on watching over you. I will kill those who go on acting, not listening to my words, not being obedient and submissive, not following the rules against sexual intercourse with later generations and the rules against sexual intercourse with previous generations, speaking lying words, going back on promises. To those who go on acting, being obedient and submissive, I will give green tender plants, seeds and crops, fruit and milk, and will watch over them with good gifts'. When they went on acting as that diviner had said, that man also whom we call: 'Kiturpayk' was born. When it happened as god said, Kiturpayk taught and gave all these things, buffaloes, cows, fire, clay pots, cloaks (i.e., clothes), smithies, all these things. When he went walking with those people, as a man with men, for fifty years, and when his three sons were not telling how they had killed (the calf) but were keeping it secret in their minds, he saw (i.e., knew as a god knows) all this, and saying: 'It is not fitting for me to be together with these people', he ceased to show himself to their eyes and went away."[1]

In this passage we are struck time and time again with the resemblance to Megasthenes' description of Dionysos: for example, the situation before the appearance of the respective gods; their contributions; the time they spent among men—all are strikingly alike. But there are also important differences. And one of these is vital, as far as our investigation is concerned. Although the god is said to have founded his cult himself, he is not identical with the god that founded the culture in question. There is a culture-hero in the picture, but in the narrative he is represented as standing outside the cult and its foundation. We conclude that this passage cannot be taken to point to the Dravidian god as the god described.

[1] *Op. cit.*, p. 41 f.

We turn therefore to the Muṇḍa traditions.

In the *Encyclopaedia Mundarica*, under the heading "Baranda-bonga," we find this formula to be used in connection with offerings to the lesser spirits (bongas): "Sing-bonga, thou who has ordered us to sacrifice to bongas, command this (name of a spirit) to accept my offering."[1]

Bodding, in *Traditions and Institutions of the Santals*, records this Santal tradition: "Marang Buru taught the two human beings to dig out medicines, to collect and prepare the stuffs for fermenting beer, to cut trees, to sow millets, to offer the first fruits of these, to invoke the spirits of the sacred grove and other matters ... Chando made the two human beings go to the Hihiri Pipiri country. He taught them the invocation in connexion with offering the first fruits of millets, and he made them prepare the sacred grove. At the foot of the trees of the sacred grove he made them fix a stone; at the stone he made them put down the ears of the *iri* millet (Lat. *panicum crus-galli*), and he taught them the invocation (as follows) ..." The name of Marang Buru is also mentioned in the invocation. Bodding comments: "The role played by Marang Buru is different from what is otherwise taught; he is here appearing as a kind of factotum of Ṭhākūr, a spirit that should be in charge of mankind and be their guide."[2] In other words, Bodding is saying that the traditions are inconsistent. The name Chando is an Aryan word meaning 'moon'; Bodding informs us however that here it is the sun who is meant, and that the sun is otherwise known as Sing-bonga.[3] It seems then that we have a parallel between Chando among the Santals and the Muṇḍa Sing-bonga as founder of the cult. It is clear from Bodding's text that Marang Buru also introduced some kind of cult, but it is not stated whether it was the cult of Marang Buru himself. But this is the implication in a tradition which we have earlier had occasion to quote: "Then Lita said to them, 'Now both of you drink this after first having poured on the ground some to Marang Buru.'"[4] Lita is reputed to be the true name of the god, Marang Buru (the great mountain) being no more than an epithet.

When we read that Dionysos taught the Indians to worship the divine, this seems to imply that there was a time when the gods were not worshipped. Although this seems to be to strain the Greek text rather, we find support in the following Muṇḍa tradition: "Before the gods were born

---

[1] *Op. cit.*, p. 424.

[2] Bodding, *op. cit.*, p. 18 f.

[3] *Op. cit.*, p. 14.

[4] Above, p. 236 f.; Bodding, *op. cit.*, p. 6.

there was great peace in the world—there was no disease, no religion, no sacrifice, no priest."[1] Another legend reads thus:

"First men were made, then the gods. But in those days men were so busy cultivating, coupling, eating, drinking, dancing that they had no time for the gods and gave them no sacrifices. The gods lived in the forest on fruit and flowers, wind and water. So, untroubled by religion, men grew rich.—But when Mahaprabhu saw the prosperity of men he was worried. 'If men are as rich as this they'll not be afraid of anyone. I must think of some way of getting their money out of them.' Mahaprabhu called the gods and made them stay with him for six months; during that time he made them very comfortable with rich meals of milk and sugar. Then he said, 'Go and live among men. There is one Seti Sisa; go to him; he is a friend of mine. He'll make arrangements for your camp and will get you all the supplies you need.'—The gods went to Sisa—it was like the coming of the police in a case of murder—and he made arrangements for them and showed them where to stay. He gave them names—he called one Dumbar and sent him to live in the sacred grove near the village. He sent Orseley, the tiger god, to haunt the approaches to the swiddens. Another god he named Runkta and put him to live in the stream where people went to bathe. He sent Saoruli to live in the hill above the village, Bugabor to the forest. Dagoi and Gurangpoi to his own house, Singraj to the spring. For Sindibor he made a stone platform.—To feed all these gods the Sisa had to levy supplies from the villagers. And the gods were not now content with roots and fruit; they had grown soft in Mahaprabhu's palace and they demanded meat and grain. Men soon became poor again."[2]

The first of these quotations deals with the Saoras, a branch of the Muṇḍas; the second with a little tribe, the Bondos, though nothing is said of their relations with other races. We learn from Elwin's *Bondo Highlander* however that they also speak an Austro-Asiatic language and thus belong to the same group.[3]

By way of summary we may say that the tradition of Dionysos as founder of a cult can be equated with both Kṛishṇa and Śiva in Sanskrit literature, and conclusively paralleled in Muṇḍa tradition; it can also be paralleled, though far from conclusively, among the Dravidians, as exemplified by the Koṭas.

s. Dionysos was accounted a god (during his lifetime).[4]

---

[1] Elwin, *Tribal Myths of Orissa*, p. 199.

[2] *Op. cit.*, p. 536.

[3] *Op. cit.*, p. 1.

[4] Frg. A 1, 2 and 6.

The Indian god who at once springs to mind when we read this statement is Kṛishṇa. There are large numbers of examples of this both in the Mbh and in other Kṛishṇa texts. Typical of these is the episode of Govardhana, which we have already mentioned on a number of occasions. No other member of the Indo-Aryan pantheon can be considered.

We have no Dravidian evidence of a god who began as a man and was deified during his lifetime, though a number of minor deities seem to have passed through this course of development in later ages. But what we are looking for now is not a minor god; on the contrary, we are seeking a major god having a position of clear supremacy in a great part of India, possibly a tribal god whose type corresponds clearly to other tribal gods. The Koṭas' Kiturpayk does not, in Emeneau's view, fulfil these conditions. He is a culture-hero pure and simple. It is true that he has divine qualities, but he never had his own cult.[1] From the evidence at our disposal we have not been able to find any South Indian god or any other personality corresponding more closely to Megasthenes' Dionysos than Kiturpayk.

The case is different among the Muṇḍas. We have already (above, p. 242) quoted a text describing how Lita orders the first humans to pour a libation to Marang Buru. But Lita and Marang Buru are identical; furthermore he is a semi-divine being, part man and part god. The description thus fits very well.

Another aspect of this statement calls for attention. Leaving aside the comment that Dionysos was worshipped during his lifetime (quoted only by Arrian in fragment A 6), ancestor-worship is at once suggested. May it not be something of this which is echoed in Diodorus' panegyric: "because of his good works he would have been deified and worshipped as a god," or "for this reason he was after his death worshipped as a god by those who had benefited by his good deeds."[2]

Our first reaction is probably that here we have the voice of Euhemerism, and not an Indian informant. This suspicion is merely intensified when we recall that much the same was said of Heracles. And it must be admitted that Euhemerism cannot be ruled out *a priori* in a country in which ancestor-worship and the cult of the dead have played such a prominent role in popular religion. This need not be a case of the Greek view of things applied to the Indian situation. Ancestor-worship is a theme constantly recurring in the RV; frequent mention is made of *pitṛi-yajña*, sacrifice to the spirits of the ancestors.[3] RV X.15 is dedicated to these spirits. The chief

[1] Cf. quotation above, p. 240 f.

[2] Frg. A 1 and A 2 respectively.

[3] RV X.16.10.

of the ancestors is naturally Yama, the first man, who is both man and god. We conclude that there is no lack of correspondence with Aryan ideas on this particular point.[1]

There is no doubt that a number of Dravidian witnesses could be produced here, but we shall limit ourselves to one, Iyengar. Writing *The History of the Tamils*, he points out that the Tamil gods flourished at the time of Karikal, and points to Murukan, to whose honour possessed women danced to the sound of flute and drum. Dead heroes were also worshipped; stones were raised, by which their shields and spears were also placed.[2]

Ancestor worship occupied the same position among the Muṇḍas as it seems to have occupied in many another part of India. This can be clearly demonstrated in the writings of Hoffmann, Roy and Elwin,[3] though this is *per se* perhaps not of very great interest.

We have no reason to suspect that the Muṇḍas were unable to distinguish between their culture-hero and the worship of their ancestors. But the Greek ambassador who attempted to understand them may not have been able to draw this distinction. We mention this in anticipation of the question, whether what we read of Dionysos fits *exactly* with what we know of Marang Buru, or whatever he may have been called, on this point as well. Now it is an undeniable fact that despite the concrete characteristics of this culture-hero, there is a great deal that is vague and intangible about him. We are never given a clear picture of him as a man.[4] But at the same time we are unable to escape the impression that we are in fact dealing with a man: a creature of flesh and blood. The introduction of the concept of "ancestor-worship" at once renders the culture-hero concrete and understandable, and gives the Muṇḍa culture-hero that combination of culture-hero and first man so characteristic of Megasthenes' Dionysos.[5]

t. Dionysos was worshipped by dwellers in the mountains.[6]

We have to some extent already dealt with this question.[7] In Part I we pointed out that the text has been misinterpreted. It has been usual to state, when trying to identify Megasthenes' Heracles and Dionysos, that Śiva was worshipped in the mountains and Kṛishṇa on the plains; and this

---

[1] See e.g. Grassmann, *Wörterbuch zum Rigveda*, s.v. Yama.

[2] *Op. cit.*, p. 355.

[3] Hoffmann, *op. cit.*, p. vii; Roy, *The Muṇḍas*, p. 467; idem, *The Khāṛiās*, p. 315; idem, *The Birhōr*, p. 305; Elwin, *The Baigas*, p. 60; idem, *The Religion of an Indian Tribe*, p. 105, Crooke, *Religion and Folklore*, pp. 157 ff., particularly p. 162, etc.

[4] Cf. below, p. 281 f., Elwin's description of Saora Kittung.

[5] See below, on the Oxydrakai, p. 275, "descended from Dionysos".

[6] Frg. A 1 and 3.

[7] Above, pp. 190 f.

has been considered adequate grounds for identification.[1] But some have said precisely the opposite, that Kṛishṇa was worshipped in the mountains and Śiva on the plains.[2] This, too, has been looked upon as adequate grounds for a diametrically opposite identification.

To do fuller justice to Kennedy's view, what he in fact said was that Kṛishṇa was worshipped in the mountains, while Śiva was worshipped all over India, and hence on the plains as well. In point of fact, it is quite impossible to limit the worship of either of these gods to the mountains or to the plains. Both were worshipped on the plains, and to judge from the oldest witnesses we have, in the mountains as well. It is of primary importance to note that the most ancient of the texts in which the two are mentioned, the Mbh, places them side by side. In other words, both Śiva and Kṛishṇa were worshipped by precisely the same people. Megasthenes' division is in fact irrelevant, and witnesses against the identification of Megasthenes' gods with either Kṛishṇa or Śiva, since their worship has never been restricted in this way.[3]

But when Megasthenes divides up the Indians into mountain- and plain-dwellers, he is in fact drawing the same distinction as we find in the Law of Manu, in which we read that the mountain country (i.e. the Himalaya and Vindhya) is the country of the *mlecchas*, while the Aryans dwell on the plains in between.[4] The situation has altered little since then. In the *Linguistic Survey* we find Konow writing that "the hill country is inhabited by Dravidian tribes, while Aryan dialects have occupied the plains".[5] But Dravidians are not the only ones to live, or to have lived, in the hills.

---

[1] *Ibid.*

[2] Kennedy in *J.R.A.S.*, 1907, p. 971.

[3] The normal argument with regard to Śiva will be clear from Meinhard, *Beiträge zur Kenntnis des Śivaismus nach den Purāṇas*, p. 3: "Auch diese Beziehung zum Himalaya wie zu den Bergen im allgemeinen legt es nahe, in Rudra-Śiva (und ebenfalls in Pārvatī) eine Gottheit der dort wohnenden bzw. von den Ariern dorthin verdrängten Urbewohner zu erblicken. Diese Vermutung wird gestützt durch die Tatsache, dass Śiva mit einem bestimmten primitiven Bergvolk, nämlich den in Himalaya lebenden Kirāta's, in Verbindung gebracht wird und scheinbar als dessen Gott gilt." P. 9: "Zusammenfassend sei also betont, dass Rudra-Śiva als eine Gottheit der Urbewohner Indiens aufgefasst werden muss, der Unterworfenen, die die unterste Schicht des Volkes bildeten, und der in Dschungel und Gebirge Verdrängten. Er steigt allmählich in die höheren Volksschichten auf und erscheint später weitmöglichst brahmanisiert. In den Purāṇa's haben wir im wesentlichen ein idealisiertes Śiva-Bild." On p. 8 Meinhard suggests that the Muṇḍas may have had to do with the rise of the Śakti cult, so closely related to the cult of Śiva.

[4] Manu II.22 and 24. Cf. above p. 190 f.

[5] *Linguistic Survey* IV, p. 278.

One author who differs on this matter is Anderson, in *The Peoples of India*, but his objection is unconvincing. He writes that "the Indo-Aryans loved to settle in the cool hills (much as the Anglo-Indian does to this day). But on the mountainous frontiers of North-East Bengal and Assam, the Mongoloid peoples have remained undisturbed till our own time".[1] This view may be dismissed.

We have endeavoured to examine the attitude of the Muṇḍas to the various points in our examination as they have come up. These are also hill peoples, not from the Himalaya and not from the Hindu Kush, but from the neighbourhood of Pāṭaliputra, Megasthenes' home for fourteen years. We have no way of knowing how large was the area they occupied in Megasthenes' day, but their traditions mention constant migrations—always eastward. In their wanderings there was one constant element: "Now, indeed, wherever the Muṇḍas settle they select some high mountain or hill in the neighbourhood on which to locate the Marang Buru Bonga—the God of the High Mountain."[2] Or, as Bodding writes of the Santals, "... they commenced to settle down on separate high-lying places".[3]

We have no reason to consider whether Kṛishṇa or Śiva may appropriately be described as a god of the mountains, since Dionysos is never so described. Thus the information that the god of the Muṇḍas, or the culture-hero Marang Buru, is a mountain god is not strictly relevant. Arbman has already dealt with this question in detail for Rudra-Śiva.[4] For Kṛishṇa, a number of suggestions have been made by Ruben in his book *Kṛishṇa*.[5]

Ruben suggests that Kṛishṇa is a Muṇḍa god (perhaps on account of the Govardhana episode). But there is little evidence to support such a view, and even Ruben maintains the mountain god Kṛishṇa to be an exception. Why should he otherwise write, "Es ist auch im ganzen richtig, dass Śiva auf den Bergen, Kṛishṇa in der Ebene verehrt wurde"?[6] But was Śiva in fact worshipped in the mountains? It is true that he is said to live in the hills, in the forests, and so on, but where is it stated that he was worshipped by dwellers in the hills? There are hymns to Rudra-Śiva in the Vedic texts (if we may without more ado identify the two deities). "An einsamen Orten treibt Rudra sein Wesen, darum wird er von den Kuhhirten und Wasserträgerinnen gesehen. Besonders nahe wird er mit der Wildnis, mit

---

[1] *Op. cit.*, p. 24.

[2] Roy, *The Muṇḍas and their Country*, p. 52.

[3] *Traditions and Institutions of the Santals*, p. 20.

[4] Arbman, *Rudra*, pp. 23–35.

[5] *Op. cit.*, p. 104.

[6] *Op. cit.*, p. 278.

Bergen und Wäldern verbunden ... Der Berg ist Rudras Heim."[1] In short, Rudra dwells in isolation up in the mountains, far from the homes of men. This, which sums up *Śaturudriyam's* view, is in fact quite different from what Megasthenes says of Dionysos, that *his worshippers* dwelt in the mountains.[2]

We are forced to conclude that in order to identify Dionysos, we must rule out *all* the gods mentioned in the literature of the Aryans, the dwellers on the plains. This of course rules out Śiva and Kṛishṇa. Priority must in theory be given to any and every Dravidian, Tibeto-Burman or Muṇḍa god over these Aryan deities. But we must issue a *caveat*, that we can attempt to deny that they had found a place in the Hindu pantheon in Megasthenes' day. This would mean that we would be forced to abandon the Śiva and Kṛishṇa of Hinduism, and fall back upon two unknown gods: unknown because unrepresented in the literature. Should we assume Megasthenes' Dionysos to be a Śiva who existed outside the bounds of the Mbh and the Purāṇas among some mountain tribe, we should have to abandon Megasthenes as a witness to the pre-Christian existence of Hinduism. We should also have to dismiss the Purāṇas from the list of literature in circulation in Megasthenes' day. For all the Purāṇas assume that both these gods were worshipped by the Aryans, the dwellers on the plains. In other words, this passage appears to hold the key to the riddle.

Megasthenes does not bear witness to the existence of a cult of the two main gods of Hinduism. Instead he paints a picture of a situation as it was before the coming of Hinduism: on one side the Aryans worshipping Indra on the plains; on the other, the pre-Aryans with their non-Aryan and non-Hindu religion, a religion which is still practised among isolated and fearful peoples. But Megasthenes' account leaves us in no doubt that the religion in question had much wider currency than it has today. In his day some of these ethnic groups lived in contact with the world around them; it was this very contact which led to their absorption into a wider Indian pattern of religion. It seems, too, to have led to the rise of Hinduism.

---

[1] Arbman, *Rudra*, p. 25.

[2] Ruben, writing in *Eisenschmiede* about the worshippers of Śiva, says (according to his own account in *Man in India* XX, 1940, p. 291): "Śiva and Durgā are the gods of the peasants *in the Ganges valley*; the tribes in the southern hills were since millenniums the enemies of these peasants and their gods." And on p. 293: "Śiva is the god of the peasants who in prehistoric times came from the west (with wheat and cows, as in Mohenjo-Daro) and from the east (with rice and buffaloes, as in Further India). Originally there was not only one Śiva or one Vishṇu, but all the numerous village gods became a Mahadev and all the protecting, fighting sun-gods became a Vishṇu."

u. The dance formed part of the cult of Dionysos.[1]

No mention is made of cultic dance in the RV, though other kinds of dance are mentioned repeatedly. Apte, in his *Social and Religious Life in the Gṛihya-Sūtras*, takes up cultic dance first of all. Note however that it is by no means certain that the Greek text implies a cultic dance. It is true that Arrian mentions dance in terms which seem to suggest cultic dance, but Polyaenus writes in such a way as to suggest profane dance, merely as an amusement.

The Licchavis danced at their religious festivals. For this information we are indebted to Law[2] (quoting *Theragāthā Commentary*, v. 62; *Psalms of the Brethren*, p. 63), who regards this particular tribe as being Indo-Aryan, despite the disagreement of other scholars.[3]

Proceeding to the non-Aryan peoples, we must first of all note that the dance formed part of the pattern of the Indus Valley Civilization. An amulet fragment has been found on which a man is represented beating a drum, while others dance. This has been given a cultic interpretation by Dikshitar.[4]

Among the Dravidians, dancing seems to have been the prerogative of women and girls. In *Dravidian India* Iyengar mentions that girls dance in order to ward off evil.[5] Referring to the god Subramanya Iyengar says, "Hypnotic dances were in vogue in honour of this god".[6] The author of the *History of the Tamils* informs us that spirit-possessed women danced to the honour of the god Murukan to the sound of the flute and the drum.[7] The *vēlan* (priest) of Murukan also performed a cultic dance: "When the priest was in communion with the god, he was also seized with the divine frenzy and sang and danced a devil-dance (*veṛiyāṭṭam*)."[8]

The Tamil work *Śilappadikāram* describes the origin of the dance as follows:

"It would appear that once Indra, the King of the Gods, gave a royal audience to the distinguished guests, sages, and seers in his ideally decorated durbar hall. Jayanta, son of Indra, was also present besides a number of heavenly actresses and dancing women like Rambhā, Ūrvaśī and others.

---

[1] Frg. A 6 and 10.

[2] See Law, *Tribes in Ancient India*, p. 315.

[3] *Op. cit.*, p. 302.

[4] *Prehistoric South India*, p. 120.

[5] *Op. cit.*, p. 91.

[6] *Op. cit.*, p. 205.

[7] Iyengar, *History of the Tamils*, p. 355; cf. above, p. 245.

[8] *Op. cit.*, p. 76.

When the *sabhā* was in session and in the presence of distinguished persons and sages, Jayanta and Ūrvaśī are said to have misbehaved in a manner that enraged the sage Agastya. The sage felt that such misbehaviour under those circumstances deserved condign punishment. Hence he pronounced a curse to the effect that Jayanta should be born as a bamboo-stick in the Vindhya mountains, and that Ūrvaśī should be born on the earth as a courtesan. But both of them fell at the feet of the wise sage, regretted their fault and begged his pardon. He would not go back on his word, but would mitigate its rigour. From that time forward the sage said that the institution of dancing would become popularly identified with Jayanta and that from Ūrvaśī would come into being a line of dancing girls and actresses in the world. So it has become a custom even at the time of the composition of the *Śilappadikāram* for dancing girls to trace their descent from the heavenly Ūrvaśī."[1]

The existence of this tradition does not of course imply that the Dravidians had no knowledge of dancing prior to their contact with the Aryans. But we have no account of the dance in Dravidian practice which is entirely free from Aryan influence. Dikshitar mentions a number of dances with purely Dravidian names: words meaning 'to shake' and the like. "In fact," he writes, "dancing was a marked feature of every incident in the life of the ancient people. It was a sure accompaniment of every joy of life and a means of efficacy and prayer."[2] He touches on the subject of the "dance of Śiva" in his account of the dance in the Tamil Literature of South India. But we do not have the impression that the dance as such was particularly characteristic of Śiva, even in the Tamil tradition; this factor can therefore be discounted as evidence of the identity of Dionysos with Śiva. The dance is so common a phenomenon that it need not necessarily call to mind the dancing Śiva.

So general a practice of course has its associations among other peoples. The Muṇḍas are said to dance by night to the sound of the *dumang*, a deep drum.[3] Roy mentions the practice of fastening bells to the feet of the young men in the *paiki* dances.[4] Ruben recalls the dances of the Muṇḍas of Chota Nagpur when he reads of how Kṛishṇa spent his nights with the herdmaidens, singing and dancing the *rāsa* dance.[5] Elwin relates the following Saora tradition of the origin of the dance: "Kittung is in the sky. He had a

---

[1] After Dikshitar, *Studies in Tamil Literature*, pp. 288–308.

[2] *Op. cit.*, p. 290 f.

[3] Hoffmann, *Muṇḍārī Grammar*, p. v.

[4] *The Muṇḍas*, p. 379.

[5] *Kṛishṇa*, pp. 109 and 111.

daughter, but she died. He buried her and after three years prepared to perform her *Karja* ceremonies. Her ghost said, 'Father, have a great dance for me, call all the neighbours, buy buffaloes and have a splendid feast.' Kittung arranged it and he himself danced like a peacock and the guests imitated him.—It was in this way that dancing began."[1] It would be possible to produce any number of examples of the occurrence of dancing among the Muṇḍas. In the circumstances it is impossible to regard the fact that Kṛishṇa and Śiva were both known as dancing gods as evidence for their identification with Dionysos. The same is true of their musical instruments.

v. The cult of Dionysos included the music of cymbals,[2]

x. kettledrums[3] and drums[4] as well as

y. processions.[5]

The musical instruments mentioned in the RV are not those mentioned in connection with the cult of Dionysos. Apte counts the following: *vīṇā* (lute), *dundubhi* (drum) and *vāṇa* (flute).[6] He does not mention the cymbals. These are however named in RV X.146.2 (*āghāṭibhir*), though they do not seem to have been widely used in Vedic religion. Thus the situation differs from that described by Megasthenes, who says nothing of either stringed or wind instruments, but mentions an instrument rarely used in Vedic practice.

A chapter in Iyengar's *Dravidian India* is devoted to Dravidian music, surprisingly enough without once mentioning musical instruments![7] I have not had access to the literature he quotes. In another context he writes that "... musical entertainments could be witnessed everywhere".[8] And in a further passage he informs us that according to the *Tolkappiyam* the tribes of herdsmen in the jungle had drums called *pambai*, while those of the desert nomads were called *tudi*.[9] We have earlier had occasion to quote a passage in which Iyengar describes how possessed women danced to the sound of flute and drum.[10] Cymbals are not mentioned, but this is of little

---

[1] *Tribal Myths of Orissa*, p. 628.

[2] Frg. A 1, 3, 5, 6 and 10.

[3] *Ibid.*

[4] Frg. A 4.

[5] *Ibid.*

[6] *Op. cit.*, p. 92.

[7] *Op. cit.*, pp. 91–93. Cf. p. 194: "There is a reference to dancing maids who press their lutes tight to their warm bosoms to heat the strings at sunset in winter ..."

[8] *Op. cit.*, p. 194.

[9] *Op. cit.*, p. 176.

[10] *Op. cit.*, p. 355; cf. above, pp. 245 and 249.

consequence, as the material is in any case so meagre. Dikshitar's *Studies in Tamil Literature*, is more detailed, but has nothing to say about cymbals.[1] Emeneau describes a Koṭa rite in which there is singing and music on the horn, drums, and clarinet, as well as dancing.[2] But this material is so sparse that no real conclusions can be drawn from it. We therefore pass on to a consideration of the Muṇḍa material.

The first thing to be said about the Muṇḍa material is that it is much more comprehensive than the corresponding Dravidian material. For example, Roy writes in *The Muṇḍas*:

"The Muṇḍa is fond of music and uses a variety of musical instruments. Among these are the *dhōlki*, a small drum made of wood and goat-skin, the *nāgerā*, a large drum made of iron and the hide of an ox or buffalo, the *dūmāng*, another variety of the drum having an earthen framework with the top and the bottom made of monkey-skin, the *dhānplā*, or tambourine made of wood and goat-skin, the *karetāl* or cymbal made of brass, the *sārāngā* or fiddle made of wood and goat-skin with strings of horse's tail, the *tūhilā* or banjo made of pumpkin gourd and wooden handle with a string of silk, the *bānōm*, another variety of the banjo consisting of two gourds and two strings and brass-guaze, the *rutu* or bamboo-flute, and the *mūrli*, a smaller flute also made of bamboo ... The principal instruments playrd upon by these Ghāsi musicians are the *dhānk*, a large drum made of wood and leather, the *narsinghā*, or horn made of copper and brass, and the *perened* or pipe made either of brass or of the bell-metal."[3]

Note the large number of varieties of drum.[4] Percussion instruments are on the whole so prominent that we are inclined to regard this as a close parallel to the musical situation described by Megasthenes. Additional material is forthcoming from a number of authors. We quote from Elwin's *Notes on a Kondh Tour*: "There was a large *nangara* drum, a small iron drum, a large tambourine of the *chang* pattern, flutes and cymbals. A group of unmarried girls came out to dance."[5] Mention had previously been made in the text of a song of the fact that the culture-hero Linga Pinnu "showed us how to beat the drum".[6]

Goswami, in an essay entitled *Music in Assam: its divine origin*, writes:

---

[1] *Op. cit.*, pp. 296–300.

[2] *Koṭa Texts*, pp. 293 ff. and 301.

[3] *Op. cit.*, p. 377 f.

[4] Note that drums were used in the Indus Valley Civilization, according to Dikshitar, *Prehistoric South India*, p. 121.

[5] *Op. cit.*, p. 52.

[6] *Op. cit.*, p. 47.

"Music ... is often held to have been first communicated by the gods (see Hastings Vol. IX p. 6). Verrier Elwin notes that the Murias sing of the 'eighteen instruments of Lingo Bai', their cult-hero ..."[1] "The drummers especially refer to musical instruments as having a divine origin."[2]

G. Ahmed Khan, in *The Bhils of Khandesh*, writes that "men in women's garb or animal skins dance to the accompaniment of drums.—The Bhils in the West Satpuras use a tambourine of an ingenious pattern and a kettle drum."[3]

The Muṇḍa material seems, unlike most of the material we have quoted from other tribes, to fit in remarkably well with what Megasthenes tells us of Dionysos; but is this impression due only to the fragmentary nature of the material? Some accounts—such as that of the Bhils—mention details which have no place in the description of Dionysos (men dressed as women, etc.); others omit all mention of cymbals; others again differ entirely.

The divine origin of musical instruments is of course found as an idea in Hinduism too. The difference is that Hinduism never attributes all the implements of culture to any *one* god—as is the case with Megasthenes' Dionysos, and with the Muṇḍas' culture-hero. Śiva is never represented as being a culture-hero: this is at once evident when we examine the standard works; had he had these characteristics, it is only reasonable to expect that one or other would have said so.[4] No mention is made of cymbals, nor of their being traceable back to Śiva. This does not of course mean that they had no connection whatever with the god in question; but it is fairly clear that they occupied no prominent place in his cult. Megasthenes however mentioned them with unusual emphasis; they in fact recur in five fragments—an almost unparalleled frequency.[5]

The *ḍamaru* of Śiva on the other hand shows a connection between Śiva and drums.

Megasthenes does not mention the fondness for singing that most ethnographers remark upon. "The woods and valleys by the side of the ancient

---

[1] *The Muria and their Ghotul*, p. 13.

[2] *Op. cit.*, p. 16.

[3] *Op. cit.*, p. 140.

[4] The motif is not to be found in Dikshitar's *Purāṇa Index*, which deals with Śiva in three pages, in Jacobi's *Mahābhārata Index*, in Dowson's *Classical Dictionary of Hindu Mythology*, or in Monier-Williams' *Sanskrit-English Dictionary*.

[5] Cymbals are mentioned in the following contexts: 1. the cultus; 2. royal campaigns; 3. Alexander's arrival was greeted with drums and cymbals. On the subject of the divine origin of music in Hinduism, see Goswami, *Music in Assam: its Divine Origin*, p. 14: "Indian *śāstrās* also hold that Naṭarāj Śiva is the ultimate source of dance and music."

Dṛishadvatī and Sarasvatī rivers appear to have rung with the Bacchanalian songs or *durangs* of the Muṇḍas ... long before the venerable Arya Rishis of old chanted their sonorous Vedic hymns."[1] "O, the songs that Lingo taught us, O, the steps that Lingo taught us! The first song is Lingo's, and the first step is Lingo's," sing the Murias, of their culture-hero.[2] He had no less than eighteen instruments, on which he played simultaneously.[3] Most were drums of various kinds.

The fact that drums are used in all branches of the Muṇḍa people may perhaps indicate their age in this ethnic group. Przyluski suggests that they were used as far back as the coming of the Aryans (in an essay *Non-Aryan loans in Indo-Aryan*):[4]

"The instrument called in Marathi *ḍámru*, in Hindi *ḍamrū*, etc. resembles a gourd, with two swellings, cut in such a way as to leave only the two hemispheric ends. The analogy of the names of this drum with those of the *udumbara* fruit in the Indian languages can therefore be explained by their common resemblances to some cucurbits ... On the whole, *udumbara*, the Sanskrit word for *Ficus glomerata*, belongs to the long series of words borrowed by the Indo-Aryan languages from the Austro-Asiatic ones."[5]

According to Jørgensen the Santals are also a musical people, well-known for their music and their song; their national instruments are the flute and the drum.[6] Once more we find a mention of song—an element of music on which Megasthenes has nothing to say. This is *per se* of little significance. But he does mention song indirectly: "When he speaks of the philosophers, he says that those of them who live among the mountains are worshippers of Dionysos ..."[7] The word ὑμνητάς, here translated "worshipper" really means "singer of praise" if taken literally. We thus have every reason to claim that this detail is in full agreement with the Muṇḍas, and with the songs of praise they sing to their culture-hero. Elwin's book *The Muria and their Ghotul* contains a number of songs of praise to Lingo, some of which we have quoted here.[8]

---

[1] Roy, *The Muṇḍas*, p. 31.

[2] Elwin, *The Muria and their Ghotul*, p. 512.

[3] *Op. cit.*, p. 524.

[4] *J.A.* 1926, pp. 25–36; Bagchi, *Pre-Aryan and Pre-Dravidian*, p. 158 f.

[5] *Ibid.*

[6] *Evangeliet blandt Santalerne*, p. 38.

[7] Frg. A 3.

[8] See above, l. 3, n. 2 (= *The Muria*, p. 512). In *Notes on a Kondh Tour* Elwin quotes the following Kondh-song, also quoted in idem, *The Muria*, p. 229:

"We will sing a song of Linga Pinnu:
Linga Pinnu made the world,

The question of the processions mentioned by Megasthenes poses a number of problems. The fact that we nowhere meet with processions in the Aryan literature is of no great significance. Iyengar touches upon the subject in passing: "The members of the Five Great Assemblies are said to have accompanied the royal processions."[1] And Roy writes of the Khāṛiās: "The whole night is spent by both men and women in singing and dancing and drinking ricebeer. Next morning the *Karam* branches are carried in procession with drumming and singing and thrown into a stream or tank."[2] The same author gives us substantially the same information about the Muṇḍas.[3] He has also described an Oraon "ceremonial procession to the sacred grove".[4]

Despite this evidence we must leave this point here without further consideration, since the Greek expression ἔξοδος (lit. exit) is obscure, and may have nothing whatever to do with processions.

z. The cult of Dionysos (διονυσιακὸν) included the wearing of fine linen garments,[5] and spotted, fine, coloured (perhaps flower-patterned) clothes,[6]

aa. a girdle (or turban),[7]

bb. and perfumes (sweet-smelling oils).[7]

Considerable difficulties are connected with Megasthenes' description of the clothes worn by the followers of Dionysos. First there is the matter of the ambiguity, not to say incomprehensibility, of the Greek text; and secondly, there is the difficulty of paralleling certain alternative translations from literary and other sources. After this preliminary *caveat* we may proceed to a consideration of such material as we have been able to gather.

Linga Pinnu made the cows,
Linga Pinnu made the roots,
Linga Pinnu taught us how to sing,
Linga Pinnu showed us how to beat the drum,
Linga Pinnu taught us how to plant roots and pulses,
Linga Pinnu taught the boys how to dance and sing.
Linga Pinnu showed us how to do the Meriah sacrifice.
Linga Pinnu was born from the ground.
He lived till he was old.
He taught us everything and died.
For our crops he gave us seed."

[1] *Dravidian India*, p. 239.

[2] *The Khāṛiās*, p. 342.

[3] *The Muṇḍas*, p. 479; cf. *ibid.*, p. 475.

[4] Roy, *Oraon Religion and Customs*, p. 206.

[5] Frg. A 3.

[6] Frg. A 3, 4 and 5.

[7] Frg. A 3 and 6.

Apte's *Social and Religious Life* makes mention of linen among other cloths, not as material specially used for cultic dress, but for everyday use.[1] The colour of the clothes worn depended upon the caste of the wearer. "Apparently the Licchavis suited the colour of their clothes and ornaments to the tint of their complexions, and dressed themselves in dark blue (*nīla*), yellow (*pīta*), red (*lohita*), or white (*odāta*) accordingly."[2] These variously coloured clothes were worn not only on important occasions but "in their ordinary daily life also".

Both girdle and turban are mentioned in the Aryan literature.[3]

Sweet-smelling oils are named in relatively early Aryan texts;[4] perfumes, on the other hand, are first mentioned in the Gṛihya-Sūtras.[5] Manu lays down that Brahmans are to be greeted with *gandhamālyaiḥ surabhibhir*, sweet-smelling garlands and perfumes (perhaps incense is also meant).[6]

We could multiply passages dealing with dress among the Dravidians. For example, we read in Iyengar's *Dravidian India* that the queen of the Tamils wore silken clothes and flower-embroidered dresses.[7] The material out of which the dresses were made is not always described. Thurston, in his *Castes and Tribes* II, p. 93, writes that Paraiyan girls wear a cotton garment around the waist until they reach puberty. Cotton is the normal material for workaday clothes in South India, with silk for special occasions. Linen is not used. In South India flowers are worn as ornaments (in the hair, etc.), but never, as far as we know, instead of clothes. We have no information about the use of the girdle or turban.

Iyengar writes, on the subject of perfumes in connection with the cult: "Adoring God with flowers and incense was an ancient practice prevalent among the Tamils."[8] We are unable to draw any definite conclusions from this sparse Dravidian material. But we are dealing with a subject which, though taken for granted, seldom rouses attention, and seldom plays any prominent role, either in travellers' tales or in scientific ethnographical accounts. Scarcity of material is thus only to be expected—always assuming that the meaning of Megasthenes' original account was as we have

---

[1] *Op. cit.*, p. 56.

[2] Law, *Tribes*, p. 312. Does not Law mean that it is the caste which decides the colour? The colour scale is the same as that of the castes, though reversed. See Apte, *op. cit.*, p. 56, with reference to Ā. G. Sūtra.

[3] Apte, *op. cit.*, pp. 55 and 111.

[4] RV X.146.6.

[5] *Op. cit.*, p. 60.

[6] III.199 with Medhātithi's commentary.

[7] *Op. cit.*, p. 222.

[8] *Dravidian India*, p. 99.

interpreted it. We shall return to the subject of the meaning of βάπτεσθαι ἄνθινα in due course.

Jørgensen's book *Evangeliet blandt Santalerne* contains a prayer, prayed by young people while the sacrifice is being offered at the Sohrae festival: "Greetings, o Great Mountain, my Father Ṭhākūr; this we give thee, reach out to thee in our autumn festival; receive this, we pray thee, with joy and pleasure ... Our fathers in the past received thee with silken garments and women's garments of red and yellow, my Father Ṭhākūr ..."[1]

Megasthenes uses the expression βάπτεσθαι ἄνθινα. Its meaning is obscure, but the most obvious interpretation is "to cover oneself with flowers". If this be correct, we have a further point of contact, since Elwin, writing in *The Baiga*, records that "flowers are also tied in the hair".[2] We learn from the same author that the Baiga are nowadays in the habit of buying their clothes and jewels, and thus do not differ from neighbouring tribes; however, he mentions in passing that the women still wear "the *kardhan* (relic of the old leaf-dress), the cord that is always worn about the waist".[3] Most of India's mountain tribes now wear woven garments, and we can thus hardly expect to find tribes still wearing the type of garment that was usual in Megasthenes' day.

We have no evidence that the Muṇḍas wore clothes made of leaves in the time of Megasthenes; nor that they wore linen garments. An interesting possibility is that the word σινδονοφορεῖν may be connected with India; it has been suggested that there is a connection between σινδών and *Sindhu*, thus meaning "Indian linen".[4]

The Muṇḍas used both the girdle and the turban. In fact the dress of a Muṇḍa man is neither more nor less than a girdle, "... a short narrow strip of cloth passed between the legs and attached to a waist-string called *ḍāṇḍā-ḍōr* made of chop fibres".[5] Shortly afterward we read that "women wear round the waist a *lāhāngā*, about one and a half to two yards long and one and a half cubits wide. A portion of this cloth is allowed to pass diagonally over the upper part of the body so as to cover the breasts".[6] Roy writes in similar terms about the dress favoured by the Khāṛiās: "Khāṛiā children remain naked till about five or six years of age, after which boys wear only a *khadiā*. This is a piece of loin-cloth seven to ten inches in width and about

[1] *Op. cit.*, p. 19.
[2] *Op. cit.*, p. 246.
[3] *Op. cit.*, p. 12.
[4] The information taken from Melander, *Grekiskt-svenskt Handlexikon*, s.v.
[5] Roy, *The Birhōr*, p. 523.
[6] *Ibid.*

one yard and a half in length ... Adult persons at home wear besides the *khadiā* and, over it, a *kārdhāni* ... This *kārdhāni* hangs down about twelve inches from the waist towards the thigh. A very old man only wears a *khadiā* like a boy ..."[1] Nothing is said by either Roy or Elwin about the material from which these garments are made.

We must note that best clothes are worn only at weddings and other festivities, and not in connection with cultic ceremonies.[2] No headdress is prescribed, but the Birhōr sometimes wears a cloth wound round his head as a protection from the sun.[3] This corresponds to the words μιτροῦσθαι and μιτρηφορέειν in the Greek text. Elwin makes express mention of the turban on a number of occasions in his book *The Baiga*. He writes: "On the head is usually a rag called *patka* or *pharria*, but some of the well-to-do have a regular turban twenty hands long."[4] A Baiga song contains these words, sung by a boy: "I am wearing a turban. Its end hangs down my back. O girl, look behind you, and your whole life will be changed."[5]

The Muṇḍas love flowers, but we seek in vain for special mention of the *perfume* of these flowers in Muṇḍa life. The flowers and oils which play such an important part in their life—and particularly in their festivities—are nowhere said to have a particularly penetrating perfume. Roy has given in his numerous books an account of most of the elements which go to make up a festival, as well as everyday happenings. He thus writes of the "oil-Test"—i.e. a ceremony in which a bridegroom allows a lock of hair to hang down in front of his face. Oil is then poured on his head; if it runs down this lock of hair it is regarded as a good omen for the future; if it spreads out in all directions, it is taken to be a bad omen. The procedure is in any case repeated until the desired result is achieved.[6]

A section of the same book is entitled "The Khāṛiā's love of flowers", and contains a song, described by the author as follows: "In the following song boys and girls express their delight at the sight of the white fragrant *gulainchi* (*plumeria acutifolia*) flowers (with a yellow tinge inside the cup) which grow wild in their native jungles and hills."[7] The song itself mentions only the "beautiful" flowers.

All these tribes have a great love of flowers, as a glance at Roy's or

---

[1] Roy, *The Khāṛiās*, p. 99.

[2] Roy, *The Birhōr*, p. 524.

[3] *Ibid.*

[4] *Op. cit.*, p. 12.

[5] *Op. cit.*, p. 248.

[6] *The Khāṛiās*, p. 259 f.

[7] *Op. cit.*, p. 484.

Elwin's books at once shows. They do not, it is true, make express mention of their perfume, and this may appear puzzling. But the mere fact of their occurrence—not to mention the obvious fact of their varied perfumes—may well be sufficient cause for Megasthenes' words μύρων ἀλοιφὰς ἐκδιδάξαι, "taught them to anoint themselves with sweet-smelling oils" and μυροῦσθαι "perfume themselves". We assume the Muṇḍas' flowers and oils to be fragrant—not an unreasonable assumption—and this point is thus capable of being connected with all three ethnic groups under discussion.

Note, however, that the Greek text is ambiguous; there is some doubt whether sweet-smelling oils, ointments or perfumes are in fact meant. And further, that there is a great deal of uncertainty as to the real meaning of the various subdivisions of this point. Thirdly, we must remember that the sources we have at our disposal cannot be expected to take up all the points raised by Megasthenes' work.

One of our greatest difficulties here is that we have been unable to produce any information about cultic practices. Our translation of Fragment A 3 has not "The cult of Dionysos includes" for Διονυσιακὸν. Translated literally, the expression has nothing whatever to do with the cultus: it says only that the point in question is also "Dionysian". Since the name of the god is expressly mentioned, it is however possible to take this as referring to something specifically religious, i.e. belonging to the cult. But we have not been able to establish any connection between the "specifically Dionysian" and any particular cult. The most plausible translation would therefore be "The custom of ... can also be traced back to Dionysos."

Unfortunately the nature of our material makes it impossible for us to penetrate more deeply into this question. If we have interpreted Dionysos correctly, then it is at least conceivable that Megasthenes is trying to pass on some general information about the tribes living in the Indian hills—that they anoint themselves, that they wear a girdle instead of ordinary clothes, and so on. This, however, must remain a hypothesis, incapable of empirical verification.

The ambiguity of the text on which this point is based renders it possible to apply its conditions to Aryans, Dravidians and Muṇḍas indiscriminately. Hence it is of no value from the point of view of identification.[1]

cc. Dionysos taught the Indians to wear their hair long in his honour[2]

dd. and to care for the beard.[3]

ee. He was therefore also called Katapōgōn.[3]

---

[1] Cf. Stein, *Megasthenes*, in Pauly-Wissowa, XV: 1, col. 257.

[2] Frg. A 6.

[3] Frg. A 2.

Apte describes the Aryans' traditional way of caring for the hair and beard as follows: "As for the hair, different fashions of keeping the hair that were oiled, anointed and combed are mentioned. Beards were kept, though shaving was known along with its indispensable accompaniments, the razor, hot water, etc. Women plaited their hair and some men also wore their hair braided and wound like a shell, e.g. the Vasishthas wore them braided on the right side of the head."[1] Thus far the RV. Unfortunately no passage references are given.

From the period immediately after the RV Apte quotes nothing save the medicines recommended in the AV for improving the growth of hair. During the Śrauta-Sūtra period it was not unusual to shave the head, either completely or leaving only a small tuft of hair. The following Gṛhya-Sūtra period was characterized by the tonsure. Obviously none of these have the slightest connection with the long hair affected by the worshippers of Dionysos.

The treatment prescribed for the beard in the Gṛhya-Sūtras can however be regarded as a parallel to the Dionysos-worshippers' care of the beard. "Brighten up my face, O barber, do not cut off my life" is quoted by Apte as evidence for the role of shaving in beautifying the face.[2] We may compare Megasthenes' words: "It is the custom among Indians to care for the beard to the end of their lives." Less of a parallel with the Dionysian is provided by the Aryan, according to the Sūtras (in Apte's version): "That a great option was allowed as regards the frequency or otherwise of shaving ordinarily, is seen from the rule in P.G.S., 'The youth should observe chastity and should not be shaved for one year, twelve nights or at least three nights,' and according to some, there was to be no shaving between the Upakarman and the Utsarga ceremonies. This means perhaps that shaving was looked upon as a luxury."[3] Nothing is said here about the care of the beard.

The information given by Megasthenes about the worshippers of Dionysos is thus flatly contradicted by what we know of Aryan practice. The long, matted hair of the occasional hermit is of course irrelevant, since Megasthenes is talking about a unit of population ("The dwellers in the hills of India": οἱ τὴν ὀρεινὴν τῆς 'Ινδικῆς κατοικοῦντες) in a definite area, and not about individual exceptions to the general rule. Medhātithi, in his commentary on Manu IV.35, says, "It is necessary to cut the hair. In this way a man

---

[1] *Social and Religious Life*, pp. 54 ff.

[2] *Op. cit.*, p. 59.

[3] *Ibid.*

becomes clean, as it is written. The man who has long hair finds it difficult to bathe." This was the Aryans' opinion of long hair.

It should be clear, from this emphasis on the necessity of caring for the *beard*, that this reference to the *hair* is insufficient to provide a clear link with Rudra-Śiva. It cannot otherwise be disputed that long hair belong to the sphere of Rudra-Śiva. In RV X.136.7, we read:

keśí vishásya pátreṇa yád rudreṇápibat sahá

The long-haired one drank poison from a bowl together with Rudra.

In his book *Rudra* Arbman has discussed this verse, taking up a number of facts which deserve our attention, since the description of Rudra-Śiva connects at a number of points with what we have been discussing.[1] One quotation—from Ward's *A view of the History, Literature and Religion of the Hindus* II, p. 190—is of particular relevance: "These mendicant worshippers of Śiva—the Sannyāsis—are very numerous in Bengal ... They smear their bodies with ashes of cow-dung, wear a narrow cloth tied with a rope round their loins and throw a cloth, dyed red, over their bodies. The artificial hair worn by some of these persons reaches down to their feet, and is often clotted with dirt till it adheres together like a rope." Elsewhere Arbman quotes from the same book (I, p. 10) to the effect that men and boys dance on the streets "having their bodies covered with ashes etc. and a long piece of false hair mixed with mud wrapped round the head like a turban". The beard, on the other hand, is never even mentioned in connection with Rudra-Śiva.

If we can ignore the overall tendency of the text, applying as it does to the entire population of a given area, then it must be admitted that this detail fits in remarkably well with Rudra-Śiva. But if the statement, "the Indians wear their hair long in honour of the god" be taken to apply *generally*, then the correspondence ceases to apply generally, and comes to be of only local significance, applicable to *sannyāsis* and other ascetics. Incidentally, these are normally characterized by their matted and unkempt hair—a detail difficult to reconcile with the statement that they cared for their beards. This is by no means characteristic of the mass of the population. Remember that we are speaking now of Rudra-Śiva, glorified in the Aryan and Hindu literatures respectively, and worshipped in those parts of India in which Aryans predominate.[2]

[1] *Op. cit.*, p. 298 f.

[2] There seems to be no names of Vishṇu and Śiva, meaning beard. *Śmaśru* beard, is never used as name or epithet of a god, nor does it form part of a name or epithet. Do Keśava and names containing -keśa belong to this context? Cf. above, p. 181 f.

Nothing can be said with certainty about the way in which the ancient Dravidians dressed their hair. It is true that Iyengar writes in *The History of the Tamils* that "Rāma's warriors bore shields black like clouds and wore flowers on their heads like southerners. The people of the ancient South India grew a whole head of hair, since the profession of the barber was unknown to them ... The Tamils loved to decorate their hair with all kinds of flowers ..."[1] Unfortunately the author does not name his sources. We do not know whether this piece of information is contained in the texts, or whether it is a piece of deduction from the fact of their having had no barbers. Should the latter be the case, then the whole passage would be worthless (see below).[2]

On the general subject of beards in India, we may first note the biological fact that all Indian races, except the Mongols of the North, are characterized by ample growth of both hair and beard. However, we have no definite information on the subject of Dravidian hair-styles, apart from a largely irrelevant passage in Iyengar's *Dravidian India.*[3] Nor is the *Tamil-English Dictionary* of any help.

Turning to the Muṇḍas, we find Roy claiming in one passage that they once wore their hair long, as certain youths do even now,[4] though he elsewhere provides us with contradictory material, drawn from the Birhōrs:

"Although women wear their hair long, men crop their hair short in order to avoid the hair being entangled in bamboo thickets and other trees and bushes in the jungles. They employ no barbers, but exchange the services of each other for cutting their hair or shaving their beards.[5] Moustaches are worn. The hair on the face is ordinarily not luxuriant; but, when it is so, the moustache is trimmed but the beard is not allowed to grow, being generally shaved clean ... As for toilet ... both men and women, bathe in some neighbouring stream or spring about once in a week and, if possible, smear over the skin some oil made either of *surgujā* (*Guizotia Olifera*) seeds or *karanj* (*Pongamia glabra*) seeds or mustard seeds. It is only after this weekly bath and on occasions of some marriage festival and the like that the women always, and men sometimes, comb their hair either with bamboo combs or wooden combs."[6]

[1] *Op. cit.*, p. 52.

[2] In a Koṭa ritual is asked the question: "Shall I roll my hair before or behind?" In the former case it means that the god comes and dwells there, Emeneau, *Koṭa Texts*, p. 303.

[3] *Op. cit.*, p. 49. [4] Roy, *The Muṇḍas*, p. 369.

[5] It follows that the mere fact of there being no barber need not mean that the hair was worn long, as Iyengar seems to claim (see above, p. 262).

[6] *Op. cit.*, p. 525.

The reason for this procedure given by Roy is not unimportant: the Birhōrs are hunters. But the worshippers of Dionysos and the Muṇḍas are farmers. Proceeding to Roy's book on *The Khāṛiās*, we find this interesting piece of information: "The Khāṛiās of either sex, as a rule, formerly used to wear long hair on the head. But at present, owing to contact with civilization and the spread of Christianity, Dudh Khāṛiā males have begun to cut their hair short. Hill Khāṛiās and Dhelki Khāṛiās of either sex still generally wear their hair long."[1]

Roy has earlier pointed out that the Hill Khāṛiās are on a low level of civilization, while the Dudh Khāṛiās are the most advanced of the Khāṛiā group.[2] The ceremony of "binding the hair" might be adduced as proof of the antiquity of the practice of wearing the hair long; in this ceremony boys and girls of about twelve years have their hair bound up with elaborate rites. This seems to indicate that the practice did not come about by chance, but has some religious significance. The nature of this significance is not so easily decided. There are no myths on the subject, apart from a hint in Elwin's summary of the character of Kittung, god of the Saoras: "He teaches boys and girls to dance. He persuades people to do their hair properly and look nice. He invents musical instruments ... When, in order to force them to do their hair, he scattered on their heads a powder which would turn into lice, they thought it was just one of his little jokes and took no notice."[3] The fact of there being no obvious connection between the god and the beard of man has its corollary in the fact that I have been unable to find any god whose name is derived from, or contains, the word 'beard'.

3. *Geographical Passages*

a. According to one source, Dionysos was three distinct persons, who lived and did their good deeds at different times.[4] The first of these "persons" is said to have been

b. Indus;[5] the others have already been named:

c. Lēnaios[6] and

d. Katapōgōn.[7]

---

[1] *Op. cit.*, p. 215 f.

[2] *Op. cit.*, p. 22.

[3] *The Religion of an Indian Tribe*, p. 90.

[4] Frg. A 2.

[5] *Ibid.*

[6] *Ibid.;* cf. above, p. 239.

[7] *Ibid.;* cf. above, pp. 259 ff.

This complex at once calls to mind the god Vishṇu and his *avatars*. He was also at least three distinct persons, living and working in separate periods. As far back as in RV VII.100.6 we find mention of the different forms which Vishṇu can adopt at will. This is evidently the same thought as that expressed by Diodorus. But is there any more substantial connection with Vishṇu and his *avatars*? Hardly. It is true that Vishṇu's *avatars*, *matsya* (fish) and *kūrma* (turtle) have to do with water; so has, in a sense, Indus. But the link is minimal: this is obviously not the source of Diodorus' statement. It must be admitted here that there exists a link between Vishṇu and Indus; and Monier-Williams' *Lexicon* quotes the word *sindhu* as describing both Varuṇa and Vishṇu: the latter, he claims, applies both to the RV and the Mbh. But Grassmann and Geldner do not share his opinion. The River Indus is mentioned in *Wörterbuch zum Rigveda* as being a goddess, it is true, but Grassmann does not seem to be acquainted with the idea of the identity of the river with Vishṇu. On the other hand he can write that "bildlich wird Indra als das die Somaströme aufnehmende Meer bezeichnet"—which places Indra in the same close relationship with the river as Monier-Williams would place Vishṇu. And although Geldner knows of the "goddess" Indus-Sindhu, he sees no reason to identify Vishṇu with the river.

The fact that some—though not all—modern Indologists have seen a connection here undoubtedly means that such an identification may have been made by the Indians themselves, or by well-informed Greek travellers. Thus although "Indus" may conceivably have referred to Vishṇu, neither Lēnaios nor Katapōgōn can have done so, resulting in the dismissal of all three from Vishṇu's sphere.[1] Hence although the details can have had no direct agreement with Vishṇu, the fact—the *avatar* concept—certainly did so.

The case of Śiva is precisely the opposite. The overall view in no way suggests Dionysos, though a number of details can be made to fit—with an effort. We have already compared the name Lēnaios with Śiva's epithet Drākshārāmeśvara,[2] pointing out, however, that the concepts are in no wise identical. Katapōgōn, on the other hand, offers no point of contact with Śiva. But we can establish a connection between Śiva and at least one of the great rivers—not the Indus, but the Ganges, the waters of which Śiva drew up in his hair.[3] We see from this that it is no easy and straight-

[1] See above, pp. 239 and 259 ff.

[2] Above, pp. 187 and 239.

[3] On Katapōgōn, see above, p. 259. On the Ganges in Śiva's hair see e.g. Mbh XIII.17.46.

forward matter to connect these passages with Śiva; the manipulation necessary justifies our dismissing Śiva from the scene.[1]

The Aryan literature as a whole otherwise contains no statement which can be said to offer a more striking agreement with these passages.

Turning to the Dravidians, we may quote Thurston, from *Castes and Tribes* VII: "The deities bestowed on this person (the one who was to kill Viśvakarman) these three names. First, Bhūmi Pālakudu or Saviour of the Earth, because he was produced by her. Second, Ganga Kulam, or Descendant of the river Ganges, by reason of having been brought forth on her banks. Third, Murdaka Pālakudu or Protector of the plough, alluding to his being born with a ploughshare in his hand."[2] But these three names are explicitly stated to be three names for one and the same person, without the slightest indication of there having been three different persons at different times. Hence there can be no question of any closer correspondence between this figure and Dionysos. Further, none of the three is nominally identical with either Indus, Lēnaios or Katapōgōn. Leaving aside the details, the final judgment is: lack of identity with any of Diodorus' three figures and lack of any statement that the three lived in different epochs.

A greater degree of similarity is to be found in the god worshipped by the Koṭas, according to a statement from Emeneau's *Koṭa Texts*, which we have quoted before: "For the one Kamatr Father-god saying another name: Elder Father-god and Younger Father-god and Mother-goddess, you must make the three gods."[3] Here we at least have three distinct persons. But they are not said to have lived in three different epochs, and their "unity" is dubious.

So our final conclusion with respect to the Dravidians is the same as that at which we arrived in the case of the Aryans: that there is no convincing correspondence with Dionysos as three persons living in three ages.

Proceeding to a consideration of the Muṇḍas, we find this passage in Bodding's *Traditions and Institutions of the Santals*:

"In the primeval age we had no bongas. During our wanderings we have got them. The Sing Bonga (Sun or Day spirit) we also got on our way in Sing duar (the Sun or Day pass). The primeval ancestors were worshipping

---

[1] The names of Rudra-Śiva are of no account here, being only eight different names for the same god, and not having anything to do with Dionysos' three different persons. Neither can be connected with Dionysos. The names Bhīma and Ugra, the terrible one and the violent one, provide a sharp contrast with the benevolent character of Dionysos.

[2] *Op. cit.*, p. 364.

[3] *Op. cit.*, p. 43; cf. above, p. 240.

only Ṭhākūr. Having got the bongas we have gradually forgotten Ṭhākūr; only the name is left. The people of the present age have mostly forgotten also the name; only we who have learnt the story of the ancestors and a few old men are remembering his name. In the present age the Santals say the Sing Bonga is presumably Ṭhākūr; therefore, when worshipping, they look towards the sun and call this their Ṭhākūr; but our ancestors of old have handed over to us, viz., to us gurus, that Ṭhākūr is different; he is not seen by human eyes; but he himself sees all. He himself has created earth and heaven, the human beings, the animals, the birds and winged beings, the insects, the snakes and reptiles, the fishes and crabs, the trees and plants, the paddy and rice, the bajra and Indian corn, all and everything, and he supports all, small and big, he feeds us all. He is the one who brings us here, he is the one who takes us away. By the word of the bongas and the mountain spirits or of a human being we are not born, nor do we go away; Ṭhākūr has measured out to us our seed, and until this is finished, no one is able to take us away. As we are living here, in the same way we shall, when we have gone to the other world, get good or bad by his order."[1] Here we have a god, Ṭhākūr, known and worshipped of old, and regarded as being identical with Sing-bonga, whom they "got" in Sing duar. In other words, we have two distinct persons in two different ages. But the resemblance with Dionysos ends there; there is no third person, and neither can be identified with any of Dionysos' "persons".

Incidentally, Thompson's *The Oral Tales of India* contains no heading under which a three-fold culture-hero is classified. Nor does the three-fold culture-hero occur in any of the books on the religion and customs of the Muṇḍas to which I have had access. Since the Greek passage as such is found only in Diodorus Siculus, it is open to serious doubt. It is not certain that it is derived from Megasthenes. Or it may come from Megasthenes originally, but have been misunderstood by Diodorus. But before we leave this point, I should like to draw attention to a passage in Tegnaeus' book *Le Héros Civilisateur*: "Dans le domain africain ce sont surtout H. Baumann et E. Brauer qui se sont occupés du héros civilisateur. Baumann cite principalement *trois aspects de ce personnage*: Le héros ancêtre ou fils du Dieu, le héros farceur et le héros thériomorphique. Brauer le présente sous l'aspect de l'Ancêtre primitif, le démiurge de la tribu, le mukuru des Héréros qui a un représentant vivant dans les chefs regnants."[2] We have of course no direct reason for coupling Diodorus with this account of the three aspects

---

[1] *Op. cit.*, p. 132. Cf. also above "a number of different Kittungs", p. 232.

[2] *Op. cit.*, p. 12.

of the culture-hero, coming as it does from Africa. But the father of the tribe, the bringer of civilization and the reigning monarch may be regarded as fundamentally one and the same person, living and active in distinct epochs. We mention this theory at this point for the sake of general interest. The culture-hero was evidently not a purely Indian phenomenon, and there may be aspects which have always existed in India, but which have not attracted attention in recent years. Our problem is most easily solved if we —following Fr.G.H.—drop this fragment. Surely Smith has interpreted it correctly when saying: Cicero distinguishes five, Diodorus three different Dionysi, evidently not limited to India.[1]

This is of course not meant as support for the identification of Dionysos with the Muṇḍas' culture-hero on this particular point. It is another matter that if this passage is authentic, it may possibly be taken as evidence for the *avatar* concept, or something similar, as far back as 300 B.C.

e. When Dionysos' army was on the point of perishing from the plague caused by the heat, he saved his men on a mountain having three peaks:[2]

f. Kondaskē[3]

g. Korasibiē,[4] and

h. Mēros.[5]

This group of passages contains the following motives, which we shall discuss in order: 1. the myth of disease and salvation, 2. the motif of the people who afterward dwelt on the mountain, 3. the motif of the three peaks, their names and connected themes.

1. We have earlier touched upon the myth of disease and salvation.[6] We found there that it was impossible to produce an exact parallel from either Aryan, Dravidian or Muṇḍa sources. But at the same time we pointed out that all three reckon with the possibility of a god or goddess intervening in case of disease or drought for the salvation of men. Myths of this type are found in all three ethnic groups.

2. We have also hinted at the motif of the people who afterward dwelt on the mountain,[7] but we may supply a little complementary material here. Lassen wrote in his *Indische Altertumskunde*: "Goṇḍa ist im Sanskrit der Name des rohen Urvolks, welches den grössern Theil dieses Landes inne

[1] Cf. also *Dema*, in Jensen, *Mythos und Kult bei Naturvölkern*.

[2] Frg. A 1 and 10.

[3] Frg. A 10.

[4] *Ibid.*

[5] Frg. A 1, 4, 5, 8, 9, 10.

[6] See above, pp. 206 ff. Cf. also the difference between Kittung and Rudra-Śiva, p. 282.

[7] Above, pp. 190 f. and 245 ff.

hat (the Vindhya mountains)."[1]—"Doch hat es für den Geschichtsforscher grosse Wichtigkeit, weil es ihm zeigt, dass Indien ursprünglich einem älteren Geschlechte roher Urbewohner angehörte; diese mussten in den offenen Gegenden dem Brahmanischen Gesetze sich unterwerfen, sie erhielten sich in den unzugänglichern Gebirgen; ... die Paharri in den Rajmahal-Bergen am Ganges sind mitten in Bengalen noch ein Überrest eines verwandten Volks, die Kola und Sura in den Gebirgen über Orissa gehören ebenfalls hieher."[2]

In our investigation we have used the collective designation "the Muṇḍas" to refer to the peoples of whom Lassen writes; they are in point of fact spread over large areas of India. In his book *The Peoples of India* Anderson writes: "The Muṇḍa languages are those of an isolated group of highlanders ..."[3] "Into the Aryan area projects the rocky plateau of Chota Nagpore, where the Muṇḍa dialects still survive, and there are a few other outlying areas where Dravidian tribes still use the original language of India."[4] On the subject of the relation between Muṇḍas and Dravidians, we may quote this interesting passage from Risley's *The People of India*: "The most important result of the inquiry was that there appears to be, from the physical point of view, no difference between the so-called 'Dravidian' and 'Kolarian' races occupying the hill country to the south of Bengal."[5] 'Kolarian' is an alternative name for the same ethnic group. Risley's view has now been entirely abandoned. The Dravidians and Muṇḍas have neither language nor race in common. But there are tribes living in the hills south of the Ganges, some of whom speak Muṇḍa, others Dravidian languages, and yet who do not belong to different races, and—most important—who have a strikingly similar culture and religion. There does not as yet seem to have been any detailed inquiry into the actual relation between the Dravidian-speaking tribes of Chota Nagpur and Orissa and the Tamil and Telugu-speaking peoples of South India. They certainly do not all belong to the same race; nor have they now any particular affinity. But may they not have done so in the distant past? The question lies well outside the bounds of our study; all we can do is to point out that the hills of India are inhabited by both Dravidians and Muṇḍas. But scholars tend to classify the tribes of Chota Nagpur and Orissa, even where they now speak Dravidian

---

[1] *Op. cit.*, I, p. 110 n. 4.

[2] *Ibid.*, p. 111.

[3] *Op. cit.*, p. 59.

[4] *Ibid.*, p. 60.

[5] *Op. cit.*, p. xiii.

or Aryan languages, as "Muṇḍas". The decisive factor, as we have pointed out, is the unity of their spiritual culture.[1]

The hills of India are nowadays inhabited by a large number of different tribes, with a variety of origins, languages and religions. Some speak Aryan languages, but have no further Aryan affinities; these are often Hindus. Others speak Dravidian languages, but are not of Dravidian stock; again, some are Hindus. We could continue on these lines, seeing how Hinduism is represented among all races and all language groups. But Hinduism, unlike Megasthenes' Dionysos-cult, is not limited to the hill-men: it cuts across all boundaries—of race, language, culture and geography. But Megasthenes describes a different situation: he informs us that the dwellers in the hills worship Dionysos, but that the plainsmen follow Heracles. The Muṇḍas provide just such an ethnic unit, including certain neighbouring peoples of similar, if not identical, race and cultural tradition—a tradition in which the culture-hero is prominent. Note, however, that we have no certain knowledge of which area in India Megasthenes meant when he talked about "India's hill country". A great deal of the subcontinent is made up of hill country. That he is speaking of the hills of the North-West, is clear from the descriptions of this area in the works of Alexander's historians. But can we therefore rule out the hilly areas north and south of Pāṭaliputra? Do the names of the three peaks give us any clue which will enable us to solve this problem?

3. We may begin by noting that the 'three peaks' motif is hinted at in the name of the ointment to be used by a *snātaka*. It is called *Traikakuda* and comes from the Himalaya.[2] The name *Traikakuda* means: "derived from (the mountain with) three peaks". The site of the mountain is not mentioned. But since one of the peaks is called "Mēros", and since this has been unanimously identified as Meru, we may start here, in the Himalaya. Law states in his *Tribes in Ancient India* that this mountain is situated in the vicinity of the sources of the Ganges and the Yamunā.[3] This becomes even clearer when we examine the map in the same author's *Historical Geography of Ancient India*, together with the text, p. 111, where we read that Kailāsa and Himavanta lie to the south of this mountain. If this is correct, then there must be more than one mountain with the same name. Since one peak was called Mēros and another Korasibiē, one name which suggests itself is Kailāsa. For no other peak in the vicinity of Meru bears a name remotely like Kondaskē or Korasibiē; and even this, the only name

[1] Above, pp. 192.

[2] Apte, *Social and Religious Life*, p. 61, from Gṛihya-Sūtras.

[3] *Op. cit.*, p. 91.

that can come under consideration, must be rejected as providing an insufficiently close parallel. Note that the difficulty we experience in localizing these hills is common to all the place-names occurring in Megasthenes' text on Dionysos.

But Megasthenes never says that these hills form part of the Himalaya. If we then turn to the Orissa area, we find a mountain called Khaṇḍagiri, which is always mentioned together with its "twin" Udayagiri, and often with a third, Nīlagiri—all three being referred to under the name of the first. Khaṇḍagiri suggests Kondaskē, even though the words are far from being identical. But since neither Mēros nor Korasibiē can be combined with the other peaks, this alternative must be rejected.

Arden mentions the following interesting tradition in his *Progressive Grammar of the Telegu Language*: "There is a tradition that the god Śiva, in the form of a *lingam*, descended upon three mountains named Kālēśvaram, Śrīśailam and Bhīmēśvaram and that these three *lingams* marked the boundaries of the country, which was in consequence called the Trilinga, Telinga or Telugu country."[1] This is interesting, particularly since it connects Śiva with a series of three peaks, one of which bears a certain resemblance to the Greek Korasibiē. But the names of the other two peaks do not fit, and we must therefore dismiss this possibility also. Incidentally, Śiva has links with both Kailāsa and, to some extent, Meru, though the latter is principally known as the dwelling-place of Brahmā.

This brief review shows how difficult it is to connect the names of the three peaks with anything to be found in Sanskrit literature. There is quite a remarkable difference between this situation and that we encountered in our Heracles section, where we were in general able to identify the names quite easily: Śūrasena, Yamunā, Mathurā, Śibi, Pāṇḍya, Pāṭaliputra. What is the reason for this?

The answer is to be found in the solution we advance of the riddle of Dionysos' identity. Dionysos is the god and culture-hero of primitive non-Aryan tribes: probably he is the principale deity of the Muṇḍas. It follows that those names mentioned in connection with Dionysos are not likely to be susceptible to explanation from Sanskrit sources. It is thus impossible even to attempt to interpret these names, since it is most likely that the peoples in question have retained no trace of the names they once used for the places under discussion. We can only suggest the lines along which a Muṇḍa interpretation might possibly be attempted. The chief god of one of the Muṇḍa-tribes is Marang Buru—the great mountain. *Marang* means

---

[1] *Op. cit.*, p. 3.

'great'; its main consonants are 'm' and 'r', like Meru. There is a Muṇḍa word *khunṭa*, meaning 'pole', which is not out of the question as the name of a mountain, and from which Kondaskē might well be derived. But these are only suggestions, and we shall not devote any more time to this line of argument. In short, we have no means of knowing what can have been the derivation of these names.

The last two names are found only in Polyaenus, and we are thus in some doubt as to whether they in fact originated with Megasthenes. Mēros, on the other hand, is named by other authors as well. We cannot draw any definite conclusions from this complex of passages, other than perhaps that the identification of Mēros with Meru is not quite so self-evident as we were led to imagine. At all events it provides us with no help for the identification of Dionysos, other than a possible indication that the god to which it refers is the god of a people whose place-names have not been preserved in Indian literature.

i. Dionysos founded a number of towns, among them Nysa, situated near Mount Mēros.[1]

All the passages in which Nysa is mentioned speak of Mount Mēros as well. The two were evidently closely connected in the minds of the Greek authors we have quoted, and should really have been considered together. If we can identify Nysa, then the chances are that we shall be able to localize Mēros too. But this fact has been overlooked. Law, who is the leading authority on India's historical geography, has stated that "the Mount Mēros of Arrian" was hard by the source of the Ganges.[2] Elsewhere he writes that "Mēros Mountain ... is also known as Mar-koh near Jalalabad in the Punjab, which was visited by Alexander the Great."[3] He thus makes it clear that he recognizes two different mountains with the same name. The second of these passages, referring to the Punjab Mēros, is however of sufficient importance to warrant an extended quotation from Law's *Tribes in Ancient India* (p. 154):

"When Alexander invaded India he found a large number of autonomous tribes and principalities in the North-Western Frontier Province and the Punjab. Among these we find mention of the Nysaeans forming a small hill-state with a republican constitution. They had Adouphis then as their President and they had a governing Body of three hundred members. Holdich in discussing the site of Nysa shows that the lower spurs and valleys of Koh-i-mor are where the ancient city of Nysa once stood. According to

[1] Frg. A 4, 5, 8, and 9.

[2] *Historical Geography of Ancient India*, p. 111.

[3] *Ibid.*

Bhāṇḍārkar, Nysa was situated between the Kophen and the Indus.[1] In the fifth book of Arrian's work, we find two relevant passages in this connection. Arrian says, 'The Nysaeans are not an Indian race, but descended from the men who came into India with Dionysos'.[2] ... In the legend the name Nysa was especially connected with Dionysos—it was the name of his nurse, or of the place where he was born or of his holy hill—and the name of this little town in the Hindu Kush, as it was pronounced to Alexander, had a similar sound. Again the legend said that Dionysos had been born from the thigh (mēros) of Zeus, and a neighbouring summit, the Greeks discovered, was called Meru."[3]

It is perfectly clear from this account that Mēros is a mountain in the Hindu Kush. The episode of Alexander the Great and the Nysaeans proves the town to have been situated in the far west of India—thus ruling out Meru, in the Himalaya, as Mēros. We are in fact in a difficult position here, since we know nothing whatever about the Indian name of the hill in question, and have no means of verifying the little information we possess.

It is possible that L. v. Schroeder's guess, that the Indian Nishādas and the Greek Nysaeans are identical, is correct.[4] Law rejects this hypothesis, but on dubious grounds,[5] and advances his own theory as to the use of the word Nishāda, as follows: "The word Nishāda seems to denote not so much a particular tribe, but to be the general term for the non-Aryan tribes who were not under Aryan control, as the Śūdras were ... The word Nishada (Nishāda) of the Vājasaneyī Saṃhitā (XVI, 27) is explained by the commentator Mahīdhara to mean a Bhīl or Bhilla, a tribe that still exists in the hills of Central India and the Vindhyan tracts ... According to Weber, the Nishādas were settled aborigines ... the name might easily be applied to the whole body of aborigines outside the Aryan organization."[6]

There seems to be a general consensus of opinion that this is a non-Aryan people. The overall picture agrees up to this point with Megasthenes' description of the religious situation and with Manu's division of the peoples of India: on the one hand the Aryans, living on the plain, and worshipping Heracles; on the other the *mlecchas*, the non-Aryans, living in the hills and

---

[1] Holdich, *Gates of India*, p. 122; Bhandarkar, *Carmichael Lectures* 1921, p. 32.

[2] Chinnock's ed., p. 399.

[3] Law, *Tribes in Ancient India*, p. 154 f.

[4] *Indiens Literatur und Cultur*, p. 366.

[5] Law, *Tribes*, p. 98 n. 5.

[6] *Ibid.*, p. 98; reference to *Vedic Index* I, p. 453 f., Weber, *Vedische Studien*, pp. 9, 340.

worshipping Dionysos. The Greek authors are unanimous in saying that the Nysaeans worshipped Dionysos, and they lived in the hills. And we learn from Indian literature that the Nishādas are a hill-people and that they are *mlecchas*, i.e. non-Aryans. This does not of course prove their identity; but it leaves the way open for such a proof. This seems to be the limit of our investigation; the general confusion surrounding certain of the tribes of India in the texts makes further progress virtually impossible.

For example, the Nishādas are non-Aryans, but the Nishadas are Aryans. Naturally the two have often been confused;[1] they both live in the Vindhya mountains, but the Nishādas are also mentioned as living in other parts of India. It is obvious that several tribes have the same name, and the confusion is perhaps natural. But at the same time it is difficult to escape the impression that authors often treat the names of tribes as no more than empty words, conveying nothing of the geographical locations in which they live. Law quotes the Purāṇas rather frequently; he is thus able to describe the situation of Mount Meru as follows:

"On the western side of this mountain stand Nishadha and Pāripātra; on the southern side stand Kailāsa and Himavanta, and on the northern side stand Śṛingavān and Jarudhi (Mārkaṇḍeya Purāṇa, Vaṅgavāsī Ed., p. 240)."[2] But on the other hand Law also writes "At the time of the Epics and Purāṇas the Nishādas seem to have had their dwelling among the mountains that form the boundary of the Jhalwar and Khandesh in the Vindhya and Satpura ranges. This is proved by the Mahābhārata (III, 130,4), which refers to a Nishādarāshṭra in the region of the Sarasvatī (!) and the Western Vindhyas, not very far from Pāripātra or Pāriyātra (!) (Mbh XII,135,3–5)."[3] The worth of such geographical statements as these is naturally open to some doubt, but we do at any rate gather that there must have been a number of tribes having the same name, among them a Nishāda tribe up in the Hindu Kush.

The Mount Nishadha which is mentioned together with Pāripātra is, according to the map in *Historical Geography*, farther north than the town of Nysa. But the mention of this mount together with Pāripātra seems to point to a desire on the part of the author to connect them geographically; when he goes on to state that there is a Nishāda-rāshṭra situated in the vicinity of Pāripātra and Sarasvatī, he brings the possibility of the Nysaeans and the Nishādas being identical very much nearer. We dare not however draw a conclusion, largely because of the element of confusion in the

---

[1] *Op. cit.*, p. 100.

[2] Law, *Historical Geography*, p. 111.

[3] *Op. cit.*, p. 291.

geographical information contained in the text. Shafer, in his book *Ethnography of Ancient India*, has drawn the consequences of these contradictory statements by providing a map on which are marked no less than three tribes with the same name—one of which lives in the vicinity of the Indus.

The name of the town Nysa has no positive value for our identification of Dionysos; it points to no Indian god in this connection. But we can perhaps go so far as to say that the positive evidence drawn from Mount Meru disappears, at least in so far as it may be taken to point to Śiva, since this god has particular connections with the Himalaya, of which Meru forms a part. There is no question of connecting Kr̥ishṇa with this particular part of India. Little more can be said. We therefore leave the possibility of the Nysaeans having been of Muṇḍa descent an open question, pausing only to note that Kuiper makes the following statement in *Rigveda Loanwords*:

"In any case, although the Austro-Asiatic component of Muṇḍa seems to point to an eastern provenance, the Proto-Muṇḍa linguistic area must have extended as far as the Indus Valley at the time of the Aryan invasion ..." A note reads: "Note the occurrence of words of apparently Muṇḍa origin in Burushaski, and of Tibeto-Burman elements in Nahali ..."[1]

We cannot rule out the possibility of there having been some connection between the Nysaeans and the Muṇḍas. We cannot advance any proof positive, largely because of the entirely different situation now to be found in the North of India. The material we have advanced seems to me to prove that Megasthenes' description of the Nysaeans' Dionysos fits in perfectly with the chief god of the Muṇḍas. Further, the mere fact that Megasthenes mentions Nysa and the surrounding area does not rule out the fact that his Dionysos may also have been worshipped in the neighbourhood of Pāṭaliputra, where the Muṇḍa of today worship Sing Bonga, Marang Buru and Kittung.

There are however other reasons apart from purely linguistic considerations for supposing there to have been a connection between the Muṇḍas and the Indus Valley people. We shall not discuss the anthropological judgment, that the Muṇḍas belong to a racial type which probably comes from the Mediterranean area.[2] An important fact has been observed by Roy and others: that there seems to have been some cultural link between the Indus Valley Civilization and a similar culture in Chota Nagpur. Chakla-

[1] *Studia Indologica*, p. 140.

[2] For anthropological discussion, see bibliography. Cf. Hutton, *op. cit.*, p. 452 and Chakladar, *Caucasic Peoples between India and the Pacific*, p. 186.

dar has expressed the matter as follows: "As Mackay has shown, copper the Indus Valley people must have obtained from Chota Nagpur, that is, the highlands of Bengal, as is demonstrated from the fact that the Mohenjo-daro copper contains a trace of nickel, and the same alloy is found in the copper from the old but still worked mines in the latter area."[1]

If we look carefully for traces of the Muṇḍas in western India, we find these on a map printed in the *Census of India* 1931, on which Hutton has attempted to describe the routes followed by the various races which have invaded India in the course of the centuries.[2] The most interesting thing about this map, for our purposes, is that the route followed by the Muṇḍas is absolutely identical with that followed by both the Indo-Europeans and Alexander the Great. Is this pure chance? Or does it mean that we can find only traces of the Indo-Europeans and the Muṇḍas in that area in which Alexander and his men heard of Heracles and Dionysos? According to Hutton, the Dravidian line of invasion was along the coast.

It is of course impossible to build a thesis on Hutton's suggestive hypothesis. But what is valuable for us is that there has been a connection established between the Muṇḍas and the west—culturally, if in no other way—and this can imply religious affinities. It is therefore not out of the question to link the Muṇḍas of the present day with the Nysaeans of the time of Alexander.

j. The Oxydrakai were regarded as having been descended from Dionysos and his men.[3]

Strabo, the only author who mentions this fact, has earlier written about the Hydrakai, whom the Persians attempted to press into service as mercenaries. Law, writing in *Tribes in Ancient India*, is of the opinion that these two words, Oxydrakai and Hydrakai, reproduce the same Sanskrit word in different Greek forms.[4] There are also other classical forms of the name, of which Sudracae and Sydracae may serve as examples. The classical authors often couple this tribe with another, called Malloi, Malli or Mallai; it has long been usual to identify these with the Mālavas and the Kshudrakas, which are often mentioned in the same breath in Sanskrit literature. Law writes that the latter "were one of the most numerous and warlike of all the Indian tribes in the Punjab".[5] Unfortunately we know

---

[1] Roy, *Caste, Race*, in *Man in India* XVII, 1937, p. 226; Chakladar, *The Prehistoric Culture of Bengal*, p. 158.

[2] *Op. cit.*, p. 460.

[3] Frg. A 4.

[4] *Op. cit.*, p. 60.

[5] *Op. cit.*, p. 394.

nothing of the race or the language of the Oxydrakai. Shafer asks in his *Ethnography of Ancient India*: "Were these 'dwarf' Mālavas the Bhils who later settled in Malwa and gave it its name?"[1] On p. 98 the words Kshudraka-Mālava are followed by the word "Bhil" in brackets and with a question mark; every time Shafer mentions the Nishāda he adds "Bhil" in brackets. What reason has he for coupling these two peoples?

The word *kshudraka* is Sanskrit and means "little". The fact of its being a Sanskrit word suggests a connection with the Aryans. But those who are known as "the little ones" are hardly likely to have been Aryans. Furthermore, though this word is said to have been Sanskrit, it is hardly an Indo-European word. It is true that it can be connected with the *skr*-root *kshud*, 'to crush', where the meaning 'to make small, reduce', may well be implied; but on the other hand Monier-Williams produces as parallels the Lith. *kūdikis*, 'child', and the New-Pers. *kūdak*, 'little, boy'. But this is not altogether convincing. The New Persian word seems irrelevant in this context. The Sanskrit *ksh-* corresponds to the Avestan *xsh-*, which in New Persian gives *sh-* (cf. *kshatra*). We might ask instead whether *kshudra* might not have to do with the Buddhistic Sanskrit word *cūḍa*. It is true that Kuiper does not take up the word *kshudra* in his examination of the different words for 'little', but the Skr. *kshudra* would not have been altogether out of place among the forms he attempts to trace back to Proto-Muṇḍa.[2]

This brief examination serves only to show the impossibility of reaching any definite conclusions concerning the race and language of the Oxydrakai on the basis of this Sanskrit word—if the word is in fact of Sanskrit origin.

It is not easy to localize the Oxydrakai in the Punjab. Law, basing his calculations on the Greek authors, suggests the area between Hydraotes (= Rāvi, Skr. Irāvatī) and Hyphasis (= Beas, i.e. Vipāśā). Map 2 in *The History and Culture of the Indian People* II includes their names entered in the vicinity of Harappa. Their allies in the struggle against Alexander, the Malloi (i.e. the Mālavas), are placed immediately north of the junction of the Rāvi and Chenab rivers. Law writes: "Indeed, the Mālavas seem to have occupied their territory in the Punjab for some time afterwards ... But before long they seem to have migrated southwards and settled somewhere in Rajputana, where the tribes seem to have held their ground at the time of Samudragupta ... According to the Purāṇas, the Mālavas are associated with the ... Arbudas, and are described as dwelling along the

---

[1] *Op. cit.*, pp. 98, 103, 105 and 128.

[2] *Proto-Muṇḍa Words in Sanskrit*, p. 152.

Pāriyātra mountains. Thus it seems that they occupied other territories besides the Punjab or Rajputana. After Samudragupta's time when, as we have seen, the tribe was settled in Rajputana, the Mālavas seem to have migrated to the Mandasor region in the north-west part of Central India. This tract of country along with the region round Bhilsa comprises what is now known as Mālwa (Mālava)."[1]

This brings us to that part of India in which the Bhils are to be found. No attempt has been made to try and show that the Mālavas were Aryans. But who were they? Was there a deeper connection than the mere exigencies of political alliance between the Oxydrakai and the Malloi? It is of course impossible to answer this question with any degree of accuracy, and we prefer not to hazard a guess. We point out merely that there was a tribe living in the Punjab at the time of the Greek campaigns who shortly afterward migrated in the direction of the hills in which live the Muṇḍas and other non-Aryan primitive tribes of today.[2] The religion they practised in Megasthenes' day has since been exchanged for Hinduism or Islam or—to some extent—Christianity. They have abandoned Dionysos, of whom no trace is to be found, either among the descendants of the Mālavas or the Kshudrakas—if these are not to be found in the Muṇḍas.

k. Before the coming of Dionysos they ate the bark of a tree called *tala*.[3]

Monier-Williams' *Sanskrit-English Dictionary* has under *tāla*: "the palmyra tree or fan-palm (*Borassus flabelliformis*, producing a sort of spirituous liquor ...)."

There is a tradition about the origin of this tree in Elwin's *Tribal Myths of Orissa*: "In Hirapali there lived a Gond and his wife. They had no children. This Gond served Bara Deo who blessed him, saying, 'You will have five sons and five daughters.' According to his word children began to be born. When they grew up, the Gond arranged their marriages, for all of them but the youngest son. For him he got the daughter of the Gond Chief of Kisnapalli. Many others asked for her but the Gond refused. In this way enmity arose between the two families. The boy's mother was a witch and she performed magic against the mother of the boy who married the girl. After the wedding the boy fell ill and died. They buried him and put his marriage-crown by his head. From this crown a toddy-palm sprang up. The parents saw it and called their Guru from Bairagarh. In their old Gondi he

---

[1] *Tribes in Ancient India*, p. 62 f.

[2] Tarn, *The Greeks in Bactria and India*, p. 240: "... whether the Oxydracae had gone south to Malva with their allies the Malli and lost their identity, cannot be said."

[3] Frg. A 6.

spoke, 'This is from the *talla* (head) and it will be called *tal*. Serve it and care for it. When it grows, it will give fruit and so spread through the world'."[1]

This is naturally popular etymology. But is there any connection between the name of the palm, characterized by a head, and a Dravidian word meaning 'head'? 'Head' in Tamil is *talai*; 'palm' is *tālam*. The latter is however borrowed from Sanskrit. The real Tamil word for 'palm' is *panai*, a word which seems to have no etymological parallel in Sanskrit, but the following in other Dravidian languages: Ma. *pana* (id.). *Ka. pane* (bastard sago-palm), Kod. *pane-mara* (toddy palm), Tu. *paṇe-kāyi* (palmyra fruit). It is interesting to note that there are Sanskrit loanwords in some other Dravidian languages: Ka. *tār* (palmyra or toddy palm), Tu. *tāri*, *tāḷi*, Te. *tāḍu*, Kol. (Kin.) *tāṭi māk*, Pa. *tāṛ*. The list compiled by Burrow-Emeneau concludes with: Cf. Skr. *tāla-*, Pkt. *tāla-*, *tāḍa-*. It is clear from this, first, that the borrowing has been from Sanskrit, and not from Dravidian, and secondly, that little reliance can be placed upon the etymology of the word given above, in which it is traced back to a Dravidian word for 'head'. The connection becomes even more unlikely when we note that all the Dravidian words for 'head' have a short 'a' in the first syllable.

Is it then possible to explain the word on a basis of the Muṇḍa languages? Kuiper does not mention it in his *Proto-Muṇḍa Words in Sanskrit*. He has however discussed a series of words having to do with water: Santālī *dalhi*, *dalahi*, etc., 'marsh, bog, marshy, boggy', *thal thal*, 'deep mud', *thala*, 'marsh, marshy'. He writes: "Many New-Indo-Aryan words are obviously derived from these Muṇḍa words, cf. Hindi *daldal*, 'marshy land, mire, mud, swamp', *daldalā*, 'marshy, boggy', Sanskrit *talla-*, m. 'small pond', Prakrit *talla-*, n., id., Hindi *tāl*, 'pool, lake', Marathi *tāl*, 'mare de liquide répandu', etc."[2]

An explanation may perhaps be found in the wine which flows like water from the tree. But the same objection arises, that there is a short 'a' in the original language or languages. But we have on the other hand a Hindi form with a long 'a', showing, if Kuiper is correct in bringing together these words, that variants are possible. No variation of the Skr. *tālam* is known; and the only variation in Dravidian words for 'head' is that Kaikāḍī seems to have a form with a short, and one with a long 'a': *talkai*, *thālī*.

Summary and conclusions

We have now come to an end of our review of those passages in which Megasthenes mentions Dionysos, and of our attempts to connect these with

[1] *Op. cit.*, p. 183. [2] *Op. cit.*, p. 138 f.

Aryan, Dravidian and Muṇḍa ideas respectively, and with Śiva and Kṛishṇa. We have seen that Dionysos has no contact whatever with the Aryan world of ideas, but that he can be connected at a number of points with non-Hindu Dravidian religion, as exemplified by the religion of the Koṭas of South India and the Oraons and others in the Chota Nagpur-Orissa area; we have however come across certain difficulties when trying to link Megasthenes' Dionysos passage with ideas current among Dravidian-speaking peoples.

Kṛishṇa is of a different type from Dionysos, despite one or two interesting parallels. Śiva at first sight appears more promising, but it proved to be the case that though the resemblances were more comprehensive than in the case of Kṛishṇa, they were still not sufficiently wide to constitute an identification. But when we turn to the hill tribes of India—who have been relatively little influenced by Hinduism—we find a quite remarkable degree of correspondence between what Megasthenes has to say about the Indian Dionysos and the tribal myths about the chief of their gods, whatever he may be called.

Our result, in tabular form, has the following figures:

Aryan	Dravidian	Muṇḍa	Kṛishṇa	Śiva
1. *Historical passages*				
3	3	5	1	0
2. *Functional passages*				
6 + (3?)	10 + (1?)	20 + (3?)	5 + (1?)	7 + (3?)
3. *Geographical passages*				
2	1?)	0	1	0
Total				
10 + (3?)	13 + (2?)	25 + (3?)	7 + (1?)	7 + (3?)

It will be clear from this table that we have been able to fix a clear connection between Megasthenes' Dionysos passages and Muṇḍa tradition on no less than twenty-five occasions: the Muṇḍa traditions in question being those to do with their sun-god/culture-hero. There were three other doubtful cases, viz. the questions of perfume, long hair and beard (2bb, cc, dd). We might summarize the areas of agreement as follows: the Muṇḍas have traditions according to which they came from the west, with a great army, including women; they have a hereditary monarchy and their gods are thought to be subject to death. Their culture-hero has bestowed upon them all manner of inventions, has changed them from hunters to farmers, taught them to harness oxen to the plough and given them seed with which to sow their fields. The fig tree occupies a prominent position in their life. Further, their culture-hero has taught them to store fruit, brew intoxicating liquors and to make use of them. He also founded a religious cult in which he himself was celebrated in some form, before his death. They worship the spirits of other ancestors, too. They live in the hills, and are skilful musicians: dancing and the music of percussion instruments (and to some extent processions) form a constant ingredient both in their everyday life and in their religious festivals. They dress in little more than a girdle, though the turban is not unknown. They have a particular fondness for flowers. They seem to have been in the habit until quite recently of wearing their hair long. The culture-hero taught them to look after their hair; he may also have taught them to care for the beard.

This information we have gathered from the ethnographical material at our disposal. Times have of course changed; a great deal can happen to a tribe in 2250 years. Hence there have been discrepancies between Megasthenes' account and that of the modern ethnographers—unavoidable discrepancies.

The maximum number of points on which Dionysos can be connected with the Muṇḍas is thus twenty-eight; the figures for Kṛishṇa and Śiva are only eight and ten respectively.[1] Note that of the ten points which can be connected with Śiva, the following have already been reckoned among those in favour of the Muṇḍas: ploughing with oxen; the fig tree; wine; the setting up of a cult; dancing; drums; the girdle; and long hair. In most cases the extent of agreement is not very large, and hardly any of these points can be called vital for Śiva and his cult. On only two occasions can we establish a connection with Śiva without being able to refer at the same time to the Muṇḍas' culture-hero: the healing of sickness and the issuing of weapons. But there is a distinct contrast here too; Dionysos is not described as one who commonly heals disease: Śiva is regularly invoked as a healer.[2] And again, while Dionysos is described as having distributed

[1] The eight pieces of information which can be combined with Kṛishṇa are: 1 f. He died at a great age, 2 r. He founded a religious cult, s. He was regarded as a god even before death, u. Dancing a part of his cult, aa. The girdle suggests Kṛishṇa's name *Dāmodara*, cc. The long hair suggests Kṛishṇa's names Hrishīkeśa and Keśava, (with more doubt) 2 c. He built towns, and 3 a. He was three different persons. The notice 1 c. He was born in India was most probably not authentic.

[2] Observe that Dionysos according to Megasthenes does not cure his sick army. He only brings it away from the perilous area. Cf. Rudra-Śiva who drive away the sickness from their worshippers. In this respect the Indian Dionysos resembles the Muṇḍa Dema more than Rudra-Śiva. Cf. below, p. 282.

weapons to the Indians generally, Śiva did so only once, to a particular individual.

Dionysos is thus unlike both Kṛishṇa and Śiva in his type. There are a number of good reasons why he cannot be an Aryan deity. The thirteen points which Dionysos and the Aryan literature have in common, are almost without exception to be connected with some new deity in the Aryan pantheon. Thus while Agni, Varuṇa and others gave away weapons, Manu made laws.

A number of the characteristics of the culture-hero are to be found in the Aryan and Dravidian Hindu literature, for example Agastya, who created the Tamil grammar and was a friend of education in all its forms. But the literature of Hinduism and ancient Aryan works have nothing resembling a culture-hero of the type represented by Dionysos, who teaches mankind everything belonging to civilization. But this is precisely the chief characteristic of the great god of the Muṇḍas. This is perhaps best demonstrated in the words of Elwin; we reproduce his summary of the character of Kittung, the god of the Saoras:

'In all he did to reform the world, Kittung is seen as generally benevolent. *He teaches men operations of agriculture* and *provides them with seed* and *ploughcattle*. He shows them how to build houses, *how to grow cotton and wear clothes, how to cook, how to extract wine from the palms*. He is quickly moved by the sight of suffering: he takes pity on an abandoned bastard child; when he sees people sleeping on the damp ground, bitten by scorpions, their ears tortured by insects, 'he feels very sorry'. He decides that people must have cots, 'for if they have trouble like this,' he says, 'they will die. Men must be happy.' At a time of drought, he 'feels sad for the misery of men'. Kittung is always ready to promote domestic happiness. He teaches a neglected wife to tickle her husband and excite him. He creates mosquitoes for no other purpose than to force a frigid wife into her husband's bed. He puts blood in the human body to prevent it drying up and make it capable of bearing children. He takes pity on the soul of an unmarried girl and sends her back as a tobacco plant, to be desired by all men. Kittung does all he can to brighten the dull existence of mankind. *He teaches boys and girls to dance. He persuades people to do their hair properly* and look nice. *He invents musical instruments* to cheer the company at weddings and funerals. He makes frogs to clean the water of tanks and wells so that people will enjoy their baths. *He makes the first shaman to save men from exactions of the spirits.* He forces a witch to cure one of her victims. Kittung is fond of animals. He gives dogs their tails and teaches them to recognize each other by their smell. He shows them how to avoid dangerous animals which would kill them. He makes horns for the buffalo so that the yoke will rest comfortably in place. He makes the cock a comb with a scarlet thread from his own loincloth. *Although he teaches men to eat meat*, he realizes what this will mean for the animals and warns them not to be too familiar with human beings but to keep them a little afraid. A lover of trees, Kittung sits down and weeps when he sees the devastation caused by the Saoras' axes, and goes to a great deal of trouble to find the seeds of new trees to grow instead ..."[1] "Kittung is, of course, lacking in many of the attributes which the more highly developed religions have given to the Supreme Being. He is far from being omnipotent: he has to go to his Mahaprabhu to get light; *he has to force a witch to cure her victim, but is not able to perform the cure himself*; he makes bees, but he cannot control them. *During a great epidemic*, when corpses are littering the villages, *he cannot stop the disease*; all he can do is to provide a vulture as scavenger. He is not omniscient, for he does not know where grain is and has to send someone to look for it; he has to send a kite to see if there are any survivors of the great flood; he has to undertake a long and rather humiliating journey in search of goats; he makes tongues for men, but only after several mistakes; he is forgetful—he makes trees, but forgets the all-important Bassia latifolia. *He is not omnipresent, for he is always shown as definitely located in some particular place*, and people have to make long journeys to see him. In many ways Kittung appears as a cult-hero of the type of Nanga Baiga or the Muria Lingo. He is a simple and thoroughly human person. He has his farm and his tobacco patch ..."[2]

This summary of the character of Kittung contains a number of striking resemblances with what we have seen of Megasthenes' account of Dionysos. We note, over and above what we have already said, that Kittung is unable to halt the course of sickness; he has to find means by which to remedy the accepted situation. He forces a witch to cure her victim; he provides a vulture as a scavenger. We find something of the same powerlessness in Dionysos, who has to take his army up into the hills in order to cure a disease which Rudra-Śiva would simply have driven away.[3]

We might summarize here, as we summarized the first part of our study: that which is told of Dionysos is also told of Kittung and the other gods/culture-heros of the Muṇḍas, and vice versa. The 2250 years which have gone by since Megasthenes first described the religious conditions in his adopted land have not altered the *type* of god worshipped by the hill-men.

---

[1] Elwin, *The Religion of an Indian Tribe*, p. 89 f.

[2] *Op. cit.*, p. 91.

[3] Another description we have quoted above p. 254 n.8 .

Details have of course changed, and not everything we have said here applies equally to all the tribes under consideration. It would be unreasonable to expect, in these circumstances, to localize every tradition narrated by Megasthenes. But what we have found seems to me to be quite sufficient to justify the conclusion that Megasthenes was describing a religion and a people—or a number of peoples—which were not Aryan and which had not been shaped by the tenets of Hinduism, a people, the religion and culture of which have been preserved by the Muṇḍas of Chota Nagpur and Orissa.

It is here that our investigation demonstrates its worth. It would be out of the question to describe the religions of India today in the same terms as those used by Megasthenes. Two conclusions are inescapable in connection with the present-day study of the religions of India: first, that there is a certain degree of unity within Hinduism, in that the worshippers of Śiva, and Kṛishṇa (or Vishṇu) live and work side by side; and secondly, that the primitive tribes of the hills are forced to occupy a position very much in the background. We call these primitives 'animists', for want of a better name, but in point of fact none but the expert knows very much about them.

But Megasthenes witnessed a different situation; on the one hand he saw the dwellers on the plains, worshippers of Indra, who were Aryans, and on the other the hill-men, non-Aryans, belonging to a variety of races and speaking a variety of languages. No mention is made of Hinduism. In short, the situation was not unlike that which we imagine to have existed soon after the time of the Aryan invasions, with a sharp distinction drawn between Aryans and non-Aryans. Megasthenes' India seems to have known nothing of the background we find in the Mahābhārata and—particularly—in the Purāṇas; but it is the same India we know from the Manu-smṛiti. We hope to take up this question in detail at some future date, in connection with our planned investigation of Megasthenes' view of the Indian philosophers.

The fact that the RV contains non-Aryan (possibly Dravidian) words need not be taken to be a contradiction of this principle of separation. An example is the eighth *maṇḍala* of the RV, which contains a number of words which come into this category: *Tirindira*, *Irimbiṭhi*, etc. The contacts between an invading people and the native tribes must have been such as to have allowed of the establishing of friendly relations at least in certain quarters.

Megasthenes and his contemporaries in Greek literature have been of enormous importance when it has come to estimating the chronology of

Indian history. By identifying Sandrakottos with Candragupta scholars found a fixed point in the Indian royal lists; in fact it is this Candragupta, together with his grandson Aśoka, who has been the pivotal figure in the chronology of the secular history of India.[1] But Megasthenes' importance is not confined to the field of profane history. His description of Heracles has been made into the foundation of certain tenacious theories concerning, on the one hand, the extreme age of the *avatar* concept in India and, on the other and most particularly, the age of Krishnaism and hence of Hinduism. A further assumption has been that certain of the great works of Indian literature had already seen the light of day, since their witness had evidently been called in as support for the identification of Heracles with Kṛishṇa.

This use of the information provided by Megasthenes in order to establish the chronology of the religion and literature of India is perfectly justifiable. But sufficient care has not always been taken to understand what Megasthenes has to say. The passages in which he refers to Heracles and Dionysos have been taken up and without more ado made to fit in with the gods the scholars have seen in 'Heracles' and 'Dionysos'. Where there have been characteristics which did not fit in with the gods in question, it has been customary to fall back upon Megasthenes' *interpretatio graeca.* It goes without saying that skilful use of this method can prove virtually anything. We have in this study applied a method diametrically opposite to that commonly in use: we have assumed that Megasthenes may have reproduced what he had seen perfectly accurately. Not until it has proved impossible to combine his information with one and the same Indian deity have we been willing to turn to *interpretatio graeca*—as an emergency measure.

We have had no occasion to apply this method. Schwanbeck was of the opinion that Megasthenes was perfectly reliable in all save his statements on Indian religion; it is strange, then, that scholars have been so sure of their identification of Heracles and Dionysos that they have not hesitated to build a chronology of Indian religion on material drawn in the first place from Megasthenes.[2] Schwanbeck draws a clear distinction between Megasthenes and other authors who have written about India on all other points. But even those who have unquestioningly accepted Schwanbeck's view of Megasthenes' reliability have at the same time accepted that *interpretatio graeca* must have played a great part in his version of Indian religion. This is hardly consistent. On the contrary, it is my considered opinion that the Greeks chose Greek names for the gods they wished to describe purely

---

[1] See further *The History and Culture of the Indian People* II, *The Age of Imperial Unity*, p. 92 f.

[2] See particularly pp. 61 and 76.

on account of the unquestionable resemblances between Heracles and Indra on the one hand, and Dionysos and sun-god/culture-hero of the Muṇḍas on the other. This is perhaps a truism, but nevertheless a necessary truism, in view of what a number of scholars have said and written on the subject.

We have already pointed out that the resemblances between the Greek and the Indian gods who go under the same name, do not need to be a burden and do not need to complicate the task of identification. But we have found characteristics ascribed to the *Indian* Heracles which have never been attributed to the *Greek* Heracles, nor to Kṛishṇa or Śiva, but which have been connected with the name of Indra. The Aornos episode and the incest story provide a case in point. This cannot be a case of *interpretatio graeca*, since both themes are unknown in the story of the Greek Heracles.

The same principle applies to Dionysos. Nilsson informs us that he was never connected with agrarian fertility in Greece.[1] He has connections with trees, but not with crops. The *Indian* Dionysos, on the other hand, was said to have provided seed for the crops—like the Muṇḍas' culture-hero, but unlike either Kṛishṇa, Śiva or any other god. So we see that at least one characteristic of the Indian Dionysos was shared exclusively with the Muṇḍas' *Dema*.

If then we are prepared to rely on Megasthenes, what is there to be said about Indian religion as it was in 300 B.C.? The final answer to this question will depend upon our examination of Megasthenes' description of the Indian philosophers, and thus must await a future occasion, but our preliminary answer is as follows:

1. *Hinduism had not yet arisen.*[2]

This result is implied in the passage in which a distinction is drawn between the dwellers on the plains and the hill-men. Our identification of the two gods Heracles and Dionysos also points in the same direction; we have been unable to demonstrate a clear case of exclusive similarity with either

---

[1] *Geschichte der Griechischen Religion* I², p. 601: "Er hat Beziehungen zur Fruchtbarkeit, *nicht der Felder*, wohl aber der Bäume."

[2] Cf. Roy, *Caste, Race and Religion*, in *Man in India* XVII, 1937, p. 249: "It was during Rāshṭrakūṭa rule that the worship of Vishṇu and Śiva became prominent" (i.e. a few centuries A.D.). According to Roy, in the centuries around the beginning of the Christian era Buddhism and Jainism became dominant, and Brahmanism in third place. "It was only during the rule of the later Chālukyas and the Kalachuri dynasty of Chedi that Pauranic Hinduism came to be firmly established in Deccan" (i.e. between 210 and 740 A.D.).

of the two chief gods of Hinduism. On the same points similarities always have been shown with either Indra or the Muṇḍa Dema. But the decisive argument is that the existence of Hinduism brought about a situation entirely different from that described by Megasthenes—a situation in which the boundaries between Aryan and non-Aryan disappeared, to be replaced by a system in which the non-Aryan was accepted, though kept in his place by the rules of caste. Thus a whole tribe was incorporated into Hinduism under the name of a *śūdra* caste. There is no distinction drawn between hill-men and plainsmen when it comes to the worship of Śiva or Vishṇu-Kṛishṇa.

2. *Kṛishṇa had not yet attained his later position.*

Note that Heracles was worshipped particularly in Mathurā. We have shown that Heracles was in fact Indra, and that it was Indra, and not Kṛishṇa, who was worshipped in Mathurā ca. 300 B.C. We know of no other place in which Kṛishṇa was worshipped with the same emphasis. Hence it follows that Kṛishṇa was unknown, or at least had not been deified, at this time. It is quite possible that he may have been some minor tribal god, but such a theory is by its nature incapable of proof or disproof.

3. *There is evidence that the avatar concept was known.*

This we deduce from the idea that Dionysos was regarded as being three different persons, living in three different ages. There is however no connection with Vishṇu. This is no new discovery; the concept can be demonstrated on other grounds, and we need not discuss the matter further.

4. *Indra had not yet been dislodged by the Trimūrti.*

In Megasthenes' day Indra was still the dominant god, as he had been ever since the Rig Vedic period.

5. *The state of Indian literature.*

Few conclusions can be drawn regarding the state of Indian literature at this time, but we can at least state that the Mahābhārata and the Purāṇas had not as yet attained even approximately the form in which we now have them, since they presuppose a situation determined and coloured by Hinduism. Since Megasthenes' India seems to have nothing of this, we are compelled to the conclusion that both the Mahābhārata and the Purāṇas must be dated later than 300 B.C. They may of course contain a great deal of older material, but that is another matter: the basic plan is more recent than Megasthenes.

This is true under the presumption that Hinduism did not originate in the Deccan. If we have understood Megasthenes correctly, he names the plains around Mathurā—where according to the Purāṇas Kṛishṇa lived, played and did his mighty deeds—as the home of the Indra-worshippers, and the hills of the Hindu Kush, the Punjab, probably the Himalaya southward to the Vindhya hills and Chota Nagpur, as the home of the other religion. But it is possible that he was not concerned with the country south of Vindhya-Chota Nagpur other than in connection with Heracles' relation to Pāṇḍya. This suggests that Indra may have been worshipped in South India, though this is far from certain. But it seems that he never mentions, or means to mention, the Dravidians—who in any case lived at a great distance from that part of India he is likely to have known as ambassador in Pāṭaliputra. Here we have a gap in the narrative, which fits in well with the view of Śiva as a god of great antiquity (perhaps coming from the Indus Valley Civilization), on the one hand, and the worship of Śiva as something particularly Dravidian, on the other.

If Hinduism developed in parts of India of which Megasthenes knew nothing, then it may well have existed in his day, despite his silence. But such is not the verdict of scholarship. It must be admitted, however, that the literature of Hinduism says nothing about the country of its origin, apart from connecting Śiva with the Himalaya and Kṛishṇa with Mathurā. The west and the south of India figure hardly at all in the Mahābhārata and the Purāṇas. We therefore maintain that Megasthenes' *Indika* is evidence that the literature of Hinduism is of more recent date than 300 B.C.

6. *Non-Aryans.*

The inhabitants of the Punjab and the Hindu Kush observed a non-Aryan and non-Hindu religion, substantially similar to that observed today by the inhabitants of Chota Nagpur and Orissa, who are mainly Muṇḍas. The nature of our material makes it impossible to draw any definite conclusions as to the language and ethnic characteristics of the Punjab tribes with whom the Greeks came into contact. They do not seem to have been Aryans—the Śibi excepted—but we are not sure whether or not they belonged to the Muṇḍa group. The migrations which we know to have taken place after the Greek invasion make it possible that there is some connection between these original dwellers in the Punjab and the Hindu Kush and those who today live in Orissa and Chota Nagpur.[1] The fact that a number of tribes which can be identified as Muṇḍas are mentioned in the Mahābhā-

---

[1] On the Mālavas, see above, p. 275 ff.

rata and the Purāṇas need not affect this judgment, particularly in view of what we have said about the difficulty of dating these works.

7. *The culture-hero.*

The most striking element in the religion of these tribes is perhaps that their culture-hero had divine attributes: a phenomenon which occurs elsewhere, but which is nevertheless noteworthy. The same dichotomy is to be observed in the figures of the Greek Dionysos and of Isis in the mysteries. It would be interesting and instructive to compare culture-heroes from Africa, India and Melanesia-Polynesia, with this in mind.[1] There is the fascinating possibility of a connection—racial, linguistic and religious—between these peoples, forming a chain reaching from the Mediterranean and Africa over India and the Far East to the Islands of the Pacific. Linguistic connections have long been supposed to have existed; ethnic relationship has been partly proved; and there are striking resemblances in certain specific religious ideas. But less interest has been accorded the Muṇḍas of India by the world's ethnographers and ethnologists than has been the case with the Polynesians, Melanesians and the tribes of Africa.

8. *The culture-hero among illiterates.*

Megasthenes' account of the Dionysos cult provides us with the most ancient record in all history of the concept of a culture-hero among an illiterate people. We hope that our investigation has made it perfectly plain that this concept is not to be dismissed as a fruit of *interpretatio graeca.*

9. *Interpretatio graeca.*

This brings us to the last result of our investigation. The suspicion that Megasthenes has been guilty of some form of *interpretatio graeca* has shown itself to be entirely unjustified. Most of the essential information transmitted by Megasthenes about Heracles and Dionysos has been paralleled in Indian literature or Indian tradition. On no occasion have we had to resort to *interpretatio graeca* in explanation of a particular statement. We have not distrusted the Greek author before proving that he was wrong. We have assumed the possibility of influence from his Greek background only when he has given us information which we have been unable to parallel

[1] Jensen, *op. cit.*, has tried to put together Indian facts with those in other parts of the world. But he has not strictly chosen Indian facts of the same sort. In the Aryan pantheon there is no real Dema.

from Indian sources—and this is very seldom indeed. In matters of religion, as in all else, Megasthenes has given us the Indians' point of view, whether or not it agreed with that of the Greeks. This does not imply that we have taken up an attitude toward *interpretatio graeca* among Greek authors in general. Scholars are convinced of its occurrence; they may be right. But not in the case of Megasthenes.

Further conclusions on the subject of Megasthenes and Indian religion must wait until we have had an opportunity of examining what Megasthenes has to say about the Indian philosophers.

BIBLIOGRAPHY

Sources

Greek with translation

Megasthenes, Indica.

Fontes historiae religionum indicarum. Collegerunt Bernardus Breloer et Franziscus Bömer. (*F.H.R.*, 7.) Bonnae 1939.

Die Fragmente der Griechischen Historiker (*F.GR.HIST.*) von Felix Jacoby. 1–3 c 2 Berlin 1923–Leiden 1958.

Megasthenis Indica. Fragmenta collegit, commentationem et indices addidit E. A. Schwanbeck. Bonnae 1846.

Ancient India as described by Megasthenēs and Arrian, being a translation of the fragments of the Indika of Megasthenēs collected by E. A. Schwanbeck and of the first part of the Indika of Arrian. By J. W. Mc Crindle. Reprinted (with additions) from the Indian Antiquary, 1876–77. Calcutta 1926.

Indian with translation

Agnipurāṇa

Śrīmaddvaipāyanamunipraṇītam Agnipurāṇam. Poona 1900. (*Ānandāśramasaṁskṛitagranthāvaliḥ*, 41.)

Āpastambagṛihyasūtra

Āpastambīyaṁ Gṛihyasūtram, The Āpastambīya Gṛihyasūtra with Extracts from the Commentaries of Haradatta and Sudarśanārya, edited by M. Winternitz. Vienna 1887.

The Gṛihya-Sūtras, Rules of Vedic Domestic Ceremonies transl. by Hermann Oldenberg. Part II ... Āpastamba ... Oxford 1892. (*S.B.E.*, Vol. XXX.)

Arthaśāstra, see *Kauṭilya*!

Ashṭādhyāyī, see *Pāṇini*!

Āśvalāyanagṛihyasūtra

Nārāyaṇakṛitavṛitti-gṛihyapariśishṭa-bhaṭṭakumārilakārikāsahitam Āśvalāyanagṛihyasūtram. [Poona] 1936. (*Ānandāśramasaṁskṛitagranthāvaliḥ*, 105.)

The Gṛihya-Sūtras, Rules of Vedic Domestic Ceremonies transl. by Hermann Oldenberg. Part I ... Āśvalāyana-Gṛihya-Sūtra ... Oxford 1886. (*S.B.E.*, Vol. XXIX.)

Atharvaveda.

Atharva Veda Sanhita herausgegeben von R. Roth und W. D. Whitney, 2. verb. Aufl. bes. von Max Lindenau. Berlin 1924.

Atharva-Veda Saṁhitā transl. with a Critical and Exegetical Commentary by William Dwight Whitney. Cambridge, Mass. 1905. (*H.O.S.*, Vol. VII–VIII.)

Bhagavadgītā.

The Bhagavadgītā. With an introductory essay, Sanskrit text, Engl. transl. and notes by S. Radhakrishnan. London 1948.

Die Bhagavadgītā. Aus dem Sanskrit übers., mit einer Einl. über ihre urspr. Gestalt, ihre Lehren und ihr Alter von Richard Garbe. 2. verb. Aufl. Leipzig 1921.

Die Bhagavadgita übers. und erläutert von F. Lorinser. Breslau 1869.

Bhāgavatapurāṇa.

Maharshivedavyāsapraṇītam Śrīmadbhāgavatamahāpurāṇam (sacitram saralahindīvyākhyāsahitam). 2nd ed. Gorakhpur 1930 (?)

Le Bhāgavata purāṇa ou histoire poétique de Kṛichṇa. Trad. et publ. par Eugène Burnouf. T. I–V. Paris 1840–1898. (*C.O.*, 6–10.)

The Gobhilagṛihyasūtra. Edited with an original Sanskrit Commentary by Srī Mūkūnda Jhā Bakshi. Benares 1936. (*K.S.S.*, 118, Haridās Sanskrit Granthamālā, karmakānda Section, No. 12.)

The Gṛihya-Sūtras, Rules of Vedic Domestic Ceremonies transl. by Hermann Oldenberg. Part II Gobhila ... Oxford 1892. (*S.B.E.*, Vol. XXX.)

Kauṭilya, Arthaśāstra

Kauṭilīyam arthaśāstram, Arthaśāstra of Kauṭilya, rev. and ed. by Dr. R. Shama Sastry. [3rd Ed.] Mysore 1924. (*B.S.*, 64.)

Kauṭilya's Arthaśāstra transl. by Dr. R. Shamasastry with an introductory note by the late Dr. J. F. Fleet. 2nd ed. Mysore 1923.

Mahābhārata.

The Mahābhārata. For the first time critically ed. by Vishnu S. Sukthankar and S. K. Belvalkar. (Only from Ādiparvan to Śāntiparvan [= I–XII: 226].) Poona 1927–58.

The Mahābhārata, an Epic Poem, written by the celebrated Veda Vyāsa Rishi (= "The Calcutta-edition"). Calcutta 1834.

Mahābhārata, Inhaltsangabe, Index und Concordanz der Calcuttaer und Bombayer Ausg. von Hermann Jacobi. Bonn 1903.

Śrīmahābhāratam śrīmanmaharshi vedavyāsaviracitam-rāyopādhikena śrīpratāpacandreṇa prakāśitam. 3rd ed. Calcutta 1887–89.

The Mahābhārata of Kṛishṇa-Dvaipāyana Vyāsa. Transl. into Engl. Prose. Publ. and distr. chiefly gratis by Pratāpa Chandra Rāy. Calcutta 1883–96.

Mahābhāshya, see *Patanjali*!

Mānavadharmaśāstra (= Manusmṛiti).

Manusmṛiti.

Manu-smṛiti with the 'Manubhāshya' of Medhātithi, ed. with the help of several manuscripts by Mahāmahopādhyāya Gaṅgānātha Jhā. Vol. I–III. Calcutta 1932–39. (*B.I.*, 256.)

Manu-smṛiti, The Laws of Manu with the Bhāshya of Medhātithi, transl. by Gaṅgā-Nātha Jhā. Vol. I–V. Calcutta 1920. Notes Vol. I–II. Calcutta 1924.

Pāṇini Ashṭādhyāyī, Ashṭakam Pāṇinīyam.

Pāṇini's Grammatik. Herausgegeben, übers., erläutert und mit verschiedenen Indices vers. von Otto Böhtlingk. Leipzig 1887.

La Grammaire du Pāṇini trad. du Sanskrit avec des extraits des commentaires indigènes par Louis Renou. Paris 1948–54.

Patanjali, Mahābhāshya.

The Vyākaraṇa-Mahābhāshya of Patanjali. Ed. by F. Kielhorn. Bombay 1880–84.

Rigveda.

Die Hymnen des Rigveda. Hrsg. von Theodor Aufrecht. 2. Aufl., Bonn 1877. (Leipzig 1955.)

Rigveda-Sanhita, the Sacred Hymns of the Brahmans; together with the Commentary of Sayanacharya. Ed. by Max Müller. London 1849–74.

Der Rig-Veda aus dem Sanskrit ins Deutsche übers. und mit einem laufenden Kommentar vers. von Karl Friedrich Geldner. Cambridge, Mass. 1951. (H.O.S., Vol. 33–36.)

Wörterbuch zum Rig-Veda, von Hermann Grassmann. Leipzig 1873.

Sāmaveda.

Sāmavedasaṁhitā bhagavatsāyaṇācārya-viracita-bhāshya-sahitaḥ ... śrīsatyavratasāmaśramibhaṭṭācāryeṇa. Vol. I–V. Calcutta [1874–78]. (*B.I.*, several numbers.)

The Hymns of the Samaveda transl. with a popular Commentary by Ralph T. H. Griffith. Benares 1926.

Śāñkhāyanagṛihyasūtra (in Sanskrit not available).

The Gṛihya-Sūtras Rules of Vedic Domestic Ceremonies transl. by Hermann Oldenberg. Part I Śāñkhāyana-Gṛihya-Sūtra ... Oxford 1886. (*S.B.E.*, Vol. XXIX.)

Śatapathabrāhmaṇa.

The Śatapatha-Brāhmaṇa in the Mādhyandina-śākhā with extracts made from the commentaries of Sāyaṇa, Harisvāmin and Dvivedaganga ed. by Dr. Albrecht Weber. Berlin, London 1849.

The Śatapatha-Brāhmaṇa according to the text of the Mādhyandina school transl. by Julius Eggeling. Oxford 1882–1900. (*S.B.E.*, Vol. XII, XXVI, XLI, XLIII, XLIV.)

Skandapurāṇa.

Śrīmatskandapurāṇāntargatā Sūtasaṁhitā 2nd ed. Vol. I–III. [Poona] 1924–25. (*Ānandāśramasaṁskṛitagranthāvaliḥ*, 25: 1–3.)

Vāyupurāṇa.

Mahāmuniśrīmadvyāsapraṇītaṁ Vāyupurāṇam [Poona] 1905. (*Ānandāśramasaṁskṛitagranthāvaliḥ*, 49.)

Vishṇupurāṇa.

Śrīśrīvishṇupurāṇa [mūla śloka aura hindī-anuvādasahita] 3rd ed. Gorakhpur 1931 (?)

The Vishṇu Purāṇa, a system of Hindu Mythology and Tradition, transl. from the original sanskrit, and illustr. by notes derived chiefly from other purāṇas, by H. H. Wilson. London 1840.

Yajurveda.

Taittirīyasaṁhitā Bhaṭṭabhāskaramiśraviracitabhāshyasahitā. The Taittirīya saṁhitā of the Black Yajur-Veda with the Commentary of Bhaṭṭabhāskaramiśra. Mysore 1894–98. (*B.S.*, No. 5, 7, 9, 12, 13, 14, 16, 17 and 18.)

Śrīmatsāyaṇācāryaviracitabhāshyasametā Kṛishṇayajurvedīyataittirīyasaṁhitā. Vol. 1–6, 2nd ed. [Poona] 1940–1948, Vol. 7–9, 1st ed. [Poona] 1904–1908. (= *Ānandāśramasaṁskṛitagranthāvaliḥ*, 42: 1–9.)

The Veda of the Black Yajus School entitled Taittiriya Sanhita ... transl. from the original Sanskrit prose and verse by Arthur Berriedale Keith. Part I–II. Cambridge, Mass. 1914. (= *H.O.S.*, Vol. 18–19.)

Dictionaries

Dravidian

Burrow, Thomas and Emeneau, M. B., A Dravidian etymological dictionary, Oxford 1961.

Tamil Lexicon. Publ. under the authority of the University of Madras. Vol. 1–6. Madras 1924–39.

A Dictionary Tamil and English based on Johann-Philip Fabricius's "Malabar-English Dictionary". 3rd ed., rev. & enlarged. Tranquebar 1933.

Percival, P., An English-Tamil Dictionary compiled by the rev. P. Percival. Rev. Madras 1953.

Greek

Liddell, H. G. & Scott, R., A Greek-English Lexicon. A new ed. rev. and augmented throughout by Henry Stuart Jones with the assistance of Roderick McKenzie and with the co-operation of many scholars. Vol. I–II. Oxford 1925–40.

ΘΗΣΑΥΡῸΣ ΤΗ͂Σ ἙΛΛΗΝΙΚΗ͂Σ ΓΛΏΣΣΗΣ.

Thesaurus Graecae Linguae, ab Henrico Stephano constructus. Post editionem anglicam novis additamentis auctum, ordineque alphabetico digestum tertio ediderunt Carolus Benedictus Hase ... Vol. I–VIII. Parisiis 1831–65.

Muṇḍārī

Hoffmann, John, and Emelen, Arthur, van, Encyclopaedia Mundarica, by Rev. John Hoffmann, S. J. in collaboration with Rev. Arthur van Emelen, S. J., assisted by the Jesuit missionaries mentioned in the preface. Vol. I–XII [= A–R]. Patna 1930–1938.

Sanskrit

Böhtlingk, Otto und Roth, Rudolph, Sanskrit-Wörterbuch, hrsg. von der Kaiserlichen Akademie der Wissenschaften bearb. von Otto Böhtlingk und Rudolph Roth. St. Petersburg 1852–75.

MONIER-WILLIAMS, A Sanskrit-English Dictionary etymologically and philologically arranged with special reference to cognate Indo-European Languages by Monier-Williams. New Ed., greatly enlarged and improved with the collaboration of E. Leumann, C. Cappeller and other scholars. Oxford (1899), 1951.

WILLIAMS, MONIER, A Dictionary, English and Sanskrit. London 1851.

Grammars

Dravidian

ARDEN, A. H., A Progressive Grammar of Common Tamil, 5th ed. Madras 1954.

—— A Progressive Grammar of the Telugu Language, 4th ed. Madras 1955.

CALDWELL, ROBERT, A comparative Grammar of the Dravidian or South-Indian Family of Languages. 1st ed. 1856, 3rd ed. rev. by J. L. Wyatt and T. Ramakrishna Pillai. London 1913. 4th ed. London 1956.

Muṇḍārī

HOFFMANN, J., Mundari Grammar. Calcutta 1903.

Sanskrit

WHITNEY, W. D., Indische Grammatik. Leipzig 1879. (*Indo-germanische Grammatiken*, II.)

Journals

American Journal of Philology (= *A.J.P.*). Baltimore 1880–.

Annals of the Bhandarkar Oriental Research Institute (= *A.B.O.R.I.*). Poona 1920–.

Anthropos. Wien 1905–.

Archiv Orientální (= *A.O.*). Budapest 1930–.

Bulletin of the School of Oriental Studies (= *B.S.O.S.*). London 1929–.

The Indian Antiquary (= *I.A.*). Bombay 1872–1933.

The Indian Culture (= *I.C.*). Calcutta 1934–.

The Indian Historical Quarterly (= *I.H.Q.*). Calcutta 1925–.

Journal of the Andhra Historical Research Society (= *J.A.H.R.S.*). Rajahmundry 1926–.

Journal of Indian History (= *J.I.H.*). London, New York, Madras 1921–.

Journal and Proceedings of the Asiatic Society of Bengal (= *J.P.A.S. Beng.*). Calcutta 1905–.

Journal of the American Oriental Society (= *J.A.O.S.*). New Haven, Conn. 1843–.

Journal of the Bihar and Orissa Research Society (= *J.B.O.R.S.*). Bankipore 1915–42.

The Journal of the Bihar Research Society (= *J.B.R.S.*). Patna 1943–.
Journal of the Royal Asiatic Society (= *J.R.A.S.*). London 1834–.
Man in India (= *M.I.*). Ranchi 1920–.
Memoirs of the Asiatic Society of Bengal (= *M.A.S.B.*). Calcutta 1905–.
Modern Review (= *M.R.*). Allahabad, Calcutta 1907–.
Le Monde Oriental (= *M.O.*). Uppsala 1906–.
Orientalia Suecana (= *O.S.*). Uppsala 1952–.
Quarterly Journal of the Mythic Society (= *Q.J.M.S.*). Bangalore 1909–.
Religion och Bibel (= *R.B.*). Uppsala 1942–.
Science and Culture (= *S.C.*). Calcutta 1935–.
Studi e Materiali di Storia delle Religioni (= *S.M.S.R.*). Bologna 1929–.
Transactions of the Bose Research Institute (= *T.B.R.I.*). Calcutta 1918–.
Transactions of the Royal Asiatic Society (= *J.R.A.S. Trans.*). London 1827–1833.
Wiener Zeitschrift für die Kunde des Morgenlandes (= *W.Z.*). Wien 1887–.
Visva Bharati Quarterly (= *V.B.Q.*). Calcutta 1935–.
Zeitschrift der Deutschen Morgenländischen Gesellschaft (= *Z.D.M.G.*). Leipzig 1847–.
Zeitschrift für Ethnologie (= *Z.E.*). Berlin 1869–.
Zeitschrift für die Kunde des Morgenlandes (= *Z.K.M.*). Göttingen–Bonn, 1–7, 1837–50.
Zeitschrift für vergleichende Sprachforschung auf dem Gebiete des deutschen, griechischen und lateinischen, hrsg. von Aufrecht, Th. und Kuhn, A. Berlin 1852–.

Literature

ACHARYA, P. K., The Origin of Hindu-Temple (*I.C.*, I, 1934, p. 89–93).
AGRAWALA, V. S., India as known to Pāṇini. Allahabad 1953.
AHMED, KHAN G., The Bhils of Khandesh (*M.I.*, XV 1935, p. 133–143).
ANDERSON, J. D., The Peoples of India (= *The Cambridge Manuals of Science and Literature*, 78). Cambridge 1913.
APTE, V. M., Social and religious life in the Gṛihya Sūtras. Bombay 1954.
—— Vajra in the Rigveda (*A.B.O.R.I.*, 37, Poona 1957, p. 292–5).
ARBMAN, E., Rudra. *Diss.* Stockholm 1922.
ARCHER, MILDRED, The Folktale in Santal Society (*M.I.*, XXIV 1944, p. 224–232).
BAHUGUNE, S. D., and MAZUMDAR, D. N., Marriage and Marital life amongst the Rawalttas (*M.I.*, XII 1932, p. 301–319).
BAINBRIDGE, R. B., The Saorias of the Rajmahal Hills (*M.A.S.B.*, II 1907–1910, Calcutta 1911, p. 43–84).
BAGCHI, Prabodh Chandra, Pre-Aryan and pre-dravidian in India. Calcutta 1929. (Cf. Lévi Sylvain: Pre-Ar.)
BANERJEA, JITENDRA NATH, The Development of Hindu Iconography. Calcutta 1941.

BANERJEE, P., Some observations on the interpretation of the Pāṇinisūtra Vāsudevārjunābhyāṁ vun and the antiquity of the Bhāgavatas (*J.B.R.S.*, XL, Patna 1954, p. 74–79).

BANERJI, KASINDRANATH, Popular Tales of Bengal. Calcutta 1905.

BARTH, AUGUSTE, Les religions de l'Inde (*Encyclopédie des sciences religieuses*), 1ère ed., Paris 1879. 2e ed., Paris 1914. The religions of India. Auth. transl. by J. Word. 4th ed. London 1906.

BARUA, K. L., Alpines in Eastern India (*I.C.*, III 1936, p. 161–171).

BASU NIRMAL KUMAR, The Spring-Festival of India (*M.I.*, VII 1927, p. 112–185).

BASU, PROVASH CHANDRA, The Racial Affinities of the Mundas (*T.B.R.I.*, VIII 1932–1933).

—— The Racial Affinities of the Oraons (*T.B.R.I.*, IX 1933–1934).

BENFEY, TH., Bemerkung zu einer Mittheilung des Megasthenes in Bezug auf indische Geschichte (*Z.K.M.*, V 1844, p. 218–31).

BENVENISTE, E., and RENOU, L., Vṛtra et Vṛthragna, Paris 1934.

BERGAIGNE, ABEL, La religion védique, d'après les hymnes du Rigvéda. Vol. I–III. Paris 1878–83.

BERGH VAN EYSINGA, G. A. VAN DEN, Indische Einflüsse auf evangelische Erzählungen. Göttingen 1909.

BERVE, HELMUT, Das Alexanderreich auf prosopographischer Grundlage. Vol. I–II, München 1926.

BHADURI, MANINDRA BHUSAN, The Aboriginal Tribes of the Udaipur State (C.P.) (*M.I.*, XXI 1941, p. 92 ff. Indian Science Congress in Benares).

BHANDARKAR, D. R., Lectures on the Ancient History of India. Calcutta 1919. (= *The Carmichael Lectures*, 1918.)

BHANDARKAR, R. G., Allusions to Kṛishṇa in Patanjali's Mahābhāshya (*I.A.*, III 1874, p. 14).

—— Early history of the Dekkan. Calcutta 1928.

—— Vaishnavism, Śaivism and minor religious systems. Strassburg 1913. (= *Grundriss der indo-arischen Philologie und Alterthumskunde* III.6).

BHATTACHARJEE, U. C., The Evidence of Pāṇini on Vāsudeva-Worship (*I.H.Q.*, I, 1925, p. 483–489).

BHATTACHARYA, S.: Review of: EMENEAU, M. B., Kolami, A Dravidian Language, University of California Publications in Linguistics, Vol. 12, Berkeley and Los Angeles 1955 and EMENEAU, M. B., Toda, a Dravidian Language, Transactions of the Philological Society. 1957. (*M.I.*, XXXVIII 1958, p. 217–220.)

BLOOMFIELD, M., A Vedic Concordance. Harvard 1906.

BODDING, P. O., A note on the "Wild People" of the Santals (*J.P.A.S. Beng.* XXVII, p. 241–263).

—— Santal Folk Tales. Vol. I, Oslo 1925. Vol. II, Oslo 1927. Vol. III, Cambridge, Mass. 1929.

—— Traditions and Institutions of the Santals (= *Oslo Etnógrafiske Museum Bulletin*, 6, Oslo 1942).

BOMPAS, CECIL HENRY, Folklore of the Santal Parganas. London 1909.

—— Folktales of Bengal. (*J.P.A.S. Beng.* XXV, p. 96 ff.)

Bonnerjea, Biren, Traces of Ugrian Occupation of India (*I.C.* III, Calcutta 1937, p. 621–632).

—— Ugrian Fishing Implements and some Indian Parallels. (*M.I.* XVIII 1938, p. 225–260.)

Bonnerjee, P., Some observations on the interpretation of the Pāṇinisūtra *Vāsudevārjunābhyam vun* and the antiquity of the Bhāgavatas. (*J. B. R. S.* XL 1954, p. 74–79.)

Bose, Sushil Kumar, Historical Notes and Questions. (2) Pāṭaliputra in the time of Patanjali. (*I.C.* II 1935, p. 56–59.)

Brandes, Edvard, Ushas og Ushashymnerne i Rigveda. *Diss.* København 1879.

Brandreth, Edward Lyall, The Non-Aryan Languages of India. (*J.R.A.S.* 1878, p. 1.)

Bréal, Michel, Hercule et Cacus, étude de Mythologie comparée. (= *Mélanges de Mythologie et de Linguistique*, 2e éd. Paris 1882, p. 1–161.)

Breeks, James Wilkinson, An Account of the primitive tribes and monuments of the Nilagiris. By James Wilkinson Breeks, ed. by his widow. London 1873.

Breloer, Bernhard, Megasthenes (etwa 300 v. Chr.) über die indische Gesellschaft. (*Z.D.M.G.*, LXXXVIII 1933, p. 130–164.)

—— Megasthenes über die indische Stadtverwaltung. (*Z.D.M.G.*, LXXXIX 1934, p. 40–67.)

Briggs, John, Aboriginal Race of India, as distinguished from the Sanskritic or Hindu Race. (*J.R.A.S.* 1852, p. 275.)

Brown, Truesdall S., The Reliability of Megasthenes. (*A.J.P.*, LXXVI 1955, p. 18–33.)

Burnes, Alexander, The Eastern Branch of the River Indus, alterations in it, the formation of the Runn (Rann?), and Alexander's route. (*J.R.A.S. Trans.* 1833, p. 550.)

Burrow, Thomas, Some Dravidian words in Sanskrit. London 1946.

Buschardt, Leo, Vṛtra. Det rituelle Daemondrab i den vediske Somakult. *Diss.* Köbenhavn 1945. (= *Det Kgl. Danske Vidensk. Selskab. Hist. filol. Meddel.* XXX, 3.)

The Cambridge History of India. Vol. 1–6, Cambridge 1922–32, Suppl. vol. Cambridge 1953.

Campbell, A., Santal Folk Tales. London 1892.

Chakladar, H. C., Caucasic Peoples between India and the Pacific. (*M.I.*, XVI 1936, p. 183–189.)

—— Pāṭaliputra (*M.R.* 1917).

—— Problems of the Racial Composition of the Indian Peoples. (*M.I.*, XVI 1936, p. 99–134.)

—— The Prehistoric Culture of Bengal. (*M.I.*, XXI 1941, p. 208–236, XXII 1942, p. 140–162, XXXI 1951, p. 124–164.)

Chanda, Ramaprasad, Archaeology and Vaishnava Tradition. (= *Memoirs of the Archaeological Survey of India*, 5, p. 151–173.) Calcutta 1920.

Charpentier, Jarl, Beiträge zur indischen Wortkunde. (*M.O.*, XXVI–XXVII, 1932–1933, p. 91–169.)

—— Indra. (*M.O.*, XXV 1931, p. 1–28.)

—— Über Rudra-Śiva. (*W.Z.* 1909.)

CHAUDHURI, NANIMADHAB, Rudra-Śiva—as an Agricultural Deity. (*I.H.Q.*, XV, 1939, p. 183–196.)

—— Some cure deities. (*M.I.*, XXI 1941, p. 72 f.: The Indian Science Congress, Benares: Anthropological Notes and News.)

—— The Indian cowherd god. (*M.I.*, XXI 1941, p. 71 f.: *The Indian Science Congress*, Benares: Anthropological Notes and News.)

—— The Sun as a Folk-God. (*M.I.*, XXI 1941, p. 1–14.)

CHRISTENSEN, ARTHUR, Smeden Kāväh og det Gamle Persiske Rigsbanner. (= *Det Kgl. Danske Vidensk. Selskab. Hist. filol. Meddel.* II, 7.)

COLE, F. T., Santhali Folklore. (*I.A.* IV, pp. 10 ff., 257 ff.)

CREUZER, J., Symbolik. 3rd ed., Leipzig 1837. French transl. by Guignaut, Paris 1825.

CROOKE, WILLIAM, Natives of Northern India. London 1907.

—— Religion and Folklore of Northern India. Oxford 1926.

—— Tribes and Castes of North-Western Provinces and Oudh. Vol. 1–4. Calcutta 1896.

CUNNINGHAM, A., Ancient geography of India, ed. Majumdar. Calcutta 1924.

DALTON, E. T., The Descriptive Ethnology of Bengal. Calcutta 1872.

DASGUPTA, S. B., Vajra and the Vajrasattvas. (*I.C.*, VIII, 23 ff.) Calcutta 1934.

DATTA, BHUPENDRA NATH, An Enquiry into the racial Elements in Beluchistan, Afghanistan, and the neighbouring Areas of the Hindukusch. (*M.I.*, XIX 1939, pp. 174–186, 218–273 and XX 1940, pp. 1–43.)

—— Ethnological Notes on some of the Castes of West Bengal. (*M.I.*, XV 1935, pp. 196–224.)

—— Vedic Funeral Customs and Indus Valley Culture. (*M.I.* XVI 1936, pp. 223–307 and XVII 1937, pp. 1–68.)

DAY, L. B.: Folk-Tales of Bengal. London 1912.

DEHON, P., Religion and Customs of the Uraons. (*M.A.S.B.* 1906, p. 121 ff.)

DEY, NUNDO LAL, The Geographical Dictionary of Ancient and Mediaeval India. (*Calcutta Oriental Series*, No. 21. E. 13.) London 1927.

DIEHL, C. G., Instrument and purpose. Studies on Rites and Rituals in South India. *Diss.* Lund 1956.

DIKSHITAR, V. R. R., Pre-Historic South India. Madras 1951. (*Madras, University, William Meyer Lectures* 1950–51.)

—— Studies in the Tamil Literature and History. London 1930.

—— The Purāṇa Index. Madras, vol. I 1951, II 1955, III 1955. (*Madras, University, Historical Series* 19: 1–3.)

DOWSON, J., A Classical Dictionary of Hindu Mythology and religion, geography, history and literature. 9th ed. London 1957. (Trübner's Oriental Series.)

DRACOTT, ALICE E., Simla Village Tales, or Folk Tales from the Himalayas. London 1906.

DUMÉZIL, GEORGES, Aspects de la fonction guerrière chez les Indo-Européens. Paris 1956. (*Bibliothèque de l'École des Hautes Études.* — Sciences religieuses LXVIIIe volume.)

—— Les pas de Kṛishṇa et l'exploit d'Arjuna. (*O.S.*, V 1956, pp. 183–188.)

—— Remarques sur les Armes des Dieux de "Troisième Fonction" chez divers Peuples Indo-Européens. (*S.M.S.R.*, 28 1957, p. 1–10.) Bologna 1957.

—— Víshṇu et les Marút à travers la Réforme zoroastrienne. (*J.A.*, 1953, p. 1–25.)

EICKSTEDT, EGON, v., The Mysore Tribes and Castes. Bangalore 1934.

ELIOT, CHARLES, Hinduism and Buddhism. An historical sketch. Vol. I–III. London 1921.

ELWIN, VERRIER, Bondo Highlander. Bombay 1950.

—— Myths of Middle India. (*Specimens of the oral Literature of Middle India*, 4.) Madras 1949.

—— Myths of the North-East Frontier of India. Shillong 1958.

—— Notes on a Kondh Tour (*M.I.*, XXIV 1944, pp. 40–58.)

—— The Muria and their Ghotul, Oxford 1947.

—— The Religion of an Indian Tribe. Bombay 1955.

—— Tribal Myths of Orissa. (*Specimens of the oral Literature of Middle India*, 5.) Calcutta 1954.

EMENEAU, MURRAY B., Koṭa Texts. Four parts. Berkeley and Los Angeles 1944–1946.

FLEET, J. F., Śiva as Lakulīśa. (*J.R.A.S.* 1907, pp. 419–426.)

FORBES, C. J. F. S., Connexion of the Mōns of Pegu with the Koles of Central India. (*J.R.A.S.* 1878, p. 234 ff.)

FRAZER, R. W., Dravidians (South India). (*E.R.E.*, V 21 ff.) Edinburgh 1925.

—— Śaivism. (*E.R.E.*, vol. XI, 91 ff.) Edinburgh 1925.

FRYE, J. P., The Uriya and the Khondh Population of Orissa. (*J.R.A.S.* 1858, p. 1 ff.)

FÜRER-HAIMENDORF, CHRISTOPH, v., Himalayan Barbary. London 1955.

—— Primitive Aboriginal Cultures in the Deccan. (*M.I.*, XXIV 1944, pp. 123–128.)

—— Problems and Prospects of Indian Anthropology. (*M.I.*, XXIX 1949, pp. 147–168.)

—— The Chenchus. London 1943.

—— The Cult of the Clan Gods among the Raj Gonds of Hyderabad. (*M.I.* XXV 1945, pp. 149–186.)

—— The Problem of Megalithic Cultures in Middle India. (*M.I.* XXV 1945, pp. 73–86.)

—— The Reddis of the Bison Hills, London 1945.

FÜRER-HAIMENDORF, ELIZABETH, v., An Anthropological Bibliography of South Asia. (*Le Monde d'outre-mer passé et présent*, quatrième Série: Bibliographies III.) Paris 1958.

GARBE, RICHARD, Indien und das Christentum. Tübingen 1914.

GEORGI, P., Alphabetum Tibetanum. Rom 1762.

GHOSH, AMALANANDA, Śiva—His Pre-Aryan Origins. (*I.C.* II 1936, pp. 763–771.)

GHOSHAL, U., A History of Hindu Political Theories. Calcutta 1923.

GHURYE, G. S., Census Contribution to the Racial Analysis of India. (*Q.J.M.S.* 1937.)

—— The Ethnic Theory of Caste. (*M.I.* IV 1924, pp. 209–272.)

GLADSTONE, M. S., Vishṇu in the Rigveda and after until the epic period. (Not printed, *diss.*) Cambridge 1928.

GLASENAPP, HELMUTH, v., Brahmā und Buddha. Berlin 1926.

—— Der Hinduismus. München 1922.

—— Der Jainismus. Berlin 1925.

—— Die Religionen Indiens. Stuttgart 1943, 2nd ed. 1956.

—— Heilige Stätten Indiens. München 1928.

GONDA, J., Aspects of early Vishnuism. Utrecht 1954.

—— Die Religionen Indiens. Stuttgart 1960. (*Die Religionen der Menschheit*, II.)

GORDON, D. H., Sialk, Giyan, Hissar and the Indo-Iranian connection. (*M.I.* XXVII 1947, pp. 195–241.)

GORDON, E. M., Indian Folk Tales. London 1908.

GORER, GEOFFREY, Himalayan Village, an account of the Lepchas of Sikkim. London 1938.

GOSWAMI, KUNJA GOVINDA, A Study of Vaishnavism. Calcutta 1956.

GOSWAMI, PRAFULLADATTA, Music in Assam: Its divine origin. (*M.I.* XXX 1950, pp. 13–16.)

GREN, ERIK, Indien. (*Kulturländernas historia.* Natur och kultur.) Stockholm 1959.

GRIERSON, GEORGE A., Language. (*Report on the Census of India*, 1901.)

—— Modern Hinduism and its debt to the Nestorians. (*J.R.A.S.* 1907, pp. 311–335 and 493–503.)

GRIFFITHS, WALTER, G., Folklore of the Kols. (*M.I.* XXIV 1944, pp. 261–268.)

GROWSE, F. S., Mathura. Mathura 1880.

GUHA, B. S., An Outline of the racial Ethnology of India. Calcutta 1937.

—— The Aboriginal Ṛaces of India. (*S.C.* 1939.)

—— The racial affinities of the peoples of India. (*XVI*[e] *Congrès International d'Anthropologie.*) Bruxelles 1935.

GÜNTERT, HERMANN, Der arische Weltkönig und Heiland. Halle 1923.

HARDY, T.: Eine buddhistische Bearbeitung der Kṛishṇa-Sage. (*Z.D.M.G.* LIII 1899, pp. 25–50.)

HAZRA, RAJENDRA CHANDRA, Purāṇas in the History of Smṛiti. (*I.C.*, I 1935, pp. 587–614.)

HESYCHII ALEXANDRINI Lexicon post Ioannem Albertum recensuit Mauricius Schmidt. Vol. I–IV. Ienae 1858–61.

HEVESY, W. v., Finnisch-Ugrisches aus Indien. Wien 1932.

—— Noms ouraliens d'animaux dans l'Inde. (*J.A.* CCXXIII, 1937.)

HEWITT, JOHN, The ruling races of prehistoric times in India, South-Western Asia and Southern Europe. Ser. 1–2. Westminster 1894–95.

The History and culture of the Indian people, ed. by *Majumdar, R. C.* Vol. 1. *The Vedic Age*, London 1951. Vol. 2. *The Age of Imperial Unity*. Bombay 1953. Vol. 3. *The Classical Age*. Bombay 1954.

HOFFMANN, J., Mundari Poetry, Music and Dances. (*M.A.S.B.* II 1907–10, Calcutta 1911, pp. 85–120.)

HOLTZMANN, A., Indra nach den Vorstellungen des Mahābhārata. (*Z.D.M.G.* XXXII, 1878, p. 290–340.)

HOPKINS, E. W., India old and new. New York, London 1901.

—— The great Epic of India, its character and origin. New York 1902.
HUNTER, W., The Hill Population in Meywar. (*J.R.A.S.* 1846, pp. 176 ff.)
HUTTEN, K., Die Bhaktireligion und der christliche Glaube im N.T. Stuttgart 1930.
HUTTON, J. H., Census of India 1931, Vol. I, Part 1—Report. Delhi 1933.
INDIA IN MAPS. Issued by the Publications Division Ministry of Information and Broadcasting Government of India. 1950.
Indien. Entwicklung seiner Wirtschaft und Kultur. Unter Leitung von Prof. Dr. Edgar Lehmann bearb. von Dr. Hildegard Weisse. (*Historisch-geographisches Kartenwerk*.) Leipzig 1958.
IYENGAR, SRINIVAS, see SRINIVAS!
IYENGAR, T. R. SESHA, see SESHA!
JACKSON, A. V. WILLIAMS, History of India Vol. IX, Historic accounts of India by foreign Travellers Classic, Oriental, and Occidental. London 1907.
JENSEN, ADOLF ELLEGARD, Mythos und Kult bei Naturvölkern. Wiesbaden 1951. (*Studien zur Kulturkunde*, Bd 10.)
JOHANSSON, K. F., Solfågeln i Indien. (*Uppsala Universitets Årsskrift* 1910.)
JONES, WILLIAMS, Asiatic Researches I. 1784 (?).
JÖRGENSEN, H. F., Evangeliet blandt Santalerne. København 1920.
KEITH, ARTHUR BERRIEDALE, Modern Hinduism and the Nestorians. (*J.R.A.S.* 1907, pp. 490–493.)
—— Denarius and the date of the Harivaṁśa. (*J.R.A.S.* 1907, pp. 681–683.)
—— Pāṇini and the Veda. (*I.C.* II 1936, pp. 735–748.)
—— Plotinus and Indian Thought. (*I.C.* II 1935, pp. 125–130.)
KENNEDY, J., Modern Hinduism and the Nestorians. (*J.R.A.S.* 1907, pp. 477–487.)
—— The child Kṛishṇa, Christianity, and the Gujārs. (*J.R.A.S.*, 1907, pp. 951–991.)
KERÉNYI, KARL, Die Herkunft der Dionysosreligion nach dem heutigen Stand der Forschung. Köln & Opladen 1956. (Düsseldorf, Arbeitsgemeinschaft für Forschung des Landes Nordrhein-Westfalen, Geisteswissenschaften, H. 58.)
—— Die Heroen der Griechen. Zürich 1958.
—— Die Mythologie der Griechen. Die Götter- und Menschheitsgeschichten. Zürich 1951.
KERN, O., Die Religion der Griechen. Vol. I–III. Berlin 1926–28.
KHAN, G. AHMED, See Ahmed, Khan G.
KIRFEL, WILLIBALD, Śiva und Dionysos. (*Z.E.* 78, 1953, pp. 83–90.)
—— Symbolik des Hinduismus und des Jinismus. (*Symbolik der Religionen*, hrsg. von Ferdinand Herrmann, IV *Symbolik des Hinduismus und des Jinismus*.) Stuttgart 1959.
KLEUKER, J., Treatise on the history and the antiquities of Asia. 2nd ed. Riga 1797. Vol. II, 1st ed. Riga 1795.
KONOW, S., Hinduismen. Oslo 1925.
KOPPERS, WILHELM, Bhagwan, the Supreme Deity of the Bhils. (*Anthropos*, XXXV–VI 1940–1941, pp. 264–325.)
—— Die Bhil in Zentralindien. Wien 1948.
—— My Central Indian Expedition, 1938–1939. (*M.I.* XX 1940, pp. 178–181.)

Krishna-lila ou Mystères de l'avatar de Krishna. (Une version tamile de Mbh.) Trad. par Sactivel. Paris 1938. (*Les joyaux de l'orient* VIII.)

KUIPER, F. B. J., Proto-Munda Words in Sanskrit. Amsterdam 1948. (*Verhandeling der Koninglijke Nederlandsche Akademie van Wetenschappen,* Afd. Letterkunde, Nieuwe Reeks Deel LI, No 3.)

—— Rigvedic Loanwords. (*Studia Indologica*, pp. 137–185.)

LAMM, MARTIN, Strindbergs Dramer II. Stockholm 1926.

LANDAU, O., Mykenisch-griechische Personennamen. Göteborg 1958.

LASSEN, CHRISTIAN, Bemerkungen über dieselbe Stelle des Megasthenes. (*Z.K.M.* V 1844, pp. 232–259.)

—— Indische Alterthumskunde. I 1st ed. Bonn 1847, 2nd ed. Leipzig 1866-67, II: 2 1st ed. Bonn 1852.

LAW, BIMALA CHURN, Historical Geography of Ancient India. Calcutta 1954 (?).

—— Tribes in Ancient India. Poona 1943. (*Bhandarkar Oriental Series*, No. 4.)

LEHMANN, ARNO, Die Śivaitische Frömmigkeit der tamulischen Erbauungsliteratur. Berlin-Hermsdorf 1947.

LEITNER, G. W., Dardu legends, Proverbs and Fables. *I.A.* I 1872.)

—— Manners and customs of the Dards. (*I.A.* I 1872.)

LÉVI, SYLVAIN, PRZYLUSKI, J., and BLOCH, J., Pre-aryan and pre-dravidian in India, translated from French by Bagchi, Prabodh Chandra. Calcutta 1929.

Linguistic Survey of India. Ed. by G. A. Grierson. Vol. IV by S. Konow. Calcutta 1906.

LÜBKERS FRIEDRICH, Reallexikon des klassischen Altertums. Leipzig, Berlin 1914.

MACDONELL, A. A., Vedic Mythology. Strassburg 1897. (*Grundriss der indoarischen Philologie und Alterthumskunde*, III: 1 A.)

MACHEK, V., Origin of the God Vishnu. (*A.O.* 28, 1960, pp. 103–126.)

MACPHERSON, SAMUEL CHARTRES, Religion of the Khonds of Gwomsur and Boad. (*J.R.A.S.* 1843, pp. 172 ff.)

—— Religion of the Khonds of Orissa. (*J.R.A.S.* 1852, pp. 216 ff.)

MAJUMDAR, D. N., Note on the traditional origin of the Hos together with a brief description of the chief Bongās of the Hos. (*J.P.A.S. Bengal*, New Series, XX 1924.)

—— Races and Cultures of India. Allahabad 1946.

MAJUMDAR, R. C., The Indika of Megasthenes. (*J.A.O.S.* 78, 1958, pp. 273–76 and 80, 1960, pp. 248–50. Cf. Sethna!)

MANNHARDT, WILHELM, Germanische Mythen, Forschungen. Berlin 1858.

—— Wald- und Feldkulte. 1st ed. Berlin 1875–77, 2nd ed. 1904–05.

MATHUR, K. S., Village Studies in India. (*M.I.* XXXIX 1959, pp. 45–52.)

MEHTA, MANUBHAI N., The Bhils of the Gwalior State. (*M.I.* XVIII 1938, pp. 264–284.)

MEILE, P., La Population de l'Inde. Paris 1948.

MEINHARD, H., Beiträge zur Kenntnis des Śivaismus nach den Purāṇas. (*Baessler-Archiv*, Band XII.) Berlin 1928.

MEYER, J. J., Trilogie altindischer Mächte und Feste der Vegetation, Kama, Bali, Indra. Zürich–Leipzig 1937.

MITRA, ACHINTA KUMAR, Indian Physical Anthropology and Raciology. (*S.C.* VIII 1942.)

MITRA SARAT CHANDRA: On the Cult of the Banyan and the Pipal trees. (*Q.J.M.S.* 1940.)

—— Studies in Plant Myths. (*Q.J.M.S.* XXVII, pp. 412 ff.)

MONIER-WILLIAMS, M., Brāhmanism and Hindūism. 4th ed. London 1891.

—— Buddhism in its connection with Brahmanism and Hinduism and its contrast with Christianity. 2nd ed. London 1890.

MOOR, EDW., Hindoo Pantheon. London 1810.

MORDTMANN, J. H., Mythologische Miscellen. (*Z.D.M.G.* XXXII 1878, pp. 552–569.)

MUIR, JOHN, Manu, as represented in Hymns of Rigveda. (*J.R.A.S.* 1863, pp. 406 ff.)

MUKHERJEA, CHARULAL, The Santals. Calcutta 1943.

MUTALIYĀR, A. CINKARAVELU, Apitāna Cintāmaṇi. Madras 1934.

NAIK, T. B., The Bhils. Delhi 1957.

NARAYANA, AYYAR C. V., Origin and early history of Śaivism in South India. Madras 1936.

NEWBOLD, THOMAS JOHN, The Chenchwars: a wild tribe in the forests. (*J.R.A.S.* 1846, pp. 271 ff.)

NILAKANTA SASTRI, A history of South India. London 1955.

—— The Pāṇḍyan Kingdom. London 1929.

NILSSON, MARTIN P:SON, Geschichte der Griechischen Religion. 2. Aufl. München, Bd 1 1955, Bd 2 1961. (*Handbuch der Altertumswissenschaft* V: 2: 1.)

—— Herakles. Stockholm 1923. (*Nordisk tidskrift* 1923.)

NOEHDEN, GEORGE HENRY, The Banyan tree as found in Greek and Roman authors. (*J.R.A.S. Trans.* 1827, pp. 119 ff.)

OLDENBERG, H., Die Lehre der Upanishaden und die Anfänge des Buddhismus. Göttingen 1915.

—— Die Religion des Veda. Berlin 1894.

OTTO, RUDOLF, The God of the Gītā, Vāsudeva—Vishṇu—Nārāyaṇa and His Origin. (*V.B.Q.* I 1935.)

OTTO, WALTER F., Dionysos. Mythos und Kultus. Frankfurt am Main 1933. (*Frankfurter Studien zur Religion und Kultur der Antike*, Bd 4.)

PARGITER, F. E., Ancient Indian Historical Tradition. London 1922.

PAULLINO À S. BARTOLOMAEO, P., Systema Brahmanicam. Rom 1791.

PAULY, A., Realencyclopädie der Klassischen Altertumswissenschaften, neue Bearbeitung, begonnen v. G. WISSOWA, hrsg. v. W. Kroll u. K. Mittelhaus. Stuttgart 1892–1956.

PAVIE, Krishna et sa Doctrine, Bhagavat Dasam Askand. Paris 1852.

PEDERSEN, J., Illustreret Religionshistorie under Redaktion af Joh. Pedersen. København 1948.

POTTINGER, WILLIAM, River Indus and the Route of Alexander the Great. (*J.R.A.S.* 1934, pp. 199 ff.)

POUSSIN, LOUIS DE LA VALLÉE, L'Inde aux temps des Mauryas et des barbares Grecs, Scythes, Parthes et Yue-tchi. Paris 1930. (*Histoire du monde*, T. 6:1)

PRZYLUSKI, JEAN, Name of the God Vishṇu and the Kṛishṇa-Legend. (*Q.J.M.S* XXV 1934–35.)

RAI CHOWDHURY, Prototypes of Siva in Western Asia. (*Acarya-Puspanjali Volume in honour of Dr. D. R. Bhandarkar*, Calcutta 1940.)

RAO, T. A. GOPINATHA, Elements of Hindu Iconography. Madras. I (1914) Gaṇapati, Vishṇu, Devī, II (1916) Śiva.

RAPSON, E. J., Ancient India from the earliest times to the first century A.D. Cambridge 1916.

RAY, GAUTAMSANKAR *et al.*, Religious Beliefs of the Hos. (*M.I.* XXXIV, 1954, pp. 288 ff.)

RAY, JOGES CHANDRA, Food and Drink in Ancient India. (*M.I.* XIV 1934, pp. 15–38.)

RAYCHAUDHURI, HEMCHANDRA, Materials for the study of the Early History of the Vaishnava Sect. Calcutta 1920.

—— Some Problems of early Maurya History and Chronology. (*I.C.* II 1936, pp. 557–564.)

—— Studies in Indian Antiquities. Calcutta 1932.

REDDY, P. C., The Yanadis of the Madras Presidency. (*M.I.* XX 1940, pp. 44–55.)

RENOU, L., & FILLIOZAT, J., L'Inde classique. Vol. I–II, Paris 1947 and 1953.

RISLEY, HERBERT, The people of India. 2nd ed. by W. Crooke, Calcutta, London 1915.

—— Tribes and Castes of Bengal. Vol. I–II, Calcutta 1891–92. (Anthropological part.)

—— Tribes and Castes of Bengal. (Ethnographical Glossary.) Vol. I–II, Calcutta 1891–92.

RODHE, STEN, Deliver us from Evil. Studies on the Vedic ideas of salvation. *Diss.* Lund 1946.

ROY, CHAUDHURI T. C., The Racial Problem of Bengal. (*M.I.* XXXII 1952, pp. 52–63.)

ROY, SARAT CHANDRA, Caste, Race, and Religion in India. (*M.I.* XIV 1934, pp. 39–63, 75–220, 271–311, and XVII 1937, pp. 147–176, 212–254.)

—— Oraon Religion & Customs. Ranchi 1928.

—— Primitive Religion in Chota Nagpur. (*J.B.O.R.S.* 1928.)

—— The Birhōrs: a little known jungle tribe of Chota Nagpur. Ranchi 1925.

—— The Divine Myths of the Muṇdas (*J.B.O.R.S.* 1916.)

—— The Gods of the Oraons. (*M.I.* II 1922, pp. 137–157.)

—— The Muṇḍas and their country. Calcutta 1912.

ROY, SARAT CHANDRA, & ROY, RAMESH CHANDRA, The Khāṛiās. Vol. I–II. Ranchi 1937.

ROY, SATINDRA NARAYAN, The Savaras of Orissa. (*M.I.* VII 1927, pp. 277–366.)

RUBEN, WALTER, Einführung in die Indienkunde. Ein Überblick über die historische Entwicklung Indiens. Berlin 1954.

—— Eisenschmiede und Dämonen in Indien. Leiden 1939. (*Internationales Archiv für Ethnographie* XXXVII Suppl.) (Cf. *M.I.* XX 1940, pp. 291–293.)

—— Krishna. Konkordanz und Kommentar der Motive seines Heldenlebens. Istanbul 1943. (*Istanbuler Schriften*, Nr. 17.)

RÖNNOW, KASTEN, Zagreus och Dionysos. (*R.B.* 2, 1943.)

Sanjana, J. E., Prohibition in Hinduism. (*M.I.* XXVII 1947, pp. 176–178.)

Sarkar, S. S., The Aboriginal Races of India. Calcutta 1954.

—— The Autochthones of India. (*M.I.* XXXIII 1953, pp. 195–211.)

—— The Negrito Racial Strain in India. (*M.I.* XXXIII 1953, pp. 19–30.)

Sastri, Nilakanta, see Nilakanta!

Sastri, K. S. Ramaswami, The Vaishnava Cult in India. (*I.C.* 1939, pp. 245 ff.)

Sastri, S. Srikantha, Hydro-Selenic Culture. (*M.I.* XXI 1941, pp. 15–32.)

Scherb, Hans, Das Motiv vom starken Knaben. Stuttgart 1930.

Schermann, Lucian, Von Indiens „Blauen Bergen" (Nīlgiri): Kurumba–Irula–Paniyan. (*Geist des Ostens* 1913–1914, and *J.A.O.S.* LXII 1942, pp. 13–35.)

Schmidt, Wilhelm, Die Stellung der Munda-Sprachen. (*B.S.O.S.* VII 1935.)

Schroeder, L. von, Herakles und Indra. Eine mythenvergleichende Untersuchung. (*Denkschrift der kaiserl. Akad. der Wissenschaften in Wien*, phil.-hist. Kl. 53, 1915.)

—— Mysterium und Mimus im Rigveda. Leipzig 1908.

Schweitzer, B., Herakles. Tübingen 1922.

Sénart, É., Essai sur la légende du Buddha, son caractère et ses origines. Paris 1882.

Sesha Iyengar, T. R., Dravidian India. Madras 1925.

Sethna, K. D., [Note on R. C. Majumdar's objections against Megasthenes and Schwanbeck]. (*J.A.O.S.* 80, 1960, pp. 243–248.)

Seydel, R., Das Evangelium von Jesu in seinen Verhältnissen zu Buddha-Sage und Buddha-Lehre. Leipzig 1882.

Shafer, Robert, Ethnography of Ancient India. Wiesbaden 1954.

Simonsson, Nils, Beobachtungen über die Bedeutung von "eka" in einigen philosophischen Texten. (*O.S.* VII 1958, pp. 159–178.)

Sinha, Surajit, Tribal Cultures of Peninsular India as a Dimension of Little Tradition in the Study of Indian Civilization: A Preliminary Statement. (*M.I.* XXXVII 1957, pp. 93–118.)

Sircar, D. C., The Dravidian Problem. (*M.I.* XXXV 1955, pp. 31–38.)

Sitapati, G. V., Religious, Magico-Religious ceremony rites and festivals of the 'Soras' (*J.A.H.R.S.* Vol. XIII 1942.)

Slater, Dravidian Element in Indian Culture. (Not available.)

Smith, Vincent A., Early History of India. 2nd ed. Oxford 1908, 4th ed. Oxford 1924.

Smith, William, Dictionnary of Greek and Roman Biography and Mythology. Vol. I–III. Boston 1849.

Somasundaram, A. M., Glimpses into Primitive Culture of India. (*M.I.* XXX 1950, pp. 28–45.)

Spiegel, Fr., *Varena*, (*Z.D.M.G.* XXXII 1878, p. 716 ff.)

Srinivas Iyengar, P. T., History of the Tamils from the earliest times to 600 A.D. Madras 1929.

Srinivasa Ayyangar, P. T., Pre-Aryan Tamil Culture. (*J.I.H.* VII 1928, pp. 80 ff.)

Stein, Aurel, Ancient Khotan. Vol. I–II. Oxford 1907.

—— On Alexander's Track to the Indus. Macmillan 1929.

STEIN, OTTO, Megasthenes und Kauṭilya. Wien 1922. *Diss.* (*Wien. Akad. d. Wissensch.*, Philos.-Histor. Classe. Sitzungsberichte, 191, 1922.)

Studia Indologica, Festschrift für Willibald Kirfel zur Vollendung seines 70. Lebensjahres, herausgegeben von Otto Spies. (= *Bonner Orientalistische Studien*, Neue Serie Band 3.) Bonn 1955.

SUDHENU, KUMAR, Das Śakti or Divine Power. Calcutta 1934.

SYAM, CHAUDHRI N. K., The Enumeration & Treatment of Tribes in the Indian Census: A Study in Retrospect. (*M.I.* XXXII 1952, pp. 160–166.)

SØRENSEN, S., An Index to the names in the Mahābhārata. London 1925.

TARN, WILLIAM WOODTHORPE, Alexander the Great. Vol. I–II, Cambridge 1948.

—— The Greeks in Bactria and India. 1st ed., Cambridge 1938. 2nd ed., Cambridge 1951.

TAUB, HANS, Strindberg als Traumdichter.. *Diss.* Göteborg 1945. (*Kungl. Vet. & Vitterhetssamh. Handlingar*, Följd 6, Ser. A, Bd 2: 3.)

TEGNAEUS, HARRY, Le héros civilisateur. *Diss.* Stockholm 1950. (*Studia ethnographica Upsaliensia*, 2.)

THIEME, PAUL, Pāṇini and the Veda. Allahabad 1935.

THOMPSON, STITH, and BALYS, JONAS, the Oral Tales of India. Bloomington 1958. (*Indian University Publications*, Folklore, Series, No. 10.)

THURSTON, EDGAR, Castes and Tribes of Southern India. Vol. I–VII. Madras 1909.

TIMMER, B. C. J., Megasthenes en de Indische Maatschappij. *Diss.* Amsterdam 1930.

TOD, JAMES, The Hindu and Theban Hercules. (*J.R.A.S. Trans.* 1833, pp. 139ff.)

VOGEL, J. PH., La sculpture de Mathura. (*Ars Asiatica* XV.) Paris 1930.

WALHOUSE, MORETON JOHN, Megalithic monuments in the Coimbatore District. (*J.R.A.S.* 1875, pp. 17 ff.)

WEBER, ALBRECHT, Über die Kṛishṇajanmāshṭamī. (*Abhandlungen der königlichen Akademie der Wissenschaften zu Berlin* 1867.) (Cf. *I.A.* III 1874, pp. 26 ff.)

WIDENGREN, G., Harlekintracht und Mönchskutte, Clownhut und Derwischmütze. (*O.S.* II 1953, pp. 41–110.)

WIKANDER, S., Der arische Männerbund. *Diss.* Lund 1937.

—— Indo-European Eschatology in Myth and Epic. (*X. Internationaler Kongress für Religionsgeschichte*, Sektion IV A, Marburg 1960.)

—— Pāṇdavasagan och Mahābhāratas mytiska förutsättningar. (*R.B.* VI 1947, pp. 27–39.)

—— Vayu. Lund 1943.

WILSON, HORACE HAYMAN, Essays on the Purāṇas (*J.R.A.S.* 1839, pp. 61 ff. and 280 ff.)

—— Historical Sketch of the Kingdom of Pāṇḍya, S. India. (*J.R.A.S.* 1836, pp. 199–242 and 387–390.)

WOODROFFE, J., Shakti and Shākta, Essays on the Shākta Tantra Shastra. Madras 1951.

ZIESENISS, A., Studien zur Geschichte des Śivaismus. Gravenhage 1939. (*Bijdragen tot de Taal-Landen Volkenkunde van Nederlandsch-Indië.* Deel 98, pp. 75–223.)

ZIMMER, H., Myths and Symbols in Indian Art and Civilization. New York 1945.

INDEX ONE

Sanskrit texts quoted in Introduction and Part II and III

INDEX TWO

Classical and modern authors quoted i Introduction and Part II and III

INDEX THREE

General Index to Introduction and Part II and III

LIST OF ABBREVIATIONS

A.B.O.R.I.	Annals of the Bhandarkar Oriental Research Institute.
A.J.P.	American Journal of Philology.
A.O.	Archiv Orientální.
Āp.G.S.	Āpastambagṛihyasūtra.
Āś.G.S.	Āśvalāyanagṛihyasūtra.
AV	Atharvaveda.
Bh.G.	Bhagavadgītā.
Bh.P.	Bhāgavatapurāṇa.
B.I.	Bibliotheca Indica.
B.R.	Böhtlingk, O., & Roth, R., Sanskrit-Wörterbuch.
B.S.	Bibliotheca Sanskrita.
B.S.O.S.	Bulletin of the School of Oriental Studies.
C.H.I.	The Cambridge History of India.
C.O.	Collection Orientale.
C.P.	Central Provinces.
E.R.E.	Encyclopaedia of Religion and Ethics.
F.GR.HIST.	Die Fragmente der Griechischen Historiker.
F.H.R.	Fontes Historiae Religionum.
Fontes	Fontes historiae religionum indicarum.
frg.	fragment.
Fr.G.H.	Die Fragmente der Griechischen Historiker.
G.G.S.	Gobhilagṛihyasūtra.
H.C.I.P.	The History and Culture of the Indian People.
H.O.S.	Harvard Oriental Series.
I.A.	The Indian Antiquary.
I.C.	The Indian Culture.

I.H.Q.	The Indian Historical Quarterly.
Ind.Alt.k.	Lassen, Indische Altertumskunde.
Jacoby	Die Fragmente der Griechischen Historiker.
J.A.H.R.S.	Journal of the Andhra Historical Research Society.
J.A.O.S.	Journal of the American Oriental Society.
J.B.O.R.S.	Journal of the Bihar and Orissa Research Institute.
J.B.R.S.	The Journal of the Bihar Research Society.
J.I.H.	Journal of Indian History.
J.P.A.S.Beng.	Journal and Proceedings of the Asiatic Society of Bengal.
J.R.A.S.	Journal of the Royal Asiatic Society.
J.R.A.S.Trans.	Transactions of the Royal Asiatic Society.
K.S.S.	The Kāshī-Sanskrit-Series.
K.Z.	Zeitschrift für vergleichende Sprachforschung.
M.A.S.B.	Memoirs of the Asiatic Society of Bengal.
Mbh.	Mahābhārata.
Meg.	Megasthenes.
M.I.	Man in India.
M.O.	Le Monde Oriental.
M.R.	Modern Review.
M.S.	Maitrāyaṇī Saṁhitā.
O.S.	Orientalia Suecana.
P.G.S.	Pāraskaragṛihyasūtra.
P.W.	Pauli, A., Realenzyclopädie der klassischen Altertumswissenschaften.
pw.	Böhtlingk, Otto, Sanskrit-Wörterbuch.
Q.J.M.S.	Quarterly Journal of the Mythic Society.
R.B.	Religion och Bibel.
RV	Rigveda.
S.B.E.	The Sacred Books of the East.
Ś.Br.	Śatapathabrāhmaṇa.
S.C.	Science and Culture.
Schw.	Schwanbeck, E. A., Megasthenis Indica.
Ś.G.S.	Śāṅkhāyanagṛihyasūtra.
Sk.P.	Skandapurāṇa.
S.M.S.R.	Studi e Materiali di Storia delle Religioni.
SV	Sāmaveda.
T.B.R.I.	Transactions of the Bose Research Institute.
TS	Taittirīyasaṁhitā.
V.B.Q.	Visva Bharati Quarterly.
Vi.P.	Vishṇupurāṇa.

VP	Vāyupurāṇa.
VS	Vājasaneyisaṁhitā.
W.Z.	Wiener Zeitschrift für die Kunde des Morgenlandes.
YV	Yajurveda.
Z.D.M.G.	Zeitschrift der Deutschen Morgenländischen Gesellschaft.
Z.E.	Zeitschrift für Ethnologie.
Z.K.M.	Zeitschrift für die Kunde des Morgenlandes.

Rules for pronunciation of Indian words

above vowels signifies prolongation. The vowels pronounced as in German.

n̄ signifies -ng- (as in "king").

ṅ, ṁ signifies *anusvara,* something like French "un", "an".

ñ signifies -ny-; cf. -n- in "punch".

ṇ, ḍ, ṭ, ḷ signifies cerebral dentals as in "hard", "horn".

c signifies -ch- as in "church".

ś pronounced as -s- in "sure".

sh pronounced as -sh- in "bush".

h is always pronounced.

ḥ is -h- at the end of a word.

ṛi signifies the vowel -r-.